"AND NOW THE NEWS, **1945"**

To Bob Scott from a lovely 2nd Lt. Navigator in the 9th Best wishes for vivid memories — Herb Harper 3/1/98

PASSPORT® COMMUNICATIONS
Suite 1945
66 Witherspoon Street
Princeton, NJ 08542

Passport Communications
Suite 1945
66 Witherspoon Street
Princeton, NJ 08542

Cover design by Sheri Barnes

All net proceeds of this book will go to the American Boychoir School of Princeton, NJ.

Library of Congress Catalog Card Number: 94-068865

ISBN: 0-9643935-0-6

Corrected Edition

Dedication

To the 20th Air Force B-29 crew of the 9th Bomb Group, 1st Squadron with whom I flew in 1945. Our lives were then inescapably inseparable as a crew resulting in a special camaraderie that has continued ever since.

About the Author

Herb Hobler was a navigator on a B-29 in the Pacific during World War II, came back to finish Princeton, and spent 18 years in television with NBC-TV, CBS-TV and as head of production of the first videotape production house in the country in New York. He then founded Nassau Broadcasting Company in Princeton, New Jersey and for 25 years owned and operated radio stations and cable companies.

He served two terms on the National Association of Broadcasters Board, was Abe Lincoln Radio Broadcaster of the Year 1975, and was a co-founder of the First Amendment Congress in 1980.

In 1985 he conceived of creating daily newscasts for 1945 by researching 1945 newspapers and historical documents mixed with his own 40 year perspective. They were aired daily in 1985 and will be aired again in 1995 on radio stations on the 50th anniversary of this significant and memorable year.

Introduction

In 1985 as owner of a Princeton, New Jersey radio station and as a World War II B-29 veteran who lived through 1945, I decided it would be edifying for young and old to live through that momentous year 40 years later with succinct day-by-day radio newscasts.

While newspapers and other media often recall certain past events as "40 years ago today," I felt it would become living history by reporting the reconstructed news as if it were happening. As a result, after months of staring at New York Times microfiche—page after page—after personal recollections and checking reference sources—I wrote a daily newscast to last perhaps 90 seconds. To make it alive every newscast opened up with "This is Herb Hobler with today's news, February 4, 1945" ending with "And that's the news this February 4, 1945, Herb Hobler reporting." That approach brought the listener—and now you the reader—into the year 1945 itself.

When these were broadcast twice a day in 1985 on WHWH Princeton, the response was excellent from those who had lived through 1945 and could recall many events. It was particularly satisfying , however, to hear younger generations say these daily broadcasts unraveled the mysteries of "history" by putting it all together in short, informative parcels to help their comprehension of what World War II, and the significant year of 1945, was all about.

As a professional broadcaster for over 40 years and for 25 years an owner of radio stations, I had thoroughly enjoyed doing sports color, editorials and special events for the sheer fun of it. I therefore decided to personally broadcast these daily newscasts.

I have written these newscasts for people of every age to recall or to be otherwise astounded or fascinated by a momentous year in our history. It's all brought into sharp focus by a radio style with which everyone is familiar.

In the spring of 1994 a good friend, former Cornell University President James Perkins, heard about the scripts which had been bound into three hard covered books. He borrowed them and returned them with an enthusiastic conviction that they should be published.

And now, a few observations about these scripts which were scheduled to be broadcast again in 1995 on WHWH Princeton on the 50th year of those historical days.

This book isn't about the war only. It's also about life and death in 1945—the stock market, the movies, the 5 cent Coca Cola or Pepsi, fashions, war efforts at home, theater, international news, and politics all written in easily comprehensible short radio newscast style.

Researching the 1945 news with a 50 year perspective provided some marvelous news items that never would have been radio news in 1945. For example, for

1

January 6th I report on the marriage of two totally unknown people—except to their friends—Barbara Pierce of Rye, New York and Lt. J.G. George Herbert Walker Bush whose brother Prescott Bush was best man. I've used many other obscure little news items that meant nothing then but now have historical attraction.

For those whose lives have been at a distance from New York City, my apologies. All my life has been near New York and while these newscasts seldom report New York City news per se, it has always been a hub for entertainment, the stock market, a major port and the important New York Times which was the source of many of these 1945 news items. Still, I've tried to create these as national radio newscasts.

It was fun to report prices of items that came out of ads which certainly would not have been normal in an actual 1945 newscast. The 35 m.p.h. war time speed limit wasn't news then, it was a way of life. That's why my associate and secretary Bonnie who typed every page over and over to be ready for the printers so enjoyed reading about the history of my time and her father's. It was an eye opener for her.

Having been a B-29 navigator flying missions out of Tinian over Japan in the early months of 1945, I could not help but inject myself as an on-the-scene reporter in several newscasts. I hope my personal recollections add some realism to a few B-29 raids.

While the March Tokyo fire raid took off from our Tinian, Guam and Saipan islands bases in the early evening of March 9th, the raid took place between 1 am and 2 am on March 10th Tokyo time early enough for papers in the U.S. to report it in their March 10th papers thanks to a 14-hour difference. Therefore, readers in the U.S. read in the March 10th papers about yesterday's March 10th Tokyo raid though "yesterday" in their minds would be March 9th. Still, the Japanese will tell you that devastating raid was March 10th, their time.

Similarily while today we recognize the Hiroshima A-bomb as August 6th (which it was in Japan at 8:49 a.m.), it was August 5th in the United States.

Keeping this in mind, there may be an inconsistency in some of the Pacific Theater dates reported in my newscasts for, with the exception of those raids in which I write as a reporter on the scene, researching news for "today" necessarily came from reading the next day's newspaper when the newspapers reported events. All the European and U.S. news reported in my newscasts are accurate as to the date. In the case of battles in the Pacific likely most, with those few exceptions, may be a day off as far as those who were in the Pacific but correct for those here in the States on American time.

In addition to straining my eyesight reading New York Times microfiche (and spending far too long with each day's paper for the sheer enjoyment of it) I referred to the Encyclopedia Britannica, to "World War II Day By Day" by Donald Sommerville (Dorset Press) a marvelous pictorial and succinctly written book, some old Life Magazines, and miscellaneous sources to confirm my memory.

2

What also is fascinating (and to qualify the accuracy of some of my information) was to find frequent spellings of Marshal Zhukov as Zhukoff while historical books spell it Zhukov. Then there were bombings of Reims and later reports that the Rheims Cathedral wasn't damaged. (The "h" apparently is an anglicized version.)

So, excepting for possible typing errors missed through proofing, I've done my best to try to spell Hermann Goering with the double "n" when sometimes I found it with one.

My sincere thanks to WHWH Princeton which was my love for 25 years until it was sold, to the Princeton town library where I spent untold hours doing research, to several agents and publishers who from samplings gave me encouragement, to thoughtful, wise Jim Perkins who urged me to published it, to my Princeton classmate John Ware for his encouragement and expertise about publishing and marketing, to Kay Bretnall and Don Bryant for their second edition editing help, to Peter Benchley, John Chancellor, Richard Challener and James Perkins for their thoughtful remarks about this book, and mostly to Bonnie Chiravalle who for 8 years has been my assistant, confidante and supporter. Since I still use my electric typewriter at about 90 words per minute with errors, Bonnie's professional expertise with word processing on computers made this book possible. It simply wouldn't have been done without her.

I hope "And Now The News, 1945" becomes a best seller because 100% of the net proceeds (except for a gift to the 20th Air Force Association which has been most helpful in this endeavor) will go to America's foremost boychoir, The American Boychoir in Princeton of which I have devotedly been Chairman for 20 years.

Since I can't think of another year in the 20th century that approaches the extraordinary events of 1945 with the ending of a world wide war, the beginning of the atomic age, the start of the United Nations and new directions for peace, I have no reason to consider doing this again. There is no other year.

And now today's news January 1, 1945.

While millions of Americans at home celebrated the new year last evening, 3500 Allied bombers bombed Germany and other bombers hit the Gestapo nest in Oslo, Norway. In spite of these continuing attacks Hitler yesterday announced he will not surrender and that the war will continue into 1946.

The Allies announced that 7000 German planes were destroyed in 1944 while the United States has noted that 11.9 million Americans are now under arms.

Last November 29th two Germans came ashore on the coast of Maine from a German U-Boat. They have just been captured and will be tried as spies.

In Greece Premier George Pompandreou has resigned and Archbishop Damaskins has been sworn in as Regent.

Good news for smokers. The War Food Administration says there will be more cigarettes available in two years.

At the movies is "Meet Me in St. Louis" with Judy Garland, and a reprise on the 1935 "Naughty Marietta" with Nelson Eddy and Jeannette McDonald. On Broadway "Life with Father" is in its 6th year, and "Oklahoma" remains a sellout.

France has been admitted to the United Nations and in England David Lloyd George, Prime Minister during World War I, has been made an Earl.

In New York at the Taft Hotel you can have lunch for 65 cents and dinner for $1.50.

The New York Stock Exchange reports that total volume for all of 1944 was 263 million shares with the highest day at 2.5 million shares last June 16th.

And that's the news this day January 1, 1945. Happy and Victorious New Year from your reporter Herb Hobler.

And now today's news, January 2, 1945

In war news, the Germans have launched attacks in the Saar Basin while General Patton's armies are attacking in Luxembourg and Belgium.

A group of German SS troops have been captured and nonchalantly admitted they were involved in slaughtering 25-30 civilians in the Belgian town of Parfoundruy last December 18th. And in Prague, 13 Czechs have been executed by Germans as a reprisal for aiding an anti-German effort.

The RAF announced they dropped 54,000 tons of bombs on German targets in December. In the Pacific, MacArthur's Navy Patrol bombers have attacked Formosa for the first time. And Chester Nimitz now sports five stars as Fleet Admiral.

Lt. Bill Rogers Jr., son of the late humorist Will Rogers—was part of a forced retreat in Belgium. Rogers left a large sign on a tree reading "Beware. We'll be back in two weeks with our new secret weapon."

Back home, First Lady Eleanor Roosevelt has challenged women to do more for the war effort.

The Government is now sending 20 million dollars a month in Social Security benefits to 1.2 million people.

Dr. John F. Condon, the man known as Jafsie during the Lindbergh kidnapping and subsequent trial, has died at the age of 84. He was the intermediary during the $50,000 ransom exchange in 1932 and later identified Richard Bruno Hauptman as the man involved.

In sports yesterday, South Carolina beat Tennessee in the Rose Bowl 25-0, the Oklahoma Aggies beat TCU in the Cotton Bowl 34-0, Tulsa beat Georgia Tech in the Orange Bowl 26-12, and in the Spaghetti Bowl in Florence, Italy, the 5th Army beat the 12th Air Force.

Sir Bertram Ramsey, hero of Dunkerque, has been killed in a plane crash in Belgium.

Popular films showing include "Keys of the Kingdom" starring Gregory Peck and "Can't Help Singing" with Deanna Durbin, while Frank Fay is starring in "Harvey" on Broadway.

Trading on the New York Stock Exchange was 1.3 million shares today and the William Waldorf Astor Estate has purchased the 36 story building at 535 Fifth Avenue for $4.5 million.

That's the news this January 2, 1945.

And now today's news, January 3, 1945

General Eisenhower and General Patton have launched the American First Army attack on the northern flank of the bulge in Belgium while Germans are threatening to drive the Allies out of the Saar. The RAF battered the Ruhr Valley with 1100 bombers.

Retreating Germans in Kuanas, Lithuania have slaughtered 10,000 remaining Jews in one night with but one survivor. Previously they had killed 30,000 Jews in the same ghetto.

The Air Force has reported that 2200 fliers who participated in the Ploesti oil field raids last April are now considered missing in action.

In the Pacific 90 B-29's have bombed Nagoya, Osaka and Hamamatsu from new American bases in Saipan in the Mariannas. The little island of Iwo Jima was bombed today for the 26th time. And in the Philippines, 25 more ships have been sunk or set afire off Luzon.

Chairman of the War Production Board J.A. Krug has reported that the U.S. produced 96,000 planes in 1944, up from 86,000 produced in 1943. 13 million tons of new shipping is expected to be built in 1945.

And now Air Force Commanding General H.H. "Hap" Arnold is sporting 5 stars.

Major General Lewis Hershey, Director of Selective Service, has ordered all state directors to re-examine all deferred farm laborers ages 18 to 25. Price Administrator Chester Bowles is concerned about inflation and plans on tighter price controls.

In sports, 1944 batting champ Lou Boudreau, classified 4F, has joined a defense factory in Harvey, Illinois.

On radio tonight Milton Berle's guest on his show "Let Yourself Go" is Fred Allen. Finally, this week's Saturday Evening Post features an article called "The Pugnacious Drew Pearson." You can buy the magazine for 10 cents.

That's the news this January 3, 1945.

Thursday, January 4, 1945

And now today's news January 4, 1945

In what is called the worst weather in the war zone this winter, the Third Army in the Battle of the Bulge has been slowed down by ice and fog. Lt. General Courtney Hodges and his infantry tanks have crashed through German outposts on a 6 mile front even as the Germans gain in the south and threaten the Alsace and Lorraine.

Russian troops are poised for an attack on Warsaw on the eastern front.

General Clare Chennault has been given the Legion of Merit for leading the China Air Task Force in 1942 and 1943.

In the Pacific, 40 B-29's based in India have hit Bangkok while U.S. carrier planes have attacked Formosa for the second day.

Lt. General George Patton has just given the Bastogne Commander, Brigadier General Anthony McAuliffe, the Distinguished Service Cross given in part for his response of "Nuts" to the German ultimatum to surrender. It became a rallying cry of his garrison of 10,000 encircled men.

Secretary of the Treasury Henry Morgenthau announced the 6th War Bond drive exceeded its goal by 54% raising $21.6 billion in subscriptions. War Mobilization Director James F. Byrnes plans to restrict large convention travel as it causes problems for troop movements and the wounded on planes, trains, and buses.

More than 30,000 sick and wounded Americans were returned to the U.S. in December alone, a 300% increase over last July. Casualties to date in the war are at 638,000 including 103,999 killed in the Army and 31,332 killed in the Navy.

F.C. Crawford, President of Thompson Products, has made a plea to the War Department to curtail censorship. He says the public isn't getting all the facts.

Swimmer Ann Curtis has become the first woman Sullivan Award winner as the best amateur athlete in the country.

Samuel Shellabarger's new book "Captain from Castile" is available at $3.00 and John Steinbeck's "Cannery Row" can be bought for $2.00. And, finally the Charlie Chaplin paternity suit in Los Angeles has ended in a mistrial.

That's the news this January 4, 1945.

And now today's news, January 5, 1945.

Field Marshal Sir Bernard L. Montgomery has been commanding the US First and 9th Armies for the past two weeks with Lt. General Omar Bradley in charge of the southern flank in the on-going battle of the Bulge in Belgium. British troops have joined in. 1000 bombers hit Berlin and Hanover today as Germans stepped up their radio controlled V-2 flying bombs over London.

The town of Oradue-sur-Glane will not be rebuilt but remain as a monument to recall the German massacre of 1100 civilians including 300 children who were herded into a church which was then set on fire. In the Philippines, 30 Japanese aircraft were destroyed on an airfield near Manila as American Forces landed on Marinduque not far from another island, Mindoro, where an attack is imminent.

President Roosevelt says the next Big Three meeting with Churchill and Stalin will take place after his inauguration for his 4th term on January 20th. Gen. Charles de Gaulle met three days ago with Churchill and Gen. Eisenhower for a military progress conference. More food is being shipped to the Italians restricted only by limited shipping facilities.

The Army Air Forces which already had taken over many Atlantic City hotels for training new inductees has now taken over the Columbus Hotel.

Senator Alben Barkley has unanimously been re-elected Senate Majority Leader. Mayor Fiorello LaGuardia of New York has called the Mayor of Kansas City to see how New Yorkers can get more meat.

In a split decision at Madison Square Garden welterweight Fritzie Zivic upset favored Bill Arnold who had won his last 31 fights.

The new production of the "Magic Flute" at the Metropolitan Opera features Mimi Benzell in a leading role along with Ezio Pinza, James Melton and John Brownlee. At the movies, Hedy Lamarr, George Brent and Paul Lukas are in "Experiment Perilous" and the March of Time's current feature is called "The French Campaign."

Robert E. Hanegan, Chairman of the Democratic National Committee, says plans for the 1946 election will start right after the inauguration.

To the soldiers, Coca Cola ads say "Glad you are back. Coca Cola 5 cents."

That's the news this January 5, 1945.

Saturday, January 6, 1945

And now today's news, January 6, 1945.

President Roosevelt's message to Congress today demands a National Service Act, draft of nurses, post-war training, and a program to train 4-F's for active service. CIO Labor leader Phillip Murray has already announced he is against such a Service Act. The President also looks for the closing of the European war this year and closing in on Japan.

Admiral Bull Halsey's Naval fleet and fliers today have sunk 83 ships and small craft and 331 planes destroyed at Formosa and Okinawa. B-29's bombed Nanking, China as well as Tokyo and Kyushu Island.

In Europe General Eisenhower says that there will be no changes in his generals as a result of the German's unexpected break through in the Ardennes. The American 8th Air Force continue to bomb in daylight and the RAF at night in a never ending assault on German positions.

An Austrian, freed from his imprisonment by the Germans, says the Germans have a cotton shortage and are using paper for bandages.

Secretary of State Edward Stettinius today strongly disagreed with a position taken by Montana Senator Wheeler who wants a negotiated peace. Stettinius notes the U.S. position of unconditional surrender is also endorsed by China, Britain and Russia.

Among the many weddings today was that of Barbara Pierce of Rye, NY who married Lt. (j.g.) George Herbert Walker Bush. Prescott Bush Jr. was best man for his brother.

A George Abbott production "On the Town" has opened at the Adelphia Theater in New York featuring Nancy Walker and Sono Osato. Ice skater Sonja Henie is at Madison Square Garden and the Radio City Music Hall film is "National Velvet" starring Mickey Rooney and Elizabeth Taylor.

January fur sales features mink furs at Arnold Constable at $1000 to $2000 while Gimbels is selling cotton dresses at $7.95. Men can buy Coward's shoes at $9.95 and an overcoat at Browning King for $50.

Finally, with the metal shortage, Illinois is making license plates out of soy bean providing a tasty morsel for dogs who often eat them.

That's the news this January 6, 1945.

And now today's news, January 7, 1945.

Tokyo radio reports they expect imminent landings by the Americans on Luzon. Intelligence indicates 150,000 Japanese hold the island. Attacks by the U.S. 3rd fleet continue.

Field Marshal Karl von Rundstedt is leading a German army in opening up a potential dangerous offensive aimed at driving out the American 7th Army and the French 1st army out of the Alsace Plain.

At a Catholic Mass in Luxembourg today a priest interrupted the service to let the organ play the Star Spangled Banner. Many of the 600 GI's in attendance had tears in their eyes.

Three miracle stories of survival today. Sgt. J.R. Krantz of Hickory Point, Tennessee was sucked out of his B-29 blister position at high altitude but thanks to having tied a rope around his ankle and leg he thrashed against the side of the plane in minus 39 degree temperatures. Crew members hauled in the unconscious gunner almost ten minutes later. He suffered frostbite and shock.

Over Germany a B-17 was damaged and burst into flames. The crew decided to stay aboard until they reach friendly territory all bailing out just seconds before the plane exploded. Americans on the ground at first thought they were Germans disguised as American flyers.

The P-51 Mustang of Lt. Emory Taylor of Austin, Texas was shot up, out of control. Struggling to get out, the wind blew him against the canopy knocking him unconscious. 6,000 feet and some minutes later he awoke unharmed in a tree, his unopened parachute still on his back.

President Roosevelt today visited the ailing former Secretary of State Cordell Hull in the Naval Hospital in Washington.

In sports, the Eastern Association of Intercollegiate Football officials met and have predicted college football will take place this fall with players who are mostly 17 years old and 4-F's.

And that's the news this January 7, 1945.

Monday, January 8, 1945

And now today's news, January 8, 1945.

In the Pacific area, two columns of the British Army are within 58 miles of Mandalay while U.S. Naval airmen have turned Manila Bay in the Philippines into a graveyard for Japanese ships. More than 50 were sunk or burned today.

Allied offensives have isolated as many as 250,000 Japanese troops in Pacific islands and 300,000 German troops have been isolated along the coast of France. The Russians have slowed the Germans outside of Budapest and destroyed 90 tanks along the north flank of the Danube.

In spite of unseasonable weather and the menace of flying bombs driving thousands into underground subway shelters nightly, the birth rate in Britain is up 29,000 over last year.

27 milligrams of radium have been found in the occupied German city of Aachen with documents signed by Mme Marie Curie, co-discoverer of radium. Amounts as little as one milligram are used in tubes for the treatment of cancer.

A new U.S. attack bomber, the A-26 Invader, carries 10 50 calibre machine guns including remote control firing by the pilot.

Admiral James H. Ingram says robot bomb attacks on American shores is not only possible but probable within 30 to 60 days. He says "we're ready for them."

Legislation to draft nurses has been reluctantly introduced by Congresswoman Edith Rogers of Massachusetts. It is being attacked by the New York City Commissioner of Hospitals who notes New York hospitals already have half the normal number of nurses available.

Auto experts say post war cars will benefit by war technology.

In sports, Sam Snead won the Los Angeles Open today ahead of Byron Nelson, Johnny Revolta, and Lloyd Mangrum. First prize was $2,666 in war bonds.

John Hersey's "A Bell for Adano" at $2.50 a book has been called the best novel of the year. Frederic March stars in the Broadway version.

On radio tonight is Ethel and Albert, Lowell Thomas News, Blind Date, Burns and Allen, Information Please and Dr. I.Q.

Finally, Macy's New York has Hickory skis at $9.98 a pair and children's double runner skates at 50 cents a pair.

That's the news this January 8, 1945.

And now today's news, January 9, 1945.

RAF Mosquitos and Beaufighters sunk 5 vessels today in a sweep over fjords in Norway while in Germany a shortage of clothing for new German defense recruits has caused Heinrich Himmler, Dr. Joseph Goebbels and Martin Borman to announce a national "sacrificial offering" for citizens to provide needed winter clothing.

In the Pacific Americans have landed 107 miles from Manila meeting little resistance. Gen. Douglas MacArthur went ashore with his troops. 800 ships participated with none being damaged.

In four years New York City has gone from a single Brooklyn Naval yard base to 7 major harbor installations making it the mightiest port of war the world has ever known.

A transport version of the B-29 known as the Boeing Stratocruiser averaging 380 mph has set a new record of 6 hours and 9 minutes from the West Coast to the East beating the old record by 38 minutes.

A 10 year old Pan American Airways Clipper has crashed in Port of Spain, Trinidad killing 23 with 7 survivors.

Staff Sgt. Joe DiMaggio, former star Yankee outfielder, arrived today at Camp Kilmer, NJ for a ten day assignment.

In Hollywood, Mary Pickford has signed Agnes de Mille to create dances and ballet numbers for the upcoming movie "One Touch of Venus." On radio tonight is Lum and Abner, A Date with Judy, the Alan Young Show, Inner Sanctum, and Fibber McGee and Molly followed by Bob Hope.

2.2 million shares traded on the New York Stock Exchange today with the volume leader New York Central with 56,000 shares. The Hotel Chesterfield in NY has single rooms with bath and radio from $2.50 to $6.00.

Finally, the War Department has announced another 6,178 casualties of killed and wounded. Call your local American Red Cross and be a blood donor. Our wounded need your help.

That's the news this January 9, 1945.

Wednesday, January 10, 1945

And now today's news, January 10, 1945.

American troops have driven 10 miles inland on Luzon in the Philippines backed by clouds of planes from carriers. So far there has been only feeble Japanese resistance. General Yamashita has promised Japan a brilliant victory and says 300,000 Americans are doomed to die. It is hoped some 6000 American civilians in Santo Tomas prison camp will be freed soon.

Three US destroyers—the Hull, Monaghan and the Spence have been lost in a typhoon recently in the Pacific. The Hull was at Pearl Harbor on December 7, 1941 and saw action at Kiska, Makin, Kwajalein, Eniwetok and Saipan Islands. 53 of the Hull's 175 men were rescued.

In Europe under the same fog and snow conditions that permitted an offense, German troops are retreating from the western tip of the Belgian salient.

74 year old composer Franz Lehar has been placed under house arrest in Vienna.

Raymond J. Albano, former ranch foreman in Idaho, has become known as the one man army killing 82 Germans in 8 days, capturing 31 along with dozens of guns. His fellow soldiers can't believe he survived.

King Peter of Yugoslavia plans to appoint a regency of 3 men and will endorse the plan of Premier Ivan Subasitch and Marshal Tito for a unified government.

A survey reports 71% of the French like U.S. soldiers with many of the negative 29% unhappy that Americans are too kind to German prisoners.

To prevent an impending coal shortage, James F. Byrnes, War Mobilization Director, has ordered a blackout of all ornamental and outdoor advertising lighting and maximum temperatures in homes and public buildings of 68 degrees.

Republican Senator Arthur Vandenberg of Michigan has proposed that the U.S., British, Soviet Russia, France and China sign immediately "a hard and fast treaty to keep Germany and Japan permanently demilitarized."

At the White House President Roosevelt today placed the nation's highest honor, the Congressional Medal of Honor, around the necks of five Army and 2 Navy service men.

And tonight on radio you can hear Mr. and Mrs. North, Henny Youngman, Eddie Cantor, Mr. District Attorney and Kay Kyser and his Kollege of Musical Knowledge.

That's the news this January 10, 1945.

And now today's news, January 11, 1945.

In the Pacific war, Japanese swimmers ferrying explosives paddled into the transport area in the Lingayen Gulf where 2.5 million tons of shipping with 50,000 sailors are located. Some of them were shoving boxes of TNT towards the ships. Some were shot, several were picked up who tried to toss grenades into the boat. Vice Admiral Thomas C. Kincaid said "We are not impressed."

Admiral Chester Nimitz has made a terse but dramatic announcement that carrier planes were attacking the enemy on the Indochina coast in the Saigon-Cam Ranh Bay area.

B-29's today hammered Singapore ship installations with good results. General Curtis LeMay, head of the 20th Bomber Command, reports no losses.

Despite a last minute British intervention, King Peter of Yugoslavia today publicly objected to a single regency tied in with Marshal Tito's anti-fascist Council of National Liberation group.

Leaders of the Greek Elas Army and the British Army have signed a truce ending the 40 day civil war.

Seven Japanese-American soldiers were given the Distinguished Service Cross today for bravery in Italy.

President Roosevelt took a rare night out to attend the Annual Radio Correspondents dinner laughing at many skits and personal affronts by such people as Jack Benny. Earlier he presented the Legion of Merit to polar explorer Rear Admiral Richard E. Byrd for a special naval aviation mission.

This weeks War Department casualties of 8,241 bring the war's total to 646,000 with 138,393 killed, 370,000 wounded, 73,000 missing and 64,000 prisoners.

Basil O'Connor, President of the National Foundation for Infantile Paralysis says treatments last year cost 11 million dollars.

Lt. Col. Eddie Eagen of the Army Air Forces will be named Chairman of the New York State Athletic Commission next week with an annual salary of $7,500.

On radio tonight listen to Suspense, the Dinah Shore Show, Abbott and Costello and the Rudy Vallee Show.

That's the news this January 11, 1945.

And now today's news, January 12, 1945.

Field Marshal Karl von Rundstedt's Belgium bulge has been reduced by 100 square miles as the Germans retreat and the British and American Third Army have joined forces. 20 German divisions have been wiped out since the battle started. While it has been speculated American losses exceed 100,000 in the bulge, it is now felt it will be under 75,000. The German V bombs killed 367 British civilians and injured 847 others in December.

RAF bombers have hit hard German U boat shelters in Bergen, Norway.

Pacific Fleet planes sunk 25 Japanese ships today off the coast and in the harbor of French Indochina. The Navy has also confirmed the sinking last October 24th in the Philippine Sea battle of the 45,000 ton dreadnaught Musashi.

General MacArthur has moved his troops another 12 miles into Luzon but reports are that the Japanese are massing troops.

Former Ambassador to Tokyo Joseph E. Grew says the invasion of Luzon does not mean an early end to the war.

Captain William A. Shomo of Huff, PA today shot down 7 planes, a record for Far East Air Forces.

Dr. C.H. Marvin of George Washington University says if the war continues into 1946 many colleges and universities may have to shut down due to financial difficulties.

The NCAA Convention in Columbus, Ohio includes football coaches Fritz Crisler of Michigan, Wisconsin Coach Harry Stuhldreher, Army Coach Col. Earl Blaik, and former Navy coach Swede Larsen.

In New York City venereal disease is rampant, with syphillis up 204% and gonorrhea up 139% since 1941 largely among high school girls.

Serge Koussevitzsky will conduct the Boston Symphony Orchestra tomorrow night at Carnegie Hall in New York.

A patent has been applied for to reduce the toxic effect of the wonder sulfa drug.

Current movies include "I Love a Soldier" with Paulette Goddard and Sonny Tufts, "Wuthering Heights" with Merle Oberon, Laurence Olivier and David Niven, and Disney's "Fanatasia" now at popular prices.

For radio tonight try the Aldrich Family, Duffy's Tavern, It Pays to be Ignorant, People Are Funny, and Amos and Andy.

That's the news this January 12, 1945.

And now today's news, January 13, 1945.

The Russian army has opened up a new winter offensive in Central Poland along a 600 mile front from the Baltic Sea to the Balkans and are within 71 miles of southeastern Germany.

The 83rd Infantry Division has spent the last two days and nights without food or sleep in an effort to cut off the Germans in Belgium.

General James Doolittle of the 8th Air Force reports a record 16,312 sorties against targets and 38,000 tons of bombs since the December 16th start of the Battle of the Bulge.

Morale has been low among American soldiers in Italy reflecting a feeling they are on a forgotten front. Gen. Mark Clark tells them they're not forgotten and morale is picking up.

An American installation in Belgium today was inadvertently bombed by B-17's. There is no report on any casualties.

The Germans have hung 2 and executed by firing squad 3 Frenchmen for persecution of pro-German Frenchmen.

Back home, 1300 soldiers at Camp Shanks, NY are relaxing after two years in battle zones abroad.

At the California Tule Lake imprisonment camp, 5000 Japanese internees have applied for repatriation to Japan.

Correspondents have been allowed in the Marietta Georgia Bell Aircraft plant for the first time to see B-29's being built in the largest room in the U.S. Some were taken up to 30,000 feet and were amazed at the warmth of the pressurized cabin, no need for oxygen masks, and no distress in rapidly descending.

The Red Cross drive starting March 1st is seeking $200,000,000 this year says head Basil O'Connor.

Arturo Toscanini conducts the New York Philharmonic tonight at Carnegie Hall in New York and opera singer Lawrence Tibbett is on the Lucky Strike "Your Hit Parade" at 9 pm having replaced Frank Sinatra.

Children's things at Gimbels NY include playpens at $4.49, boy's snow suit at $8.87, girl's pinafore at $1.98 while at Bloomingdales you can buy 2 dozen cans of 18 ounce grapefruit juice for $3.12, sardines at 87 cents, and a 30 ounce tin of hearts of palm for 88 cents, no ration points required.

That's the news this January 13, 1945.

Sunday, January 14, 1945

And now today's news, January 14, 1945.

In the Pacific the Lingayen gulf base on Luzon has been widened to 45 miles, one column moving 19 miles closer to Manila still with little Japanese resistance. B-29's smashed targets on Formosa with no losses.

In Europe the Russians have captured 200 towns in southern Poland and have wiped out German-Hungarian defenders in Budapest. And, finally, the Battle of the Bulge is in its last stages as the Germans continue to retreat.

The German Luftwaffe suffered one of its worst days today as the Allies destroyed 232 planes while losing 45.

It is reported that the Germans have mined many historical Prague buildings and are ready to destroy them even if the Czech capital doesn't become a battle center.

Hundreds of American built planes are regularly delivered to Ladd Field in Alaska where Soviet pilots then fly them for Allied use on the Russian front.

50,000 Yugoslavians have denounced King Peter for rejecting a regency proposal of Marshal Tito. Crowds chant "We don't want a king. We want Tito."

At least 50% of Pisa, Italy is now uninhabitable, food is short, and local American soldiers are blamed and find it necessary to be armed.

America's leading air ace, Congressional Medal of Honor winner Major Richard Bong, has been welcomed home to be married in Superior, Wisconsin.

The American Medical Association reports that 70 doctors were killed in action last year and another 113 died in the service.

Sir Alexander Fleming, discoverer of penicillin, regularly stops in to visit wounded troops in hospitals in England.

Leopold Stokowski conducts the New York City Symphony at the New York City Center tomorrow night while pianist Rudolf Serkin performs tonight at Carnegie Hall.

In sports, Byron Nelson has won the Phoenix open at ten under par followed by Denny Shute. Nelson wins $6,666 in war bonds.

Finally, don't expect to find hotel space in Washington for the upcoming January 20th inauguration of President Roosevelt's fourth term. 94% of the hotels are already booked for the curtailed ceremonies.

That's the news this January 14, 1945.

And now today's news, January 15, 1945.

The U.S. Third fleet has bombed enemy ports in China including Amoy and Hong Kong following the attacks two days ago that sunk 41 ships, damaged 28 others and destroyed 112 planes. The U.S. lost 16 planes.

In Poland, Russian troops are within 51 miles of the German border, 21 miles from Cracow.

While there is little left of the bulge in Belgium and Luxembourg, the Germans have increased their assaults in the Saar and Alsace.

Here in U.S. prisoner of war camps, it has just been reported that there have been six murders of Germans who were anti-Nazis. The Germans were convicted by a kangaroo court and killed by their fellow Nazi prisoners.

2100 Allied bombers, including many from Italian bases, have bombed oil supplies, communications and rail yards. 600 of the bombers were escorted by U.S Mustangs and Thunderbolts.

With the tobacco shortage, the National Association of Tobacco Dealers has announced plans to have dealers distribute ration cards hoping to get consumption to an average of 15 cigarettes a day. Last year 33 million packs a day were sold for 38 million smokers who average 17 a day.

When Captain Eddie Rickenbacker was lost for weeks in the Pacific Ocean, one of the men who found him in a small life raft was Captain William Eadie who has now been killed in combat.

Pope Pius has addressed the Roman nobility with new declarations on democracy and social and political thought. Some feel they are as important as the liberal advances made by his predecessor Pope Leo XIII.

While March 15th is the deadline for paying taxes, the government moved up the last 1944 quarter payments to today. Lines are long at the post office and internal revenue offices.

With President Roosevelt proposing to draft 20,000 nurses, 4000 nurses have signed up this week.

At the Capitol Theater in New York tonight is "Music for Millions" starring Margaret O'Brien, Jimmy Durante, Jose Iturbi and June Allyson with Tommy Dorsey and his orchestra on stage.

Finally, 2 million shares traded on the New York Stock Exchange today with Graham Paige leading with 114,000 shares. Other top ten traders were Packard Motors, Hupp Motors, Studebaker and Hudson Motors.

That's the news this January 15, 1945.

Tuesday, January 16, 1945

And now today's news, January 16, 1945.

In Philippine action, General MacArthur's 6th Army has widened the wedge on Japanese positions meeting with opposition for the first time since the invasion.

U.S. carrier planes continue to strike at Hong Kong, Swatow and Canton during the last three days with 87 enemy planes destroyed or damaged as well as 100,000 tons of shipping sunk or damaged.

Lingayen Bishop Mariano Madriaga regrets the invasion damage of his homeland but says the Americans are friends and the Japanese enemy is evil.

The Red Army including Marshal Gregori Zhukov's First White Russian Army and General Ivan Chernyakhovsky's Third White Russian Army are smashing across Poland, nearing Warsaw as hundreds of towns have fallen.

Norwegian troops opened their first big attack against the Germans in the extreme northern part of Norway.

Defense Minister of liberated Hungary says he met with Hitler last September calling him deranged and prepared to fling the last man and last drop of blood to defend Germany.

Officers of the French War Crimes Commission will call as many as 20,000 Germans to trial after the war.

Another 4023 U.S. casualties have been announced by the War Department. The British Empire has had over 1 million casualties since September 3, 1939 to December 1, 1944 with 200,000 United Kingdom killed, 28,000 Canadians killed, 9000 New Zealanders, 17,000 from India and 4500 from the colonies.

Lt. Cecil Harris, the Navy's #2 ace, is home on leave after destroying 24 Japanese planes in 82 days.

One for the books in the Pacific as a B-24 Liberator accidentally dropped a bomb on another Liberator below. Gunners improvised a crow bar out of 50 calibre machine gun barrels to pry the bomb free from the waist of the plane, then watched the armed bomb drop into the water below.

In Cleveland, Ohio and Trenton, New Jersey several workers who went on strike were re-classified as A-1 for deterring the war effort and inducted into the service.

And Dodger Dixie Walker who batted .357 has been named baseball player of the year by the New York Chapter of Writers Association.

That's the news this January 16, 1945.

20

And now today's news, January 17, 1945.

Russian and Polish troops have captured Warsaw, the first capital overrun by Hitler. German troops are hastily retreating as survivors are freed of 5 years of tyranny. German radio has reported the loss of Warsaw as a collapse and a catastrophe and also says the new Russian super tank, the Joseph Stalin, is the best in the world.

700 Liberators and Flying Fortresses have bombed by daylight today and 1200 RAF bombers by night on submarine bases, rail yards, and fuel depots. 10 American planes and 28 British bombers were lost. Additional B-17's are going to Europe having been totally replaced in the Pacific by B-24 Liberators.

The weather is so cold in the Ardennes hills that U.S. First Army troops are using dynamite and mortar shells to dig slit trenches.

A native of Paterson, New Jersey, Major Thomas B. Maguire, who was the leading active war ace with 38 Japanese kills, has been shot down and lost.

The government says it may add another hour to daylight savings time to reduce electric power use and coal consumption.

Secretary of Commerce Jesse Jones says the government is producing synthetic rubber at less cost than natural rubber and expects it will compete with natural rubber after the war.

In sports, miler Gil Dodds, who holds the world indoor record of 4.06.3, is retiring just as great Swedish miler Gunder Haegg is planning to arrive in the U.S. February 2nd.

Gene and Kathleen Lockhart are returning from Hollywood to star in a Broadway show "Happily Ever After." A new movie opening up in a few days is "Sunday Dinner for a Soldier" starring Anne Baxter and John Hodiak. Randolph Scott has signed for the lead in "Captain Kidd" and Angela Lansbury for "The Harvey Girls."

Volume on the New York Stock Exchange today was 1,984,000 shares led by Radio Corporation at 12 with 60,200 shares.

Finally, three service men with a C priority are upset that they got bumped off their airplane at Memphis for an A priority passenger—an English bulldog owned by Colonel Elliott Roosevelt in a large crate that took up 3 seats.

A few current prices include Gilbey's Gin at $3.30 and Hiram Walker Imperial Whiskey at $3.55 and rayon and silk ties at DePinna's, NY marked down to $1.65.

That's the news this January 17, 1945.

21

Thursday, January 18, 1945

And now today's news, January 18, 1945.

Winston Churchill has warned the Germans to surrender unconditionally now as the Allies have powerful offensives going on three fronts with the Russians going west, British and Americans going East as well as going north from Italy.

As the Russians drive into the Silesian border, a German radio war reporter has noted an all-out effort by the Germans which includes using men over 50 and youths of 16 and 17.

French prisoners of war in Germany are reported starving and reduced to eating rats and mice and boiling dahlia bulbs to make soup.

A final curtain has fallen on the French Vichy government as furnishings, dinner services, and carpets have been returned to the Elysee Palace in Paris.

Brigadier General Frederick W. Castle, an 8th Air Force pioneer, went down in his B-17 after being attacked by seven Messerschmitts and after ordering all his crew to bail out.

In the Pacific, 24 more Japanese ships have been sunk by U.S submarines making a total to date of 958 including 103 combat vessels.

The U.S. 14th Air Force pilots from the Kunming, China area have damaged or destroyed another 131 Japanese airplanes, many at the Shanghai airdrome. Also destroyed were 26 locomotives while hundreds were killed by strafing.

Gas shortages on the east coast have resulted in many dry gas stations making ration coupons useless. Heating oil seems to be adequately available at the moment.

The Regional War Labor Board says the American Federation of Musicians is feather-bedding with excess musicians required of employers and will take corrective steps.

1936 Presidential candidate Alfred M. Landon has urged greater teamwork among the U.S., British and Russia political and military leaders. The final tally in last November's election was 25,600,000 votes for Roosevelt to 22 million for Thomas E. Dewey. Socialist Norman Thomas got 80,000 votes.

J. Edgar Hoover says bank robberies were up to 37 compared to 22 in 1943. The highest ever was in 1932 with 606 bank robberies.

In Hollywood, Universal has borrowed Ralph Bellamy to star with Deanna Durbin in "Lady On a Train."

That's the news this January 18, 1945.

22

And now today's news, January 19, 1945.

Over 100 B-29's from Saipan have bombed the Kawasaki aircraft plant in the Kobe-Osaka area in a daylight raid. No losses were reported.

The Russians have reached the border of German Silesia capturing Lodz, Cracow, and Tarnow after a 28 mile advance.

More than 100,000 Poles have returned to Warsaw with picks and shovels to dig in ruins for bodies of relatives and household articles. Only one prominent building remains standing in the city.

Four months after the liberation of Bulgaria, 45,000 Jews are in desperate condition. Many are clotheless, shoeless and starving with 3 to 4 families crowded together in small quarters with no heat.

Secretary of State Edward Stettinius will join President Roosevelt along with Presidential Advisor Harry L. Hopkins in the upcoming summit meeting with Winston Churchill and Joseph Stalin.

Prince Humbert of Italy has decorated Lt. General Mark Clark for his role in the landings at Salerno, Anzio and in the liberation of Rome.

Chester Bowles, head of the Office of Price Administration, says he doesn't think cigarettes will have to be rationed. As to the rationing for an average of 15 cigarettes a day he says he smokes more than that himself.

St. Louis Cardinal baseball player Stan Musial, father of two young children, has been accepted for Naval service. Over 25,000 U.S. servicemen are playing basketball in Britian hoping to be part of 16 teams in the upcoming United Kingdom championships in March.

Quick thinking has saved the life of 2nd Lt. Wilbur Madison of Anderson, North Carolina. Madison was trying to pull out the pin of a hand grenade as Germans were approaching. As a German came around a corner, he pulled it out, handed it to the German who was stupefield giving time for Madison to run. The grenade exploded in the German's hand killing him.

Faye Emerson, wife of Colonel Elliott Roosevelt, gets the lead in a new movie "Danger Signal" while Humphrey Bogart and Barbara Stanwyck have signed to star in "The Fountainhead."

That's the news this January 19, 1945.

Saturday, January 20, 1945

And now today's news, January 20, 1945.

Bareheaded with no overcoat in 33 degree weather, President Franklin D. Roosevelt was sworn in as President for an unprecedented fourth term today by Chief Justice Harlan Stone. Minutes before, former Vice President Henry A. Wallace gave the oath to new Vice President Harry S. Truman. Several thousand spectators standing on a light snowfall heard a short inaugural address in which the President declared isolationism is dead commenting "We have become citizens of the world."

In separate news, Vice Admiral Ross T. McIntire, Surgeon General of the Navy, stated that Roosevelt is in fine shape.

To minimize enemy raids, the Japanese Diet has approved 2 billion yen to build air shelters and fire fighting facilities while adding new controls to prevent factory workers from leaving the cities.

A year ago today Anzio, Italy was invaded by Allied troops. Today, with remnants of that bloody battle in evidence, more bodies are found daily to be interred in either the British or American cemetery. 2400 Germans are also buried there.

Feared riots have now occurred in Italy as a draft of young men has started for a reconstituted army to fight the Germans.

Of 15,000 Canadian draftees given an embarkation holiday leave, 6300 are currently reported AWOL.

In sports, the U.S. Lawn Tennis Association has given #1 ranking to Sgt. Frank Parker and to Pauline Betz.

In New York young American conductor Leonard Bernstein will start a four day engagement with the Philharmonic Symphony Orchestra next Thursday the same day new tenor Richard Tucker makes his metropolitan debut in "La Giaconda."

A week from tonight a new Broadway show "Up in Central Park" will open starring Wilbur Evans, Betty Bruce, Noah Beery and Charles Irwin. Music is by Sigmund Romberg with lyrics by Herbert and Dorothy Fields. And Myrna Loy and William Powell in "The Thin Man Goes Home" opens this week.

On radio tonight try the National Barn Dance, the Judy Canova Show, or the Danny Kaye Show with Harry James and his orchestra, and listen to Lt. Robert Taylor on a Report to the Nation.

That's the news this January 20, 1945.

And now today's news, January 21, 1945.

The Red Army continues to roll over German opposition from East Prussia to Hungary. The First White Russian Army and First Ukrainian Army have plunged into German by driving into Silesia while taking over 1000 communities.

From what is left of the Belgian Bulge, Field Marshal von Rundstedt's men are pulling back quickly to the protection of the Siegfried line.

9000 Allied bombers and 500 fighters have hit three links in the German rail system while planes based in Italy have hit Vienna and Flume oil targets.

In the Pacific, the U.S. Sixth Army on Luzon is within 65 miles of Manila and only 22 miles from Clark Field.

In Japan, Premier Koiso has warned the Japanese people of an American invasion and says Japan stands at a dividing line of survival and death. New mobilization plans now include children.

President Roosevelt has nominated former Vice President Henry A. Wallace to succeed Jesse Jones as Secretary of Commerce.

A Congressional Medal of Honor has been posthumously awarded to Sgt. Truman Olsen of Cambridge, Wisconsin for holding off 200 Germans and firing 3200 machine gun rounds while saving his company from annihilation.

Corporal Gerald Wade of Lewiston, Idaho has become the first survivor of the Bataan Death march to cross into American lines on Luzon. He lived on rice for three years.

The 48th Medical Battalion of the 2nd Armored Division near Belgium treats frostbite with whiskey and notes a lot of ambulance drivers are now claiming frostbite.

Mayor Fiorello LaGuardia of New York has made Tuesdays and Fridays meatless days except for hamburger and frankfurter stands.

In sports, Roy Mangrum has won the Tucson open with a 12 under 268 and first prize money of $1000. Byron Nelson was second, Jug McSpaden fourth and Sam Snead 5th.

On radio tonight try Quick As a Flash, Ozzie and Harriet, The Great Gildersleeve, Fanny Brice, Jack Benny, and Edgar Bergen and Charlie McCarthy.

That's the news this January 21, 1945.

And now today's news, January 22, 1945.

Russian troops have advanced 53 more miles and are within 150 miles of Berlin while taking another 1750 towns. Nazi radio and press has beseeched all Germans to take up arms in defense of the Third Reich.

The German High Command claims their U boats have sunk another 6 merchant ships and 3 corvettes prompting Winston Churchill to note the Germans remain resourceful and dangerous.

The U.S. First Army says their U.S. Sherman tank crews perform brilliantly but admits that German Panthers, Tigers and Royal Tiger tanks have firepower superiority and better defensive armor.

Scores of Britons were killed today in southern England by German V-bombs that hit buildings, factories and private homes.

In Japan, Foreign Minister Sigemitsu says relations between Japan and Russia are "securely maintained in accordance with the neutrality pact."

Major General Curtis LeMay has moved from the B-29 command in China to take over the 21st B-29 Bomber Command from Brigadier General Hayward S. Hansell in the Marianas.

Herbert Brownell, head of the Republican National Committee, has laid out a four year plan to fight the Roosevelt New Deal.

Negro baseball last year had its greatest attendance says J.L. Wilkinson, co-owner of the Kansas City Monarchs. He says the Negro American and National Leagues will start their 100 game schedule in mid-May and hopes that great pitcher Satchel Paige—who he claims is better than most major leaguers—will be fully recovered from a stomach condition.

On Broadway tomorrow night Gloria Swanson and Conrad Nagel open up in "A Goose for the Gander" and current movies include 62 stars in "Hollywood Canteen," "Keys of the Kingdom" starring Gregory Peck, Vincent Price and Thomas Mitchell, and "Winged Victory" starring Jeanne Crain, Lee J. Cobb and Red Buttons.

Finally, 100 year old Mrs. Adaline Judd of Sag Harbor, NY recalls how young folk would go by stagecoach and horseback to see whaling ships off and comments that today's younger generation is no worse than others. She says "All this talk of juvenile delinquency is so much poppycock."

And you might tune in tonight to hear the perfect fool, Ed Wynn.

That's the news this January 22, 1945.

And now today's news, January 23, 1945.

The Soviet Union's mighty armies have reached the Oder River on a 37 mile front near Breslau, German Silesia. Most of Poland's liberated cities are almost without damage as Germans have made hasty retreats. Another 2000 Polish towns and 1500 German towns have been occupied. As German refugees are streaming into the German interior, Hitler has dispatched Gestapo head Heinrich Himmler to East Prussia with instructions to make drastic decisions.

Meanwhile, the Polish government has asked Great Britian and the United States to set up an Allied Military Council until free elections are held.

General Eisenhower's troops are within five miles of recapturing all of the former Ardennes Bulge territory while at the same time abandoning a sizeable strip of the Maginot line north of Strasbourg.

In the Pacific Camp O'Donnell, where American prisoners suffered disease and starvation, has been freed. So far 4000 graves have been found.

B-29's have bombed industrial targets in Nagoya, Japan and Iwo Jima with one plane lost. Navy and Army bombers have pounded Formosa again.

Prime Minister William L. MacKenzie King of Canada says due to political pressures he likely will dissolve Parliament next week and ask for new elections.

Governor Ellis Arnall of Georgia has asked the General Assembly to repeal the $1 poll tax on voting.

With home canning critical, the War Food Administration has assured housewives they will get the same sugar, pressure canners and containers as in 1944.

The Boxing Writers Association tomorrow night will honor Lt. Commander Benny Leonard, the only living retired undefeated world lightweight champion along with Private Beau Jack, a former lightweight champion.

Col. Larry MacPhail, former President of the Brooklyn Dodgers, will be discharged February 10th and Danny Kaye has been signed for a musical fantasy of Hans Christian Andersen which will also feature Virginia Mayo.

The New York Stock Exchange traded 1,365,000 shares with 20th Century Fox the volume leader with 47,800 shares.

That's the news this January 23, 1945.

Wednesday, January 24, 1945

And now today's news, January 24, 1945.

With the Red Army only 4 miles from Breslau, some 200,000 Germans in East Prussia are facing the danger of being entirely cut off from Germany.

The Nazis have announced the execution of 19 American and British agents charged with being sent to Slovakia to carry out sabotage.

Vice President Harry S. Truman has returned from the European theater with two Senators have deemed impractical Representative Clare Booth Luce's proposal that there should be fixed tours of duty in combat.

The red star emblem of Marshal Tito is replacing Yugoslavian blue, white and red tricolor flags around the world.

Major General Patrick Hurley, arriving in Chungking, China as U.S. Ambassador to China, was greeted by General Chiang Kai-shek.

The A-20 attack bombers are now being equipped with a super camera for taking pictures at night of German ground movements using large flash units capable of taking up to 100 sequential pictures.

Britain is spending 57 million dollars a day prosecuting the war and New York City is receiving over 1000 wounded a month arriving from Europe in Douglas C-54s in 18 hours.

The House Military Affairs Committee has approved 20 to 5 a Limited National Service bill giving the option to men 18 to 45 to join or not join a union in defense factories.

Outgoing Secretary of Commerce Jesse Jones says his proposed replacement, former Vice President Henry A. Wallace, is unfit to handle the financial dealings of the department. President Phillip Murray of the CIO backs Wallace.

A Zenith Vice President says television is a riddle that will have difficulty in developing and surviving relying only on advertising revenues. First, sets must be built and sold to provide an advertising audience.

Charles E. Merrill, General Partner of Merrill, Lynch, Pierce, Fenner and Beane reports 1944 profits of $4.4 million down from 1943.

And finally, international skating star Sonja Henie continues her ice show at Madison Square Garden, NY. Tickets range from $1.25 to $2.50 each.

That's the news this January 24, 1945.

And now today's news, January 25, 1945.

General Douglas MacArthur, who will be 65 tomorrow, has announced the taking of Clark Field and Fort Stotsenburg in Luzon while troops have suffered first casualties.

B-29 Superfortresses and B-24 Liberators today dropped 187 tons of bombs on Iwo Jima.

In Europe German troops have lashed out at American troops in the Strasbourg area driving 2000 yards into the U.S. 7th Army positions. American counterattacks wiped out most of their progress.

Dr. Joseph Goebbels has warned the German public of anarchy and sees more Russian inroads into Germany offering little cheer regarding the war.

Secretary of War Henry Stimson has announced the loss of 765 Americans on a troop ship. 1400 were saved, 517 are missing with no further details provided.

Some 13,000 American troops are AWOL on an average day in the ETO, many gravitating to Paris where some get involved in the black market.

In Greece 200 butchered bodies have been found, victims of the recent Elas communist period of occupation. American correspondents are now free to interview leaders of Eam, the Greek political resistance group.

President Roosevelt has named 103 generals including a promotion from Brigadier General for Anthony C. McAuliffe of the 101st Airborne Division who said "Nuts" to the Germans. Col. Elliott Roosevelt, the President's son, has been named a Brigadier General.

King Farouk of Egypt is visiting King Ibn Saud of Saudi Arabia.

The House panel continues to question Henry A. Wallace on his political views in considering him for Secretary of Commerce.

Three years after it opened, the New York Canteen has just entertained its one millionth service man and woman.

In Hollywood, Ingrid Bergman and Bing Crosby will star in a new movie "Bells of St. Marys" and a new movie just opening is "Woman in the Window" starring Edward G. Robinson, Raymond Massey, and Joan Bennett.

And, Beardsley Ruml's new book for $2.50 is entitled "Tomorrows Business."

That's the news this January 25, 1945.

Friday, January 26, 1945

And now today's news, January 26, 1945.

The Red Army has reached the Baltic and is within 8 miles of the Junker capital of Konigsberg. On other fronts they are close to Hindenburg in Silesia and within 93 miles of Berlin.

The American 9th Army has joined British forces north of Aachen driving the Germans out of the west bank of the Roer River. The American 7th Army in the Alsace has wiped out German wedges north of Strasbourg while the French First Army has further reduced the Colmar pocket.

It is now estimated that some 30,000 Jews remain alive in Poland compared to a pre-war total of three million.

German radio announced evacuation of civilians in Danzig and the Polish Corridor with the Nazi Gaulieter there calling on home recruits to report to mobilization centers.

In the Pacific the Japanese are shelling the newly taken Clark Field slowing U.S. progress towards Manila.

Japanese forces continue to advance on U.S. 14th Air Force bases in Hunan Province, China.

B-29's today from Saipan attacked Tokyo and destroyed or damaged 75 planes with a loss of 5 planes. General Lauris Norstad says fleets of B-29's will increase air strikes on Japan. It's now officially disclosed that B-29's carry 20,000 pounds of bombs. 135 planes are being built monthly.

Presbyterians will be asked to raise $20 million for a five year reconstruction plan for churches abroad and ministry to disabled veterans.

"Big Tom" Pendergast, Kansas City political boss who supported Vice President Truman's political career, has died at 72.

General Motors Vice President and inventive genius C.F. "Boss" Kettering says he sees the GM Allison engines important for post-war aviation use.

In New York today radio engineers, including Major Edwin H. Armstrong, inventor of FM, are arguing the merits of the FCC proposed move of FM frequencies.

Giovanni Martinelli, 32 years as a leading tenor, makes his seasonal Met debut tonight in Verdi's "Il Trovatore."

That's the news this January 26, 1945.

Saturday, January 27, 1945

And now today's news, January 27, 1945.

The on-rushing Russian armies have overrun Silesian war arsenals, have surrounded Posen and are close to Brandenburg as German radio announces they have abandoned industries of Upper Silesia.

The American Third Army has swept to the German border in five areas, overrun 11 Belgian and Luxembourg towns and have pushed the enemy back close to the Siegfried Line.

Field Marshal Baron Carl Gustav Mannerheim will resign as President of Finland in March to be succeeded by Premier Juho Passikiva.

American submarines have sunk another 21 Japanese ships inflicting total losses to date of 5.5 million tons leaving an estimated 3.5 million tons.

In London Lt. General Carl Spaatz says 12,500 Nazi planes have been destroyed in the last three years but at the expense of 5000 American bombers and 2500 fighters with the loss of 50,000 men.

In Bastogne, Burgomaster Leon Jacqumain says while Americans were idolized just three weeks ago after freeing the town, now American soldiers are looting stores taking watches, blankets, and mattresses. In apologizing, General Maxwell Taylor also noted some American MP's had been involved.

Judge Phillip Sullivan has ruled unconstitutional President Roosevelt's seizure of Montgomery Ward because of a labor strike. It's considered a victory for Board Chairman Sewell Avery. Montgomery Ward's stock rose 2 3/4 to 52 7/8's.

Gloria Vanderbilt diCicco, heiress to a $4.5 million fortune when she becomes 21 on February 20, has broken off her marriage to Pasquale "Pat" diCicco.

At Bloomingdales in New York beds are selling at $35 each, high chests at $62, studio consoles at $179.50 and walnut veneer chairs at $9.00. At Arnold Constables women's alligator shoes are $14.95 and pure wool suits are $49.95.

Kirk Douglas and Peggy Conklin open up Wednesday on Broadway in "Alice in Arms" and composer-conductor Igor Stravinsky will conduct the Philharmonic in four concerts next week.

On radio tonight try Truth or Consequences or Your Hit Parade.

That's the news this January 27, 1945.

31

Sunday, January 28, 1945

And now today's news, January 28, 1945.

Troops of the First Infantry Division of the American First Army have attacked north of St. Vith in a blinding, whirling snow storm with 7 foot drifts but had support of Allied planes in spite of the weather. The 8th Air Force celebrated its third birthday today by sending 1000 bombers with 3000 tons of bombs and 250 fighters over Germany. The RAF added 2000 tons on a Berlin night raid.

Figures on last week's raids report British and American planes destroyed 7300 German road and rail vehicles, including 521 tanks and armored vehicles, 2000 transport vehicles with a loss of 18 fighter bombers.

Adolf Hitler has conferred with his Norwegian puppet Vidkun Quisling apparently indicating Norwegian Nazis will be abandoned.

In the Pacific, the American military command headed by Admiral Chester Nimitz as Commander in Chief of Pacific Ocean areas has been moved several thousand miles west from Honolulu to a recaptured island.

Australian losses to date are 40,757 men in the Japanese war and a total overall of 84,396. The United States has reported another 2,980 casualties this past week.

The twin engine twin tailed Lockheed P-38 fighter has become the equivalent of a medium bomber able to carry two tons of bombs—as much as the earlier B-17—and flies at 425 mph with an increased range of 1800 miles using wing tip gas tanks.

A P-47 Thunderbolt fighter today says from high altitude he headed in a deep dive to join combat and hit 700 mph.

3 1/2 billion dollars was paid out last year in dependency allowances for wives and dependent children—a total of 6,450,000 persons.

Dana Andrews has signed for "Leave Her to Heaven" with Gene Tierney. Dennis O'Keefe and Don De Fore have joined with Robert Cummings and Elizabeth Scott to make "You Came Along."

Stock leaders for the past week were New York Central with 114,200 shares traded closing at 23 1/8, Graham Paige 110,000 shares at 7 1/4, IT&T 98,800 shares at 22 5/8 and Curtis Publishing 91,200 at 11 1/2. Packard has declared dividend number 129 at 15 cents per share.

Finally, at a National Press Club Show in Washington, the entertainment is Jack Benny on the violin accompanied on the piano by Vice President Harry S. Truman.

That's the news this January 28, 1945.

And now today's news, January 29, 1945.

The U.S. Third Army has broken back into Germany from the Ardennes bulge for the first time as 3500 flights have smashed railroad systems over a 350 mile stretch. 668 railroad cars and 47 locomotives were destroyed or damaged. Thanks to the support of fighters, U.S. bomber crews have been reduced from 10 to 9.

The Red Army is now 93 miles from Berlin and has invaded Pomerania in northeast Germany on the eve of Hitler's 12th anniversary as Chancellor. Streams of refugees arriving in Berlin are trying to escape the third night in a row of RAF bombing.

On Luzon, the 14th Corps troops are within 34 air miles of Manila while in the north the First Corps has savagely repulsed tank-led Japanese counterattacks.

The U.S. cost of the war is going at a rate of 84 billion dollars a year.

Elements of the British 14th Army are clearing the ways along the Irrawaddy River in Burma before an all-out attack on Mandalay.

Henry A. Wallace spoke at a testimonial dinner tonight in an all or nothing fight for his nomination as Secretary of Commerce. Mrs. Eleanor Roosevelt brought a ringing personal expression of confidence from the President.

General Joseph Stilwell says the Japanese war will be a long one. He believes the Japanese can field 4 million men and will never surrender unless beaten in a battle. Vice President Harry Truman says any compromise to conclude the war with Germany or Japan would be fatal in the long run.

Two Brooklyn gamblers have been taken into custody for paying $1000 each to five Brooklyn College basketball players to throw a game against the University of Akron.

The Duke and Duchess of Gloucester have arrived in Sydney, Australia for a two year stint as Governor General of the Commonwealth.

Gloria Swanson was married today to her fifth husband, George W. Davey, by a Police Recorder in Union City, NJ.

And Lionel Barrymore has replaced Cecil B. deMille as host on the Lux Radio Theater on tonight due to a disagreement with the AFTRA union.

That's the news this January 29, 1945.

Tuesday, January 30, 1945

And now today's news, January 30, 1945.

Russian troops continue unchecked 73 miles from Berlin as they have invaded Brandenburg and encircled the flaming East Prussian capital of Koenigsburg.

A Hitler speech from his headquarters says he expects the German people to die in their tracks to preserve National Socialism. He says maintaining unity gives a chance for final victory and preserving the moral destiny of Europe.

The German high command may withdraw certain troops from Italy to compensate for losses on the eastern front.

Tokyo reports that B-29's have bombed Luzon, and the homeland Honshu and have put reconnaissance over Korea.

The Americans have made a second landing on Luzon with five beachheads without firing a shot or seeing an enemy uniform. Troops include members of the 38th Division of Kentucky and Arkansas Mountaineers as well as the 24th Division, veterans of fighting in the jungles of New Guinea.

Presidential Advisor Harry Hopkins today spent 40 minutes with Pope Pius and Presidential personal Vatican envoy Myron C. Taylor discussing Poland, Germany and war rehabilitation.

The Wendell L. Willkie One World Award for Leadership has been given this year to AP Executive Kent Cooper, RCA President General David Sarnoff, and 20th Century Fox production Vice President Darryl Zanuck.

In Boston, divorces are up 10% to 2265 in 1943 due mostly to hasty war-time marriages says Suffolk County Registrar Arthur Sullivan. He says cases have arisen where the husband was unable to tell his wife's first name.

Large quantities of marijuana and some heroin have been seized in New York. Four major mob groups are supplying the drugs including the 107th Street mob formerly run by Lucky Luciano.

20-year-old Nora Eddington, former aircraft factory worker and cigar stand sales girl, has given birth to Diedri Flynn Eddington. She says she was married to actor Errol Flynn in 1943. In Mexico, Flynn declined to comment.

Finally, for President Roosevelt's 63rd birthday today Hollywood stars have gathered in Washington including Ella Logan, Joe E. Brown, Veronica Lake, Gale Storm, Linda Darnell, Jane Wyman, Danny Kaye, Myrna Loy, Charles Bickford, Ralph Edwards, Alan Ladd, Gene Kelly, Kay Kyser, Monty Woolley and Victor Borge.

That's the news this January 30, 1945.

And now today's news, January 31, 1945.

Capturing 200 prisoners in the past two weeks, the U.S. 1st Division of the First Army is three miles inside Germany while Red armies are just 63 miles from Berlin. The German army is on the defense from the Netherlands to Switzerland. SHAEF, Supreme Headquarters Allied Expeditionary Force, says a common front may be formed by the U.S. and Russia before German resistance is stamped out.

Cairo radio says terrified Berliners can hear sounds of big guns and the red glow of battle in the distance.

General MacArthur's troops have captured Olongapp, former U.S. naval base on Subic Bay on the Bataan peninsula.

A first convoy has started moving along what was known as the Ledo Road—now renamed the Stilwell Road—a lifeline from Assam, India to Kunming, China.

The Romanian council of ministers has approved arresting the first 100 generals, politicians and officials on charges of Nazi collaboration. Heading the list is former Premier Marshal Ion Antonescu.

1218 bodies have been exhumed in the Athens area since the liberation of Greece from the Nazis. Half bore signs of torture, 62% died of knifing and the rest were shot.

Japanese troops have sealed off the Chinese coast of Canton-Hankow guarding against possible Allied landings.

The Seabees, famous for building airfields, docks and highways almost overnight, are using their talents to build a major new Pacific headquarters base on a yet-to-be-identified recaptured island.

The War Production Board says all civilian tires may cease to be available after mid-year due to war needs.

The Brock triplets of Clarendon, Texas, enlisted together and now, all within 5 days, one has been killed, one is missing, and one is seriously wounded.

Commander Jack Dempsey, Chief of the Coast Guard physical fitness program, says sports are important and baseball in particular must go on during the war.

In New York City a new $80 million north tunnel has opened next to the south Lincoln tunnel used last year by 5.7 million vehicles.

Worsening weather on the east coast is part of the reason for a nationwide brown-out starting today to conserve coal.

That's the news this January 31, 1945.

Thursday, Feburary 1, 1945

And now today's news, February 1, 1945.

In a bold raid 407 Rangers and Filipino guerillas have rescued the first 513 gaunt and ragged survivors of the Bataan death march and Corregidor. Two freed prisoners died of heart attacks during the rescue while 523 Japanese and 27 U.S. soldiers were killed. Prisoners said 5000 of the 10,000 attacking Japanese on May 5, 1942 taking Corregidor were killed.

The Red Army is 57 miles from Berlin as women in Berlin are helping man anti-aircraft guns. French and American troops are in the suburbs of Colmar.

Ludwigshafen was hit by 700 Flying Fortresses while 1000 RAF night bombers hit Mannheim and Berlin.

Since D Day the U.S. has captured 868,982 Germans.

B-29's have knocked out the world's largest drydock in Singapore.

Nine Americans have been sentenced to death by U.S. Court Martial for diverting gasoline to the black market. 11 others received terms from 5 to 25 years.

Former Under Secretary of State Sumner Welles is speaking today at the 25th anniversary of the League of Nations as plans have been announced to change the name to the United Nations.

Following King Farouk's visit to Saudia Arabia, the Egyptian government has invited all Near Eastern Ministers to an Arab Union conference in Cairo in two weeks.

Lauren Bacall and Humphrey Bogart have just completed "The Big Sleep," Robert Montgomery "They Were Expendable" and Errol Flynn has been signed for "Target—Japan" about B-29's. Young Elizabeth Taylor has signed to join Bing Crosby in "The Bells of St. Mary."

John Gunther, called by Thomas Mann as "the greatest living man of letters" has a new book "The Troubled Midnight" available at $2.50 a copy.

Wall Street today reports silver at 44 3/4 cents an ounce and mortgages at 4 1/2%.

And in Chicago, the world's largest hotel, the 3000 room Stevens, is being sold to a syndicate headed by C.N. Hilton of Hilton Hotels for $7,500,000.

That's the news this February 1, 1945.

And now today's news, Februlary 2, 1945.

On the war front today, the U. S. First Army is within 4 miles of Sebleiden as American troops are battling in the streets of Colmar. On the Russian front, Marshal Zhukov's First White Russian army is within 12 to 14 miles of Frankfort.

In the air, 1200 RAF planes are bombing Wiesbaden and Karlsruhe with another 3000 Allied planes bombing and strafing German reinforcement troops.

And finally in Europe reports out of Germany indicate propaganda chief Dr. Joseph Goebbels is fleeing Berlin.

In the South Pacific the American First Cavalry has rapidly covered 32 miles on Luzon in a race to recapture Manila. The Navy Department reports another 10 Japanese ships have been sunk, bringing the total in the war thus far to 989.

The War Department reports today that American Forces have suffered 737,341 casualties to date including a total of 134,365 dead. Currently there are 5.1 million American troops overseas.

In Newark, an investigation has begun into the flourishing cigarette black market.

In Washington, Republican leaders are moving strategically to restrict Secretary of Commerce nominee Henry A. Wallace from putting a number of government agencies under his direction.

Looking towards a post war economy, General Motors has forecast Americans will have a pent-up demand for 12 million cars.

In sports, Larry MacPhail of the New York Yankees has urged the appointment of either Ford Frick or James E. Farley as baseball conmissiomer to replace the late Kenesaw Landis. In golf, Craig Wood leads in the $5000 Corpus Christi Open with a 6 under par 64.

In New York City, Frederic March is starring on Broadway in "A Bell For Adamo", Bobby Clark is in "Mexican Hayride", and the Astor Theater is ending the first run of the new Judy Garland movie, "Meet Me In St. Louis".

On the Stock Exchange, Radio Corporation closed at 12 5/8 with total trading on the Exchange reaching 1,871,100 shares.

That's the news this February 2, 1945.

Saturday, February 3, 1945

And now today's news, February 3, 1945.

While an estimated 3 million refugees have jammed into Berlin, the 8th Air Force today dropped 3000 tons of high explosive and incendiaries into the heart of that beleaguered city. An additional 400 B-24 Liberators blasted a synthetic oil plant at Rothensee.

Troops of the 9th Infantry waded into icy waters of a 14th century moat to trap a German garrison in a castle 7 miles from Monschau.

A Red army is within 11 miles of Frankfort having killed 8000 Germans and taken 9450 prisoners in an encircled pocket.

Rumors out of Ankara and Cairo say peace feelers from the Germans have been extended to the Big Three—Churchill, Stalin and Roosevelt who are meeting in the Black Sea area. It is felt to be premature.

More than 2/3's of the U.S Senate agree Germany and Japan should be permanently demilitarized.

In spite of sniper fire the people of Colmar, the last major French city to be liberated, are calm one day after their new freedom.

As the impending battle for Manila grows nearer, Filipino agents report all but a few thousand Japanese have withdrawn from the city.

In Rome Lt. Commander Douglas Fairbanks, Jr. has received the British Distinguished Service Cross for landings in Sicily, Salerno and Elba.

A lucky B-29 crew got home today on two and half engines with 147 holes in its fuselage and an unexploded Japanese shell lodged in one of its fuel tanks.

Statisticians of Metropolitan Life say Axis death losses to date are 1,250,000, of which 75% are German, to 880,000 for the Allies of which 65% are Russian.

The U.S. government says the birth rate in the U.S. is declining but inevitably will increase after the war with the reunion of families.

With the coldest winter in 25 years east of Chicago, Mayor Fiorello LaGaurdia of New York says he may close all theaters. Meantime, the Lyric Theatre has a load of cordwood on hand.

A new movie this week is the "Princess and the Pirate" with Bob Hope, Virginia Mayo and Victor McLaglen while on Broadway Jane Wyatt and Franchot Tone open in "Hope for the Best."

For radio tonight, try Nick Charles, the Andrews Sister Show with Abbott and Costello, The Shadow, Blondie or the Eddie Bracken Show.

That's the news this February 3, 1945.

And now today's news, February 4, 1945.

First, exciting news on the war front in the South Pacific. American troops have covered 100 miles in 66 hours to capture Manila in the Philippines and free a civilian interment camp. Then in a room by room battle at Santo Tomas University, they freed 3000 Americans. As Gen. MacArthur was forced to leave the Philippines three years ago on March 21, 1942 he stated "I shall return." Today he has said "I have returned."

Meanwhile B-29's from the new bomber bases in the Marianas hit Kobe, Japan for the first time in daylight from 25,000 feet. No losses were reported but in a Tokyo raid several days ago Capt. Waddy Young, a former All-American footballer at Oklahoma University, has been lost.

At home, the fuel crisis continues in the northeast with Buffalo having had 91 inches of snow already this year. New York's Governor Thomas E. Dewey feels the crisis is about over.

In sports, Byron Nelson celebrated his 33rd birthday today by winning the $5000 Corpus Christi Open with a 16 under par.

In New York, Dr. Harry Emerson Fosdick of the Riverside Church has predicted a slump in religious interest when the war is over.

On Broadway, Milton Berle is on stage at the Roxy, Myrna Loy and William Powell are on the screen with "The Thin Man Goes Home," and Sonja Henie is in the last five days of her ice show at Madison Square Garden.

A reminder to our listeners about two new radio shows tomorrow night—the Eddie Bracken Show and the Joe E. Brown Show. Jack Benny's weekly show of course starts at 7 pm on NBC opposite Kate Smith on CBS.

Finally, for the ladies, Franklin Simon in New York will give you a circular haircut for $1.50. National Airlines announces new flying time from New York to Jacksonville in four hours and 50 minutes, while inflation and shortages in China has the cost of a single egg at $24.

That's the news this February 4, 1945.

And now today's news, February 5, 1945.

Highlights on the war: In Europe, the Russian Red Army has reached the Oder River on a 75 mile wide front as U.S. and RAF bombers have hit Regensberg and Bonn again. Meanwhile, the U.S. Third Army has smashed through the Siegfried Line with an astounding lack of resistance by the Germans.

In the Pacific, Americans have freed another 1350 prisoners in Manila making a total of 5000 U.S., British and other nationals freed thus far.

Many internees are in tears as they see Old Glory for the first time in 3 years. Amazingly, all of the nurses known as the Angels of Bataan in 1942 have been accounted for. General MacArthur's latest statement is now "on to Tokyo."

While no decisions have been forthcoming from the secret conference of Churchill, Roosevelt and Stalin, General Charles de Gaulle in France has publicly stated their decisions will not be binding on France until he reviews them.

In New York City, many restaurants are balking at the introduction of a third meatless day this week after meatless Tuesday and Friday of last week.

At the Waldorf Astoria over 1000 people are celebrating today the 4th anniversary of the USO.

At Radio City Music Hall today is "A Song to Remember" starring Paul Muni, Merle Oberon and introducing Cornel Wilde. Artie Shaw's band is on stage at Warners' Strand, while in many area theaters Spencer Tracy and Van Johnson star in "30 Seconds Over Tokyo." And Edna Ferber's new book, "Guest Son," is available at $2.50 per copy.

Finally, in New York, Kings County District Attorney William O'Dwyer is tossing his hat in the New York City mayoralty race.

On Wall Street, margin accounts have increased from 40 to 50% as national employment has hit 51,800,000. On the New York Stock Exchange, Packard led trading volume with 97,400 shares and closed at 7, up a half.

That's the news this February 5, 1945.

And now today's news, February 6, 1945.

The war in Europe continues to move rapidly as 1300 U.S. bombers have hit Magdeburg, Leipzig and Chemnitz while American troops are moving in on five big dams on the Cologne Plain. A call to the home front has requested 6000 more WACS to relieve fighting troops for front line battle.

In the Pacific, Americans have entered Bataan and are in hand to hand combat in Manila. Military leaders are trying to determine if the Japanese will try a last ditch stand as did the Americans at Bataan and Corregidor.

In other news, there's still no clue as to exactly where Churchill, Stalin and Roosevelt are having their conference.

In Yugoslavia, Marshal Tito has rejected three of King Peters' nominees to the regency council.

At home, Washington is proposing a one billion dollar lend lease program to France.

James C. Petrillo, President of the American Federation of Musicians, has put the Interlochen Music Camp on the unfair list.

In sports, Columbia and Fordham will introduce a novel experiment tonight on the basketball court by giving 3 points for a shot from 21 feet or more. The idea was conceived by Howard Hobson, Oregon coach and Julian Rice, Columbia alumnus.

Big Bill Tilden and Vinnie Richards will put on a tennis exhibition on February 17th followed by a dance. On the same night at Madison Square Garden you can see the great sprinter, Corporal Barney Ewell, in action.

In business, America's major railroads announced income of 660 million in 1944, down 213 million from 1943 due to increased expenses. Volume on the Exchange today was 1,598,000.

Finally, the great British battleship Nelson has been refitted at the Philadelphia Navy Yard and is again at sea.

That's the news this February 6, 1945.

41

Wednesday, February 7, 1945

And now today's news, February 7, 1945.

Well, the news is finally out. Roosevelt, Churchill, and Stalin have been meeting in the Black Sea area with their chiefs of staff. The timing of this conference is critical since both the Americans and Russians are pouring into Germany.

Today we have word that Berliners have bricked up their famous Brandenburg Arch so that the Russians cannot have a victory march through it.

Another sign of disarray is that no word of Dr. Joseph Goebbels has been reported for some time.

Meanwhile, four of General George Patton's divisions have smashed over the German border in 10 places as the Russians under Marshal Zhukov are 31 miles from Berlin. U.S. assault troops have pushed across the Oder and Saar Rivers in boats under bitter Nazi fire.

In the Pacific, MacArthur has entered Manila and is handshaking old friends. Quezon City has been taken amid fires and destruction caused by the retreating Japanese.

In the air, B-29's have hit Saigon in French Indochina targeting the Rama VI bridge with good results.

On the home front, the government reports ration books are being lost at an ever greater rate.

In Washington, Col. Thomas Turin of the Civil Public Health Service has spoken out critically of those people who—and I quote— "under the banner of moral force," would keep a low profile on spreading information about new controls on the disease syphillis.

The National Red Cross headed by Colby Chester says they will need $200 million for 1945.

In sports, the King of Swat, Babe Ruth, is 51 today.

On Broadway, Lauritz Melchoir sings tonight at Town Hall and Alexander Brailowsky will appear on February 13th at Carnegie Hall.

A review of current retail prices includes men's suits at Gimbels for $40 and $50 apiece.

That's the news this February 7, 1945.

Thursday, February 8, 1945

And now today's news, February 8, 1945.

From Tokyo today comes word that the Japanese believe their Axis partner, the Third Reich, will survive and win the war notwithstanding the present situation. Meanwhile, American B-29's have hit Kobe in Japan for the 5th day in a row while B-24 Liberators have hit Iwo Jima south of Japan for the 63rd time.

In Europe, Field Marshal Bernard Montgomery's British and Canadian units supported by 2200 RAF and US planes have mounted a major offensive in the west and northern end of the Siegfried Line as RAF units also hit Berlin again. The Russian armies are heading towards the Baltic and are cutting off Danzig.

The food situation in Germany is becoming desperate and the Nazi government has now commandeered all German grain stocks. With people nearing the breaking point, Heinrich Himmler has personally taken over the defense of Berlin.

Insiders say the most powerful of the Big Three conference in the Black Sea has been Marshal Stalin. A more complete report of these conferences is expected any day.

Secretary of War Henry Stimson predicts that notwithstanding new freedom of American naval vessels in the Philippines and around Formosa, winning the war against Japan will be extremely difficult. Japan is being assailed for their treatment of just released prisoners in Manila.

Joseph Grew, Acting Secretary of State, reports the Italian Armistice is not yet settled.

Americans have been giving their blood generously in 1944. The Red Cross reports 5,371,000 pints donated but says they need more in 1945.

In sports, Phillip K. Wrigley of the Cubs and Sam Breadon of the Cardinals are on the committee to select the new baseball commissioner.

In New York, Victor Borge is at the Waldorf Astoria with the Leo Reisman and Mischa Borr orchestras. The hit show "Oklahoma" is being repackaged for foxhole tours abroad and Schenley Distillers has slashed quotas to retailers due to shortages.

Finally Daniel Harris, the last of 8,000 Jewish Civil War Veterans, has died at the age of 98.

That's the news this February 8, 1945.

Friday, February 9, 1945

And now today's news, February 9, 1945.

There's fierce fighting house to house on the streets of Manila today as U.S. troops gained another 200 yards. Fires are burning in three sections of the city. General Jonathan Wainwright was one of the 17 generals, 119 colonels, 6 navy captains and 34 enlisted men who were to have been moved by the Japanese from a prison camp in Formosa to Mukden prison in Manchuria.

China is preparing for Allied landings on the Asiatic coast by establishing headquarters at Kunming.

In Europe 1300 American bombers with 900 fighters blasted oil refineries at Lutzendorf, factories at Weimar, and rail yards at Magdeburg. 19 bombers were lost along with 3 fighters.

The Red Army is 9 miles from Stettin as Canadian and British troops under Field Marshal Montgomery are within 4 miles of Cleve.

Heinrich Himmler has told the garrison at Schneidemuhl to "hold fast for me" as the mayor of Koenigsburg has been hanged for leaving his town without evacuation orders.

Rampaging rivers on the Our and Sauer Rivers are holding up U.S. Army engineers from building bridges. At the Big three meeting, Churchill, Stalin and Roosevelt have been making plans for immediate occupation should there be a sudden German military collapse.

Malnutrition in France has caused a 48% rise in tuberculosis.

15 more Norwegian hostages have been executed by the Germans for committing sabotage making a recent total of 34.

Arab leaders now realize a need to make some concessions to Jews not just in Europe but worldwide which might also enlist better appreciation of their own nationalist viewpoint.

Republicans say they think Thomas E. Dewey may run again for President in 1948. William R. Barnes, Chairman of Barnes and Noble booksellers founded by his father in 1994, has died at age 78.

No-hitter baseball star and now Chief Specialist Bob Feller has gone east to receive new naval orders.

General Motors reports since 1940 it has manufactured one million machine guns, 2.4 million carbines, and 180,000 canons.

In Hollywood Humphrey Bogart and Barbara Stanwyck have been signed for the "Two Mrs. Carrolls" and Bruce Cabot and Kay Francis for "Divorce."

That's the news this February 9, 1945.

44

And now today's news, February 10, 1945.

Moscow Radio reports German naval personnel have revolted at Bremen Harbor as they have been dragged from their ships to be sent to the front in the army.

Lt. General Jacob Devers says the entire German 19th Army has effectively been eliminated after a 21 day assault on the Colmar pocket with 18,000-20,000 prisoners and 3000 dead. The Polish Government in exile has proposed 29 amendments to the Dumbarton Oaks world security plan.

The largest B-29 raid, 100 planes, have hit Tokyo, shot down 20 enemy planes and lost three right after Tokyo endured a large 3 hour earthquake. It's also been reported that from June to October Japanese airplane losses in the Pacific area were 20 times that of the U.S.

8000 square miles of Luzon have now been regained in the first month.

The Archbishop of Paris has issued instructions to parish priests to discourage hasty French war marriages to American and Britons.

The United Nations Relief and Rehabilitation Administration says 2000 representatives are ready to go to France to help millions of displaced persons.

The head of immigration of the Jewish Agency for Palestine says most of the 1.2 million survivors of the original 6 million Jews under German rule are eager to go to Palestine.

Secretary of State Edward Stettinius is going to Mexico for the Inter-American Conference on Problems of War and Peace with a large entourage including congressional leaders Senator Warren Austin of Vermont, Rep. Sol Bloom of New York, Sen. Tom Connally of Texas, and Rep. Edith Nourse Rogers of Massachusetts.

A $1000 gift from the United Auto Workers of Detroit to the first all-Negro squadron now flying in Italy has been returned by the flyers.

Big Band leader and trombonist Tommy Dorsey is rehearsing for an appearance with the Philharmonic in New York conducted by Leopold Stokowski.

On radio tonight, try the Mysterious Traveller, the Al Pearce Show, and Herbert Marshall in The Man Called X and tomorrow afternoon Nelson Eddy is now on CBS with Robert Armbruster's orchestra and ventriloquist Shirley Dinsdale and dummy Judy Splinters.

That's the news this February 10, 1945.

Sunday, February 11, 1945

And now today's news, February 11, 1945.

Two famous generals of recent years are in the news today. Gen. Jonathan Wainwright, imprisoned by the Japanese after the capture of Corregidor, has arrived in Formosa after his rescue several days ago. Elsewhere, Secretary of War Stimson has honored "Vinegar Joe" Stilwell, the General who was in charge of the China-Burma-India Theatre.

On the war front, 90 B-29's from the 21st Bomber Command in the Mariannas have today hit the Nakajima Aircraft Factory in Ota, Japan after blasting Tokyo yesterday. B-29's are now based on Guam, Tinian and Saipan as the beautiful city of Agana on Guam is being rebuilt.

In Europe today 125 B-24 Liberators and 250 Mustang fighters have blasted Nazi fuel dumps near Muenster.

Washington reported today that the total cost of the war is now up to 238 billion.

The American Legion and the ODA are meeting today to discuss ways for retraining war veterans for peacetime work.

In New York Archbishop Francis Spellman is telling 4000 Boy Scouts today he thinks the 1600 Protestant churchmen who have stated that religious sects should not take part in world politics is un-Christian. At the Cathedral of St. John the Divine, Protestant Episcopal Bishop Harry S. Kennedy spoke highly today of the loyalty of the Japanese living in Hawaii.

In sports, the New Orleans $5000 Open Golf Tournament has been cancelled due to rain.

On Broadway Olson and Johnson have 'em in the aisles with their zany antics in "Laffing Room Only."

On a sad note, Composer Al Dubin, age 54, has died. His most familiar number was "Dancing With Tears in My Eyes."

Finally, nothing is getting cheaper anymore even though DePinnas in New York has marked down their $350 Muskrat coats to $268. Broadcloth men's shirts at Sterns are $3.95 and four hot cross buns at Hanscom Bake shops are now 40 cents.

I'll be back again tomorrow with more news of our turbulent times.

That's the news this February 11, 1945.

Monday, February 12, 1945

And now today's news, February 12, 1945.

Details of the Big Three meetings in the Black Sea at Yalta continue to be released. President Roosevelt who was accompanied by his daughter, Mrs. John Boettiger, had with him advisor Harry Hopkins, Secretary of State Edward Stettinius, Chief of Staff Admiral Leahy, and James Byrnes. Prime Minister Churchill was accompanied by Anthony Eden, Foreign Secretary. Marshal Stalin had similar top advisors and military people with him.

Their discussions have concerned how to seal the doom of Nazi Germany and its militarism, occupation plans by the Allies, the establishment of popular governments, and reparations. Some discussion also occurred regarding the role the Russians might play in winding up the Pacific war.

Back home, former President Herbert Hoover has lauded the Yalta agreements.

The Senate has approved promoting Elliott Roosevelt, the President's son, to Brigadier General based on his war record.

General "Wild Bill" Donovan, Director of the Office of Strategic Services better known as the OSS, has proposed a peace-time spy plan organization for continuing intelligence. While some fear possible Gestapo tactics, the idea has been well received by Congress.

President Roosevelt has sent Congress a message regarding worldwide money plans as discussed at the Bretton Woods conference.

The War Department has released weekly casualty lists including 3,997 Army and Air Corps and 320 Navy and 64 Merchant Marine casualties.

In New York, Broadway hits include "The Late George Apley," "Up in Central Park," and "I Remember Mama."

The government today has released federal taxes for 1944 amounting to $42 billion of which $34 billion was from corporate and personal taxes.

Finally, as the situation worsens for Germany, the Nazis are drafting women and girls for auxiliary work.

That's the news this February 12, 1945.

Tuesday, February 13, 1945

And now today's news, February 13, 1945.

In Europe the Red Army has taken Budapest ending a 50 day siege in what is called a major war catastrophe with 159,000 Germans killed or wounded. Hitler had vowed to make Budapest another Stalingrad.

Meanwhile, 1400 RAF planes today have hit Dresden in support of the Russian ground forces.

In the Pacific, Americans have taken the big Cavite Naval base with the end of the fierce battle for Manila in sight. U.S. Navy experts estimate that 244,000 Japanese troops are holding on in bypassed islands.

In Washington, former Secretary of State Cordell Hull will represent the U.S. at the San Francisco convening of the United Nations to help draft world security plans. Others to attend are Commander Harold Stassen, Senator Tom Connally, Senator Arthur Vandenburg, Dean Virginia Gildersleeve, and Rep. Sol Bloom.

At the Crimean conference, Stalin agreed to a simple majority vote of 11 nations on the Security Council so long as it includes the U.S., Russia, Britain, and France voting with the majority.

In London, the Polish government in exile has denounced the decisions of the Big Three regarding Poland's future. Also in London it has been reported that 32-year-old Viscount Elveden, heir to the Guiness Brewery millions, has been killed. His 7-year-old son, Arthur Francis Guiness, becomes heir.

In sports, boxer Corporal Billy Conn is touring Europe. Here in the states a popular new movie is "To Have or Have Not" starring Humphrey Bogart and Lauren Bacall.

Today's retail prices include girdles at Best and Company for $7.50 each, men's stadium boots at Saks for $10.95 and Canada Dry's new Spur Cola is 5 cents a bottle.

In the business world, the Shawmut Bank of Boston has issued notes bearing 3.6% interest and Lily Dache will show her Spring fashions tomorrow.

Finally, from Washington, the consensus on the outlook of the war is that there will not be an early end in Europe and Russia is expected to enter the war against Japan soon.

That's the news this February 13, 1945.

And now today's news, February 14, 1945.

In the South Pacific, the U.S. First Cavalry has reached Ft. McKinley in the Philippines as the Japanese in their retreat have been setting fires and bayoneting and massacring civilians. Thirty one more Japanese ships are sunk by U.S. submarines.

In Europe, 8000 planes of the RAF and the U.S. 8th and 15th Air Forces have battered the Nazis in ten cities in one of the most powerful raids of the war. Dresden has been hit today three times. The Red Army has surrounded Breslau as Canadian forces are reaching Goch.

At home, two German agents who infiltrated U.S. shores by submarine will die by hanging after sentencing today at Governor's Island.

President Roosevelt is scheduled to stop and visit with Pope Pius on his way home from the Crimean conference as Secretary of State Edward Stettinius visits Moscow today.

In Budapest, many historical buildings have been severely damaged or destroyed including the Royal Palace, the Parliament and museums as citizens are leaving their cellars. 49,000 German bodies are lying in the snow in that city.

A number of Nazi radio stations are faking broadcasts as BBC stations and giving false reports.

The British have announced a new Spitfire capable of flying 400 m.p.h. with a 300 mile range.

At New York's Capitol Theater Anne Baxter and Ralph Bellamy star in "Guest in the House" featuring Marie "The Body" MacDonald with Ralph Edwards of radio's "Truth or Consequences" fame on stage.

Stocks are highest in five years with 2.0 million shares trading today as Secretary of the Treasury Henry Morgenthau predicts a tax cut after the war.

That's the news this February 14, 1945.

Thursday, February 15, 1945

And now today's news, February 15, 1945.

Today 1200 U.S. Navy planes have hit Tokyo airfields at tree top level bringing the war home to 8 million Japanese residents. To the south the small island of Iwo Jima is being bombarded by ships for the 69th day as B-29's from Saipan and Tinian have hit Nagoya in Japan. Tokyo radio reported 60 planes hit the Mitsubishi Aircraft Factory.

In the Philippines, U.S. guns are now within range of Corregidor.

In Europe, the aerial offensive continues night and day over Berlin, Dresden, and Nuremberg. 80% of all German oil refineries are now inoperative leaving only 4 synthetic plants operating.

In New York harbor, a B-29 has crashed in the water at La Guardia airport with 5 of the 10 man crew killed.

The New York Times reports from a 5000 sample survey that the average Japanese thinks Japan will win the war based upon their spiritual superiority. They do concede stronger U.S. industrial might.

Casualties reported today include 8848 Americans killed, 41,000 wounded, and 11,800 missing on the German war front alone.

The Hindu, Sabu, who became known as the Elephant boy in the movies, is now a ball turret gunner in the 13th Air Force. Metropolitan opera star Kirsten Flagstad's husband has been arrested in Norway by Germans, Charlie Spivak's band is at the Commodore, Frank Fay is starring on Broadway in "Harvey," and Kate Smith has been honored for her 1944 goodwill broadcasts.

Weber and Heilbronner men's hats are on sale at $6.50 to $15 and Coca Cola is still 5 cents a bottle.

The American Federation of Labor has agreed to re-admit the United Mine Workers if John L. Lewis is not put on their Board.

Finally, a new technique now permits taking of penicillin by mouth instead of by injection.

That's the news this February 15, 1945.

And now today's news, February 16, 1945.

American troops have made a surprise landing on the southern tip of the Bataan peninsula and have taken beach front across from Corregidor.

1200 carrier planes have attacked Tokyo at dawn today. Battleships and cruisers continue to shell Iwo Jima 750 miles south of Tokyo as Tokyo says it expects an invasion soon.

In Europe more than 1000 planes have hit Dortmund and Gelsenkirchen in Germany. Dresden has already been reduced to shambles by previous attacks.

Adolph Hitler has declared martial law on all fronts and in Berlin to curb panic and chaos.

It's been reported that a Japanese ship was torpedoed last October while moving American prisoners from Luzon. 1800 Americans were lost with only five survivors. And another 4186 Army and 249 Navy casualties this week have been announced by the War Department.

In aviation news, two Japanese planes can do 400 mph though they cannot keep up with the B-29 at 40,000 feet.

Today's papers are carrying a picture of Churchill, Roosevelt and Stalin outdoors in overcoats at the Lavadia Palace in Yalta.

San Francisco's 1500 hotels will be overbooked in April when 44 nations gather to draw up a charter for a permanent world security organization.

Former Congressman Maury Maverick testified today that $10,000 a year is not enough for congressmen and he endorses the $12,500 proposed by Representative Emmanuel Celler of New York.

In Hollywood Deanna Durbin and Charles Laughton have signed for "Catherine the Last." Mary Martin will star in "One Touch of Venus" and Linda Darnell in "Fallen Angel."

In an auto accident actress Marjorie Rambeau has a broken leg and possible skull fracture.

Sam Snead is 6 under par in the $5000 Gulfport, Mississippi Open and in New York a tennis benefit for serviceman overseas features 52 year old Big Bill Tilden and Vinnie Richards in singles and Tilden also will team in doubles with Hollywood's best tennis player, Errol Flynn.

That's the news this February 16, 1945.

Saturday, February 17, 1945

And now today's news, February 17, 1945.

General MacArthur's troops have landed on Corregidor where America suffered its bitterest defeat three years ago.

Heavy bombardment continues on Iwo Jima. Tokyo says landings have been made, though Admiral Chester Nimitz has made no such mention. This rocky fortress will be critical to put fighters within range of Japan and for emergency B-29 landings.

General Charles de Gaulle of France has declined an invitation to meet with President Roosevelt after the Big Three Yalta conference. He apparently feels France should have been included. His action has dismayed the French cabinet.

Argentina is taking steps to declare war on Germany.

Senator Robert F. Wagner of New York says the U.S. will not block U.S. membership in the United Nations as it did in the League of Nations after World War I.

Premier Achill Van Acker of Belgium says more Allied aid is needed and will ask for 500,000 tons a month to save the nation.

Ruins of Monte Cassino where a Benedictine Abbey was destroyed a year ago— will only be partially rebuilt leaving the rest as a monument.

The Swiss Federal Council has frozen all German and Lichtenstein assets pending further accounts examination.

A 9 story building on 40th Street in New York City originally purchased for $450,000 for the now discontinued New York Club has been purchased for $250,000 to become the Wendell Willkie Memorial Building dedicated to his causes.

In music, Johann Strauss' "Der Rosenkavalier" will be performed Friday night at the Met in New York featuring Rise Stevens and Lotte Lehmann while Robert Shaw will conduct the Collegiate Chorale tomorrow night at the City Center.

The top four seeds in the Eastern Lawn Tennis Association tournament have all won. There are Bill Talbert, Sidney Wood, Gilbert Hall and Frank Broida.

And when planning ahead, Phoenix Mutual is advertising a lay-away plan that will permit you to retire at age 60 with $150 a month.

That's the news this February 17, 1945.

And now today's news, February 18, 1945.

Over the weekend naval air attacks continued over Japan and MacArthur's troops have landed on Corregidor.

Today, the 4th and 5th Marines stormed ashore on Iwo Jima in the Volcano Island group under the direction of Admiral Chester W. Nimitz who called this invasion a momentous step on the road to Tokyo. Bitter Japanese resistance was encountered.*

As B-29's continue to hit Japan, Tinian has become the world's largest airport with 8000 foot runways built in 60 days by the Seabees.

In the Philippines, Americans have seized the Manila hospital and freed 7000 people amid reports of laughing Japanese who were bayoneting a priest and civilians last week.

In Europe, the Nazi base at Goch is doomed by British action as the American 7th Army has re-entered Germany southwest of Saarbruken. The Red Army is nearing the border of Saxony.

Washington has announced a new draft program that will take men under 38 in a "work or fight" plan. Qualified men will of course see combat.

In sports, Sam Snead set the pace yesterday in the $5000 Gulfport, Mississippi Open and today is tied with Byron Nelson at 275. There'll be a playoff tomorrow of 18 holes.

Young screen actor Roddy McDowell grows up to be Gregory Peck in a new movie "Keys to the Kingdom," and rehearsals for a new Broadway show called "Carousel" have started. "Dear Ruth" and "Voice of the Turtle" are other Broadway hits today. On radio tonight, you can listen to the Philco Radio Hall of Fame featuring Bob Hope, Judy Canova, Paul Whiteman, Janet Blair and Eddie Cantor.

A newspaper ad today is promoting the February 26th Red Cross benefit with pictures of volunteer stars including William Gaxton, Victor Moore, Hazel Scott, Victor Borge, and Gypsy Rose Lee.

Macy's ad today features 3 side tables and a sofa for $249 while Lane Bryant offers woman's grey jerkin suit for $8.25. At the bookstores you can buy Earl Browder's new book "Teheran."

That's the news this February 18, 1945.

*Feburary 19th Pacific Time.

53

Monday, February 19, 1945

And now today's news, February 19,1945.

The fighting on Iwo Jima has intensified as American troops are nearing the airfield along side Mt. Suribachi. 800 naval vessels have helped establish a 2½ mile beach head including 6 ancient U.S. Battleships—the New York, Arkansas, Texas, Idaho, Nevada, and Tennessee. Passing nearby Iwo on the way to bomb Tokyo today were 150 superforts who destroyed 66 Japanese planes under the direction of General Curtis LeMay and his 20th Air Force flyers.

While rumors of possible peace feelers continue, Admiral Bull Halsey has warned of being tricked by Japanese industrialists who would sue for peace. He says we shouldn't accept if this occurs.

In Europe, rugged Scottish troops have swept the Germans from Goch as the Red Army moves in on Breslau. Elsewhere, Russian troops have freed American prisoners in German camps in Poland. 2000 RAF, 8th and 15th Air Force planes have hit railroad yards all the way to Vienna today. Destruction by guns and planes on the Siegfried line has made it virtually a mausoleum for trapped Germans.

In London, Czechoslovakian President-in-exile Eduoard Benes hopes to establish a temporary capital at Kosice until Prague is freed, and Churchill and Anthony Eden have returned today from the Crimean conference.

In Washington, U.S. diplomatic relations have been re-established with El Salvador after a lengthy investigation into its ties with the Axis.

The house today has approved increasing interest on the debt to $4.5 billion, up $750 million.

In sports, Willie Pep, world featherweight champion, retained his title today at Madison Square Garden. Actor Fred Stone will appear for two weeks on Broadway in "You Can't Take It With You" and Arturo Toscanini and his famous son-in-law Vladmir Horowitz appear tonight at Carnegie Hall in a benefit for the National Foundation for Infantile Paralysis.

The stock market was up 2 points on 1,880,000 shares.

Finally, Mrs. Calvin Coolidge has returned to her home in Northampton, Massachusetts after loaning it for the past two years to Smith College.

That's the news this February 19, 1945.

And now today's news, February 20, 1945

In the Pacific war American Marines have taken the Iwo Jima airfield as 4th and 5th Marine divisions gained only 100 yards today. The U.S. now holds 4500 yards on one side and 2000 yards on the west side of the island.

In Europe 900 U.S. B-17 Flying Fortresses have hit Nuremberg as big British Lancaster bombers hit Dortmund in the Ruhr Valley last night.

It is now known that Prime Minister Churchill and President Roosevelt conferred in Alexandria, Egypt after their Crimean conference. Churchill pledges an all-out Pacific British effort as soon as the European war is over.

Ex-Minnesota Governor and Flag Secretary to Admiral William Halsey—Commander Harold Stassen, has accepted an assignment to the upcoming United Nations Security Conference in San Francisco.

Enemy casualties on Luzon are reported as 92,000 compared to U.S. casualties of 2676 killed and 10,000 wounded.

In France, the purge continues of over 60,000 who have collaborated with the Germans. One third are expected to be reprieved.

In Washington the War Labor Board has ordered the minimum pay scale of 55 cents per hour to be paid textile workers equal to a 5 cent per hour raise.

In sports, Ford Frick, President of the National league, met today with War Mobilization Board Director James Byrnes regarding travel restrictions which could drastically affect this year's baseball season.

In New York, the Ballet Russe de Monte Carlo opens today for five weeks at the City Center with tickets priced at 90 cents to $2.40. Abbott and Costello in "Here Come the Coeds" is at Loew's Criterion featuring Peggy Ryan plus Phil Spitalny and the Hour of Charm All-Girl Orchestra.

Ladies, at Lambert's Jewelers you can get a diamond solitaire for $100 and at Abercrombie and Fitch's a check tweed skirt at $18.75.

On Wall Street, Halsey Stuart and Company has issued bonds bearing a 2 3/4% interest return.

And finally, Gloria Vanderbilt de Cicco—estranged wife of Hollywood agent Pat de Cicco whom she married when she was 17, becomes 21 today and will inherit a $4.5 million trust.

That's the news this February 20, 1945.

Wednesday, February 21, 1945

And this is today's news, February 21, 1945.

On the European war front American P-47 Thunderbolt fighters hit Bertchesgaden for the first time. It was only after the raid that the pilots found out they had hit Hitler's secret hideout.

Patton's tanks moved today between the Moselle and Saar Rivers as the Third Army gained 5 miles. Elsewhere, Russian forces are threatening Cottbus and Guben.

In the Pacific theater 3 U.S. Marine Divisions totaling between 45,000-60,000 troops are inching up the slopes of Iwo Volcano. The Americans report taking only one Japanese prisoner thus far on the 7.9 square mile island.

The Navy reports another 25 Japanese ships sunk, a total of 1045 thus far in the war. Further south, British tanks are moving within 35 miles of Mandalay.

In other news, 1209 repatriates—wounded soldiers and sailors—have arrived in New York harbor on the Swedish American Liner Gripsholm. There were tears in the eyes of many as they passed Miss Liberty.

The Attorney General's office is cooperating with the New York State Tax Department after seizure of over 205,000 black market cigarettes in retail stores.

In Washington, the Frequency Modulation Broadcasters, Inc. are at odds with the FCC regarding FM spectrum allocation for what many feel will be an exciting new industry after the war.

In New York, Park Bernet Galleries has sold a Van Dyck portrait for $10,000, a Gilbert Stuart for $5,500 and George Romney's famous Blue Boy was sold for $9,250.

An A&P grocery ad today lists Campbell's vegetable soup at 12 cents, Wheaties at 14 cents, Shredded Wheat 22 cents, a dozen donuts at 19 cents, 2 bags of Red Circle Coffee at 47 cents and six 12 ounce bottles of Pepsi Cola for 23 cents.

New York Stock Exchange volume today was 1,700,000 as Socony Vacuum closed at 17.

Finally, German food rations have been cut by one-eighth as Berlin women are building barricades to defend against the on-coming Russians.

That's the news this February 21, 1945.

And now today's news, February 22, 1945.

Washington's 213th birthday will be celebrated today without a holiday as war production continues at full blast. The stock exchange will be closed.

On Iwo Jima the 28th Marine Regiment has captured Mt. Suribachi and raised an American flag in what has been the hardest fight in the 168 year history of the Marines. B-29's have flown over Japan on reconnaissance flights.

In Europe more than 700 aircraft involving 5 Allied air forces, dropped 100 tons a minute battering German rail yards. British Mosquito bombers have hit Berlin.

Marshal Stalin today says full victory is near. He puts Nazi losses in the last 40 days at 1,150,000 men. The 5.5 million bewildered citizens of Berlin are busy building barricades.

German inflation is soaring as thousands of Gestapo agents have been reassigned from helping to control inflation to the defense of Berlin.

France's Foreign Minister Georges Bidault has been invited to London to be briefed by Anthony Eden on the Yalta talks. In Geneva, the International Red Cross reports they have handled almost 35 million pieces of mail for war prisoners since the start of the war.

At home, the National Foundation for Infantile Paralysis has authorized 1.8 million dollars for research, education and training of physical therapists.

In sports, Sugar Ray Robinson is favored in his 4th bout with Jake LaMotta. The Philadelphia Eagles report five of their players have been killed in the war.

At the movies, Errol Flynn is in "Objective Burma," Rosalind Russell and Jack Carson in "Roughly Speaking" and George Sanders is in "The Picture of Dorian Gray."

At Macy's, classical records are 39 cents, a dozen pencils are 22 cents while A&P has bananas at 12 cents a pound and sirloin steak at 44 cents. Finally, AT&T reports earnings of $169,000,000 last year on sales of $1.76 billion.

That's the news this February 22, 1945.

Friday, February 23, 1945

And now today's news, February 23, 1945.

In a great offensive to put Allied troops on the Rhine, the American 1st and 9th Armies launched a powerful attack east of Aachen and 20 miles west of Cologne. Troops stormed across the Roer River in the most spectacular operation since D-Day.

Newly captured German prisoners say Germany is eager to surrender.

6000 Allied planes struck rail systems in many German areas. Marines gained 300 yards in the bloody and savage battle on the little island of Iwo Jima—yard by yard over an area strewn with Japanese bodies. The Japanese are using 1000 pound rockets in counter attacking.

On the southern tip 28th Marine Regiment has surrounded Mt. Suribachi and 3rd Division Marines have occupied the southern airstrip.

Turkey, sitting on the sidelines for 6 years, has declared war on Germany and Japan so as to win a seat at the UN conference table.

An American Airlines plane has crashed near Cedar Springs, Virginia killing 17 early today.

Under Secretary of War Robert Patterson says we need another 900,000 men in the Army and Navy within 6 months. New York City alone has contributed over 850,000 men in service since 1940.

Reception of cable communications between Guam and Hawaii has been repaired and started again over a 3981 mile stretch.

Congressional resentment against the power of James C. Petrillo over music and radio has brought proposals to limit his authority.

Alexei Tolstoy considered by many as Russia's greatest contemporary author died today at 67.

Retail sales nationwide are up 24% over the same period last year.

Welterweight Harlem Negro Ray Robinson outpointed Jake LaMotta at Madison Square Garden. Paul Robeson's performance in "Othello" on the west coast is a sell-out for four weeks.

And, to keep further informed listen tonight to Bill Stern for sports and H.V. Kaltenborn and Lowell Thomas for news.

That's the news this February 23, 1945.

And now today's news, February 24, 1945.

The Marines have gained another 600 yards on Iwo Jima fighting through a maze of pillboxes, land mines and fortified caves many 40 feet deep and good reason why 74 days of bombardment failed to decimate the garrison.

The three week fight for Manila has ended with more than 12,000 Japanese dead and now 2146 civilians rescued from the Los Bunos interment camp.

2300 Allied planes have blasted Dortmund, Hanover and Hamburg paving the way for the final drive of the war against Germany.

300 German U boats are still based in Norway in part to protect the German Navy no matter if there is a German military collapse elsewhere.

A Hitler speech to the Old Guard Nazis threatens traitors even as he predicts a German triumph.

Many great cities in the Netherlands have severe famine. Amsterdam is without telephones, electric lighting and gas. No civilian autos, buses or trollies are in operation. Water is doled out every 24 hours.

A pro-Axis 28 year old man has assassinated Egypt's Premier Ahmed Maher Pasha in Cairo.

67 American nurses who were prisoners on Bataan in the Santo Tomas Philippine prison have arrived at Hamilton Field, and will have a medical check-up at Letterman Hospital in San Francisco.

For the first time in 26 years the death rate in Italy is higher than the birth rate.

A spectacular photo taken on Mt. Suribachi of Marines hoisting a victorious American flag is in newspapers coast to coast taken by Joe Rosenthal, Associated Press photographer, who has been commended for his outstanding pictures of the Iwo Jima invasion.

At the movies Eddie Bracken and Veronica Lake are in "Bring on the Girls" while in New York this week two well known conductors take the stage, Conductor George Szell with the Budapest String Quartet and Eugene Ormandy conducting the Philadelphia Orchestra at Carnegie Hall.

And finally, when you need a treat, those five flavored Life Savers are still only a nickel.

That's the news this February 24, 1945.

Sunday, February 25, 1945

And now today's news, February 25, 1945.

Over the weekend 1600 Naval aircraft hit Tokyo again and B-29's bombed the same target today. On the front page of most newspapers today is a striking photo of five U.S. Marines raising the American flag atop Mt. Suribachi Iwo Jima. Marines have captured the east-west runway and two-thirds of the north-south strip on the embattled island as Secretary of Defense James V. Forrestal toured the island today.

In Europe, American 1st and 9th armies have crossed the Roer River and established a 25 mile beachhead only 17 miles from Cologne. 16 more towns have fallen to Gen. Simpson's 9th Army and Gen. Courtney Hodges 1st Army assault troops. In the air, Munich has been blasted by 6000 planes in daylight raids on rail, aviation, tank and industrial targets.

From Rome, British Resident Minister Harold McMillan has announced drastic changes giving the Italian government more controls over their destinies.

A European source indicates they expect 6 million of the 15 million displaced persons in Europe to get home by walking.

Helen Hayes starts a new Mutual network drama series and Katharine Cornell and Brian Aherne will star on Broadway in a revival of the "Barretts of Wimpole Street."

On radio on the NBC Blue Network tonight, you can hear Transatlantic Quiz featuring from New York author Christopher Morley, Harvey star Frank Fay and Moderator Alistaire Cook while from London film player Lt. Col. David Niven will be along with two others.

Finally, Pan Am has ordered for post war delivery 15 six engine land based clippers from Consolidated Vultee capable of holding 204 passengers with a cruising speed of 350 and a range of 4200 miles. It's wing span of 230 feet is twice that of the B-24 liberator.

That's the news this February 25, 1945.

And now today's news, February 26, 1945.

On the war front, Filipinos have regained full civil control as General MacArthur today turned over all controls to President Sergio Osmena after bitterly denouncing the Japanese for destruction of churches and cultural centers during the war. Farther north, a small American airplane was used for the first time today on a captured Iwo Jima airfield.

In Europe, American guns are shelling Cologne from 10 miles away as troops near the Rhine are using a superhighway built by Hitler. 1900 planes of the U.S. Air Force are hitting Berlin in the heaviest attack of the war today. Only moderate flak and no Luftwaffe fighters have been encountered.

Following Egypt's lead, Syria has now declared war on Germany and Japan. Lebanon is expected to follow shortly.

At home John L. Lewis, head of the United Mine Workers, has filed notice of a strike three days from now. Nationwide, a midnight curfew has started to conserve fuel. Night club bands are playing Good Night Ladies and bars offer last drinks at 11:45 pm.

In Albany, New York, Governor Thomas E. Dewey is meeting with Commander Harold Stassen to discuss Republican strategy in regard to the upcoming United Nations conference in San Francisco.

Even though the present war is not yet over, General H.H. "Hap" Arnold, head of the Air Force, predicts that in the next war the United States will be hit first because of growing air power capabilities.

Movie producer Samuel Goldwyn is in London today not on movie business but on a fact finding mission for the Foreign Economic Administration. New books out include "The Thurber Carnival" by James Thurber at $2.75 and John Steinbeck's "Cannery Row" at $2.00.

Finally in the news here in the United States, World War I flying ace, Captain Eddie Rickenbacker, now President of Eastern Airlines, has announced that all revenues of the airline for 24 hours will be donated to the Red Cross.

On the stock exchange, RCA earnings for 1944 were $1.2 million up one cent from 1943. Volume on the exchange was a slow 1.2 million shares.

That's the news this February 26, 1945.

Tuesday, February 27, 1945

This is Herb Hobler with today's news, February 27, 1945.

Today's papers reported the B-29 incendiary raid yesterday burned out a section of Tokyo equal to 240 square blocks of New York City. This reporter was on that B-29 raid with explosive bombs dropped from 25,000 feet with minimum accuracy due to a 210 knot tail wind. En route to the target at 2 am the island of Iwo looked like a Fourth of July display.

In Europe Russian troops have advanced 44 miles in 4 days through Pomerania towards the Baltic. The Germans have reported sinking 57 Allied merchant ships, 27 destroyers and two light cruisers while the Swiss Air Force reports shooting down two American bombers and forcing down 7 bombers that were flying over Switzerland.

Another kind of tragedy is happening in the city of Rotterdam as 400 people a day are dying of hunger. It's reported Nazi troops are providing soup kitchens for children under 10.

In London, Prime Minister Churchill has asked Commons to affirm the decisions made by the Big 3 in Yalta as the best hope for the cause of future peace.

At home, the War Labor Board has approved the raising of 4 million more workers to 55 cents per hour. The War Department is releasing 90,000 men a month but with peace expects it will rise to 200-250,000 after VE day. And, the 68 just released Bataan Nurses who were prisoners for 3 years will get back pay averaging $6500.

In sports, Cornell gets a new football coach, Ed McKeever from Notre Dame replacing Carl Snavely who returns to North Carolina. Big Bill Tilden has called insufferable the U.S. Lawn Tennis Association ban on amateurs playing professionals at army camps and hospitals.

In New York, actor Raymond Massey and Mayor Fiorello LaGuardia have urged 5000 people today to give blood to the Red Cross.

Also in New York you can have lunch today at the Barbizon Plaza for 45 cents, cocktails from 65 cents.

The U.S. government says the average American will have 5½ pounds less chicken available this year due to military demands.

By the way, the New York Times 7 days a week now costs $17 a year.

That's the news this February 27, 1945.

And now today's news, February 28, 1945.

At the top of the news, President Roosevelt has returned to Washington with a prophecy of peace after his Yalta conference with Marshal Stalin and Prime Minister Churchill. The President was gone 5 weeks, covered 14,000 miles and looked tanned and refreshed. He speaks to Congress tomorrow.

On the war front, U.S. tanks are 7 miles from Cologne as German forces fade under determined attacks by the Canadian first Army near Hochwald. German field Marshal Karl von Rundstedt is pulling his troops back as 6000 U.S. planes hit rail yards on a broad front.

In the Pacific, the hell of the Iwo Jima battle has been complicated by the island's volcanic ash choking rifles, clogging men's eyes and requiring men to crawl rather than walk with heavy equipment.

In Washington $2.5 billion in lend-lease has been approved for France for now and postwar reconstruction.

A posthumous award has been presented to the widow of Scripps Howard columnist and famed journalist Raymond Clapper killed a year ago on Kwajalein.

The Navy Department has announced the loss of the 38th and 39th submarine of the war, the Shark and the Escolar.

Air Force Chief Gen. Hap Arnold has announced America's first jet fighter, the P-80 Shooting Star, designed and built and flown in 143 days. The British jet fighter, the Meteor, has been operational since last summer and presumably flies at over 500 m.p.h. America's pressurized P-80 reputedly approaches the speed of sound.

In sports, Marine Major Tuss McLaughrey will be released April 1st to return to Dartmouth as head football coach.

For entertainment, you can now buy a 6 record album of the "Song of Norway" for $6.75 on Decca Records. Elsewhere Major Edwin F. Armstrong, inventor of FM, has urged the FCC to put the new FM band in the mid band and put TV at the upper end of the spectrum for postwar development of both mediums.

On the political scene, Congressman Adam Clayton Powell of New York says Henry A. Wallace, new Secretary of Commerce, has taken a first step towards the presidency.

Finally, a new movie has opened called "A Tree Grows in Brooklyn." It stars Dorothy Maguire, Joan Blondell, James Dunn and Peggy Ann Garner.

That's the news this February 28, 1945.

63

Thursday, March 1, 1945

And now today's news, March 1, 1945.

President Roosevelt is addressing Congress today on the Big Three conference at Yalta. He notes that the U.S. no longer can take unilateral action but must collaborate with other countries for peace.

In the Philippines, General MacArthur's troops have landed on Palawan with veteran troops of the New Guinea and Biak invasions a year ago. A tragic story was then revealed of how 150 American troops several years ago had been forced into sandbagged tunnels, fueled by gasoline and set fire. Attempting escape, some were shot and a few escaped to tell the story.

The Navy revealed today the loss of the small salvage vessel U.S.S. Extractor accidentally sunk by one of our own submarines. 6 men were lost.

In Paris, pending trial for treason, the courts have ordered seizure of personal belongings of Marshal Henri Petain and many of his ministers including the wealthy Pierre Laval.

Here in New Jersey, 125 newly commissioned army nurses have arrived at Ft. Dix. All volunteers, they range in age from 20 to 45.

Secretary of War Stimson announced another 11,870 casualties today while also noting that during the Italian campaign from September 9, 1943 to February 25, 1944 19,989 Americans were killed with 70,000 more wounded.

In sports, among the leaders in the $5000 Jacksonville Open are Craig Wood, Byron Nelson, Sam Snead and Denny Shute. In New York the internationally known Swedish distance runner, Gunder Haegg, has arrived for indoor track meets.

Two new movies showing are "Hotel Berlin" starring Faye Emerson, Helmut Dantine, Raymond Massey and Peter Lorre plus "Hollywood Canteen" featuring Bette Davis, John Garfield, Jack Benny, Eddie Cantor and many others.

A story reported today concerns a German citizen and his wife who was about to give birth. They reached out to men of the U.S. Third Army who assisted in the birth of a boy that the German couple named—Franklin Delano Ludwig.

That's the news this March 1, 1945.

And now today's news, March 2, 1945.

Three years after being defeated, General MacArthur today returned to Corregidor to raise a flag stating "Hoist the colors, let no enemy haul them down." Luband Island has been seized by American troops.

On Iwo Jima the Third Marine Division moved ahead 200 yards into enemy lines virtually cutting the island in two.

The level of German resistance is crumbling before a flood of Allied might with the American 1st Army within 5 miles of Cologne, the 3rd nearing Coblenz while Nazis have been ordered to leave a scorched earth defending ruins with ruins.

For the 18th consecutive day Allied air raids are pounding Germany—6000 planes hit 9 targets with 67 fighters shot down, 37 wrecked on the ground and gunners on bombers shooting down another 6. Cologne was battered again, next to Berlin the most bombed city in the world.

Generalissimo Francisco Franco of Spain has let it be known that 867 British and American flyers downed on Spanish soil have been delivered to Gilbraltar.

After weeks of controversy and hearings Henry A. Wallace has been confirmed as Secretary of Commerce.

The UAW has given a strong warning to the National Labor Board that in addition to the 34,000 already on strike, a total of 126,000 workers of Chrysler and Briggs Manufacturing may be on strike by tomorrow.

David B. Smith of Philco told the FCC that television would be "a large post war industry providing job opportunities for a great many people."

Bernard Baruch, appointed as an advisor to James F. Byrnes almost two years ago, says he is no longer connected with the government.

General Joseph Stilwell says the GI's daily prayer is "Oh Lord, distribute the bullets as you do the pay; let the officers get most of them" and says the GI doesn't understand while risking his life why workers back home go on strike for more pay.

An average of 34 WACS and doughboys are married each week in Paris.

15-year-old Richard Button has won the National Men's Junior figure skating championship.

A new movie is "Riocabana" starring John Payne and June Haver.

That's the news this March 2, 1945.

65

Saturday, March 3, 1945

And now today's news, March 3, 1945.

American carrier planes have hit the Ryukyu Islands southwest of Japan as 150 B-29's have hit Tokyo again. In Britain German flying bombs have started in daylight again as Spitfires immediately attacked launching sites in the Netherlands.

General Dwight D. Eisenhower has warned the Germans to stay west of the Rhine River for to be east would put them in mortal danger.

Hanson Baldwin of the New York Times says the battle west of the Rhine has been won and 75,000 prisoners have been taken since February 1st.

An unauthorized strike of 7000 dock workers in London is affecting critical shipping.

In northern Italy a speech by a thinner Benito Mussolini says "what could be worse on our soil than to have the scum of the earth—Negroes, Jews, Indians, New Zealanders, South Africans, Britons and Americans."

The greatest sea search ever is under way in the Pacific looking for Lt. General Millard Harmon and his crew who were en route to Hickam Field, Hawaii in a C-87 converted B-24.

Flyers off the carrier Fighting Lady tell of shooting down 67 Japanese planes while losing 4 in strikes over Tokyo.

The Inter-American Conference in Mexico City has unanimously adopted a proposal wherein all 20 countries will guarantee territorial integrity of each other.

The E.R. Squibb Company reports the War Production Board's approval to release penicillin for civilian use is imminent.

The War Labor Board has refused a blanket wage increase for 300,000 General Motors workers and the War Production Board say tire production is up 46% with praise for workers doing superhuman efforts.

Swedish miler Gunder Haegg, holder of 7 world records, came in last in the Louis Zamperini Mile while James Rafferty won in 4.16.4.

New movies include Rita Hayworth and Jack Cole in "Tonight and Every Night," Dick Powell and Mike Mazurki in "Murder, My Sweet," and in New York Gladys Swarthout returns after a two year absence to sing "Carmen" this week at the City Center.

Finally, baseball fans, be proud of the 4000 baseball players now in various services.

That's the news this March 3, 1945.

66

And now today's news, March 4, 1945, Herb Hobler reporting.

On the war front in Europe, the Russian Army is in a 62 mile race to the Baltic as U.S. troops have occupied Neuss and have confined 30,000 civilians to their homes until further notice.

In Switzerland, both Basel and Zurich have been hit by U.S. B-17 and B-24 bombers. The Swiss radio says the bombing was precise and not accidental. Americans have now admitted the bombing was in error, thinking they were hitting German cities. Meanwhile, German radio reports Dresden has been wiped out by Allied raids.

In the Pacific, Marines have moved only 40 yards today as Japanese continue to stiffen their resistance on Iwo Jima. Also today the first B-29 landed on Iwo when their bomb bay doors would not close after a mission over Japan. Of interest to this reporter is that the B-29 airplane commander Lt. Raymond Malo and the Navigator Lt. Bernard Beninson are serving in the same Squadron as this navigator, and living in an adjacent tent here on Tinian.

The dramatic picture of 5 Marines raising an American flag atop Mt. Suribachi on Iwo Jima will be the basis of a permanent monument modelled after the striking photo. Gen. MacArthur also raised a flag over the weekend at Corregidor.

In Europe, Finland has declared war on Germany while in England 18-year-old Princess Elizabeth has joined the ATS, Britain's version of the U.S. WACS.

Washington reports new drugs may soon be released to combat malaria that affects over 800 million around the world.

Tommy Dorsey's Orchestra featuring Buddy Rich on the drums is at the 400 Restaurant in New York City, while nearby Oscar Strauss celebrated his 75th birthday today conducting at Carnegie Hall.

Down the street at Bloomingdales, you can buy a man's shirt at $3.95 and a tie at $1.50, and in Paris there's a boom on French perfume thanks to the demand of American Forces.

In FCC channel allocation hearings today in Washington, Philco Corporation testified that the television will become a large post-war business.

That's the news this March 4, 1945.

Monday, March 5, 1945

And now today's news, March 5, 1945.

Leading General Eisenhower's broad offensive today were three columns of American troops smashing into Cologne. First reports indicated the city's famous cathedral is intact. Eisenhower also hailed Danish saboteurs whose efforts have seriously slowed down every German train withdrawing German troops from Norway.

In Burma, the British have travelled 85 miles in 11 days, and are within 80 miles south of Mandalay.

In Washington Secretary of the Navy James V. Forrestal says the Allies will have to face 5 million Japanese troops on their home soil to defeat them. He did not see the enemy giving up easily.

The post office today reported that 45 million pieces of mail go overseas every week to troops. Such volume no longer guarantees even an air mail stamp on V mail will go airmail.

Rep. Clare Booth Luce is flying to London today to do survey work of British women in war.

In the medical field, through the American Cancer Society a nationwide $5 million fund raising effort for the first time is going on to search for answers to cancer.

And on the international scene, 39 nations have been invited to the United Nations Security Council in San Francisco. Poland has not been invited.

In sports, Nat Holman, City College basketball coach for 26 years, testified before Kings County Judge Samuel Leibowitz that he has always been in control of his players. His appearance was part of hearings regarding the five Brooklyn College players each of whom took $1000 to throw a game in Boston. Swedish miler Gunder Haegg says he hopes to do a 4:10 mile next time out.

And Frank Sinatra, bobby soxer idol, who has had an occupational deferment not physically qualified for service, has been reclassified by his Jersey City draft board as 4-F, not liable for war service but now liable for war work.

Rita Hayworth is in "Tonight and Every Night" at Radio City Music Hall, the "Song of Bernadette" is showing in area movie houses, and a smash hit Broadway show is at the Century Theater called "Up in Central Park."

That's the news this March 5,1945.

And now today's news, March 6, 1945.

Germany's fourth largest city has fallen today to the American troops. Headed by General Hodges' troops, Cologne has finally been taken after incredible damage throughout the city. Elsewhere, General Patton's Armored Division has gained 30 miles to get within 20 miles of Coblenz. Prime Minister Winston Churchill also arrived today in Germany to look at the ruins of Aachen City near the Rhine River.

A prison camp near Stiringwendel was the scene of over 1000 dirty, diseased, and crippled Allied prisoners bursting forth out of the German hell camp as the U.S. 274th Regiment men approached the camp. Included among the prisoners were 800 Russians and Italians, Yugoslavs, French and Poles, some of whom had been there since 1939.

In New York State today, Governor Thomas E. Dewey has pegged the state's annual budget at $369 million and in Washington Fred Vinson has been confirmed by the Senate as Federal Loan Administrator.

In sports, 17-year-old Vince Boryla, Notre Dame basketball center, scored a record 31 points today while also establishing another Notre Dame record of 322 points in a single season. After the game he announced he is going in the Navy. Chief Navy Specialist Bobby Feller, former Cleveland Indians great pitcher, is at the Mayo Clinic in Rochester, Minnesota for a check-up.

Lt. Dave Breger, cartoonist known by millions of GI's for his hapless misfit cartoons in Stars and Stripes and Yank Magazine, has a new cartoon book out called "GI Joe." You can get it for a buck.

And, Dick Powell, Clair Trevor and Anne Shirley are starring in "Murder My Sweet" at neighborhood theaters.

The Hotel Chesterfield at 49th Street New York has single rooms for $2.50 and $3.50, doubles from $3.50 to $6. Macy's Drug and Cosmetic center has shave cream at 20 cents, men's talc for 14 cents, cold cream at 49 cents and lipsticks for 44 cents.

Chrysler has reported 1944 sales at just over $1 billion with a profit of 24 million and all but $612 million in sales was in war production.

This is the news this March 6, 1945.

Wednesday, March 7, 1945

And now today's news, March 7, 1945.

In Germany, the city of Cologne is lifeless. It's famous cathedral still stands, but the RAF bombing last October destroyed its hospital, though only 4 patients were killed. Paving the way for the Allied advance into Germany, the Ludendorff Bridge at Remagen on the Rhine was captured today by the 9th Armored Division moments before the Germans had planned to destroy it.

Elsewhere, the Russians have mounted an all-out push and have formed bridgeheads on the Oder River en route to Berlin.

In the Pacific, Marines are fighting hand-to-hand with the Japanese on Iwo Jima who continue to dig in after 17 days of battle.

Benito Mussolini, head of the Italian Fascist Republic, said today the Germans may use gas in a last ditch stand and says they will be justified in doing so. He said the Italians are on their own and don't expect German help. Meanwhile, American troops have passed north of Florence and are approaching Bologna.

In Iran, the youthful Shah of Iran has asked for the backing of the Allies since Iran has been supportive since 1941.

In Washington, the house voted today 347 to 42 to draft nurses and the War Production Board has tripled the availability of penicillin for the public. The army has announced a new tank called the Pershing with a 90mm gun and more armor and gun power than the famed Sherman Tank.

In sports, golf balls have gone to war—the pros and civilians continue to use old balls and pay $4 per new ball if they can be found. 300 GI's headed by Sgt. Vic Ghezzi began a 4 day tournament in Rome today.

On Broadway, everybody's favorite ballet choreographer , George Balanchine, is staging his new work called "Mozartiana" with the Ballet Russe de Monte Carlo. Leopold Stokowski is conducting at the New York City Center next week and Arlene Francis is starring in the "Overtons" on Broadway.

If you like one of those footlockers widely used by GI's and service wives for storage on your summer vacation, you can get them for $9.90 at Gimbels.

Finally, the cigar shortage is getting worse thanks to the OPA cutting back production.

That's the news this March 7, 1945.

And now today's news, March 8, 1945.

Since D Day at Normandy last June, American armies have lost $500 million in equipment including 6200 combat vehicles, 34,000 general purpose vehicles, 167,000 rifles, 75,000 binoculars and thousands of other items. It's estimated German losses have been 2 to 10 times as much.

Marshal Zukhov's Russian troops are now within 26 miles of Berlin.

Air Force General Carl Spaatz is meeting today with Swiss High Command to prevent future Allied bombardments like that of last week. In Cologne, notwithstanding orders not to fraternize, some American troops feel sorry for civilians many of whom seem glad to see the GI's.

While German Propaganda Minister Joseph Goebbels says the war is reaching a climax and the Germans will suddenly win, a February 24th speech by Hitler blames Japan for Germany losing the war by Japan not declaring war on Russia.

In the Pacific, Indian and British troops have entered the fabled city of Mandalay in Burma while U.S. Admiral Nimitz has intimated that there may be landings on the Chinese coast preceding landings in Japan.

A congressional medal of honor winner, Sgt. John Basilone of Raritan, New Jersey, has been killed on Iwo Jima. After his gallantry on Guadacanal in October 1942, he toured the United States on bond rallies.

Among five nurses sworn in today to the Navy Reserve Nurse Corps is Phyllis Mae Daly, the first Negro nurse in the Corps.

On Broadway, tap dancer Bill "Bojangles" Robinson has signed a 2 year contract to star in a new show called "Memphis Bound."

Rita Hayworth, Janet Blair and Lee Bowman are in a new movie "Tonight and Every Night."

President Roosevelt is back in Washington after 4 days in Hyde Park and bestowed medals on the U.S. Rangers who rescued prisoners recently on Luzon. Admiral William F. "Bull" Halsey also received a gold star.

Washington says there's an acute shoe shortage for adults with only 8% of cattle hide now available for civilian use.

Finally, Mrs. Douglas MacArthur and her son have left Australia and have joined General MacArthur in the Philippines.

That's the news this March 8, 1945.

Friday, March 9, 1945

And now today's news, March 9, 1945.

Russian troops today are nearing the outskirts of Danzig and Stettin as the Americans have captured the university town of Bonn and have captured the bridge at Remagen. First across was Sgt. Alexander Drabik, a young butcher from Holland, Ohio, who was followed by 10 riflemen running and shooting at the surprised Germans who were about to blow up the bridge.

A new American army, the 15th led by Lt. General Leonard T. Gerow, will join Lt. Gen. Bradley's lst and 3rd Army.

Adolf Hitler has paid a visit to the Oder River front and reports he is heartened by the spirit of his German troops.

A nuisance raid on the coast of Normandy has been made by Germans apparently coming from the Channel Islands.

The Japanese have wiped out the last vestige of French control in Indochina.

Two American Navy PT boats have been sunk in the Philippine area by our own forces in an inadvertent attack. Casualties were light.

5400 veterans of the forgotten Italian campaign have arrived at Camp Kilmer, New Jersey.

President Roosevelt and Prime Minister Churchill say merchant shipping losses in February were moderate and more U-Boats were sunk by the Allies than in January.

12 Japanese ships have been sunk by U.S. submarines raising the total of ships sunk thus far by the Navy in the war to 1,057.

Robert Walker has been signed to play Jerome Kern in a movie soon to start production entitled "Till the Clouds Roll By" and Eve Arden has signed to begin "Janie Gets Married."

Rocky Graziano has scored an upset knockout in the fourth round of Negro Bill Arnold in a fight at Madison Square Garden attended by Vice President Harry S. Truman.

IBM has announced earnings in 1944 of $37,700,000 with taxes paid of $28 million leaving a profit of $9,700,000 or $8.90 per share on the 1,039,000 shares outstanding.

That's the news this March 9, 1945.

This is Herb Hobler with today's news, March 10, 1945.

This reporter got back today (March 10th Tokyo time) after a 17-hour mission as navigator on a B-29 over Tokyo in what probably was the most devastating raid in history. Gen. Curtis LeMay ordered up a maximum effort of 325 B-29's for a fire raid on Tokyo.

At a 4 pm briefing, the bombing altitude was set at 5000 feet instead of the usual 25,000 feet, intelligence reported no knowledge of barrage balloons, weather was reported poor all the way requiring reliance on dead reckoning over 1500 miles of ocean, non-formation individual area bombing was ordered with no ammunition allowed in the B-29 guns, and a full load of 7500 gallons of gas and tons of incendiaries were carried. Like many others, this reporter went back to his tent and wrote what might have been a last letter to his young bride back in the states.

After a 6 pm takeoff huge fires were sighted at 2 am 100 miles ahead. The city of Tokyo was already a sea of flames. Within sight of the Emperor's Palace, a target ordered to be avoided, searchlights covered each plane while billowing smoke permeated the air in and out of the first pressurized airplane in history. There was an occasional tinkling sound throughout the plane caused by ineffective flak. The sight of a whole city in roaring flames was incredible. 17 hours after takeoff the plane returned to Tinian.

Photo reconnaissance shots today showed a 15 square mile section of Tokyo turned into ashes—an area equal to the size of the Bronx or Queens. It was an obvious holocaust. Amazingly, only 12 B-29's were lost.

And that's a special newscast for March 10, 1945, Herb Hobler glad to be reporting to you.

* * * * * *

(An historical postscript to that Tokyo fire raid of March 10, 1945: In a 1957 Army-Navy-Air Force Journal article the full story was told. 325 B-29's had dropped 2000 tons of incendiaries. The raid was more devastating than either atomic bomb raid on Nagasaki or Hiroshima or any single raid in Europe. 15.8 square miles of Tokyo were consumed, 267,000 buildings destroyed, 84,000 people died, 41,000 wounded, and over one million made homeless according to Japanese records. In that single sudden shocking loss it became evident to the Japanese that the war was lost according to the article.)

73

German divisions trapped between Coblenz and Remagen are being systematically destroyed as Americans cross the Rhine in assault boats.

On the 26th day of non-stop aerial bombardment, another 1350 bombers dropped 3000 tons on railways and communications in central Germany. Russians are now 38 miles to the east of Berlin while their Baltic offense is nearing the former free city of Danzig.

Marines on Iwo Jima have reached the beaches on the northeast part of the island after 21 continuous days of fighting.

Indian and British troops attacking Mandalay have now taken half of the city.

Prime Minister Churchill has sent congratulations to General Eisenhower on his victories. Similar messages were sent by Secretary of Defense James Forrestal and Speaker of the House Sam Rayburn.

The 250 new Pershing tanks that went into action last month are reported as being very effective with greater destructive power.

The Bonn, Germany birthplace of Ludwig van Beethoven is now in ruins.

British radio reports that Hitler's favorite General, Marshal Erwin Rommel, was one of the conspirators in the assassination plot of Hitler last July.

With the appointment of a Republican Senator to succeed the late Senator Moses of South Dakota, the Democrats are down to 55 Senators with 40 Republicans and one progressive Senator Robert La Follette of Wisconsin.

In entertainment, Wagner's "Das Rheingold" at the New York Met will feature Blanche Thebom and Martha Lipton and Sir Thomas Beecham will conduct the Philharmonic at Carnegie Hall next Saturday.

The annual visit by Ringling Brothers, Barnum and Bailey Circus to Madison Square Garden starts April 4th with tickets starting at $1.20.

In the movies Roy Rogers is in "Utah," and Laraine Day, Susan Peters and Lana Turner are in "Keep Your Powder Dry."

And that's the news this March 10, 1945.

And now today's news, March 11, 1945.

41st Division troops under Lt. General Robert J. Eichelberger's 8th Army have landed on Mindanao just east of Zamboanga as 6 more nuns have been freed from Santo Tomas prison.

Major U-boat pens and oil plants have been hit by 3200 Britain based planes of the 8th Air Force with RAF bombers hitting Essen, the heart of German armament industry.

A single plane, probably inadvertently, dropped bombs on Basel, Switzerland killing four with many injuries and extensive damage.

A human interest story in the midst of the terrible death and wounds of GI's on Iwo Jima. Because blood donations carry the name and address of the donor, many grateful GI's are writing back home with thanks to the donor. Some, we are told, are letters to women the GI's hope to meet upon return.

The non fraternization of American troops with Germans in occupied towns was broken today as many of both sides attended a Catholic mass.

U.S newspapers are carrying the names of American prisoners freed from German prisons.

President Getulio Vargas of Brazil will not run again ending 15 years of rule.

73 surplus DC-3 transports and 9 Lockheed Lodestars will be used by U.S. Airlines increasing service by 1,750,000 trips a year.

A New York Times editorial following the fire raids in Japan says "We cannot conquer her by destroying her cities. We must occupy them."

Mahmound Reza Pahlavi, 19-year-old brother of the Shah of Iran, has been at the Choate School in Connecticut for the past ten weeks away from the unsettled political and social conditions in Iran.

King George, Queen Elizabeth and Princess Elizabeth have planted oak trees in Windsor Great Park to mark the raising of $25,000,000 for the Red Cross.

Byron Nelson and Jug McSpaden overwhelmed Sam Byrd and Denny Chute 8 and 6 in the $7000 International Four Ball Tournament in Miami worth $1100 each to the winners and $750 to second place.

And a well reviewed new book is "The Lost Weekend" by Charles Jackson available at $2.50 each.

That's the news this March 11, 1945.

Monday, March 12, 1945

And now today's news, March 12, 1945.

A second major fire raid by B-29's at an unprecendented low level has left Japan's third largest city Nagoya in flames. Smoke still rises thousands of feet in the air from the Tokyo raid 34 hours ago.

In Europe, 3500 planes have hit Berlin and Dortmund almost half of which is now destroyed. Bombers include British Mosquitos, Lancasters and Halifaxes along with U.S. B-17 Flying Fortresses and B-24 Liberators.

At home, the midnight curfew to save fuel has spawned all night speakeasies as Washington announces a 20% cut-back in coal use. Editors and·writers of Stars and Stripes claim First Amendment infringements as an order from above now requires review of GI gripe letters on Mail Call before publishing.

The U.S. Supreme Court today dismissed a 15 million dollar lawsuit by the Shoshone Indians who claimed ownership of lands in the northwest.

Camp Kilmer here in New Jersey today received over 1900 wounded evacuees—the largest group thus far.

In New York at the Capitol Hotel, two famous billiard champions, Willie Hoppe and Welker Cochran, meet today in a 3 cushion challenge. In Washington, Washington Senators owner Clark Griffith handed President Roosevelt his usual season pass as the President endorsed the idea of night baseball. In Philadelphia, invitations have gone out from Penn Relay Officials to schools and colleges only within 20 miles to save transportation costs.

In Hollywood, 4 major studios are tied up by an AFL union dispute putting thousands out of work. In an air raid on Dresden in Germany, German movie actress and favorite of Hitler, Dorothea Wieck, has been killed. She made pictures also in Hollywood. Anne Baxter and Linda Darnell have been signed by 20th Century Fox to star in the "Fallen Angel."

Finally, if you want some reasonable entertainment, try the Hotel Taft in New York. Dance to the music of Vincent Lopez and have lunch for 65 cents or dinner for $1.50.

That's the news this March 12, 1945.

And now today's news, March 13, 1945.

In Europe, the Red Army has created a trap for 100,000 Germans near Danzig as reports say Field Marshal Von Rundstadt is being replaced as head of the German army on the western front.

In just captured Cologne, American sound trucks are touring the streets with the first non-Nazi news for citizens in years while giving instructions not to leave the city, not to drive cars, and be indoors from 6 pm to 7 am.

The German general who demanded surrender of paratroops under the command of Gen. McAuliffe who responded with the now famous word "NUTS," has been captured. His name is Lt. Gen. Von Rothkirch.

The Germans are using more and more flak to knock down Allied planes as compared to use of fighters. The word flak comes from a shortened version of the German word meaning anti-aircraft gun —fliegerabwehrkanone (flee-ger-abwerk-anone). In the city of Duisberg, the Germans were escaping through an underground coal tunnel. Now the Americans have made captured Germans seal it up. And a sample poll taken by Allied forces of principally Catholic Germans in a captured area indicated the people blame the Nazis for the war and are convinced the Allies will win.

In Washington, Chester Bowles, head of the Office of Price Administration, has put a ceiling on movie prices which have risen almost 40% since June 1941. Americans spent over $1.5 billion at the gate in 1944 alone.

While there are now four four-star generals—Generals Eisenhower, George C. Marshall, H.H. Arnold and MacArthur, President Roosevelt today recommended three stars to eight generals including Omar Bradley, Carl Spaatz, Mark Clark and Jacob Devers.

In sports, Will Harridge, President of the American League, says there will indeed be a full 154 game schedule of baseball this year.

Tonight on radio, tune in Dick Haymes with guest star Betty Hutton, or hear the Alan Young Show, Inner Sanctum mystery, Fibber McGee and Molly, or Bob Hope with guest star Frances Langford.

Finally, a 99-year-old Union veteran died today leaving only one GAR veteran left in Massachusetts.

That's the news this March 13, 1945.

Wednesday, March 14, 1945

And now today's news, March 14, 1945, Herb Hobler reporting.

The victory flag was raised today on Iwo Jima after 23 days of bitter battle that killed some 4000 American Marines and over 20,000 Japanese. Fighting continues on one part of the island south of Japan.

In Europe, the RAF has dropped the world's largest bomb on Dortmund—an 11 ton bomb measuring 25 feet by 3 feet.

In the Pacific the third fire incendiary raid in five days has hit Japan's second largest city, Osaka. As a member of one of the crews, this reporter can again confirm the destruction was severe. The billowing fires from refineries hit our ship at 5000 feet with such updrafts that the ship was tossed up another 3000 feet almost onto its side. Indeed, one B-29 literally was thrown up over 5000 feet, did a slow roll, and came out at 3000 feet. Boeing engineers on Tinian believed such a maneuver with a B-29 was impossible. 20th Air Force officials reported that over 24 square miles of Tokyo, Nagoya and Osaka have been wiped out by these three low level fire raids.

It was also announced today that no American will be buried on Nazi soil. In England, the conservatives have endorsed Prime Minister Churchill. And at home a new destroyer has been launched called the Ellison. It's named after one of the Navy fliers lost during the Battle of Midway in which all 15 planes of the now famous Squadron 8 were lost. The one survivor, Lt. J.G.—then Ensign—George H. Gay was present at the launching.

In New Hampshire all 225 towns have voted overwhelmingly in favor of the U.S. being part of an international police force for peace after the war. In Paris, the courts plan on starting the trial of Marshal Petain and Pierre Laval soon.

And in Washington, Vice President Harry S. Truman will sub for President Roosevelt on opening baseball day, April 16th, and toss in the first ball at the Senators-Yankees game. 82-year-old Connie Mack says his Philadelphia Athletics have a chance to win this year.

Franchot Tone and Jane Wyatt are in a new play "Hope for the Best," on Broadway. Gene Lockhart is in "Happily Ever After" and in the movies Anne Baxter and John Hodiak are in "Sunday Dinner for a Soldier."

Stocks today traded only 750,000 shares as Studebaker closed at 23½, up one.

Once again safely back from a mission, this is Herb Hobler reporting the news this March 14, 1945.

And now today's news, March 15, 1945.

As 6000 planes including 440 heavy bombers tossed 300,000 incendiary bombs on Zossen, Prime Minister Churchill says the war should be over by summer—perhaps sooner. Unofficially, a Nazi peace feeler through Sweden has been turned down. And Gen. Eisenhower conferred today in Holland with Gen. Omar Bradley and British Field Marshal Bernard Montogmery.

The Soviet Tass news agency reports through its Japanese sources that Tokyo has been in a panic since the Tokyo fire raid last week. Thousands of refugees are trying to leave as Japanese radio reports thousands were burned to death. The Air Force also released information that these incendiary bombs were made by the National Fireworks Plant in Mays Landing, New Jersey, each being 19 inches long with 3 pounds of gasoline, jelly, and a secret thickening agent.

In Italy, a year after the total destruction of the Monte Cassino Abby, one hundred new houses have been built and dedicated.

In the Bahamas, the Duke of Windsor has resigned his post after five years as Governor and Commander in Chief of the Bahamas. He may reside in the U.S. or Canada.

The soft coal industry back home has offered the union $1.69 per week raise plus liberalized vacations.

Secretary of War Stimson reports that since D Day Americans have lost 70,000 killed and 297,000 wounded. And the Navy reports that since Pearl Harbor 91,000 men have been killed with total casualties of 839,000. Finally, in Washington, Secretary Frances Perkins advocates the public vote for the U.S. delegate to the United Nations.

The Academy Awards have just announced Oscars for 1944—best picture was "Going My Way," best actor Bing Crosby in the same film, best actress Ingrid Bergman in "Gaslight," best supporting actor Barry Fitzgerald in "Going My Way," best supporting actress Ethel Barrymore in "None But The Lonely Heart." NBC President Niles Trammell says news is a public service and, therefore, says no more commercial breaks in the middle of the news. And sportscaster Ted Husing will host a Red Cross benefit on April 18th.

Finally, the OPA reports the theft of over 2 million gas coupons today in Chicago.

That's the news this March 15, 1945.

79

Friday, March 16, 1945

And now today's news, March 16, 1945.

Organized resistance on Iwo has ceased but only after 20,000 of 61,000 American combatants were casualties including 4,189 killed.

The American First Army in the Remagen bridgehead has cut the Frankfort-Ruhr highway while the Third Army has slashed from the Moselle to beyond Simmern with German armies in the Saar facing disaster.

President Roosevelt, who says there is nothing to the rumors of peace feelers from the Germans, is sending Bernard Baruch to see Churchill in England regarding postwar economic and reparations problems.

The immediate problems of the Allied Military Government is in re-educating German youths who have been Nazi indoctrinated.

One of the greatest skiers of all time, Torger Tokle, has been killed leading his infantry platoon of the Tenth Mountain Division. He became a U.S. Citizen in April 1943, and joined the army. In 3 years he lost only five of 41 ski events.

A report from Stockholm says that Vaslav Nijinsky, one of the world's foremost ballet dancers, has been executed by Germans in Budapest.*

The Navy has an urgent call for 3000 more doctors for mounting casualties.

U.S. Citizens of Japanese ancestry are required by Selective Service to foreswear any allegiance to the Japanese Emperor before induction.

Little Margaret O'Brien was handed a tiny Oscar by Emcee Bob Hope at the Academy Awards for "best little actress."

Basil Rathbone and Nigel Bruce's new Sherlock Holmes movie is "The House of Fear."

The sounds of bombers and crews on missions is being recorded by combat reporters for airing on radio.

And the manpower shortage may have Dodger Manager Leo Durocher back playing second base this year.

And that's the news this March 16, 1945.

*Historical Footnote: Nijinsky lived until 1950.

80

And now today's news, March 17, 1945.

Japan's fourth biggest city, Kobe, was hit by over 250 B-29's in the fourth low level attack in a week. 2500 tons were dropped on shipbuilding causing 12 square miles of destruction. Fires are still so intense from the Kobe fire raid that photo planes cannot get clear pictures of the damage.

A photo in the New York Times shows the first B-29 to land on Iwo Jima surrounded by amazed Marines.

Lt. General George Patton's Third Army hard bitten veterans of the 87th Infantry started out today at 3 am and have overrun the historic city of Coblenz. 25% of the Germany of 1935 is now held by the Allies.

Antwerp, Belgium was hit by German V bombs for four months until January 31st and caused great destruction.

The Ministry of Justice in Paris says 679 collaborators have been sentenced to death and 1172 found not guilty.

President Edouard Benes of Czechoslovakia, a political refugee for 6 years, is in Moscow hoping to return home to Prague soon.

The Hungarian Minister of Agriculture says all estates and property of war criminals will be confiscated and all estates over 140 acres nationalized.

The War Labor Board has approved raises for 50,000 textile workers and will raise the minimum wage from 50 to 55 cents.

The 33,000 ton battleship Pennsylvania peacetime leader of the fleet has shot more main batteries ammunition at Japanese positions than any other ship.

The civilian meat supply has been lowered 12% to support the military.

President and Mrs. Roosevelt are celebrating their 40th wedding anniversary today at a family luncheon.

Paul Porter, Chairman of the Federal Communications Commission, says he thinks broadcasting has excessive commercialism.

A new movie coming out this week stars Spencer Tracy and Katharine Hepburn in "Without Love."

It's planting time around the country. So for those of you who haven't started this year's victory garden, get out the spades and seeds and grow your own fresh vegetables once again.

And that's the news this day March 17, 1945.

Sunday, March 18, 1945

And now today's news, March 18, 1945.

There's been an incredible collapse of the center span of the Ludendorff Bridge at Remagen captured by Americans just 10 days ago moments before the Germans were to blow it up.

General Patton has sent four divisions into enemy territory in an attempt to destroy 80,000 men of the German First Army.

Berlin got its worst daylight bombing raid of the war as 1300 American heavy bombers with 700 Mustangs dropped 3000 tons on the beleaguered city.

In a daring foray into a fjord in Norway, four British destroyers have made a bold rescue of 525 Norwegian patriots who have been hiding in caves.

Even after Americans on Luzon have captured an area and moved on, Japanese remain in caves and using shotguns and rifles snipe at and often kill careless American soldiers.

Foreign Minister Henri Spaak will head the Belgian delegation to the San Francisco peace conference next month.

A group of women in Indiana are planning a cooperative program to study war and post-war problems of women workers.

Baseball notable PeeWee Reese is in the Navy on Guam while in New York great Yankee shortstop Frankie Crossetti may soon retire.

In movies about to go into production June Allyson and Robert Walker have been signed to star in "For Better or Worse" while Cornel Wilde and Anita Louise will be in "The Bandit of Sherwood Forest."

Tonight on radio is Edgar Bergen, Gabriel Heatter, Walter Winchell, and Jimmie Fiddler on Hollywood.

If you find things confusing with ration stamps figuring out how much for foods, gasoline, clothing or any other item, keep checking your daily newspaper or call your local ration board.

That's the news this March 18, 1945

This is Herb Hobler with today's news, March 19, 1945.

In Germany, it's reported that Heinrich Himmler has been linked to the unsuccessful plot to kill Hitler last July when a bomb was exploded under the Fuhrer's chair. The U.S. 8th Air Force today has bombed German jet-propelled aircraft factories while 1000 tanks of the U.S. 3rd Armored Division are sweeping across the Saar-Moselle-Rhine area towards a great victory.

In the Pacific, more devastating fire bomb raids over Japan, the fourth and fifth in ten days. This reporter again has safely returned as a B-29 navigator first over Tokyo, then Nagoya, Osaka and two days ago Kobe which was also hit by 300 Superfortresses with over 2500 tons of bombs. Key Kobe transportation and locomotive works were hit as Japanese fighters were reluctant to take on the B-29's. Reports taken say fires are still raging 20 hours later. Happily for this reporter after 66 hours of navigation over the Pacific on four 15 hour individual sortie missions in 8 days, our crew was not assigned to today's second fire raid over Nagoya. Again, severe destruction was dealt Japanese targets, and 9 disabled B-29's were saved by being able to land on the way home on the just-captured and enlarged air field on Iwo Jima. These fire raids have caused the Japanese to close all schools for the next 12 months in order to press into service everyone over 6 years of age to do war work.

In Washington, Secretary of State Edward Stettinius will probably include John Foster Dulles in the U.N. conference in San Francisco.

The Philadelphia Navy Yard is building two new Essex type aircraft carriers each 850 feet long capable of speeds of 30 knots and carrying 80 planes. They are to be named the Valley Forge and the Princeton.

In sports, big George Mikan of DePaul hit 33 points today in basketball against W. Virginia at Madison Square Garden. Byron Nelson and Sam Snead are tied in the Charlotte $10,000 open.

In music Sir Thomas Beecham is conducting at Carnegie Hall, Artur Rodzinski will start his third year as permanent conductor of the New York Philharmonic Symphony Society, and diminutive opera singer Lily Pons just completed her 5th concert for GI's in Germany especially picking out music by Jewish composers to perform in captured German concert halls. On Broadway, Tallulah Bankhead, Henry Hull and Donald Cook have opened in "Foolish Notion" and John O'Hara has a new book "Pipe Night" for $2.50.

Finally, Republic Aviation has reduced the cost of building P-47 Thunderbirds in 3 years from $66,000 down to $43,000. Last year they built 6,900 planes.

That's the news this March 19, 1945.

83

Tuesday, March 20, 1945

And now today's news, March 20, 1945.

Lt. Gen. George Patton is now the ruler of the Rhineland as the American 3rd and 7th Armies smashed through the Saar-Moselle-Rhine triangle into struggling masses of frightened German soldiers. Eighty thousand already have been captured as the 90th infantry swept into Mainz and the 10th Armored division has cleared the great railroad center of Kaiserlautern. Meanwhile, the 33rd Army also reached Worms, the home of Martin Luther.

Even as another 5,000 sorties over Berlin occurred today, it is reported that Berlin is now 87% destroyed.

In the South Pacific, all of Mandalay has been taken by the British exactly 2 years, 10 months and 2 days after it fell to the Japanese. Americans caught Japanese warships in the Japanese Inland Sea damaging or sinking 6 freighters, a battleship, light carrier, 2 or 3 aircraft carriers plus a destroyer and a submarine.

In England, the House of Lords says Hitler should be tried as a war criminal while the Archbishop of York says...death with no trial. Herbert C. Pell, U.S. Representative on the U.N. War Crimes Commission says the Nazis have been responsible for over 20 million deaths.

At home, President Roosevelt today backed Jimmy Byrnes in his argument with New York's Mayor LaGuardia regarding LaGuardia extending the midnight curfew. The War Department has ordered all personnel to observe the midnight time notwithstanding.

Virginians are up in arms today regarding the possibility of army engineers building a 53 mile long lake and dam in the Shenandoah Valley.

At Newport News, Virginia, the world's largest aircraft carrier, the U.S.S. Midway, was christened today.

In the Midwest, Sister Elizabeth Kenny, the Australian nurse who founded treatment centers for Infantile Paralysis, is leaving the United States after disagreements with a Minneapolis hospital.

In sports, Brooklyn Dodger owner Branch Rickey has offered manager Leo the Lip Durocher $1,000 to play ball again in the first 15 games. On Broadway, "Bloomer Girl" stars Celeste Holm and Joan McCracken, "The Tempest" stars Vera Zorina and Canada Lee, and "Hats Off to Ice" stars skater Sonja Heinie.

Finally, for those cool days yet to come this winter, you can get a pair of BVD's at Gimbels for $1.25.

That's the news this March 20, 1945.

And now today's news, March 21, 1945.

In Europe, the Soviets are within 6 miles of the former free city of Danzig as 4500 planes of the 8th Air Force bombed key targets while being attacked by German jet planes, 12 of which were shot down. The U.S. lost 9 bombers and 21 fighters.

France estimates that the Germans have left behind over 100 million land mines. Youth volunteers may be trained to locate and defuse them.

S. Pacific Vice Admiral Marc Mitscher's carrier planes today sank 6 ships and damaged 22 off the coast of Japan. Far south, the Australians have captured a key airfield on the north coast of Netherlands New Guinea near Wewak.

In Rome, the Vatican has protested to Japan the execution of Franciscan monks and nuns in Manila, while in Japan the Imperial Diet has been asked to let the army turn the whole nation into an armed camp under military law.

India's Governor General, Marshal Viscount Wavell, is en route to London for political discussions. And Chinese General Chiang Kai-shek has endorsed peace proposals based upon justice and freedom equally for all.

Today, Queen Wilhelmina returns to her own Netherlands after 4 years and 10 months exile in England as Dutch citizens cried, sang and laughed in celebration.

At home, the Navy reports the 40th submarine lost, the U.S.S. Barbel, with crew of 65 to 70 men. Herbert Lehman, Director of the U.N. Relief and Rehabilitation Administration, says 938,000 pounds of food will be distributed abroad in the next 3 months with 42% coming from the U.S.

In sports, the War Manpower Commission has given approval to let professional baseball players leave off-season part-time jobs to return to play baseball this season. Manager Mel Ott and Director of Operations Carl Hubbell are getting the NY Giants into spring training today at Lakewood, New Jersey.

In Washington, Sen. Robert A. Taft of Ohio says there's a vital need to recognize the need for an independent Jewish state and John Foster Dulles says he will not be an official delegate to the U.N. conference in San Francisco, preferring an unofficial role.

Finally, Western Union will shortly test relay of messages by radio from Camden to Bordentown to New Brunswick to New York.

That's the news this March 21, 1945.

Thursday, March 22, 1945

And now today's news, March 22, 1945.

Field Marshal Karl von Rundstedt has been replaced by Field Marshal Albert Kessering as Commander in Chief of the West for Germany as German losses of over 100,000 are reported in the Saar. Today 3100 bombers escorted by 1500 fighters scourged Germany from the Western front to Russian lines in an unparalleled blitz from British and Italian bases. In Berlin, Propaganda Minister Joseph Goebbels says the crisis is severe.

In Tokyo some 3 million of a total 7 million citizens are expected to be evacuated from Tokyo as B-29's again hit the mainland as well as Rangoon to the South. Australian troops have landed at Bougainville, the scene of a bloody defeat 3 years ago.

Chile is expected to declare war on Japan today.

In Washington, IRS agents are after the free spenders who made fortunes in the black market in Miami and Miami Beach resorts.

Former Secretary of State Cordell Hull will be a delegate to the U.N. conference in San Francisco as Rep. Emanuel Celler of New York says the trials of German war criminals should be given wide publicity.

In New York, notwithstanding a nationwide government ordered curfew at midnight, Mayor Fiorello LaGuardia says New York bars can stay open to 4 am with no entertainment. The Army and James Byrnes are reported very upset.

For entertainment, Cab Calloway is at the Strand in New York as the life of Gen. Chennault is the subject of a new movie called "God Is My Co-Pilot" starring Dennis Morgan, Dane Clark and Raymond Massey.

An update on real estate values today from ads in the New York Times. In Plainfield, New Jersey, for rent is a house with 4 master bedrooms, servants quarters, 3 car garage and 11 acres for $150 per month. In Old Greenwich a 4 bedroom, 3 bath house for sale at $20,000 and nearby a beautiful home on 3 acres with 3 master bedrooms, 3 baths, wine cellar, 4 car garage, fruit trees, and shuffleboard courts for $35,000. Taxes are $600 per year.

In New York City you can apply for switchboard operator working 5½ days for $25 per week, retail saleslady $26, bookkeeper $45, and bartender $40, meals included.

That's the news this March 22, 1945.

And now today's news, March 23, 1945.

The USS Bismarck Sea, an escort aircraft carrier, was lost to enemy attacks on February 21st off Iwo Jima as reported by Admiral Nimitz. Most of the crew has been saved.

Lt. Gen. George Patton's 3rd Army has stormed across a bridgehead over the Rhine incurring no losses and getting no shots from the Germans.

12th Army Commander Lt. Gen. Omar Bradley says the Allies can now cross the Rhine virtually anywhere at any time.

A powerful fleet of RAF bombers has battered German troops and positions on the east side of the Rhine and have hit Berlin for the 32nd straight night with an estimated 50,000 killed and 400,000 made homeless.

The Italian government has confiscated 114 apartments owned by Count Ciano, the late son-in-law of Mussolini, who was executed last year for treason to Mussolini. Since June Italian-Americans have sent 11 million dollars to kin in Italy.

Brigadier General Lauris Norstad says the B-29 raids on Tokyo, two on Nagoya, and on Kobe and Osaka in 8 days was the greatest destruction ever inflicted on any people and will cost Japan one million industrial man-days lost.

Premier Kuniaki Koiso told the Japanese Diet that Japan is fully prepared to hold off any invasion and promised an offensive to take back Iwo, Saipan and the Guadacanal Islands.

The World War I battleship Tennessee, slightly damaged at Pearl Harbor, continues in battle operations and was at Iwo Jima.

The Japanese envoy in Berne, Switzerland recently approached diplomatic representatives of the Allies with peace proposals according to a Berlin source though it may have been an unofficial approach.

The death rate from cancer has more than doubled since 1900 possibly due to more older people and better medical records.

Heavyweight Tami Mauriello won a unanimous decision in 10 rounds over Lee Oma and in golf Johnny Revolta leads the $7500 Greensboro open by two over Sam Byrd and Byron Nelson.

A new movies is "Rough, Tough and Ready" with Chester Morris and Victor McLaglen.

That's the news this March 23, 1945.

Saturday, March 24, 1945

And now today's news, March 24, 1945.

With his familiar cigar in his mouth, Winston Churchill visited the banks of the Rhine today giving his V sign to the troops. Last night General Eisenhower watched crossings from a ruined church. 669 small storm boats were ordered on February 1st and boat manufacturers in Michigan, Minnesota and Florida completed and rushed them to the Rhine for the crossings.

In history's biggest airborne operation, 1500 troop-laden planes and gliders landed thousands of paratroopers on the Westphalian plains. For the first time the C-46 planes emptied 1st Airborne paratroopers out both sides.

225 B-29's have hit Nagoya again this time with high explosive bombs on Mitsubishi aircraft factories.

The first trainload of 3500 freed French prisoners liberated by the Russians have arrived in Paris.

In uniform, Mrs. Gertrude Legendre, the first woman to be captured in Luxembourg last September, has fled from German captivity across the Swiss border.

Captain Jack Chevigny, 39, Notre Dame football star from 1926 to 1928, later Head Coach of the Professional Chicago Cardinals and then the University of Texas, was killed February 19th on Iwo Jima.

Joe Rosenthal's already famous photo of the Iwo flag raising on Mt. Suribachi is being used in sketch form for a War Loan Drive.

On Broadway starting Monday is Katharine Cornell and Brian Aherne in "The Barretts of Wimpole Street." New movies are "Between Two Women" with Van Johnson, "Colonel Blimp" with shining new star Deborah Kerr, and "The Corn is Green" with Bette Davis due Thursday.

Arturo Toscanini is 78 tomorrow.

Chanteuse singer and piano player Hildegarde now has a show on NBC Tuesday evenings.

6'9" George Mikan, one of the greatest basketball players ever, is injured and may not play for De Paul against Bowling Green in the national invitational tournament tomorrow.

And broadcast columnist Jack Gould in the New York Times reports Radio Corporation has a TV set for post war that projects a 16 x 21 inch picture on a screen.

That's the news this March 24, 1945.

And now today's news, March 25, 1945.

In Europe without loss of manpower, Gen. Patton in a bold move has crossed the Rhine with support of tons of Allied bombs.

Frankfort radio stations are announcing warnings that Patton is coming. A report says that Propaganda Minister Goebbels barely missed losing his life as a time bomb placed by saboteurs went off in his air raid shelter. And, it's estimated 50,000 Berliners have lost their lives in air raids.

In the Pacific, 225 B-29's have hit Nagoya again with high explosive bombs, Admiral Spruance's 5th fleet has bombarded the Rykuyus Islands, and planes hit Formosa. In China 60,000 tank-led Japanese have opened an offensive northwest of Hankow.

In Washington, the House has extended the draft for another year. Draft violators after 60 days will be reclassified as available for combat and for conscientious objectors there'll be special service assignments.

15th Air Force Gen. Ira Eaker says that 20,500 men and 2050 bombers have been lost this past year equal to a 100% turnover. The air raids have, however, grounded virtually every German airplane saving thousands of Allied troops on the ground.

The Blue Network has retained former Under Secretary of State Sumner Welles to cover the U.N. in San Francisco. At the movies Fred MacMurray and Claudette Colbert are in "Practically Yours," and on Broadway Nancy Walker is in "On the Town." 56-year-old Al Jolson has taken a 4th wife, this time 21-year-old starlet Erle Chennault. Jolson's last marriage was to actress Ruby Keeler.

Eastern Airlines now has 6 daily flights to Boston from N.Y. Silver closed today in London at 44½ cents.

Our real estate reporter says in Mt. Kisco, New York, that there is a 21-room house on 10 acres with pool and a 6 room caretakers house for sale at $65,000.

Finally, the average GI ate 307 pounds of meat in 1944, 160 pounds more than his civilian counterpart.

That's the news this March 25, 1945.

Monday, March 26, 1945

And now today's news, March 26, 1945.

In Europe while Generals Eisenhower, Bradley, Patton and Hodges are meeting, hundreds of thousands of the finest U.S., British and Canadian troops are pouring over the Rhine striking disorganized resistance. There's a feeling of victory by the Generals who are staying at the Petersburg Hotel where former English Prime Minister Neville Chamberlain stayed in 1938 when he was negotiating with Hitler. King George VI has hailed the crossings and declared thanks to Eisenhower and Field Marshal Montgomery. Elsewhere the Russians are within 31 miles of Austria.

An RAF error caused an unfortunate raid on The Hague killing 800 Dutch and injuring 1000 others on March 3rd with one sixth of the city destroyed. Bombs were intended for nearby German launching sites and the British have called the error a "deplorable catastrophe."

200 B-29's have joined the attacks on Okinawa as the U.S. fleet has swarmed all over the Ryukyu (Re-ou-key-ou) Islands.

In Washington, Congress has raised the debt limit from $260 to $300 billion. Argentina is likely to declare war today on Germany and in England, Lloyd George, England's Prime Minister during WW I, has died in North Wales at the age of 82. He has been called the man who won the last war in 1918.

In a poll of 500 U.S. veterans, 95% of them said they would fight again to preserve peace.

In Germany, Hitler is reported calling an emergency cabinet meeting with party leaders and, as Allies talk to citizens and soldiers, it's becoming obvious they have had no real news for 5 years since they don't understand why they are constantly bombed.

At home, the heads of 34 national churches have called for a day of prayer on April 22 for the success of the U.N. and President Roosevelt has declared April cancer control month.

At Madison Square Garden DePaul's basketball giant, 6'9" George Mikan, faced Bowling Green's 6'11½" giant Don Otten as DePaul won 71-54.

Mrs. Bruno Walter, wife of the great conductor, has died. They were married in 1901 and came to the United States from Berlin in 1939.

After the war, Britain plans to buy U.S. wines, apparently feeling many are comparable to good French wines.

That's the news this March 26, 1945.

And now today's news, March 27, 1945.

Gen. Eisenhower today says the Germans are whipped but the war isn't over even as the Red Army is 20 miles from Vienna.

For the 36th consecutive night, Berlin was hit again by British Lancaster bombers, this time with huge 11 ton bombs. Americans are fighting block by block in Frankfort.

In a town near Duisberg, 7000 German civilians, old and young, raised a white flag to surrender causing German soldiers to rake them with machine guns. At least 10 were killed.

In Britain Lord Vansittant says the Allies have only two problems with German war criminals— "the location of the gallows and the length of the rope." Today's New York Times shows a picture of Hitler giving the Iron Cross to one of his 12-year-old boy soldiers.

In Washington, Office of War Information Director Elmer Davis says the agency will continue after the war to educate Germans. Fleet Admiral Ernest J. King reported today on 72 naval engagements during the past year including Normandy, Saipan, Tinian and Guam, Leyte Gulf, Ulithi, Wake Island, Corregidor, Iwo Jima, and the Philippines. The Navy also announced the loss of its 41st submarine, the Albacore, presumably in the Pacific.

Former President Herbert Hoover is making recommendations regarding the upcoming U.N. conference. He says the U.S. made a mistake in 1918 letting the Germans have armies of 100,000.

Mayor Frank Hague of Jersey City today defied a subpoena to appear in court in a libel suit against him.

At the movies, Van Johnson, Lionel Barrymore and Gloria deHaven are in "Between Two Women" while "Belle of the Yukon" stars Randolph Scott, Gypsy Rose Lee, Dinah Shore and Bob Burns. On stage at the Paramount in New York is Benny Goodman's band with Teddy Wilson and Red Norvo. In testimony in Washington, Juan Trippe, President of Pan Am, says only one airline is affordable for overseas travel—competition would be too costly. And Vincent Bendix, founder of Bendix Aviation, is dead at 62.

Major General Lewis B. Hershey, Selective Service Director, said today a large factor in rejecting 4.5 million men has been poor nutrition.

Finally, notwithstanding the cigarette shortage here in the States, some 3000 American civilians in England are buying cigarettes freely at 5 cents a pack.

That's the news this March 27, 1945.

Wednesday, March 28, 1945

And now today's news, March 28, 1945.

German radio today at first conceded defeat and then reported that German defenses are stiffening. Frankfurt citizens, much like similar peace demonstrations in 1918, held large peace rallies today and caused the SS elite guard to shoot down many citizens.

Elsewhere U.S. troops freed 290 half starved, tattered but smiling prisoners held in an insane asylum. In another prison camp, in order to prevent American fighters from strafing, 1000 prisoners bared their backs in the sun and formed human letters spelling out P-O-W. It worked.

Two interesting surrenders were reported today. In Duisberg, Germany, 100,000 residents surrendered to just seven GI's. At another location, Lt. Paula Krull of Fitchburg, Massachusettes was more than a nurse as two jerries came out of the woods and surrendered— "You are a lady and women wouldn't hurt us."

In Washington, Gen. Lucius D. Clay is expected to resign as Deputy to James F. Byrnes.

Soft coal miners today came out in favor of a strike supporting John L. Lewis, President of the United Mine Workers.

In London, Prime Minister Churchill spoke today at the funeral services for Lloyd George as Lord Beaverbrook spoke of the role of Britain's World War I leader in The House of Lords.

The War Department announced today the highest one day casualties in the war— 14,443 Army and 721 Navy including 3,200 dead. In Harrisburg, PA, D. Victor Emanuel got word today that his third son in a year had been killed.

In sports, in a pre-season Brooklyn Dodger versus Army game at West Point, Big Ralph Branca walked a man in the 9th and lost the game. Manager Leo Durocher was playing second base and announced the trade of Whitlow Wyatt to the Phillies.

Italian heavyweight boxer giant, Primo Carnera, is now under surveillance by the Gestapo in Rome. And Coast Guard Commander Jack Dempsey is in the Pacific theater. Testifying before Judge Samuel Leibowitz, acting president of Madison Square Garden, Ned Irish, says he is paid $12,500 a year.

On Broadway, Bea Lillie and Bert Lahr are in "Seven Lively Arts" with music by Cole Porter.

And on the New York Stock Exchange, volume was 720,000 shares led by Hudson Motors.

That's the news this March 28, 1945.

And now today's news, March 29, 1945.

In the European Theater, Russian troops have reached the Austrian border while Lt. Gen. Hodges 1st Army has moved so fast towards Paderborn that jeep-riding reporters literally couldn't keep up with them. The Allies are capturing so many Germans the captured German soldiers don't believe it is happening to them!

In New York today, former President of Cuba Gen. Batista would not comment on present Cuban problems regarding a plot to overthrow the constitutional government of Dr. Ramon Martin.

In Washington, it was announced that Gen. Lucis D. Clay will join Gen. Eisenhower as his deputy in charge of civil affairs in Europe. In preparation for the U.N. Conference in San Francisco, both the U.S. and Russia will try to get 3 votes each in the Security Assembly as proposed by Russia at Yalta. And President Roosevelt appointed Jonathan Daniels in charge of White House press relations. In Rome, the Pope has received Rep. Clare Booth Luce of Connecticut.

The cost of human life in the war today passed the total losses of the Civil War. Since Pearl Harbor, 189,541 men have been killed, 3000 more than the Civil War.

The GI Bill of Rights which gives veterans education subsidies is being studied to see how and why more veterans aren't taking advantage of their rights.

And in the Bahamas, the recently resigned Governor, the Duke of Windsor, today urged the development of tourism not only on New Providence but in the outer islands as well.

In sports, sportscaster Red Barber, and head of the New York Red Cross, gave blood today to help set an example. The Dodgers still don't have an agreement with Dixie Walker who is holding out for $21,000.

On Broadway, the "Earl Carroll Vanities" stars Constance Moore and Dennis O'Keefe. The new movie "The Corn is Green" stars Bette Davis, John Dall, Nigel Bruce, Rhys Williams and Mildred Dunnock, and, after a 6 month search, 10-year-old Claude Jarman has been signed to play the lead in Marjorie Rawling's "The Yearling."

From Detroit, Ford Motor Company, producer of thousands of B-24 Liberators, plans to get out of the aircraft business after the war. General Motors today announced record sales in 1944 of $4.2 billion with a net of $171 million.

That's the news this March 29, 1945.

Friday, March 30, 1945

And now today's news, March 30, 1945.

Approximately 300 tanks struck deep into the Reich today in a victory offensive involving six American and 3 British armored divisions. With disaster after disaster, some Germans are being sent to the front with orders to find their own guns.

The Red Army surged across the Austrian frontier 52 miles from Vienna to make Austria—the last country dominated by Hitlerite Germany—a battleground. The German SS has imposed iron discipline on the Viennese and is suppressing peace demonstrations. Red armies have also captured the naval base at Danzig.

2300 8th Air Force bombers hit five U boat yards at or near Bremen, Wilhelmshaven and Hamburg with 4000 tons of bombs.

Since August 1942, the 9th Air Force has shot down 11,082 German planes, more than twice the American losses, while noting the greatest American losses in one month was April 1944 with 361.

Historic Heidelberg has been taken by the 44th Infantry Division after sustaining only light damage.

Some 300 American soldiers celebrated Passover in the former home of Propaganda Minister Joseph Goebbels, one of the most zealous Jewish prosecutors. Said one soldier, "Retribution comes home."

40th Division American troops have landed on Negros Island in the Philippines and have advanced 14 miles.

In China, Japanese troops continued a major offensive and have forced evacuation of American forces in the Laohokow area. U.S. submarines have sunk a large Japanese carrier and 10 other enemy ships.

75-year-old James Cox, Democratic presidential candidate in 1920, sees promise of a long peace and a new age.

Heavyweight Joe Baski defeated Lou Nova tonight on a decision. Dixie Walker who hit .357 has accepted the Brooklyn Dodger offer of an estimated $18,000 for his 19th year in organized baseball.

Some double feature theaters are showing "Jesse James" with Tyrone Power, Henry Fonda and Randolph Scott and "The Return of Frank James" with Henry Fonda, Gene Tierney, Jackie Cooper, Henry Hull and John Carradine.

Lockheed Aircraft reports 1944 earnings of $4.5 million, down from almost $8 million while the stock market is closed today, Good Friday.

That's the news this March 30, 1945.

94

And now today's news, March 31, 1945

A new American 15th Army has joined 8 other Allied armies in a bid for a knock-out victory. General Eisenhower has urged Germans to surrender emphasizing the hopelessness of their armies. 1,142,000 Germans have been captured since December 16th.

The U.S. and Britain have rejected Russia's request to invite the Soviet supported Polish provisional government to the San Francisco peace conference.

While Germany is depicted as a land of gloom by travellers and refugees with political terrorism and despair, paradoxically they continue to fight without a thought of quitting. They say neurotic Hitler is holding them together.

The Navy continues for the 9th day to bomb Ryukyu Islands sinking 18 ships. Tokyo says American forces have landed on Formosa as 150 superfortresses have hit Kyushu and Honshu.

War Mobilization Director James F. Byrnes promises a return to free enterprise as soon as possible and is optimistic about the war ending soon. He says the ban on horse racing will end soon after V-E day.

Travelling third class as usual, Mohandas K. Gandhi has arrived in Bombay to meet with Trustees of the National Memorial Fund.

Russia is pouring a stream of propaganda into Cuba bidding for influence in South America. 86 year old King Gustav of Sweden will become his country's longest reigning monarch tomorrow with over 37 years beating a predecessor 16th century Norwegian king though not as long as Austrian Emperor Franz Joseph who ruled 68 years.

Thousands of Allied fighting men are being received today by Pope Pius XII the day before Easter.

Author Beardsley Ruml, proponent of pay-as-you-go-plans, says post war taxes should be as low as possible to stimulate purchasing power.

Jimmy Rafferty has run a 4.10.9 indoor mile eclipsing Paavo Nurmi's record.

In New York "Oklahoma" celebrates its second anniversary. A new movie arriving this week is "I'll Be Seeing You" with Joseph Cotton and Ginger Rogers.

On radio today you might try Quincy Howe for news, Grantland Rice for Sports, and note that the "Alan Young" show starts Tuesday on the NBC Blue network.

Finally, ideal weather is predicted for Easter tomorrow on the east coast.

That's the news this March 31, 1945.

95

Sunday, April 1, 1945

And now today's news, April 1, 1945.

Following several days of huge naval bombardments and air strikes, United States troops of the 10th Army today invaded Okinawa, 362 miles from Japan with minimal resistance. This greatest invasion of the war involved 1400 ships. B-29's again hit Nagoya yesterday as a U.S. submarine reported sinking the 15th Japanese aircraft carrier.

In Europe Russian troops have invaded Austria as Vienna is reported under German SS rule. 3000 Allied tanks have struck deeply into the Reich in what is called Ike's 7 day victory offensive. The historical and beautiful city of Heidelberg has been captured with only light damage.

Allies report capturing over 1.1 million Germans since December 16th as Germans are leaving behind poisoned sugar, chocolate, coffee and explosive cigarettes.

In San Francisco two proposals for major post war airports include one by Henry J. Kaiser Industries.

In Paris, 2 million people flocked into the Champs Elysee today as Paris lights went on for the first time since the war started.

The Air Force today reported the lowest 8th Air Force monthly losses in the war—1338 bombers and 99 fighters from 45,000 sorties or a loss of ½ of 1%.

In baseball the oldest of 3 baseball playing brothers, Vince DiMaggio, has been traded from Pittsburgh to the Phillies.

Good Friday at the Met featured Lauritz Melchior in "Parsifal," 20th Century Fox has given a new contract to 13-year-old Peggy Ann Garner, and the Sammy Kaye Orchestra is at the Westchester County Center.

On radio tonight try Ozzie Nelson and Harriet Hilliard in "Blondie" or Phil Baker in "Take It Or Leave It."

By last Easter the United States had incurred 162,000 casualties in the war while today on Easter the number has skyrocketed to a total of 870,000.

That's the news this April 1, 1945.

And now today's news, April 2, 1945.

American doughboys have cut Okinawa in half meeting only scattered resistance from 60-80,000 Japanese. The Okinawa invasion is required in expectation of launching an invasion of the mainland of Japan in the future. B-29's hit the Nakajima aircraft factory near Tokyo today with a loss of 2 planes. The Japanese reported another 14 more admirals have lost their lives, now a total of 108.

The Samaritan, known as the White Lady hospital ship, has arrived in Honolulu after a 7000 mile trip carrying hundreds of wounded troops from Iwo Jima.

In Germany, Gen. Eisenhower has told the Germans to quit or be starved as food stocks and farms may be destroyed.

In Washington, influentials are uneasy about relations with Russia even before the first U.N. meeting in San Francisco. James Byrnes today resigned as Director of the Office of War Mobilization and will be succeeded by Fred Vinson who was just made Federal Loan Administrator last week.

In London, U.S. Emissary Bernard Baruch met with King George and Winston Churchill today. German radio says Baruch will be promptly killed if he sets foot in Germany.

Mayor LaGuardia in New York urges donation of 50 million pounds of clothing for the new overseas war relief campaign.

In Washington the War Production Board is releasing freon for theaters, bars, restaurants and movie theaters who have had no cooling since 1943.

In sports, former Georgia football and now Detroit Lions star Frank Sinkwich beat out Don Hutson of the Green Bay Packers to be named Most Valuable Player of the National Football League for 1944.

The Governor of the Virgin Islands, which was purchased from Denmark by the U.S. in 1917, sees the islands as a great tourist area after the war.

For your radio entertainment tonight, your choices include the Jack Kirkwood Show, Cavalcade of America, Lum and Abner, Burns and Allen, Information Please, Longines Symphonette, and you can hear a live broadcast from the WAC section at Saks 5th Avenue featuring Jimmy Durante and Bill Goodwin.

Finally, Dr. John Dill, given six months to live when discharged from the Union Army in 1864, died today at age 102. His first vote was for Abraham Lincoln.

That's the news this April 2, 1945.

Tuesday, April 3, 1945

And now today's news, April 3, 1945.

On Okinawa American Marines have reached the east coast as 300 B-29's from the Marianas hit targets in the Tokyo area for the third time since March 10th. Gen. Chennault's 14th Air Force planes today destroyed 122 Japanese planes at air bases in China while Gen. MacArthur's headquarters reports the Japanese have had over 300,000 casualties thus far during the recapture of the Philippines.

In Europe one million Allies have crossed the Rhine as the British are 25 miles from the Zuider Zee and the British 2nd Army 63 miles from Bremen. 1400 Allied planes blasted submarine yards at Kiel.

Near Bad Orb, Germany Allies found 6500 prisoners at Stalag 9-B including 3200 Americans who had been driven by Germans like cattle into a 400 square foot area awaiting slow death from starvation amid foul degradation. Most were like living skeletons. Elsewhere 9500 Russian prisoners were treated equally badly as 12 to 15 died daily from lack of food.

In Washington, the War Food Administration says meat cutbacks are necessary to feed liberated people even as major meat shortages already exist.

An airplane carrying Marshal Jan Christan Smuts of Pretoria, South Africa was hit by lightning just before landing today in Cairo. He was unhurt.

Washington says the cost of the war in March was a record $8.2 billion or about $300 million a day.

In London, the government says when V-E day comes all government employees will get two vacation days with pay.

And would you believe, Babe Ruth turned up today as a referee in the wrestling ring.

For your radio entertainment tonight there is Edwin C. Hill news and Ted Husing Sports at 6:15, Fred Vandeventer news at 6:30, Lowell Thomas news at 6:45 at the same time as Stan Lomax Sports, Fulton Lewis News and Comment at 7:00 and Raymond Graham Swing News at 7:15. At 8:00 Ginny Simms sings followed by Ted Malone, A Date with Judy, Hildegarde, and then the Bob Hope Show. Tomorrow a further report on popular radio shows.

That's the news this April 3, 1945.

And now today's news, April 4, 1945.

In the Pacific, the 3rd Marine Amphibious group and U.S. 10th Army now have won one sixth of Okinawa, as GI's are having a big battle with Okinawa mosquitoes.

From Tinian, Guam and Saipan B-29's today hit 4 targets in the Tokyo area leaving great fires.

Japanese losses are so heavy at sea that Emperor Hirohito's sailors are being told not to commit hari-kari because so many of their best sailors have already done so. In the Indian Ocean, the British Navy is massing a huge fleet for the invasion of Sumatra and South Thailand.

Soviet guns are shelling Vienna and they have pushed the last Germans from Hungarian soil.

Bernard Baruch sees five years of post-war prosperity. Maj. General Patrick Hurley, U.S. Ambassador to China is in London today on the way home. Britain, Russia and the U.S. have not yet agreed to include France in on the German armistice signing. As the war goes north in Italy, the city of Venice has asked both sides not to make the ancient city a battlefield.

In a captured German tunnel used as an air raid shelter, Allies today found great art works including paintings by Rubens, Rembrandt, Van Gogh and Van Dyke.

The Navy has cut its April draft quota by half.

In Nassau the retiring Island Governor, The Duke of Windsor, gave a farewell speech today.

On April 18th a huge Red Cross benefit will feature Ted Husing, Babe Ruth, Joe McCarthy, Leo Durocher, Mel Ott, Branch Rickey and Larry MacPhail of baseball fame, plus basketball coach Joe Lapchik, tennis star Lt. Helen Jacobs of the WAVES and movie stars Joan Fontaine, Ethel Merman, Joan Bennett, plus Perry Como, Milton Berle and Fred Waring's orchestra.

On radio today hear Quincy Howe news and Bill Stern sports followed by One Man's Family, Curt Massey, Inner Sanctum, Mr. District Attorney, Dale Carnegie and Eddie Cantor.

On Wall Street, Eastern Airlines' President Capt. Eddie Rickenbacker has reported 1944 sales of $18.6 million and profit of $1.5 million.

That's the news this April 4, 1945.

Thursday, April 5, 1945

And now today's news, April 5, 1945.

Today Russia shocked the Japanese and Russian citizens by denouncing their mutual neutrality pact of 1941. This announcement, in combination with many defeats, caused the entire Japanese cabinet to resign as Emperor Hirohito called on Elder Statesman Kantaro Suzuki to form a new cabinet.

President Roosevelt today named Gen. Douglas MacArthur and Admiral Chester Nimitz as Commanders of all Army and Navy Forces in the Pacific settling the question of whether Gen. Eisenhower might be put in charge at the conclusion of the European war. For the second day Hong Kong has been bombed by B-24's sinking 9 freighters in the harbor.

In Europe, the Nazi Gestapo newspaper says complete collapse of German forces is only days or weeks away.

At home, John Foster Dulles has been appointed advisor to the U.S. delegation to the upcoming U.N. conference in San Francisco. Greece today reported that the country's population has been reduced by 13% due to starvation, execution and guerilla warfare under German rule. 60% of the reduction was due to the Germans, 40% to the Italian and Bulgarian occupation.

Pravda has called former President Herbert Hoover's proposals for Dumbarton Oaks and the U.N. suspicious and Hoover an enemy of the Soviet people.

The Air Force today announced a new Thunderbolt combination fighter and bomber called the P47N with a 2000 mile range.

82-year-old author and philosopher George Santayana has been awarded the Columbia University Nicholas Murray Butler Gold Medal.

On radio late this afternoon, shows for Mom and the kids include Terry and the Pirates, Uncle Don, Superman, Dick Tracy, Jack Armstrong, Adventures of Tom Mix, Hop Harrigan and soaps Young Widder Brown, Portia Faces Life, and Just Plain Bill.

TWA is boasting of its new $400,000 Stratoliner which cuts off 3 hours to the west coast. You leave New York at 11:15 pm, stop at Pittsburgh and arrive next afternoon at 12:15, with total elapsed time of 10 hours. We live in a remarkable age.

That's the news this April 5, 1945.

And now today's news, April 6, 1945.

Londoners heard live coverage today of the shelling of Vienna by Russians, hearing the announcer telling citizens to hold fast while old Austrian songs were sung.

The American 9th Army is within 20 miles of Hanover while the British 2nd Army is 35 miles from Bremen.

650 Flying Fortresses and Liberators escorted by 600 Mustangs and Thunderbolts attacked rail networks in front of the 1st and 3rd Army spearheads. There were no German Luftwaffe interceptors and little flak.

General Omar Bradley today said "Germans will know that the brutal Nazi creed they adopted has led them ingloriously to total defeat."

First Army troops captured a trainload of German V-bombs which can now be studied.

The Russians are amazed at the lack of German resistance on the Western front while still offering strong resistance on the Eastern front.

Generalissimo Chiang Kai-shek's Chinese troops in southwest Honan Province have launched counter offensives against the Japanese while battling towards Shensi Province.

While the U.S. will support the Dumbarton Oaks proposals as the basis for discussion at the San Francisco United Nations Peace Conference, it will, along with other countries, reserve the right to offer amendments.

12-year-old Donald Gift has been signed to play Fodder Wing in the movie version of "The Yearling."

Marine Rene Gagnon, the only survivor of the six men raising the American flag on Mt. Suribachi on Iwo Jima, is homeward bound to take part in a bond rally.

Volume on the New York Stock Exchange today was a slow 610,000 shares.

Finally, as we watch World War II winding down in Europe, today is the 28th anniversary of America entering World War I.

That's the news this April 6, 1945.

Saturday, April 7, 1945

And now today's news, April 7, 1945.

The U.S. Naval fleet has made a shattering attack on Japanese positions in Okinawa and in the East China Sea having sunk 6 warships. 300 B-29's and Mustangs have again attacked Tokyo and Nagoya.

In Burma, the 50,000 man Japanese 15th Army has now been destroyed.

The U.S. Marine dead on Iwo Jima of 4189 would have been doubled except for the whole blood flowing in by the Red Cross.

General Joseph Stilwell says don't expect the Japanese to quit after the war in Europe is over.

On Luzon General MacArthur says forces continue to push forward in Visayas and Zamboanga areas of Mindinao.

In Europe General George Patton's diverse tactics in taking, surrounding or by-passing German cities is adding to German morale problems.

American soldiers have found 100 tons of gold and cash in a salt mine said to be the entire German gold reserve. Cash included American, British, Norwegian and French currency.

A transport full of Iwo Jima wounded arrived in San Francisco recently and as ambulances met them at gangplanks the GI's cheered when greeted by smiling American women. American military officers see the European war as won with no more major engagements and expectations of soon meeting the Russians coming from the east.

Former President Herbert Hoover says there's tragedy for cities in Europe with the current disorganization of UNRRA trying to ship food through 8 different agencies in Washington.

A Piper cub pilot in Germany spotting for artillery was attacked by 5 German ME-109's, so he went into a steep dive causing one MC-109 to crash into the ground. The other four planes immediately left.

Half the fleet of all commercial airlines have been taken over by the military and have flown 2.5 billion miles overseas for the army and navy while the remaining commercial planes have increased business by 37.8%.

The British feel the United States should be the home of the new United Nations and that headquarters should be in Washington.

Finally, your spare clothing can be helpful for the war devastated countries so give your clothing to the United National Clothing Collection.

That's the news this April 7, 1945.

And now today's news, April 8, 1945.

In the last two days, B-29's with first time fighter protection have hit Japan. 50,000 Japanese troops have been wiped out in Burma in three weeks, and the U.S. Navy has sunk Japan's largest warship, the Yamamoto, in the East China seas. That, plus the capture of 309,000 Germans in three weeks, is the weekend news.

August Cardinal Hlond, Roman Primate of Poland, has been rescued after 5 years in the hands of the Gestapo and U.S. troops have overrun an extermination center near Ohrdruf and found 4000 prisoners clubbed and burned to death.

The British report German V-bombs have finally been stopped after killing 8436 since June of 1944. In Paris 2700 Frenchmen have been tried as collaborators.

Details have been released regarding last October 24th's rescue attempt by the light cruiser Birmingham when the aircraft carrier Princeton was aflame from Japanese bombs. The Princeton suddenly exploded and sank causing 639 casualties to the Birmingham.

In Washington, Harry Hopkins, President Roosevelt's assistant and former Secretary of Commerce, has received a $5000 raise bringing him up to the same $15,000 level of other Cabinet members.

Current radio shows are Mary Margaret McBride, Maggie McNellis, Galen Drake and John J. Anthony, with popular soap operas including Helen Trent, Our Gal Sunday, Life Can Be Beautiful, Guiding Light, Big Sister, Ma Perkins, Young Dr. Malone, Ethel and Albert and Perry Mason. This week Lionel Hampton is in a jazz concert at Carnegie Hall, and new books include Booth Tarkington's "Image of Josephine" and Taylor Caldwell's "The Wide House."

In sports, Connie Desmond and Red Barber will broadcast Brooklyn Dodgers baseball while Al Helfer and Bill Slater will do Giants and the Yankees. Two Negroes have tried out for the Brooklyn Dodgers but were unimpressive to President Branch Rickey.

Finally, there's an acute shortage of fats. Salvage them for your country and turn them in for red points at your butchers.

That's the news this April 8, 1945.

Monday, April 9, 1945

And now today's news, April 9, 1945.

The Russians have captured the heart of Vienna in hand to hand street fighting capturing City Hall, Parliament and the Opera House. The Russians are telling the Austrians they will maintain their freedoms and social systems after Soviet occupation.

American planes have blasted Germans in the Po Valley aided by the Japanese-American 442nd Regiment and the 92nd Negro Division. Meanwhile, the RAF is operating out of Crete for the first time in 5 years.

President Roosevelt has told Norway and Denmark their liberation is at hand after 5 years.

South American countries and the U.S. have resumed diplomatic relations with Argentina. Spruille Braden, present Ambassador to Cuba becomes U.S. Ambassador to Argentina.

Casualties announced today include 8453 Army and 598 Navy troops.

American troops are bringing home at least 20,000 British brides—all at the expense of the U.S., and 1500 American troops arriving in Boston from liberated prison camps have reported on their starvation, lack of clothing and shelter.

In Paris, a meatless week has been announced including no horse flesh.

The Massachusetts Legislature has upheld the death penalty today.

On radio tonight, hear commentary by Morgan Beatty or R.H. Baukage. At the movies, Hal Wallis' new movie "The Affairs of Susan" starring Joan Fontaine and George Brent, Wallace Beery is in "This Man's Navy," and Ernest Lubitsch's latest is "A Royal Scandal" starring Tallulah Bankhead, Anne Baxter, and William Eythe. Celeste Holm and Joan McCracken are on Broadway in "Bloomer Girl" and Artur Rodzinski conducts the N.Y. Philharmonic Symphonic Orchestra at Carnegie Hall.

King George and Queen Elizabeth have visited their 19-year-old ATS grease monkey Princess Elizabeth.

On Wall Street today in a dull session, trading was only 510,000 shares with the Dow Jones ending at 156.

That's the news this April 9, 1945.

And now today's news, April 10, 1945.

Flame throwing British Crocodile tanks surged today through the Po Valley as 100 bombers attacked the Germans. U.S. fliers smashed 397 Nazi aircraft after fighting through the new German jet aircraft.

In the South Pacific, Americans hurled back Japanese attacks on Okinawa as further south Gen. MacArthur's troops in the Philippines took control of the Sulu Archipelago. Tokyo broadcasts continue to deny any interest in peace negotiations.

U.S. Naval Lt. William E. Delany of Detroit was picked up after 4 hours in the water right in the midst of Japanese ships after 4 of his airplanes' bombs had hit and help sink the Yamamoto battleship.

In Germany, Rembrandt, Holbein and Titian art treasures have been found in salt mines. Moscow today reports the war has cost it $50 billion thus far.

In Seattle, Washington, Boeing aircraft has built its last B-17 Flying Fortress and converted full production to the B-29 Superfortress. Boeing had built 6,981 B-17's.

In Britain, Prime Minister Churchill reported today total war casualties to date are 1,100,000 including 306,000 dead in all areas of combat.

In Washington Secretary of War Henry Stimson has proposed merging the Army an Navy into one department after the war; and in Mississippi in a German prison camp, Maj. Gen. Von Schubert has died and has been buried 4000 miles from his fatherland.

At local book stores Emily Dickinson's latest book of poems is "Bolts of Melody." On Broadway Tennessee Williams' "Glass Menagerie" has been named best play of the year. Coming in second was "Harvey." Ingrid Bergman and Raymond Massey have been signed for Maxwell Anderson's new play "A Girl From Lorraine" about Joan of Arc while at the Roxy Theater Hazel Scott and Jackie Miles are on stage.

Knox the Hatter has men's felt hats for $5 each, men's shirts at Sterns' are $2.50 each and the cost of beer is going up to 11 cents a pint and 27 cents a quart.

For radio entertainment tonight try Henny Youngman. Carol Bruce and Eddy Howard at 8:30 and Boston Blackie at 10 pm.

That's the news this April 10, 1945.

105

Wednesday, April 11, 1945

And now today's news, April 11, 1945.

The last German pocket battleship, the Admiral Scheer, has been sunk by RAF planes, the U.S. 2nd Armored Division is 63 miles from Berlin, and Soviet troops are heading towards Hitler's Bertesgaden retreat.

On Okinawa in the South Pacific, Japanese resistance has stiffened but little resistance has been noted on Luzon in the Philippines. B-29's have hit Tokyo again, this time again accompanied by U.S.fighter planes out of Iwo Jima.

Inadvertently, a U.S. sub has sunk a Japanese relief ship travelling under safe conduct but without lights or proper ID. The U.S. has also apologized for an inadvertent attack on Portuguese Macao in China.

London has an unconfirmed report that Hitler is dying and Heinrich Himmler is taking over.

The Polish ministry has confirmed at least 1.7 million Jews have been exterminated at Birkenau with a probable total of over 5 million at all concentration camps.

Singer Lily Pons and conductor husband Andre Kostalanetz are back from France predicting revolution by the poor if they don't receive food soon.

In sports, the 10 National Football League teams plan on 10 games this season starting September 23rd while there remains doubt right now whether the Kentucky Derby even will be run on May 5th unless the war has ended.

In New York the Philharmonic Symphony Society has sent $1000 to composer Jan Silbelius in Finland after hearing of his wartime deprivations.

Some of the popular radio shows today are Mary Marlin, Martha Deane, Pepper Young's Family, Right To Happiness, Backstage Wife, Stella Dallas, Lorenzo Jones and for news and commentary tonight you can try Westbrook Van Voorhees.

In business, today's heavy volume on the New York Stock Exchange of 1,060,000 shares put the averages up 1.55. And, Old Gold cigarettes will shortly start using aluminium foil in their packaging for the first time since the start of the war.

A final story tells of the German mother who went into the woods, found her soldier son, took him by the hand and turned him over to the U.S. troops as a prisoner for safekeeping.

That's the news this April 11, 1945.

And now today's news, April 12, 1945.

The news for this day is indeed tragic. President Franklin D. Roosevelt died today at 3:35 pm at the Little White House in Warm Springs, Georgia.

The 63-year-old President was in excellent spirits at 9:30 am this morning. At 1 pm, as he was being sketched he suddenly said "I have a terrific headache"—his last words. Mrs. Roosevelt and his daughter, Mrs. John Boettinger, were in Washington at the time and the First Lady immediately left the White House for Warm Springs. Sons, James, Elliott and John Roosevelt are all overseas.

He died in the 83rd day of his unprecedented fourth term.

At 7:09 pm, standing straight-backed with determined features, Vice President Harry S. Truman was sworn in as 32nd President by Chief Justice Harlan Stone in a ceremony lasting less than a minute. Deferring any press conference, he merely confirmed there will be no change in policies.

Now standing second in line for the Presidency is Secretary of State Edward R. Stettinius. President Truman is the 7th man to become elevated to President due to a Presidential death.

Reaction around the world was immediate. Foreign Minister Georges Bidault of France called it "a great disaster," Gen. Charles de Gaulle said "I am shocked more than I can say," and Winston Churchill said Britain had lost a gallant friend. Speaker of the House Sam Rayburn and Senate Majority Leader Alben Barkley were too shocked to comment. A 36-year-old Congressman from Texas, Lyndon Baines Johnson, had tears in his eyes. Typical of the shock of American troops around the world was Corp. Israel Goldberg of St. Louis who said, "We're so close to victory it's a terrible time to happen."

Franklin Delano Roosevelt served his country over 30 years as Assistant Secretary of the Navy, Governor of New York, and his critical Presidency during the war years. His radical new policies at the depths of the depression set the country in new directions. His Vice Presidents were two term John Nance Garner, Henry A. Wallace, and Truman.

Funeral services for President Roosevelt will be in the East Room of the White House with interment on the 15th at Hyde Park.

That's the news this April 12, 1945.

Friday, April 13, 1945

And now today's news, April, 13, 1945.

Crowds are gathering at every station along the route from Warm Springs, Georgia as the train bearing the body of President Roosevelt nears Washington. Funeral services will be held tomorrow in Washington. New President Harry S. Truman will accompany the body thereafter to Hyde Park with the family for burial on Sunday.

President Truman worked a hard 9 to 5 on his first day as President conferring with military heads that included Secretary of War Henry Stimson, Secretary of the Navy James Forrestal, Fleet Admiral Ernest J. King, Army Chief of Staff George C. Marshall, and Lt. General Barney Giles of the Army Air Forces. He has already authorized Secretary of State Stettinius to say there will be no changes in US foreign policies. The President will address Congress on Monday and has declared tomorrow as "a day of mourning and prayer throughout the United States."

Cities throughout the country are arranging their own special memorials and prayer services. Flags are at half mast in Switzerland, and grief is universal in Britain, France, New Zealand and Australia. Winston Churchill in a faltering voice addressed Commons speaking of "the great departed statesman and war leader."

The Soviet people considered Roosevelt their great friend.

The radio networks have cancelled all their regular programs through Sunday.

The Trumans have moved from their apartment on Connecticut Avenue to Blair House across from the White House giving Mrs. Roosevelt all the time she needs for moving.

On the war front, U.S. Flyers destroyed 321 more German planes, a total of 1392 in the last week as RAF bombers attacked Kiel.

In the Pacific, a great fleet of B-29's dropped more incendiaries on Tokyo as crews said they could hear explosions one hundred miles away.

Fleet Admiral Chester Nimitz says the Japanese are using suicide planes to hit ships. Called Kamikaze Corps—meaning Divine Wind Corps, he says they are not effective.

After two minutes of silence at the opening, the stock market gained, banks were open, and the nation seemed confident of the future.

While many theaters will be closed tomorrow, a new movie just opened starring Wallace Beery and James Gleason in "This Man's Navy."

And that's the news this beginning day of a new administration at a time of world-wide sadness, April 13, 1945.

And now today's news, April 14, 1945.

Simple funeral rites were held today in the East Room of the White House for the 31st President of the United States, Franklin Delano Roosevelt. Mrs. Roosevelt was a calm central figure with her family including daughter Anna R. Boettiger, son Brigadier Elliott Roosevelt, daughter-in-law Mrs. James, Mrs. Elliott, Mrs. Franklin, and Mrs. John Roosevelt and son-in-law Lt. Col. John Boettiger.

In addition to President Truman, others present were Anthony Eden of Britain, former Chief Justice Charles Evans Hughes, and Russian Ambassador Andrei Gromyko. An estimated 500,000 people watched the coffin borne through the streets of Washington with military honors. The train, with President Truman aboard, left at 11 pm for Hyde Park. Foreign newspapers were filled with tributes and an estimated million New Yorkers outdoors in the rain paid honor to the late President.

Japan's Premier Kantaro Suzuki voiced sympathy noting President Roosevelt was responsible for "America's advantageous position today." The Nazi press called President Roosevelt a war criminal and his death a divine justice. The French are concerned for fear the Russians will gain throughout Europe without Roosevelt's restraint.

Since Rudolf Hess bailed out into Britain on May 10, 1941, he has been constantly moved for safety purposes from one prison to another. Franz Von Papen, the gray fox of German diplomacy and notorious international figure since he was expelled from the United States in 1951, has been captured in Germany by the U.S. 9th Army.

In the Pacific, the Marines have over run Japanese positions in the northern tip of Formosa. It's been reported that 6 B-29's were lost in yesterday's Tokyo raid. In Manila Bay, American troops dumped thousands of gallons of gasoline inside the old Fort Drum on El Fraile Island with an explosion that assured no survival of any Japanese inside.

At Carnegie Hall in New York, Serge Koussevitsky conducted the Boston Symphony Orchestra in a memorial service to President Roosevelt to a silent audience. Backed by black drape on stage with an American flag the tribute included music by Beethoven, Randall Thompson, Shostakovitch and choral performance by the Harvard Glee Club.

The New York Red Cross benefit cancelled due to the President's death has been rescheduled for May 4th at the Waldorf Astoria with feature sportscaster Ted Husing as producer with Babe Ruth, Leo Durocher, Larry MacPhail, Joe McCarthy, Branch Rickey, Eleanor Holm, WAVE Lt. Helen Jacobs, Joe Lapchik, Lou Little, Lt. Benny Leonard and others.

That's the news this April 14, 1945

And now today's news, April 15, 1945.

As B-29's again firebombed Tokyo, the Soviets captured Vienna and the U.S. First Army nears Leipzig, the world continues to mourn the death of President Roosevelt. Following yesterday's White House funeral services the carefully guarded 17 car funeral train carrying President Roosevelt's body proceeded to Hyde Park accompanied by family and virtually every key government official including President Truman. Tearful thousands watched as the train passed through the countryside and cities.

At Hyde Park today President Roosevelt was buried. As planes flew overhead, West Point cadets stood at attention and a 21-gun salute preceded taps. In attendance were Mrs. Eleanor Roosevelt, daughter Mrs. John Boettiger and Brig. Gen. Elliott Roosevelt. Government officials included new President Harry S. Truman, cabinet members Edward R. Stettinius, Secretary of State, Henry Morgenthau, Treasury, Henry Stimson, War, James V. Forrestal, Navy, Claude Wickard, Agriculture, Henry A. Wallace, Commerce, Frances Perkins, Labor, Harold Ickes, Interior Francis Biddle, Attorney General, Frank C. Walker, Postmaster General, Fleet Admiral William D. Leahy, physician and Vice Admiral Ross McIntyre, Alice Tully, the President's personal secretary, and the entire Supreme Court including Chief Justice Harlan Stone, and Justices Owen J. Roberts, Hugo Black, Wiley Rutledge, Robert H. Jackson, Frank Murphy, Stanley Reed, William O. Douglas, and Felix Frankfurter. Prime Minister MacKenzie King of Canada also was present. In Philadelphia, the tower bell at Independence Hall was tolled 63 times, one for each year of President Roosevelt's life—the first time the bell has been rung since the death of Calvin Coolidge in 1933.

Today radio stations resumed regular programming including commercials for the first time in 3 days. Condolences continued to pour in from around the world on this day of sadness in the United States.

That's the news this April 15, 1945.

And now today's news, April 16, 1945.

With a standing ovation both before and after addressing a joint session of Congress plus cabinet members and the Supreme Court as well as Mrs. Truman and daughter Margaret, President Harry Truman today asked for unity as peace nears. In Grandview,, Missouri, his 92-year-old mother said "Harry will get along all right." The President speaks via radio to the Armed Forces around the world tomorrow. Mrs. Roosevelt then gave a tour of the White House to Mrs. Truman.

In Germany, 218,000 prisoners have been taken in the last 72 hours, another 845 Luftwaffe planes were destroyed in one raid as 6000 Allied planes attacked, Red Army paratroopers are within 18 miles of Berlin, U.S. troops smashed into Nuremberg, and among prominent prisoners taken is former German Chancellor Franz Von Papen. One million residents of Leipzig may be in for a terrible doom unless the Nazis give up as few defenses remain.

Two GI's stumbled upon a salt mine entrance that contained, 950 feet below, an entire jet aircraft factory capable of producing 700 jet planes per month which could out perform the U.S. propeller drive aircraft. The Nazi manager stated "One more year and all these jets would have turned the war around."

Hitler has warned his eastern armies they have one final chance to defeat "the Jewish Bolshevik archenemy." Among the 17,000 Allied prisoners freed in Orbke, Germany are 2800 Yanks.

In sports, well known 41-year veteran and ailing baseball umpire Bill Klem will miss his first season's opener. Boston Red Sox manager Joe Cronin gave try outs to three Negroes, one named Jackie Robinson, former UCLA baseball and football star who has served 31 months as an Army Lieutenant. 82-year-old Mr. Baseball, Connie Mack of the Philadelphia Athletics, says the team to beat this year is the St. Louis Browns.

At Camp Shanks, New York where 10,000 wounded arrive a month, 50 telephone operators have become personal message carriers of hope, sorrow, death, marriages and broken engagements to the returning GI's.

At Gimbels you can buy a ready-made 10 x 10 garage for $188.00

That's the news this April 16, 1945.

And now today's news, April 17, 1945.

In Europe, the British have taken Hamburg, Gen. Omar Bradley's U.S. 12th Army has footholds along the Elbe and Mulde Rivers and historic Rothenburg has been captured by GI's. 720 parked apparently gasless German planes have been destroyed in the last 10 days.

From nearby Weimar, 1200 civilians have been taken into Buchenwald concentration camp to find 20,000 survivors of what had been 80,000 prisoners. The unbelievable horrors caused tears and fainting.

Japan has started large scale manufacturing of suicide planes in Manchuria to carry 2200 pounds of explosives which detonate upon plane contact. Suicide pilots will be given 3 months final leave, then, without parachutes, will be locked into the plane, will circle the field 3 times, and head for an absolute doom no matter what.

In Bombay, India, Mohandas K. Gandhi today said "an indisputable preliminary to peace is the complete freedom of India from all foreign control."

In Washington President Truman held his first press conference today appointing 36-year-old Atlanta radio executive J. Leonard Reinsch his press secretary and Matthew J. Connelly his confidential secretary.

President Truman also today elevated 3 star generals George Patton and Courtney Hodges to four stars and 2 star general Lucius D. Clay to Lt. General.

On Guam, Major Winthrop Rockefeller is recovering from flash burns following wounds suffered during a Japanese air attack off Okinawa.

In London, a memorial service for President Roosevelt was attended by King George and Queen Elizabeth, Princess Elizabeth in her ATS uniform and Prime Minister Churchill among hundreds.

New movies include "God is My Co-Pilot" with Dennis Morgan, Dane Clark, Raymond Massey and Alan Hale, and Bette Davis in "The Corn is Green."

Mrs. Roosevelt today resumed her daily newspaper column "My Day."

And finally, in Italy the navigator and bombardier of a B-24 dropped their bombs on target and then literally dropped a kitchen sink.

That's the news this April 17, 1945.

And now today's news, April 18, 1945.

Russian troops are within sight of Berlin, the American 9th is in Magdeburg, the German Luftwaffe is almost immobile as 96% of German gas output has been destroyed, and over 2 million German prisoners have been taken since D Day last June.

A German ringleader has been captured responsible for suffocating and burning 1000 political prisoners as another infamous concentration camp, Belsen, has been taken freeing 29,000 prisoners suffering from typhus, typhoid, tuberculosis, starvation, nakedness. Allies found dumps of unburied bodies including 500 children. Back in the United States the first 10 U.S. freed men have told of their prison mistreatment.

As European troops and facilities are being sent to the South Pacific, at home there are sweeping cutbacks planned in producing B-17 and B-24 bombers.

A New York City High School continues to emphasize required rifle practice and swimming for boys, while making commando practice less strenuous. Girl students continue nursing, homemaking and secretarial training.

A sad casualty of the war today was famed correspondent Ernie Pyle who was killed instantly by Japanese machine gun fire on Ie Island west of Okinawa. He was best known for chronicling the American GI story.

In Europe, RAF Wing Commander Douglas Bader, famous legless flier, has been freed. After escaping three times, the Germans took his legs away to prevent a fourth escape.

Opening baseball day yesterday at Yankee Stadium featured a tribute to the late President Roosevelt. Together in the stands were Col. Larry MacPhail, Yankee owner, Mayor Fiorello LaGuardia, former Cuban President Batista, and James A. Farley. Outside the stadium were 20 Negroes picketing with signs saying "If we can pay, why can't we play?"

Tennis matches featuring top stars on April 22nd will enjoy the pantomine entertainment of Al Schacht.

A 20-year-old designer of costumes for Ringling Brothers Circus has married 59-year-old composer Deems Taylor. Taylor was divorced in 1934.

That's the news this April 18, 1945.

Thursday, April 19, 1945

And now today's news, April 19, 1945.

In Europe the U.S. First Army has taken Leipzig, Germany's fifth largest city, as a wave of suicides, including the Burgomeister, is occurring. The U.S. Third Army has captured Germany's complete roster of all prisoners since the beginning of the war including dates of capture and whereabouts. 6 ton bombs have been dropped on the island of Helgoland with an ultimatum to surrender or be invaded.

In Buchenwald concentration camp, freed prisoners continue in great despair as the Red Cross is rushing aid to a camp where many atrocities are too horrible to report.

As the city of Halle was captured by Americans, so too was one of its defenders, the almost legendary sea devil Count Felix Von Luckner. Credited with sinking 25 Allied merchant ships in World War I yet claiming rescue of every crew, Von Luckner toured the United States in the 1920's and was a national hero in Germany. To the Americans yesterday he said "By Joe—you Americans are wonderful."

The Prime Minister of Syria opposes any expansion of a Jewish state concept in Palestine. Passing through New York en route to San Francisco for the United Nations conference were Jan Christian Smuts of South Africa and Georges Bidault of France. The U.S. has disagreed with Russia that the provisional government of Poland be invited to the U.N. conference.

Washington announced another 11,500 casualties, a total of 912,000 since Pearl Harbor including 162,000 Army deaths, 38,000 Navy deaths, almost 100,000 missing and 75,000 taken prisoner.

In Philadelphia, Dr. Harlow Shapley of Harvard College Observatory, has been honored with the Franklin Medal.

Union employees of a Kansas City company have asked the War Labor board to approve a pay cut of 5 to 7 cents per hour in order to minimize layoffs during reconversion to peacetime production.

In Britain, the lights are on again after 5 years and 7 months of blackouts. The light on Big Ben is on for the first time since August 31, 1939.

Have you become a blood donor yet? Help keep our casualty list down and volunteer today!

That's the news this April 19, 1945.

And now today's news, April 20, 1945.

Nazi radio reports the Russians are 7 miles from the bomb torn, flaming city of Berlin as American and British planes continue to blast the city. The Nazi shrine city of Nuremberg was captured today on Hitler's 56th birthday—a desolate city in ruins. General Eisenhower sees the Germans tottering on the threshold of defeat.

American and French armies are 10 to 20 miles further into Bavaria on a 200 mile front and expect Hitler to make his last stand in that area.

In Italy, American troops smashed into the Po Valley.

In the Pacific, Americans moved ahead another 1000 yards on Okinawa as Admiral Nimitz reveals the loss of 15 American naval vessels in the last four weeks . General MacArthur says the U.S. now controls all of the central Philippines while British troops are now only 200 miles from Rangoon.

60,000 Japanese troops are driving towards the U.S. 14th Air Force base at Chunkiang.

B-29's have bombed nine Kyushu airfields and towns including one called Usa, so renamed several years ago so that toys could be shipped from U.S.A.

President Truman will address by radio the first plenary session of the San Francisco United Nations Conference on International Organization on Wednesday. Descriptions of the atrocities at Belsen concentration camp in Germany where 60,000 dead, dying and starving may be shown to the conference. Meanwhile Josef Kramer, known as the Beast of Belsen is under 24 hour guard.

750 Americans freed from prisons by the Russians have arrived in Boston.

Britain says that 146,000 civilians have been casualties since the war started with 60,500 killed.

Ernie Pyle, the doughboy's reporter, was buried today on Ie Island where he was killed. Hundreds of Marines attended even as mortar shells passed overhead.

President Truman has appointed Charles G. Ross at his press aide and Mrs. Roosevelt left her White House home today after 12 years of residency.

Speaker Sam Rayburn threw out the first ball at the Washington Senators and Yankees game with Clark Griffith and great pitcher Walter Johnson watching.

Harry Davenport will have a part with Fred McMurray in "Pardon My Past" and a new movie has just opened called "The Horn Blows at Midnight" starring Jack Benny and Alexis Smith.

That's the news this April 20, 1945.

115

Saturday, April 21, 1945

And now today's news, April 21, 1945.

Russian tanks and troops are three miles inside Berlin with three-quarters of the city encircled as American armies moved closer.

Joseph Goebbels is cajoling Berliners to fight to the death even as shells fall and they face starvation and lack of water.

American military officers say that even after the fall of Berlin they expect bloody battles in southeastern Bavaria and in the North Sea areas.

American, Polish and Italian troops surged into Bologna today gaining the greatest victory since the fall of Rome.

Only one church remains standing in the ruins of Nuremberg, now 95% destroyed.

Stockholm reports that Hermann Goering and his wife have fled his palatial mansion 40 miles northeast of Berlin with $20 million in jewelry mostly looted from the Lowlands and France.

The encirclement of the Ruhr is described by Lt. General Walter Bedell Smith an almost perfect battle, the "largest double envelopment in military history."

France hopes to use 2 million Germans for labor as reparations.

New York Times reporter Frederick Graham and Stars and Stripes reporter Andy Rooney have described the horrors of the small town of Thekla in an April 18th report telling of 300 Allied prisoners forced by SS troops into a building. Gasoline was poured inside, it was set on fire, and escapees were shot before Americans arrived on the way to Leipzig.

The Grand Duchess Charlotte and Princess Elizabeth and Princess Marie Adelaide of Luxembourg have left London to return to their homeland.

Lt. Bernard C. Duffy, whose Duffy's Radio Tavern in New York City was the inspiration for the radio show of the same name, has been killed in Burma.

Gloria Vanderbilt di Cicco married conductor Leopold Stokowski today in Mexico.

Gimbels New York is selling 8 glass tumblers for $1.49, 3 jars of marmalade for $1.92, and a dozen 46 ounce cans of orange juice for $5.76.

At the movies, Robert Young, Dorothy Maguire and Herbert Marshall star in "The Enchanted Cottage" and for radio tomorrow night try Phil Baker and "Take It or Leave It."

That's the news this April 21, 1945.

And now today's news, April 22, 1945.

Over the weekend, the Russians drove 7 miles inside Berlin and now control one sixth of the city. Germany's last pocket battleship, the 12,000 ton Luetzow, has been sunk by RAF Lancaster bombers in the Baltic port of Swinemuende, and 8th Air Force bombers have begun using new rocket-propelled bombs in Germany.

In the Pacific, General MacArthur has announced American forces have now won control of the entire central Philippines.

While Russia and Poland have signed a mutual aid pact, Edward Stettinius, Anthony Eden and Vyacheslav Molotov are conferring about Poland's representation in the United Nations Conference on International Organization.

Brazil has repaid the United States 35 million dollars for lend lease aid.

If you're looking for bargains, Gimbel's has women's pigskin sandals for $2.98, and six sugar sack towels for $1.41. And, you can buy a detached Colonial house in Forest Hills for $17,500.

Spencer Tracy and Katharine Hepburn are starring "Without Love" at Radio City Music Hall, and Franchot Tone and Jane Wyatt are at the Royale Theater in "Hope for the Best."

That's the news this April 22, 1945.

Monday, April 23, 1945

And now today's news, April 23, 1945.

The Russians have taken 1/3 of Berlin and only 16 miles separate them and the Red Armies. In the South, the Allies have reached the Po River in Italy.

In the Philippines, the Americans have cut off the Japanese garrisons from Dravo to the south. B-29's from the Mariannas have bombed the Hitachi Aircraft plant in Tokyo in the first raid since the great fire raid of April 16th.

Sixty-four year old former King Ferdinand of Bulgaria has been killed in an auto accident while he was fleeing from Slovakia en route to Austria.

The Argentine government has re-established press censorship on outgoing news after General Arturo Rawson was arrested.

There will be a shortage of smoking pipes for the public since the armed forces are now taking 1/2 of the 2 million pipes now being produced each month.

In Washington the War Labor Board has okayed the new soft coal miners' contract calling for a raise of $1.02 a day for a 6-day week.

In sports, major league baseball owners are still trying to decide on a successor to Kenesaw Mountain Landis as commissioner.

In New York at the movies, Maria Montez, Jon Hall and Turhan Bey are now playing in "Sudan" at Loew's Criterion. And, if you want a bigger laugh, try Olsen and Johnson in "Laffing Room Only" at the Winter Garden.

That's the news this April 23, 1945.

And now today's news, April 24, 1945.

Two Russian Army groups took 8 more districts of Berlin today and joined up inside the city limits. 25% of greater Berlin is now in Soviet hands. German propaganda minister Joseph Goebbels is urging Berlin' defenders to hold on, saying that reinforcements are on the way.

NBC news commentator Lowell Thomas, flying over Berlin today, says the city is "in flames from one end to the other."

The blackout in London has officially ended with the relighting of the famous Big Ben clock tower.

In Italy, the American 5th Army has crossed the Po River at several points, and the 15th Army Group is massed at various places along the river from Ferrara to Borgoforte.

In the Pacific, Army troops have taken an important hill at the eastern end of the Naha line on Okinawa. Lt. General Barney Giles has been promoted to Commanding General, Army Air Forces in the Pacific.

President Truman will address the United Nations Conference in San Francisco today. The 46 nations on hand will meet tomorrow to organize the peace.

The Joint Chiefs of Staff are formulating plans for a naval blockade of Japan coupled with air strikes from land and carrier-based planes.

Marshal Henri Phillipe Petain has surrendered in Switzerland and will return to France to face charges of high treason.

The U.S. Senate has overwhelmingly voted to ban the use of 18-year-olds in Army combat duty until they have had at least 6 months training.

Charles Jundt, founder of the Charles of the Ritz beauty salons, has died at 64. He suffered a cerebral hemorrhage last week.

And, Senator Albert "Happy" Chandler of Kentucky has been named the new commissioner of major league baseball, succeeding the late Kenesaw Mountain Landis.

That's the news this April 24, 1945.

Wednesday, April 25, 1945

And now today's news, April 25, 1945.

The United Nations Conference on International Organization opened in San Francisco today. President Truman addressed the group from the White House asking them to rise above personal interests.

On the war front, the Russians have completely encircled Berlin and now occupy nearly all the city. Captured Lt. General Heinrich Kirchheim has urged the High Command to surrender.

American troops are advancing on Okinawa and recaptured Kakuzu in the center of the island.

Here at home, black market wholesalers are getting $100 plus the OPA ceiling price for beef carcasses. Vegetable prices posted by the OPA show strawberries going for 34 cents a pint, new potatoes, in bulk, for 36 cents.

Acting under an order from President Truman, the Navy has seized the United Engineering Company plant in San Francisco where a labor dispute has tied up work on vitally-needed ships.

The name of the new 45,000-ton supercarrier Coral Sea has been changed to the U.S.S. Franklin Delano Roosevelt.

The War Production Board says rumors of clothing rationing are farfetched and should be discounted.

Lionel Hampton and his orchestra are at the Cafe Zanzibar in New York. The dinner show and dancing costs $1.

New York Mayor LaGuardia will get no support for renomination from Republican leaders.

That's the new this April 25, 1945.

And now today's new, April 26, 1945.

Russian Foreign Minister Molotov has rejected a suggestion that Edward R. Stettinius be made permanent chairman of the U.N. Conference in San Francisco, suggesting instead there be 4 chairmen, including himself, Stettinius, Anthony Eden and T.V. Soong of China.

Reichsmarshal Hermann Goering has been relieved of his command, the first of the German hierarchy to fall.

German defenses are crumbling all over, and Berlin is a shambles.

Italian dictator Benito Mussolini has been captured by Italian patriots as he tried to escape in Northern Italy.

A 10-man Congressional team has visited the concentration camp at Buchenwald.

General Erwin Rommel's widow said her husband died of a heart attack on October 14th as he was recovering from a head wound received in France.

Americans will get less meat next month and have to give up red points for all kinds except mutton. Margarine and most cheeses will cost more points, too.

Freddie Schott will seek his 37th straight win as a professional fighter tonight against Billy Grant at St. Nicholas Arena.

Fritz Kreisler presents a recital tonight for a benefit of the Musicians Emergency Fund at Carnegie Hall.

The Danny Kaye Radio Show will be heard at its new time tonight at 10:30 right after the Jimmy Durante Show.

Walter B. Cooke Funeral Homes are advertising dignified funerals for as low as $150.

That's the news this April 26, 1945.

And now today's news, April 27, 1945.

The U.S. and Red Armies have joined forces splitting Germany and sealing the doom of the German army. After battling 700 miles from Normandy men of General Courtney Hodges' 1st Army met troops of the First Ukranian Army at the Elbe River at 4:40 pm on the 25th.

The Red Army has overwhelmed the southern part of Berlin and has taken Tempelhof Airport. Berliners have started looting.

Marshal Gregori Zhukov's First White Russian Army has entered Potsdam and seized Spandau. The American 5th Army has entered Genoa, Italy after partisans gained control.

German General Dittmar, who surrendered with his son by paddling across the Elbe River, says Hitler is still in Berlin and intends to die there.

Brigadier General Julius Ochs Adler, back as Vice President of the New York Times, is in Europe inspecting concentration camps. He describes Buchenwald as worse than a battlefield. A British white paper says 51,000 have died there since 1937, 17,000 since January 1st.

89-year-old Marshal Henri-Phillipe Petain has returned to Paris as a prisoner to be tried for treason.

Fleet Admiral Chester Nimitz reveals that there are Japanese rocket bombs with humans inside guiding them. Launched from the underside of bombers, GI's call them baka bombs since baka means stupid. One GI said "They don't get a chance to practice so they're not too accurate."

Edwin Pauley, Democratic National Committee treasurer, has been named to head the U.S. Reparations unit meeting in Moscow next month.

46 nations continue to meet in San Francisco as Secretary of State Stettinius keeps a direct wire to former Secretary of State Cordell Hull ill at the Bethesda Naval Hospital.

The Navy has relaxed its restrictions on sea assignments for Negroes and will permit up to 10% of crew of all auxiliary crafts. There are 160,000 Negro officers and enlisted men in the Navy.

Virginia Mayo and Vera Ellen will star with Danny Kaye in "The Kid From Brooklyn,"and the Marx Brothers will make a movie after 3 years as yet untitled.

That's the news this April 27, 1945.

And now today's news, April 28, 1945.

While President Truman says there is no basis for the rumor, a Heinrich Himmler report says Hitler is dying, that he, Himmler, is in charge and in a position to surrender. According to Swedish sources Himmler has sent an offer through Count Folke Bernadotte of Sweden.

Two Red armies have captured 27,000 Germans as the inner defenses of Berlin have collapsed.

Lt. General Alexander Patch's 7th Army has crossed the Austrian border.

Lt. General Leonard T. Gerow's 15th Army will take over as occupation troops in sections of Germany with no pampering of the conquered.

Japanese fighters furiously attacked B-29 bombers today head on and dropped phosphorous bombs on them over southern Japan.

In the Philippines, Americans have captured Baguio, the summer capital and one-time Japanese headquarters on Northern Luzon.

6 German tugboats, 10 river barges and 14 other boats sailed up the Elbe River to surrender to Americans.

While it originally was to be called the USS Coral Sea, tomorrow the USS Franklin D. Roosevelt carrier will be launched in New York as sister ship to the Midway. Mrs. Roosevelt will be on hand.

Holland is still occupied by Germans as underground resistance continues in the midst of starvation and tragic conditions.

48 of the 58 major German cities have now been captured, 42 by the Americans.

Churches and synagogues countrywide are making plans to celebrate V-E day.

French women will vote for the first time in municipal elections tomorrow.

U.S. Delegate Commander Harold Stassen says the San Francisco peace conference is off to a good start. Justice, human rights, and the dignity of man are key subjects. Foreign Commissar Molotov of Russia presided as one of the four presidents of the U.S. Conference.

Fred Waring and his entire musical group performs tonight at Carnegie Hall.

Baseball's new Commissioner Senator A.B. "Happy" Chandler says President Truman wants to keep baseball going during the war.

Current quiz shows include "Dr. I.Q.," "Quick As A Flash," Kay Kyser's "Kollege of Musical Knowledge," and "Truth or Consequences."

That's the news this April 28, 1945.

123

Sunday, April 29, 1945

And now today's news, April 29, 1945.

Over the weekend, the U.S. and Red Armies met on the Elbe River splitting Germany. Three-fourths of Berlin is now in Russian hands. Berliners are looting as their food supply runs low.

The Russians have also captured Potsdam and Spandau, and the U.S. 7th Army has entered Munich.

The Germans killed 5000 prisoners in Buchenwald as a human roadblock to advancing tanks.

President Truman says there is no truth to reports of German surrender. In Italy, Benito Mussolini has been executed by Italian Partisans. His mistress and 12 men were also executed.

At home, the War Production Board has revoked 40 of its lesser controls on industry.

The Carrier Franklin Delano Roosevelt was christened today at the New York Navy Yard in Brooklyn.

The Rev. Dr. Donald Aldrich has warned us to "beware of Russia." Movie actor George Sidney, best known for his antics in the old Cohen and Kelly series, died today at 68.

Philco Corporation's annual report released today shows a 31% sales increase in 1944.

Louis Bromfield will be a guest on the "Information Please" radio show tonight.

And, it's the 4th big week for Shirley Temple, Ginger Rogers and Joseph Cotten in "I'll Be Seeing You."

That's the news this April 29, 1945.

And now today's news, April 30, 1945.

The Russians have captured the German Reichstag and run up their victory flag. Reports of German surrender are increasing.

The U.S. 7th Army is smashing toward Innsbruck, and General Mark Clark says the German Army has been virtually eliminated in Italy.

Germany's most-dreaded concentration camp, Dachau, has been captured and 32,000 prisoners freed.

Italian partisans have reportedly executed Marshal Rodolfo Graziani.

Machinato Airfield on Okinawa has been taken from the Japanese, and an Allied Force has invaded Borneo.

New red and new blue ration stamps go into effect today for buying processed foods, meats and fats, along with a new sugar stamp. Sugar rationing has been reduced 25%.

The War Labor Board has ordered John L. Lewis and his United Mine Workers to extend their hard coal contract.

Edward D. McKim today became President Truman's Chief Administrative Assistant.

In sports, Phillies pitcher, Ken Raffensberger, has been called up for pre-induction examinations.

Betty Grable will be the guest star tonight on the Dick Haymes radio show at 7:30...and Clifton Webb stars in "My Man Godfrey" at 8:30.

United Aircraft Corporation has reported earnings of $3.5 million for the first quarter of this year.

That's the news this April 30, 1945.

Tuesday, May 1, 1945

And now today's news, May 1, 1945.

Adolph Hitler has reportedly died at his command post in the Chancellery in Berlin. Grand Admiral Karl Doenitz has proclaimed himself the new Fuhrer and said the war will continue. The Russians say the death report is a Fascist trick, and the British Foreign Office says it will demand production of Hitler's body after the end of hostilities.

German Field Marshal Karl von Rundstedt has been captured by the U.S. 7th Army which also captured Admiral Nicholas Horthy, the former regent for Hungary.

Benito Mussolini, executed by Italian partisans yesterday, has been buried in a paupers grave in northern Italy.

Henri Petain has been hanged in effigy in Paris...and the Russians have revealed the world's heaviest artillery weapon in their May Day Parade.

Sister Elizabeth Kenny has charged the National Foundation for Infantile Paralysis with boycotting her treatment of the disease.

The War Labor Board has ordered the United Mine Workers to resume full production of hard coal. President Truman has recommended government seizure of the mines.

Baseball Commissioner Happy Chandler says baseball will have to provide jobs for baseball's war veterans. He wants to locate leagues near government hospitals and in high schools and colleges.

Comedian Hugh Herbert will start rehearsals this week for "Oh, Brother," opening in New York in June.

Lady Hawthorne cigarettes are selling for $1.93 a carton.

That's the news this May 1, 1945.

And now today's news, May 2, 1945.

The war is over in Italy, as one million German and Italians surrender in Italy and Austria.

Berlin has fallen to the Russians, and Denmark's cutoff is now complete. German surrender is expected at any time.

Air raid warnings have been discontinued in London.

It's been revealed that Adolf Hitler and Joseph Goebbels have indeed committed suicide.

Joachim von Ribbentrop has been removed as Germany's foreign minister. Pierre Laval of France has been interned in Spain for disposition by the Allies.

In the Pacific, British forces have landed south of Rangoon, while American troops continue their drive in Okinawa.

At home, plans are being formulated for construction of new civilian vehicles in Detroit.

Consumer groups are opposed to any general increase in ceiling prices.

President Truman has informed Congress the Office of Civilian Defense will stop operating on June 30th.

The War Labor Board is taking steps to seize the anthracite coal mines in Northeast Pennsylvania tomorrow.

New onions are now 3 pounds for a quarter and 18 cents for old ones. California oranges are up 1 cent to 13 cents a pound.

Following one of the biggest publicity campaigns in show business, "Billy Rose's Diamond Horseshoe," with Betty Grable opened today at the Roxy Theater in New York.

That's the news this May 2, 1945.

Thursday, May 3, 1945

And now today's news, May 3, 1945.

The German government has moved to Copenhagen, and Dr. Albert Speer says Germany is defeated. Admiral Doenitz has declared Prague an open city. Denmark and Norway are in confusion with German commanders trying to keep their armies intact.

Moscow Radio says Adolph Hitler shot himself and Joseph Goebbels poisoned himself, but their bodies have not been found.

The British 8th Army has formally occupied the city of Trieste. Rangoon has fallen to the British 14th Army, and Burma is virtually liberated from the Japanese, while Australian troops have advanced in Borneo.

Secretary Ickes has taken possession of the hard coal mines in Pennsylvania and the miners have been asked to return to work. They'll go back if John L. Lewis gives the word.

Baseball Commissioner Happy Chandler says he'll move his office to Cincinnati and he may remain a U.S. Senator "longer than expected."

Paul Waner, in his 23rd year in baseball, has been released by the Boston Red Sox.

Popular Tony Janiro will fight Sammy Parrotto tonight at St. Nicholas Arena.

The egg scarcity is getting worse and the black market in eggs is spreading.

After the end of the war in Europe, gasoline rations in the U.S. may be increased 50% and fluorescent lighting will be available for most homeowners within a year or two after the war.

Judge William Pecora has ruled that ASCAP is the sole owner of public performance rights of songs written by it members.

That's the news this May 3, 1945.

And now today's news, May 4, 1945.

More than 500,000 Germans have surrendered to Field Marshal Sir Bernard Montgomery including all in the Netherlands, Denmark, and northwest Germany. With a 48 hour total of 1 million surrendering, General Eisenhower says the Germans are thoroughly beaten.

It appears that Grand Admiral Karl Doenitz gave the order for Denmark to surrender to keep them out of Russian hands and he will likely now give up Norway.

General George C. Marshall was warned that U.S. Armed Forces will not be reduced as much as many hoped since General MacArthur needs more troops to fight the war against the Japanese.

Japanese planes have sunk 5 more U.S. light ships off Okinawa as the U.S. shot down 150 planes. 600 Japanese troops have landed behind U.S. lines on Okinawa.

With the fall of Rangoon, Admiral Lord Louis Mountbatten says the Burma campaign has ended with 350,000 Japanese casualties including at least 97,000 killed.

The Soviet press reports that when their troops entered the German Chancellery Wednesday they were driven back by the flames of the building and if Hitler were still inside he would be cremated.

In New York over 15,000 police are being readied to handle V-E day celebrations. Captured Field Marshal von Runstedt says Allied bombings of oil, gas and transportation prevented the Germans from any effective repulse of D-Day invasion.

The Italians want Maestro Arturo Toscanini to return to La Scala Opera House in Milan but he says he would only return as a free citizen and not a subject of a degenerate king.

U.S. aircraft plants turned out 6,900 planes in April down slightly from March. B-17's and B-24's will not be produced after the summer in favor of the mightier B-29 and B-32.

A boom in the sale of postwar FM radios at prices as low as $59.50 is predicted by a vice president of Metropolitan TV, Inc. of New York. The company owns frequency modulation station WABF and television station W2 XMT.

Hedy Lamarr is signed to star in "Strange Woman," and new movies include Gregory Peck and Greer Garson in "The Valley of Decision" and Joan Fontaine and George Brent in "The Affairs of Susan."

That's the news this May 4, 1945.

Saturday, May 5, 1945

And now today's news, May 5, 1945.

The end of the war seems to be hours away. 200-300,000 more Germans have surrendered to Lt. General Jacob Dever's 6th Army with capitulation due tomorrow noon. Only 1 major German army remains in Norway and it's expected Grand Admiral Karl Doenitz is said to be ready to surrender.

There are a few pockets of continued resistance on the Atlantic Coast. The Red Army took the last Nazi Baltic port of Swinemuende. British troops entering Copenhagen were cheered by thousands of Danes.

Here in the U.S. plans are to discharge 2 million men a year but 6 million men will be sent to the Pacific to help win that war.

Among those freed today in Austria are former French Premiers Eduoard Daladier, and Paul Reynaud, Generals Gamelin and Weygand and a sister of General de Gaulle. Near the Brenner Pass others freed are former Austrian Chancellor Kurt Schuschnigg and Rev. Martin Niemoeller who defied Hitler.

War Production Board Chairman Krug says the nationwide brownout will end with V-E Day. There is a political crisis in Belgium as the Socialist party backed by the Communist newspaper are fighting the Catholics who want their king back.

Sandbag barricades are coming down in London, Victory flags are going up, and floodlights are in place to illuminate Parliament and Buckingham Palace.

Among the 2000 prisoners taken at the Hitler hideout at Berchtesgaden is Poland's #1 Nazi Hans Frank who has tried to commit suicide.

As citizens in the Netherlands started celebrating their liberation remaining Germans fired into crowds killing an unspecified number.

The Russians have found an elaborate underground headquarters of the Nazis not in Berlin but in a small village of Zossen south of Berlin.

Ezra Pound, American born poet under indictment for treason, has been captured in Genoa, Italy.

The $70 million 27,000 ton aircraft carrier Kearsarge was launched today at the Brooklyn Navy Yard 14 months after construction started.

Finally, in case you ever tuned in short wave during the last 12 years to Propaganda Minister Dr. Joseph Goebbels short wave operations, it is now kaput. Off the air. Gone.

That's the news this May 5, 1945.

And now today's news, May 6, 1945.

In the last two days over 1 million Germans have surrendered, and General Eisenhower says the foe is whipped. British troops are in Copenhagen as armed Danes are fighting the Nazis while civilians sing and cry in the streets. It's reported the Nazis are ready for a full surrender momentarily as Eisenhower has been authorized to accept capitulation on all fronts.

Germany's Admiral Doenitz, now acting as Reichsfuhrer, wants to continue the fight against the Russians but has ordered all German submarines back home. German newspaper headlines are shocking citizens stating— "Adolf Hitler is dead, Mussolini has been hanged, Goering resigns, Goebbels is said to have killed himself." The U.S. flag now flies over Hitler's headquarters retreat in Berteschgarden. Freed prisoners in Austria include former French premiers Leon Blum and Maxime Weygand.

Also freed in Austria was the son of the American Ambassador to England, Lt. John G. Winant, Jr.

Army officials in Washington plan to discharge 2 million men a year, 1,900 more liberated GI's have arrived at Camp Kilmer, the Air Force is cutting back on the air cadet program, and European bombers are being deployed to the South Pacific.

Freedom of speech and worship has been granted to Spaniards by its government, and Premier Chiang Kai-shek in China says he's dedicated to a better livelihood for the Chinese after Japan is defeated.

Bob Hope's disagreement with Paramount has been cleared up. In New York, "Kiss Them For Me" starring Judy Holliday is moving from the Belasco to the Fulton Theater.

Newspaper ads today for Old Dutch Cleanser features its famous ingredient Seismotite.

That's the news this May 6, 1945.

Monday, May 7, 1945

And now today's news, May 7, 1945.

The war in Europe is over! The Germans have capitulated on all fronts.

At a little red schoolhouse in Reims just 5 years, 8 months and 6 days after the Germans invaded Poland, Col. General Gustav Jodl, new German Chief of Staff, signed for Germany, Lt. General Walter Bedell Smith for the U.S. along with generals from France and Russia. Col. General Jodl appealed for mercy for the German people and armed forces. German troops have given up in Norway.

President Truman, Prime Minister Churchill and General Charles de Gaulle of France will make broadcasts tomorrow.

King George has lauded General Eisenhower for his brilliant leadership. Crowds went wild on Wall Street and Times Square and in London. Synagogues and churches, of course, are full.

The world heard of the surrender thanks to Associated Press Western Front Chief Ted Kennedy having a scoop by breaking security. ETO officials have restricted him to any further news coverage noting that his leak could have cost lives.

In Washington, the capitol dome and the Washington Monument are flooded with light for the first time since December 8, 1941. The government forecasts continued shortages as the war continues. In the Pacific B-29's battered Kyushu for the 18th time.

In Washington, Robert E. Hannegan has been named Postmaster General.

During the war, 355,000 Jews fled from Germany and Europe to Palestine.

In sports, a 6 team U.S. Negro Baseball League has been announced including the Brooklyn Brown Dodgers.

Pulitzer prizes have gone to Mary Chase for "Harvey," John Hersey for "A Bell for Adano," James B. Reston for national reporting, Sgt. Hal Boyle for war reporting, Joe Rosenthal who took the Iwo Jima Suribachi photo, Sgt. Bill Maudlin for cartooning and Aaron Copeland for music.

We repeat...the war is over in Germany. V-E day has arrived.

That's the news this May 7, 1945,

And now today's news, May 8, 1945.

Yesterday's unconditional German surrender at Reims has now been ratified in Berlin even as Germans in Prague and Zagreb fight to avoid capture by the Russians.

President Harry S. Truman in a national radio address today said... "a solemn but a glorious hour." He bid the Japanese to quit as he spoke to over 36 million Americans—with a 64.1 share of audience, the highest in radio history. One of his listeners was elderly General John J. Pershing, head of American troops in World War I.

Meanwhile, the British have told the Germans how to surrender their Navy consisting of only 2 cruisers, several destroyers and 250-300 subs at sea. Churchill has hailed the victory and said— "Now Japan." Pope Pius will speak at noon tomorrow.

President Truman has also laid a wreath at the tomb of the late President Roosevelt and declared Sunday a day of national prayer.

And, the national brownout has been revoked—lights are on in Times Square and the Statue of Liberty.

An unconfirmed report by the Russians says that Hitler's body has been found.

Washington reports U.S. losses in the war are over 150,000 dead and 750,000 injuries in the European Theater alone. Total cost of the war to date is over $275 billion. Former President Herbert Hoover has appealed for food immediately for war ravaged people in Europe.

At the movies, Dorothy Maguire, Robert Young and Herbert Marshall are in "Enchanted Cottage," Paul Muni and Merle Oberon in "Song to Remember."

Finally, former world boxing champion Commander Jack Dempsey is home after a 3-month world tour.

That's the news this May 8, 1945.

Wednesday, May 9, 1945

And now today's news, May 9, 1945.

Bemedaled, pompous, overweight Marshal Hermann Goering, head of the German Luftwaffe, gave up today to the U.S.7th Army. He insisted on both a bath and a fresh uniform before pictures were taken. Meanwhile, Heinrich Himmler, Hitler's #2 man, is reported in Sweden or Norway.

Senior U.S. officers at SHAEF are concerned that German generals and Admiral Doenitz remain a threat because of their prestige with the German people.

In Oslo, Norway, Vidkun Quisling and six of his so-called cabinet officers are now in the same jail to which he sent so many of his countrymen. His name has become synonymous with the word traitor. He arrived in a silver-plated Mercedes Benz given to him by Hitler.

In Berlin, Russian Marshal Zhukov included today among 25 toasts at dinner one to General Eisenhower as "...one of the greatest generals of present time."

The Pope today also spoke with a prayer for peace.

General Frank Allen, head of Public Relations for SHAEF, said the Associated Press early release on the surrender by Bureau Chief Ted Kennedy was "a deliberate violation against good faith and security invoking possible loss of American and Allied lives." Three AP correspondents have been suspended.

Travel restrictions to Bermuda for bona fide business or by property owners has now been lifted.

A new book by Margaret Landon called "Anna and the King of Siam" is on sale at $3.75 per copy.

Finally, while the world wonders if the Russians will now interfere in the Japanese war, a Marine Corsair pilot found his guns frozen at 45,000 feet and attacked a Japanese plane with his propellers causing the Japanse plane to go into a spin and crash!

That's the news this May 9, 1945.

And now today's news, May 10, 1945.

As the Russians attack Germans in Czechoslovakia who refuse to surrender, the first German U-boat has surrendered in Britain. The Channel Islands fell today after a skinny, stubborn German Navy Lt. gave in. Churchill says the draft will continue until the Japanese conflict is over. In Japan, another 250 B-29's blasted an aircraft factory near Kobe.

Washington has announced how the GI can become a civilian by earning 85 points through time served at home, abroad, for combat, medals, and parenthood for children under age 18. One million, three hundred thousand men are expected to be released this year.

In the New Jersey, New York and Delaware areas, the sale of beer, cigarettes and candy has been banned for German prisoners of war.

The War Production Board has dropped 73 controls on civilian products and warns industry not to convert to civilian products too fast.

A quick trial for Hermann Goering of Germany is predicted. He has said Hitler was arrogant and narrow-minded—that Von Ribbentrop is a scoundrel, and Rudolf Hess is an eccentric with energy.

Plans were found today for a fantastic plan for 75,000 German prisoners in England to break out last Christmas and capture London!

American troops have been given a guidelines booklet on the occupation restricting fraternization.

The Soviets are making some hard-nosed demands of the British regarding the use of the Dardanelles and other areas.

While the war is over, another 3,600 casualties are reported today including many dead being confirmed over recent months and weeks.

That's the news this May 10, 1945.

Friday, May 11, 1945

And now today's news, May 11, 1945.

It's been revealed that B-29's have had 19 mining missions dropping Navy mines into the Japanese Inland Sea and all major ports. Large mines are dropped by parachute with locations marked by a Naval officer aboard for future clearing with different explosive timings as ships pass over.

8th Air Force Gen. James Doolittle predicted that 2000 B-29's carrying 20,000 tons of bombs will be in operation before the end of the war.

While three million men will move to the Pacific from Europe, General Eisenhower says those who fought both in North Africa and Europe will not fight again.

The War Crimes Commission says that from 4 to 6 million Germans may suffer punishment. High on the list is Hermann Goering who already claims innocence on ordering the raid on Canterbury Cathedral in England and claims no knowledge of the concentration camps.

In Berlin, diehard Germans are setting fires and flooding subways.

In the Pacific, American liberation forces have made their 4th landing on Mindanao again without enemy opposition.

18 separation centers have been set up around the country with the first 2500 discharged tomorrow.

Tokyo radio today admitted that Japan started the war for her own reasons as compared to past stories it was provoked by Britain and the United States. Simultaneously, Japan says it is out to avenge Germany's defeat.

Frau Lucie Maria Rommel has now said her husband Erwin Rommel did not die of a heart attack but by murder on orders of Hitler.

6000 American flyers have been liberated by Russians at Barth on the Baltic coast from the Stalag Luft I prison.

President Truman's 92-year-old mother Martha Truman took her first airplane flight today to see her son for the first time as President. Arriving in Washington from Missouri with dozens of clicking press cameras, her reaction was "Fiddlesticks."

The California racing commission has authorized resumption of horse racing for a 40 day meeting at Santa Anita starting Tuesday.

A new movie features Stan Laurel and Oliver Hardy in "The Bullfighter" and Peter Lorre will be seen soon in "Three Strangers."

That's the news this May 11, 1945.

And now today's news, May 12, 1945.

In a mop-up on the Eastern front, Russian soldiers have captured 700,000 Germans since the surrender Tuesday. Many captives have been taken to Russia to help rebuild homes.

With the advent of V-E Day, lend lease to Russia has ceased.

On Okinawa the 6th Marine Division fought its way today into the Naha suburbs, the second largest city on Okinawa. Cruisers and destroyers bombarded nearby islands.

A dramatic photo obtained by Life Magazine shows a blindfolded Allied airman on his knees about to be beheaded by a Japanese captor. Just released POW's of Bataan say they were forced to watch beheadings of comrades.

Chinese troops are rolling back retreating Japanese on all sides of the Hunan front as General Chiang Kai-shek says Japan will soon meet the same fate as Germany. President Truman is keeping the door open for peace requests with assurances that the Japanese people will not be harmed.

Crown Prince Olaf and three princes have returned to Norway from Great Britain. King George and Queen Elizabeth will give thanks tomorrow for the first peace-time Sunday in 6 years starting with a royal procession from Buckingham Palace to St. Paul's Cathedral.

The Channel Islands are getting tons of food with liberated citizens of Guernsey enthusiastically singing "There'll Always Be An England."

An Alabama soldier has amassed a record 158 discharge points for 55 months of service, 27 months overseas, a bronze star, 7 battle stars and 3 dependent children.

The Queen Elizabeth and Queen Mary took a million soldiers to Europe and now will be used to bring back veterans.

In San Francisco they've decided on a U.N. Security Council of 11 nations.

With V-E Day past, air raid wardens across the country are being demobilized.

Paul "Pops" Whiteman starts his hot weather music show on the NBC Blue Network tomorrow night as Martha Graham and her dance repertory start their second annual engagement at the National Theater on Monday.

That's the news this May 12, 1945.

137

Sunday, May 13, 1945

And now today's news, May 13, 1945.

In Norway high level Nazis have blown themselves up rather than be captured. To the east Russians have captured another 200,000 Germans including 64 generals, all of whom are being sent to Russia to help rebuild devastated cities.

B-29's have been mining the Inland Sea for months raising havoc with Japanese shipping lanes. The 6th Marines are in the suburbs of Naha on Okinawa in bitter battle as the Japanese have lost another 165 planes even as they continue to hit U.S. ships.

Today 500 B-29's have hit Nagoya with 3,300 tons of incendiary bombs, the biggest incendiary raid in history.

A German U-boat has surrendered to the Navy off Cape May, New Jersey.

King George and Queen Elizabeth joined in prayer services for peace at St. Pauls in London yesterday.

Unconfirmed reports say Himmler has been captured and Goering has been indicted as a war criminal.

In Washington today, President Truman joined GI's in Bethesda for national prayers.

In Germany the remaining generals are asking Allies to exonerate the German High command of all war guilt. Cheering masses of people today in Oslo, Norway greeted the return of Crown Prince Olaf while returning GI prisoners of war have spoken of brutalities to them as compared to treatment of German prisoners here in the U.S.

In New York, Rev. Henry Sloan Coffin retires this week as President of Union Theological Seminary. At the movies, Betty Grable and Dick Haymes star in "Diamond Horseshoe."

Every single retail ad in the first 22 pages of today's New York Times supports the beginning of the 7th War Loan Drive for 14 billion dollars—7 billion from individuals is targeted, 7 billion from corporations. You have from now to June 30th to help make the goal. So buy war bonds—and help finish the fight.

That's the news this May 13, 1945.

And now today's news, May 14, 1945.

The U-boat 858 that surrendered off Cape May yesterday claimed sinking 16 Allied ships as part of the German wolfpack.

Gen. Eisenhower has reprimanded senior U.S. officers for being too friendly to German prisoners—he insists on a just but hard peace.

The U.S. and Britain have told Marshal Tito of Yugoslavia that the Italian port of Trieste must stay under Allied control until its future is decided.

Lt. Gen. Jimmy Doolittle has relinquished command of European 8th Air Force and may be sent to the Pacific theater. B-29 airfields in the Mariannas can now handle 800 planes. Other American planes are pounding retreating Japanese in East Burma.

Among 900 released prisoners today from Stalag I near Berlin are two American aces—Lt. Col. Francis Gabreski with a record 28 planes downed in the air plus 3 on the ground and Col. Hubert Zemke with 19 air and 11 ground kills.

The War Crimes Commission and Gen. Eisenhower have invited 6 man teams from Czechoslovakia, Yugoslavia, Poland and Greece to gather evidence at Buchenwald, Dachau and other concentration camps. The Czechs' war criminal target list includes Hitler, Joachim von Ribbentrop, Heinrich Himmler, Admiral Karl Doenitz, Hermann Goering, Hjalmar Schact, Walter Funk, Field Marshal Wilhem Keitel and Arthur Seyss-Inquart.

In Oslo, Crown Prince Olaf has directed that Vidkun Quisling, the traitor, be tried as an ordinary criminal.

In Washington, the War Production Board has increased automobile tires for civilian use by 50% for May. And, plans are being discussed for independence for the Philippines.

Finally, the GI newspaper Stars and Stripes reports that last election day, a German U-boat in the Atlantic launched a V-bomb towards New York City, but it fell short.

That's the news this May 14, 1945.

Tuesday, May 15, 1945

And now today's news, May 15, 1945.

In Okinawa hundreds of Japanese have been killed by U.S. 77th division as U.S. troops captured Chocolate Drop Hill after a 5-day battle.

U.S. carrier planes have destroyed 284 Japanese aircraft on 17 airfields on Kyushu. Chinese troops have captured Foochow on the China coast as General MacArthur reports 90% of Mindinao in the Philippines is in U.S. hands as fierce hand-to-hand combat continues.

President Truman and Prime Minister Churchill are hopeful of meeting soon with Stalin to discuss peace plans. Gen. de Gaulle of France is not to be included. Truman also announced there will be no tax reductions until the war is over.

In London, General Eisenhower and General Bradley were acclaimed today by thousands in the lastest V-E celebration. Along with son John Eisenhower and Eisenhower's secretary, Lt. Kay Summersby, the generals will attend the theater tonight.

Lt. Gen. Ernest Kaltenbrunner, accused of the gas murders of over 4 million Europeans has been captured in Austria. And, an enormous fortress 70 feet underground has been found in Berlin previously occupied by Goering, Hitler, Goebbels and the site of many recent suicides.

Secretary of the Interior Harold Ickes has asked for federal funds to permanently preserve the Hyde Park, New York home of the late President Roosevelt.

In business, Ralston Purina is offering a new preferred stock with a 3 3/4% inherent return.

At the movies Judy Garland and Robert Walker are in "The Clock," and Gregory Peck and Greer Garson star in "Valley of Decision."

The #1 fiction best seller is "Captain from Castille" by Samuel Shellabarger. Lunch at Jack Dempsey's restaurant starts at $.65 and dinner starts at $1.25.

Finally, the war must be over—the Loch Ness monster has been sighted again off the coast of Scotland.

That's the news this May 15,1945.

And now today's news, May 16, 1945.

500 B-29's again have hit Nagoya and the Mitsubishi aircraft factory. Fires could be seen 100 miles at sea. On Okinawa the Japanese are using the tombs of their ancestors as pillboxes and halting U.S. advances with withering fire.

500 miles east of Newfoundland a German U-boat has surrendered with two escaping Japanese who committed suicide before capture.

Prime Minister Eamon DeValera of Ireland today defended his position and his country of neutrality in the war.

Berlin has been closed by the Russians to both the Americans and the British as frictions continue. And, an eyewitness said Hitler jumped with joy and laughter when he heard of the death of President Roosevelt last month.

In the Pacific, Admiral Kincaid says the Japanese suicide Kamikaze airplane attacks are persistent and bothersome but generally are controlled by heavy naval gun power.

In Washington, Charles G. Ross is President Truman's new press secretary, 50% more cigarettes should be available by June 1st and if you hold an A gas ration card your gas allowance will be increased soon.

Peace production of autos is starting up again with expected production of 200,000 cars in the 4th quarter and 400,000 in the first quarter of 1946.

Two days ago Paul Whiteman hosted a tribute to George Gershwin who died in 1937 with those in attendance including Mildred Bailey, Leonard Bernstein, Jane Froman, Mimi Benzell, Gladys Swarthout, Paul LaValle, Morton Gould, Alexander Smallens and Walter Damrosch.

At the grocers, watermelons are now 6 cents a pound, McIntosh apples 13 cents, green peas 20 cents, eggplant 15 cents and onions 19 cents a pound.

That's the news this May 16, 1945.

Thursday, May 17, 1945

And now today's news, May 17, 1945.

Today the 17,000 ton aircraft carrier U.S.S. Franklin limped into Brooklyn Navy yard scarred and blackened in what now has been reported as one of the ugliest naval catastrophes of the war. Japanese bombs caused the carriers' own bombs and octane gas to explode with some men burned to a crisp, many drowned—a total of 832 dead and some 300 missing. No carrier ever survived such destruction.

On Okinawa the 6th Marines have captured the capital city of Naha.

In Portsmouth, New Hampshire, a 25-year-old German U-boat surrendering commander says his men should be treated like brothers, that Hitler was a great man, and Germany has not lost the war notwithstanding the May 7th surrender.

The Soviet government has asked the Swedish government to confiscate a recent issue of a weekly periodical critical of Stalin.

At the U.N. conference in San Francisco, the U.S. has opposed guaranteeing independence of all colonial peoples as President Truman met in Washington with present and past Secretaries of State Edward R. Stetinnius and Cordell Hull, our present U.N. representatives.

Eight-year-old actress Margaret O'Brien who gets $300 a week, will now also get $12,500 per picture.

"Life With Father" is now in its 6th year on Broadway and, while hit shows "Oklahoma" and "Up in Central Park" continue, "Carmen Jones" closes in two days.

Parke Bernet Galleries has auctioned a Pissaro for $8,000, a Degas pastel for $3,500 and a Renoir for $4,000.

Teachers in New York are suing the School Board to eliminate the requirement of a tuberculosis x-ray examination.

Finally, Washington says you're living longer. The average at death in the U.S. 1930 was 48.9 years, is now up to 56.9 years.

That's the news this May 17, 1945.

And today's news, May 18, 1945.

300 B-29's have battered Hamamatsu at a medium altitude while another group hit the western outskirts of Tokyo. One quarter of Nagoya has now been destroyed.

President Truman has told French Foreign Minister Georges Bidault that the United States will let France take over part of the American occupation zone and further says he looks forward to meeting with Charles de Gaulle soon.

The War Manpower Commission has an emergency campaign to find 1600 workers to finish two new 27,000 ton carriers, the Valley Forge and the Princeton.

As American casualties approach one million with 40,000 coming home monthly, a new nationwide bond rally will be called Bonds for Mercy.

Fred M. Vinson, Director of the Office of War Mobilization, has announced a program to get more beef and pork for civilians.

Four Burke brothers from New York City are all serving together in the 27th Division. The Sergeant, Captain and two Lt. Colonels share 68 years of service.

Five British destroyers have attacked and sunk a 10,000 ton Japanese heavy cruiser of the Nati class off the Malayan and Sumatra straits as an estimated 44,000 bedraggled Japanese soldiers are withdrawing in Burma.

Britain now reveals it had located the launching site of a German V-3 rocket with a 100 mile range firing 600 rockets per hour from guns 400 feet long. The RAF bombed out the site last year.

Czechoslovakia has added field Marshal Wilhelm Keitel, Chief of the German High Command, to a list of more than 500 war criminals.

A general election may be held in England soon with Conservative Foreign Secretary Anthony Eden and Laborite Deputy Prime Minister Clement Attlee starting public debate.

Papers across the country which have regularly listed casualties by name and hometown, are now doing the same for liberated prisoners.

Australia, New Zealand and India have provided over 3 billion pounds of food for our armies since the lend-lease program started in March 1941.

In San Francisco, smaller nations are arguing against the veto power of the 5 permanent members of the Security Council.

In the movies, Evelyn Keyes will star in "The Kansan" and Alan Ladd will be reporting for Army induction on Tuesday.

That's the news this May 18, 1945.

And now today's news, May 19, 1945.

On Okinawa elements of the 6th Marine Division pulled off Sugar Loaf for the fourth time today and then fought their way back.

The important coastal town of Foochow has been recaptured for the second time in two years by the Japanese. Trapped Japanese are being pounded by Americans east of Manila at Sas Airfield.

The Western Allies are accusing Tito of violating his word on Trieste in accepting peaceful terms of his territorial claims. Tito says he has the same right as other Allies in staying in territory they liberated. Field Marshal Harold Alexander compares his tactics to those of Hitler, Mussolini and the Japanese.

Approximately 125,000 American prisoners have been flown from German prison camps, 85,000 by the RAF and 30,000 by American Flying Fortresses.

Canada is likely to send 30,000 troops plus naval support to the south Pacific. 500 UNRRA centers have been set up in Europe to provide relief, repatriation and resettlement.

It's now reported that German slave labor working in underground bomb proof factories kept Germany going in spite of destruction above ground.

Dr. Alfred Rosenberg, arch philosopher of Nazism, has been caught at Flensburg in a continuing Allied dragnet looking for fugitive leaders.

U-Boat U234 has been brought into Portsmouth, New Hampshire with its crew of 57 and 9 passengers.

It has now been revealed that an air raid shelter was built under the White House for President Roosevelt and his family with entrance from the basement on the East Wing.

The War Production Board says it will permit production of 530,000 gas and electric refrigerators in the last half of this year.

On Broadway a return limited engagement of "Othello" starts Tuesday with Paul Robeson, Jose Ferrer and Uta Hagen while an all Negro musical "Memphis Bound" starts Thursday starring Bill "Bojangles" Robinson and Avon Long.

Ida Lupino, Sidney Greenstreet, and William Prince open Friday in "Pillow To Post" and on radio tomorrow night be sure to tune to Phil Spitalny and his 35 all-girl orchestra on NBC.

Finally, while President Roosevelt's famous Scottie Fala is gone, now Margaret Truman, daughter of the President, has brought home Mike, a young Irish Setter.

That's the news this May 19,1 945.

And now today's news, May 20, 1945.

Elements of 3 American divisions are encircling Shuri fortress on Okinawa, advancing against a network of caves, ridges and pillboxes. Meanwhile, American forces have captured Sasa Airdome on Mindanao.

American troops have withdrawn from Trieste and Yugoslavia has agreed to withdraw from the disputed province of Carpathia.

You may not have known that Hermann Goering was an art connoisseur, but his private collection went on exhibition today at a requisitioned hotel outside of Berchtesgaden. The collection is valued at over $2,000,000.

Here at home, the hard coal miners have agreed to accept a wage hike of $1.37½ a day to end their 3-week strike. Coal prices will probably rise anywhere from 50-75 cents a ton.

Preliminary operations are expected to start at the new Idlewild Airport around October 1st, and at least a dozen major airlines have indicated they will sign leases.

In the world of entertainment, Frances Langford is going to have her own summer radio show. She'll fill in for Edgar Bergen in the 8:00-8:30 pm slot on Sunday. And, Fred Allen has signed for a new program series starting in September.

Back in August 1943, the Allies staged their biggest air raid on Milan, Italy, badly damaging the famous LaScala opera house. It's now being rebuilt, and it's hoped that Arturo Toscanini can be induced to come home to conduct the reopening.

That's the news this May 20, 1945.

Monday, May 21, 1945

And now today's news, May 21, 1945.

Japanese troops, some of them wearing American uniforms, were thrown back at Naha on Okinawa in fierce fighting. In Japan itself, some 20,000,000 students have been mobilized for defense of the homeland.

The U.S. 1st Army, which was first across the Rhine River, is being transferred to the Far East, but the troops will get furloughs first before taking off to fight the Japanese.

There never was a plot against Gen. Dwight Eisenhower. Supreme Headquarters of the Allied Expeditionary Force now says it was an elaborate and astonishing but unsuccessful German commando operation. In any event, Eisenhower was replaced with a double in his car at the time.

On the home front, meat and poultry are still virtually unobtainable, even on the black market. And black market ham has just jumped 5 cents to 80 cents a pound.

The Red Cross says it is discontinuing sending food and relief packages to French, Polish and Yugoslavian POW's in Germany.

David Lilienthal has been confirmed by the U.S. Senate as director of the TVA.

With the war over in Europe, men over 40 will now be able to get out of the army just by applying for release.

Lauren Bacall and Humphrey Bogart were married today. The ceremony took place at the farm home of Louis Bromfield in Mansfield, Ohio.

William Simmons, the first Imperial Wizard of the Ku Klux Klan, died today in a hospital in Atlanta.

That's the news this May 21, 1945.

And now today's news, May 22, 1945.

The War and Navy Departments have revealed that in the past several months, Japanese long-range free balloons, carrying bombs, have fallen in the Northwest States. The only reason for releasing the information now is to warn civilians not to handle the bombs if they find any.

In the fighting, American troops have captured the village of Taira on Okinawa in 3 surprise attacks.

Representative Mike Mansfield predicts that Russia will enter the war against Japan, and the Japanese have warned against "peace agitation" in that country.

Selective Service has announced that men 18-29 will be drafted in larger numbers, including some now classed as 4-F. Men 30 or older are expected to get more sympathetic consideration.

Because of shortages in meat, poultry and eggs, some 500 New York Manufacturers, distributors and retailers of deli meat have voted to close their doors next week on Monday until they can be assured of relief from price squeezes in regulations.

Britain has announced lower rations of fats, milk, soap, bacon and meat, reducing consumption about 100 calories a day.

Charles "Lucky" Luciano's attorney says his client helped military authorities for 2 years before the Allied invasion of Sicily. Luciano is serving a 30-50 years sentence as a vice king. He allegedly used his connections to supply valuable intelligence information.

CIO President Philip Murray today urged a 20% increase in wage ceilings.

That's the news this May 22, 1945.

Wednesday, May 23, 1945

And now today's news, May 23, 1945.

Winston Churchill has resigned in preparation for a general election and was promptly reappointed as Prime Minister, First Lord of the Treasury and Minister of Defense. General elections have been set for July 5th.

550 B-29's, the largest force ever to take part in a single mission, bombed Tokyo with 700,000 fire bombs, at the rate of 40 tons a minute. The attack was deemed highly successful. The raid comes exactly 6 months after Tokyo was hit by B-29's for the first time.

Marine units have driven into Naha on Okinawa under cover of heavy naval fire.

The German high command was dissolved by the Allies today and its members have been arrested.

President Truman has reorganized his cabinet. Attorney-General Francis Biddle, Labor Secretary Frances Perkins and Agriculture Secretary Claude Wickart are out, and Thomas Clark, Louis Schwellenbach and Clinton P. Anderson are in.

Gasoline rations for motorists with A and B coupons will increase next month. "A" coupons will be good for 6 gallons.

The retail ceiling price of nearly all kinds of poultry goes up 1 and 2 cents a pound as the OPA tries to ease the shortage.

Pitcher Mort Cooper has been sold by the St. Louis Cardinals to the Braves. He'll join them in Pittsburgh on Friday.

Van Johnson and Esther Williams' new film, "Thrill of Romance," premiered today in New York at the Capitol Theater. The stage show will feature Guy Lombardo, comedian Joey Adams and actress June Havoc.

That's the news this May 23, 1945.

And now today's news, May 24, 1945.

Heinrich Himmler has committed suicide in Lueneberg, Germany. He took poison as he was being examined by doctors after being caught while trying to escape. The poison capsule had been hidden in his mouth. He was wearing a disguise when captured.

Australia is demanding the indictment and execution of Emperor Hirohito as a war criminal. China will support this demand.

Warships are rushing Japanese reinforcements to China's east coast in an effort to hold that strategic area.

A Big Three meeting is definitely in the works, but still in the projection stage.

German war dead has been estimated at 4,000,000 soldiers and 500,000 civilians. U.S. war casualties on both fronts are almost 1,000,000.

A wider Social Security plan is expected to include 15,000,000 more people under new bills in Congress which would federalize jobless pay, and establish health insurance. Four percent would be deducted from workers' pay.

The increase in gasoline rations is expected to be a big blow to the black market. The new ration will add about 12 miles of driving per week for the average motorist.

Secretary Morgenthau will ask for at least 5,000 more Treasury agents to ferret out income tax evaders. It would be the biggest such drive ever put on by the government.

In sports, Rocky Graziano takes on Al Davis in a middleweight bout at Madison Square Garden tonight.

Eighteen major symphony orchestras in this country say they are losing money. The deficit totals almost $2,000,000.

That's the news this May 24, 1945.

Friday, May 25, 1945

And now today's news, May 25, 1945.

While Japanese planes hit 11 U.S. ships today off Ie Island, the Americans knocked down 111 of their planes.

In a second giant raid in 48 hours, some 500 B-29's hit Tokyo with incendiaries some of which may have hit the Emperor's Palace.

Britain has asked the U.S. for a greater role in the Pacific war.

In Europe, surly Germans in towns not hit with major destruction consider the American victory a fluke.

At home the War Production Board has cut back the production of new planes by 17,000 while saving 4 billion dollars.

In San Francisco as smaller nations show concern, differences continue between U.S. and Britain and Russia regarding the veto power of the Big Five.

The destroyer U.S.S. Laffey has arrived in Seattle, a miracle survivor of 6 Japanese suicide planes and two direct bomb hits. 31 officers and men were killed or missing.

After being released from a German prison camp in Norway, the husband of Norwegian opera star Kirsten Flagstad has been arrested for Nazi collaboration.

Two days after Heinrich Himmler committed suicide by biting into a poison vial, no decision has been made on whether he should have any kind of ceremonial burial. Over $1 million in currency he hid has been found.

Marshal Henri Petain has sent a letter to U.S. Admiral William D. Leahy, former U.S. Ambassador to the Vichy government asking him to testify on his behalf.

5000 men of the 15th Air Force along with 1000 wounded have arrived on a transport ship in Boston. After leaves, many will be sent to the Pacific.

A committee in Paris has asked that Generalissimo Francisco Franco resign in favor of all the Spanish Democratic groups.

President Truman has approved the Naval Academy going back to a four year curriculum.

36 years after they joined Admiral Robert E. Peary on a North Pole expedition, Captain Robert A. Bartlett and Commander Donald B. MacMillan have been honored on Bartlett's ship in Boston with the Peary Polar Expedition Medal.

At the movies is "The Body Snatcher" with Boris Karloff and Bela Lugosi and "Molly and Me" starring Monty Woolley, Gracie Fields and Roddy McDowall.

That's the news this May 25, 1946.

And now today's news, May 26, 1945.

In spite of being in the middle of a re-election campaign, Winston Churchill says he will meet with President Truman and Marshal Stalin before July 5th.

Lt. General Jimmy Doolittle will take the 8th Air Force to the South Pacific to help finish up the bombing he started in April 1942 with the famous B-25 flights that bombed Tokyo from an aircraft carrier.

The last section of Tokyo was hit by 500 Superfortresses destroying the government and central business district. A monstrous wind escalated the damage. 19 B-29's were lost.

A B-29 on that raid named Uncle Tom's Cabin was mortally wounded by a Japanese Tony fighter which smashed into it. Struggling to stay aloft, the B-29 shot down 11 fighters and finally crashed. The pilot will be honored with the Congressional Medal of Honor and the crew with Silver Stars.

Washington says Japan is capable of a long war despite destructive raids and naval losses.

The body of Heinrich Himmler was dumped into a truck, taken into some woods and unceremoniously buried by U.S. soldiers.

Vidkun Quisling, Norway's puppet Premier during the German occupation, has shouted "not guilty" at the beginning of the trial.

There are 2.8 million displaced persons in the Allied Headquarters Zone.

Former President and World War I Food Relief Administrator Herbert Hoover will meet with President Truman on Monday to discuss relief and food problems in Europe.

The Army Transport Command expects to fly home 50,000 men a month at the rate of one flight every six minutes.

Six of the ten most active stocks on the New York Stock Exchange today were railroads all on the plus side.

At Gimbels New York women's bathing suits are from $3.98 to $7.95, a pair of Tiffany silver candlesticks at $20, and a large Sheffield silver tea tray at $200.

On Broadway Zero Mostel is in "Concert Varieties."

That's the news this May 26, 1945.

And now today's news, May 27, 1945.

Over the weekend, Superfortresses wiped out Tokyo in record pre-dawn attacks at a cost of 31 of the big planes. The last undamaged areas of the world's 3rd largest city were reported in smoking ruins. Washington has warned not to expect a quick victory in the Pacific—there's lots of fighting still ahead.

While giving awards to 14 members of the submarine silent service, Admiral Nimitz says 1119 ships have been sunk in the war.

For the first time in history an entire army is moving by air—China's new 6th Army from Burma into China.

General Robert Ritter von Greim, successor to Hermann Goering, has committed suicide in a Salzburg hospital.

Two women Nazi radio propaganda broadcasters have been captured. One broadcast to Allied troops in Holland, the other was educated in and lived in Staten Island for 13 years.

Fewer than 100,000 American troops remain in Europe in hospitals and all are expected to be home by July 1st.

The first nine crewmen of a B-29 having flown 31 missions are now eligible to come home from Saipan.

Tokyo fires are still burning 36 hours later after the latest B-29 raid.

The Japanese have suffered 378,427 casualties in the Philippines, mostly killed.

New York Governor Thomas A. Dewey says he will not tolerate what he calls "the cold and clammy hand of Bureaucracy" in veterans' affairs.

Brokers say the shortage of lard, shortening and vegetables will continue for some months.

Dancer Ray Bolger will host a summer radio program on Friday nights when Jimmy Durante and Gary Moore go on a summer tour.

Singer Ginny Simms will move from NBC radio to CBS in September.

Mind-reader Dunninger takes over the Amos 'n Andy slot on Friday night, starting in June.

In a new movie Barbara Stanwyck stars with Robert Cummings in "The Bride Wore Boots."

That's the news this May 27, 1945.

And now today's news this May 28, 1945.

Two-thirds of Naha on Okinawa is in American hands following a lunge by the 6th Marine Division.

Yokohama, Japan's great port, was hit by more than 450 B-29's. It was the first attack on the city.

The Russians are reportedly building an air base on the Danish island of Bornhalen in the Baltic Sea and apparently intend to remain there.

Harry L. Hopkins conferred with Premier Stalin for the 3rd day in Moscow in an effort to smooth out misunderstandings and pave the way for a Big 3 meeting.

President Truman talked with former President Herbert Hoover about the food situation in Europe and invited 1936 Presidential candidate Alf Landon and Thomas Dewey to confer with him.

New York's fruit and vegetable dealers will vote Friday on whether to close their shops in protest against wholesale overcharges and other black market practices.

Carole Landis has received a leave of absence from her 20th Century Fox contract and has been withdrawn from the lead in the forthcoming "The Spider."

Montgomery Ward & Company profits for the quarter ended with April were four and 3/4 million dollars, an increase of 44% over a year ago.

That's the news this May 28, 1945.

Tuesday, May 29, 1945

And now today's news, May 29, 1945.

Five ships carrying more than 10,000 American soldiers from Europe arrived in New York today, representing the largest daily contingent since V-E day.

Lord Haw Haw, born William Joyce, who broadcast for the Germans during the war, is a prisoner in British hands. He was picked up in Germany near the Danish border. He has been wounded and is in an Army hospital in Lueneberg.

1st Marine Division troops have smashed a Japanese keystone position in Okinawa, reaching Shuri Castle.

Japan has shaken up its naval command and replaced its commander-in-chief.

French mortars are reportedly shelling Damascus, and clashes between irregulars and French troops are spreading southward in Syria.

Relaxation of control over alien travelers will go into effect June 1. Aliens, regardless of nationality, will be able to go to Canada without a departure permit.

The public cannot expect any more $500 cars after the war, but GM says it will keep the price of the new Chevy as low as possible. Brand new post-war cars, however, probably won't be available for 2 years.

Unemployment is expected to double to about 1.9 million within 3 months as the armed forces continue to reduce their requirements of arms and ammunition.

Mary Martin is reported seriously ill in New York and an appeal for blood donors has been issued. She has already received 4 transfusions.

A book published by Louis Rougier says Churchill and Henri-Philippe Petain reached a secret agreement in 1940 to keep France from joining the Axis and the French fleet from falling into German hands.

That's the news this May 29, 1945.

And now today's news, May 30, 1945.

The Allied Control Commission for Germany will meet in a few days. Differences between Russia and the Allies are expected to be cleared up at the meeting, and the final limitations for the four zones of occupation will be announced.

The crisis in the Near East has grown worse. Open conflict is raging between French troops and Arabs.

Iran has asked the United States, Britain and Russia to remove their troops in line with a treaty agreement.

Generalissimo Chiang Kai-shek has resigned as premier of China and is succeeded by T.V. Soong. Chiang, however, remains as President and Head of State.

On Okinawa, American troops have now captured the ancient castle of Shuri.

Research experts of the American University in Washington estimate that direct war expenditures so far total over 1 trillion dollars.

Educators are warning that fly-by-night schools and colleges may try to exploit returning veterans.

According to the OPA, the meat supply for American civilians will be 7% less in June than it was this month.

Ten West Pointers and the widow of Franklin D. Roosevelt gathered at Hyde Park today for a simple ceremony honoring the late President.

Teamster President Daniel Tobin today urged his union's members to disregard picket lines unless otherwise directed by the International.

Faye Marlowe has been named to replace Carole Landis in the lead role in the forthcoming remake of "The Spider."

That's the news this May 30, 1945.

Thursday, May 31, 1945

And now today's news, May 31, 1945.

Great Britain has demanded that Gen. Charles de Gaulle order a cease-fire in the Middle East. President Truman approved the Churchill note in advance.

Osaka, Japan's second largest city, was set ablaze by 400 B-29's that dropped 3,200 tons of fire bombs, and it's reported that 80% of Formosa's industrial capacity has been knocked out.

The Japanese have announced that all naval branches will now be used in suicide attacks against the Americans.

It's reported that totalitarianism in Argentina has exceeded even that of Fascist Italy.

At home, the OPA has started a drastic program to end a racket in sugar supposedly used for home canning.

Dr. Robert Wilson,, Chairman of Standard Oil, says better quality gasoline for civilians should be available soon.

Almost 5,000 federal employees were dropped from the government payroll in April. Many of these people held temporary war jobs.

Warner Brothers has resigned from the Motion Picture Producers and Distributors of America. The organization is better known as the "Hays Office."

Commander Jack Dempsey, former heavyweight champion, may return to the Pacific to supervise Coast Guard physical training programs and arrange service bouts.

That's the news this May 31, 1945.

And now today's news, June 1, 1945.

President Truman says the Big Three Conference will take place soon at an as yet undisclosed location.

450 Superfortresses hit the Sumitomo Aircraft Factory and main rail yards in Osaka today. It's reported the Yokohama raid last Tuesday destroyed another 6.9 square miles of the city.

Major General John Hodge says Japanese organized resistance on Okinawa is on the verge of collapse.

Russia is reported to reject the Anglo-American interpretation of the Yalta Agreement which would have exempted a French-Soviet alliance from world security control.

On June 9, 1942, the entire village of Lidice was destroyed by Germans with a massacre of all but 2 of the 667 villagers. Today Col. General Kurt Daluege who ordered the massacre has been captured by the British.

The Red Cross now says that 99% of all American prisoners survived German prison camps.

The War Production Board says that while there may be new cars later this year, they will not have spare tires while the war continues.

In sports, Red Grange, the great Galloping Ghost All-American from Illinois, has resigned as President of the proposed U.S. Football League due to commitments and lack of confidence in its future. Meantime, players are holding out for $400 to $600 per game.

Reports from both the East and West Coast say the resort business will be much better this year now that the lights can be on.

In the movie world, Jack Oakie, Peggy Ryan, Gene Lockhart, Andy Devine, Arthur Treacher and Buster Keaton are in "That's the Spirit." Another new movie stars John Wayne and Ann Dvorak in "Flame of the Barbary Coast" while Anne Baxter has been signed for the lead opposite Randolph Scott in the upcoming "Smokey."

Lt. Col. David Niven was given leave by the British to star in another film called "The Way Ahead" written by Peter Ustinov and Edir Ambler.

That's the news this June 1, 1945.

Saturday, June 2, 1945

And now today's news, June 2, 1945.

Troops led by tanks have gained another 1000 yards on Okinawa as they close in on the Naha Airfield and are within sight of the beaches in southern Okinawa.Admiral Bull Halsey, after four months of rest and planning, has taken command again of the Third Fleet replacing Admiral Raymond Spruance.

General Eisenhower goes to Berlin tomorrow to meet with British Field Marshal Sir Bernard Montgomery, Soviet Marshal Gregory Zhukov and French General Jean de Lattre. The General is also coming back to the States June 18th first with a June 19th stop in New York, then Kansas City and then to visit his mother in his hometown of Abilene, Kansas.

The British have revealed a war secret called FIDO— "Fog Investigation Dispersal Operations," a system of burning petroleum around airfields dissipating the fog and permitting planes to take off and land.

Lt. Audie Murphy of Texas has now received the Congressional Medal of Honor and the Legion of Merit tying him with Capt. Maurice Britt of Arkansas as the war's most decorated soldier.

King Haakon will return to Oslo on June 7th when the Norwegian cabinet will meet on native soil for the first time since 1940.

Cartiers in Paris says they outwitted the Nazis by hiding $10 million in gems.

The Argentine opposition says the government has closed 14 newspapers and arrested 10 editors.

99-year-old General Julius Howell, Commander of the Civil War United Confederate Veterans, had his picture taken today with President Truman.

Ford has announced that 1946 models, the first since 1942, will be in production in 60 to 90 days with new features and styling changes.

West Point has graduated 280 men with wings who trained at Stewart Air Field.

In sports, the National Football League's Brooklyn Tigers, owned by Dan Topping, will play in Yankee Stadium as finally agreed to by the New York Giants.

Two new movies this week— "Out of this World" with Eddie Bracken and Cass Daley, and "Where Do We Go From There" with Fred MacMurray, June Haver and Joan Leslie.

Great Yankee pitcher Red Ruffing will be discharged as an Army Sergeant Monday or Tuesday.

That's the news this June 2, 1945.

And now today's news, June 3, 1945.

President Truman has pledged to double the size of the American army from 3.5 million to 7 million in order to smash Japan. In Russia-controlled Berlin, the Mayor has announced any continued disorders by citizens will result in the execution of 50 Nazis for each incident. A special warning has been given to Hitler Youth.

Including last Tuesday's B-29 Yokohama raid, over 82 square miles of principal Japanese cities have been burned out including over 50 square miles of Tokyo. Japanese government leaders say they will stay in Tokyo no matter what. Meanwhile, B-29's are daily dropping 750,000 leaflets over Japan urging surrender.

As a result of U.S. meat shortages, all meat shipments to Europe will cease on July 1.

At the U.N. conference in San Francisco, Russia has rejected the Anglo-American understanding at Yalta about rights of big power voting. This is the first severe crisis at the new U.N.

Word has been received that in December 1943, 11 American missionaries and one 9-year-old boy were beheaded by the Japanese.

As troops are arriving home from Europe so too are Generals Carl Spaatz and Omar Bradley. General Eisenhower is due back on June 18th.

At the movies Robert Montgomery is starring in the fantasy "Here Comes Mr. Jordan," Danny Kaye and Vera Ellen are in a new comedy "Wonder Man," and Roland Young, best known for his "Topper" movies, stars in the same role on NBC radio.

The War Production Board says when the new cars arrive, there will be only 4 tires—not enough available for a spare. Ford is the first to unveil its 1946 model which will be the first cars built since 1942. Most people will have to wait 1 to 2 years to get a car.

That's the news this June 3, 1945.

Monday, June 4, 1945

And now today's news, June 4, 1945.

Kobe, Japan has been firebombed for the third time by B-29's. Kobe handles 40% of Japan's import and export trade. U.S. Marines have won half of the Naha airfield in Okinawa and found little resistance as many Japanese are committing suicide in anticipation of defeat.

President Truman has asked Harry Hopkins to visit with Marshal Stalin in Moscow to present the U.S. British desire not to have a veto power for the Big 5 at the U.N. conference in San Francisco.

In England, conservative Prime Minister Churchill is running for office again warning voters that if the Labor Party is elected there will be Socialism.

In Washington, President Truman has approved $4.4 billion in lend-lease aid for the coming year for those countries at war with Japan or aiding the Allies in redeployment. Russia, which has received $8.8 billion in past aid, will not receive aid.

Washington has announced another 1,500 American casualties and the loss of two destroyers making a total of 313 ships since the start of the war. Both the Morrison and the Luce lost about 200 men each.

The American Consulate in Manila is feeding American civilians with 2,000 calories a day at a cost of $1.80 per week each.

Women now smoke 69% of all cigarettes sold to civilians, Treasury bills now pay 3.75% interest and the English pound is valued at $4.02.

CBS Vice President Frank Stanton has been made General Manager and a Board member.

At Warner's Strand is "Pillow to Post" starring Ida Lupino, Sidney Greenstreet and William Prince with Shep Field's Orchestra on stage plus Borrah Minavitch's Harmonica Rascals.

Venetian blinds are $2.99 at Bloomingdales, Nettleton men's shoes are $14.95 and a new book about the life of Alexander Woollcott is $3.50.

In New York, Vincent Lopez's orchestra is at the Taft Grill with lunch starting at $.65 and dinner at $1.50 Harry James Orchestra is due soon at the Astor Roof.

That's the news this June 4, 1945.

And now today's news, June 5, 1945.

General Eisenhower has arrived in Berlin for the first Allied Control Council for Germany to meet with Russian Marshal Zhukov, British Field Marshal Montgomery and French General de Lattre.

The Japanese are on the verge of collapse on Okinawa and Admiral Nimitz has sent congratulations to General Simon Bolivar Bruckner. On the Chinese mainland, Japanese troops have abandoned 4 cities west of Hong Kong.

The unmanned Japanese balloons floating across the ocean and over the U.S. have already caused the deaths of 5 children in Oregon who found one on the ground as it accidentally exploded.

In England, Labor Party candidate Clement Attlee says Churchill's fear of Socialism is ridiculous. In New York politics, the Democrats are running William O'Dwyer for Mayor and Lawrence Gerosa as Comptroller.

Task Force 58 Admiral Marc Mitscher met with Secretary of Defense James V. Forrestal today in Washington to provide assurance that Japanese Kamikaze suicide planes are causing minimal damage to U.S. ships with less that 1% getting to their targets. Kamikazes are also ramming B-29's.

The War Department estimates over 60 million casualties by all participants in the European war with some 14 million deaths compared to 8.5 million in World War I not including civilians.

Today King Haakon of Norway and his family leave Britain for the first time since June 1940 to return to their homeland in Oslo.

Dr. Harry Emerson Fosdick of the Riverside Church in New York will retire next May while 83-year-old Nicholas Murray Butler, President of Columbia University, presided at his last graduation ceremony today before retirement.

Cowles Publishing has given $100,000 for a Negro Community Center near Des Moines, Iowa to honor Wendell Willkie, unsuccessful Republican presidential candidate in 1940.

That's the news this June 5, 1945.

Wednesday, June 6, 1945

And now today's news, June 6, 1945.

D-Day was a year ago today as the Allies invaded France signaling the beginning of the end for the Germans. In Berlin the Russians have released a map outlining their boundaries for what will be East and West Germany. They also report with almost surety that they have found the burned and charred body of Hitler in a Berlin underground fortress.

The FBI has seized 6 Americans as spies including two in the State Department. One, John Stewart Service, formerly was stationed in China.

Guatemala and Salvador today announced a merger of their countries with both presidents to resign. It is hoped that Honduras, Nicaragua and Costa Rica will also become part of the new federation.

Eight hundred women in the WAVES today became the first women in history to become qualified navigators to serve on military air crews.

Former Brooklyn Dodger catcher Mickey Owen is now in the Navy. The top three jockeys in the country racing today are Johnny Adams, Ted Atchison, and Eddie Arcaro.

A rundown on the best known Broadway shows today include "A Bell for Adano," "Anna Lucasta," "Bloomer Girl," "Carousel," "Dear Ruth," "Follow the Girls," "Harvey," "Hats Off to Ice," "I Remember Mama," "Life With Father," "Oklahoma," "On the Town" with Paul Robeson, "The Glass Menagerie," "Voice of the Turtle," and "Up in Central Park."

The now famous February photograph of Mt. Suribachi with Marines raising the American flag will be put on a new 3 cent stamp. At Macys men's summer lightweight cotton suits are $14.50 and Dunhills fine cigars $6.95 for 25—with a limit of 400 per customer. You can buy a silk tie at Bloomingdales' for $5.

Frank Folsom has been elected Executive Vice President of RCA Victor Division as announced by Brigadier General David Sarnoff.

And finally, returning GI's got a break today. They'll receive an extra gallon of gas each day while on furlough.

That's the news this June 6, 1945.

And now today's news, June 7, 1945.

The first major U.N. crisis in San Francisco has been resolved as Russia has yielded on their insistence for a veto right for the Big Five and will allow freedom of discussion in the World Security Council.

As Germans hear about and see films of the concentration camps, a widespread feeling of shame is developing according to several sources.

In Washington, Congress has approved the same $2,500 expense money per year for members while consideration is being given to raise congressional salaries from $10,000 to $15,000 or $25,000 per year.

Franklin D. Roosevelt, Jr. has been reassigned to the Navy War College after serving 78 days in battle areas at sea.

Washington reports that over 700 German U-boats were sunk in the war while less than one out of 1,000 Allied ships in convoys were sunk. In Boston, General George Patton was greeted by over 1 million people today as he returned from Germany. His son, George, Jr., a West Point cadet, joined him in the parade along with Mrs. Patton.

The Navy has a new twin engine F7F Tigercat fighter bomber rated at 425 mph. It is due in combat on supercarriers soon.

A 33-year-old woman born in the U.S. who left and became an Italian citizen in 1941 has been seized in Rome. Known to millions of GI's in Europe as Axis Sally, she broadcast for the Fascists in English and, instead of lowering GI morale, she became must listening. The New York Times reports the reputedly attractive woman is, among other features, cross-eyed.

In sports, Byron Nelson shot a 63 today in the $10,000 Canadian PGA in Montreal with Jug McSpaden in at 69. Former tennis star Big Bill Tilden will play an exhibition at Forest Hills June 22nd.

A new book, "Commodore Hornblower" by C.S. Forrester, is now in bookstores.

Finally, Washington says there will be 25% to 40% less canned food this year so keep those victory gardens going.

That's the news this June 7, 1945.

Friday, June 8, 1945

And now today's news, June 8, 1945.

150 B-29's have hit Osaka, Kobe and Nagoya with high explosives as U.S. Naval planes once again attacked Kyushu.

Japanese suicide planes have resumed their attacks on shipping off Okinawa but in response Americans shot down another 67 Japanese planes. The last main Japanese defenses on the southern part of the island are under heavy naval, air and ground attack.

In the Philippines, a drive continues on Luzon towards the Cayagan Valley, the last large area still held by the Japanese.

An agreement with Marshal Tito of Yugoslavia gives the Allies full control of the city of Trieste.

Acting Secretary of State Joseph Grew denies that an understanding was made at Yalta to give Korea to Russia along with other concessions in exchange for Russia entering the Pacific war.

About 250,000 men in Europe have earned 85 points or more and are thus eligible for discharge.

A.P. correspondent Edward Kennedy, who released the news of German's surrender 1 day before it was officially released, says he'd do it again but merely notes that censors had not yet approved it.

The Houses of Parliament in London was hit 12 times during the war causing 3 deaths and 15 injuries. Additionally, a British aircraft shell damaged Big Ben.

Generals George Patton and Jimmy Doolittle are being honored across the country having just left Boston and are now in Denver with Los Angeles the next stop.

The Maritime Engineers Union has filed suit to retroactively collect travel pay over 4 years for their members covering the distance from the gate 50 to 200 yards to the time clock when work starts.

3 million motorists with B ration cards will get increases up to 650 miles a month. Current limits in the west are 400 to 475 miles and in the east 325 miles.

New movies include "It's in the Bag," with Fred Allen, Jack Benny, Don Ameche, William Bendix, Victor Moore, and Rudy Vallee plus "Delightfully Dangerous" with Jane Powell, Ralph Bellamy and Constance Moore.

The Kentucky Derby tomorrow is likely to be very slow considering the track today is a sea of mud.

That's the news this June 8, 1945.

And now today's news, June 9, 1945.

150 to 200 B-29's for the second day in a row have hit Japanese industrial plants on Honshu Island. A Japanese report says the Allies have invaded northwest Borneo but this is not confirmed by General MacArthur.

Chinese troops have reached the Indochina frontier while Japanese are fleeing towards Cao Bang north of Hanoi, the capital.

Marshal Gregori Zhukov, conqueror of Berlin, says there is no trace of Hitler but says he married Eva Braun and escaped.

Yugoslavia has accepted the Anglo-U.S. policy of Trieste area with details to be worked out by Marshal Tito and Field Marshal Sir Harold Alexander.

The Philippine Congress met for the first time since liberation to hear President Sergio Osmena pledge continued support for the U.S.

The liquid assets of Germany and Japanese in the U.S. worth $220 million which were frozen after Pearl Harbor will be seized by the U.S. Treasury. Physical properties were previously disposed of.

It is estimated that 80% of the Jews in Germany have been exterminated as part of a Hitler plan to wipe out 12 million Jews in Europe, a plan that called for a Jew-free Europe by April 1, 1942 as a birthday present for Hitler.

General George Patton and General Jimmy Doolittle received a thunderous welcome in Los Angeles today by 1½ million people along a downtown parade route as 36 Warhawks flew over. Fellow General Omar Bradley was simultaneously welcomed in Moberly, Missouri today.

In sports, Eddie Arcaro, the country's leading jockey, won the 71st Kentucky Derby today atop Hoop, owned by Fred Hooper.

The First 1946 Nash, one of two models, has been shown. It has room for 6 passengers.

A new movie features Sidney Greenstreet and Humphrey Bogart in "Conflict." In New York, blues singer Josh White sings at Town Hall and Edwin Franko Goldman conducts summer concerts for the 28th year.

Finally, as Father's Day is coming up get him a silk tie available at $1.50 to $2.50, white shirts at $2.50, rayon sports shirts at $4.98 or lisle socks at $1.25.

That's the news this June 9, 1945.

Sunday, June 10, 1945

And now today's news, June 10, 1945.

For the first time B-29's have simultaneously hit three major Japanese mainland cities—Osaka, Nagoya, and Kobe inflicting serious damage. On Okinawa the U.S. has destroyed 67 Japanese planes while on mainland China the Chinese have trapped 200,000 Japanese in the Liuchow area.

Contrary to earlier Russian reports, Marshal Zhukov reports that they have not found Hitler's body but do have evidence he married Eva Braun two days before the fall of Berlin and they may have been able to fly out. Eisenhower has also received Russia's highest award from Zhukov.

U.S. Ambassador Joseph Grew denies that the U.S. and Britain gave up Korea to the Russians in exchange for Russia's entry into the Japanese war. The U.S. position is for Korean independence.

Recently liberated former Austrian Chancellor Kurt Schuschnigg has announced his opinion that the German people hated war—that they too were victims of the Nazis.

The New York Times today carried a picture of returned General George Patton wiping tears from his eyes after a state dinner in Boston two days ago. Yesterday he and General Jimmy Doolittle were hailed by hundreds of thousands in a Los Angeles parade.

The queen of the Merchant Marine, The West Point, has circled the globe 14 times during the war, carried 350,000 troops, crossed the Atlantic 24 times.Originally planned to be an elite cruise ship, it carries a crew of 800 and 7,200 passengers on these crossings.

At the movies, "Son of Lassie" is starring Donald Crisp, Peter Lawford and June Lockhart while "Thrill of Romance" stars Van Johnson, Esther Williams and Tommy Dorsey's orchestra. Two newspaper photos today show Spike Jones with his washboard, the other with singer Frances Langford and guitarist Tony Romano.

Finally, today is the third anniversary of the German massacre of the village of Lidice in Czechoslovakia.

That's the news this June 10, 1945.

And now today's news, June 11, 1945.

In the South Pacific, Lt. General Simon Bolivar Bruckner has demanded the Japanese surrender in anticipation of utter defeat on Okinawa. In the south, four landings by Australian troops on Borneo have been announced by General MacArthur.

In Washington, President Truman has submitted a 1946 budget of $39 billion, down 25% from 1945 now that the war is over in Europe. Incredibly, in the last 11 months of war in Europe, the Yanks fired over one billion bullets, 48 million artillery shells and over 1.3 million bazookas. Bazookas, of course were named after the one-of-a-kind musical instrument of the same name created by comedian Bob Burns.

Truman has also received thanks from Marshal Stalin on the 3rd anniversary of lend-lease to the Russians. And, in France, Marshal Petain who signed the armistice with the Germans in 1940, has told a high court of investigation that he was a savior for the French and that Pierre Laval was forced on him.

Five hundred seventy-nine new U.S. casualties have been announced plus the names of 3,600 liberated GI's. The Navy announced the loss of the destroyer Longshaw which was caught on an Okinawa reef and shelled by the Japanese. Two-thirds of the crew of 250 were lost.

Congress has voted out of committee a bill to outlaw the poll tax as a requisite of voting. Southern Democrats have opposed it.

In sports, Col. Frank Shields returns to play tennis in the Red Cross benefit at Forest Hills. Others include Big Bill Tilden, Alice Marble, Pauline Betz and Pancho Segura. On the coast, the California tennis title has been won by Margaret Osborne over Louise Brough.

If you're in Manhattan this week, Jimmy Savo and Josh White are appearing at Cafe Society Uptown.

Telephone service has just started between Calcutta, India and Kunming, China, a distance of 1,750 miles.

And, oh yes, Nash today is showing its first 1946 model car.

That's the news this June 11, 1945.

Tuesday, June 12, 1945

And now today's news, June 12, 1945.

A big day today in London for General Eisenhower as he is feted and honored with a huge parade, the Order of Merit hung around his neck by King George, and a private reception by Queen Mary. Coincidentally, he released a letter written in January to the American Society of Newspaper Editors making a plea for a free press for all nations.

In the Pacific, the battle for Okinawa is almost over. Japan has lost a minimum of 4,000 planes in all areas in just the last 3 months. The Mexican Expeditionary Air Force in support of American infantry troops has blasted Japanese troops in the Manila area using U.S. Thunderbolt planes.

In Rome, the Pope today revealed how he had ceaselessly tried to keep Italy out of the war including a personal appeal to Mussolini.

In Washington, the American Legion and the Veterans of Foreign Wars denounce the quality of treatment of veterans in veteran hospitals at a Congressional hearing.

The first operational area for B-29's was in India but today the last 150 B-29's successfully and without loss covered the 3,600 miles from India to Tinian in the Mariannas with only one stop.

Swedish inventor Sven Lindequist says that current guns will be obsolete for the next war. He sees rocket propelled ten-ton shells from underground factories being a principal weapon. He says the gun barrel is outdated.

If you like New York dancing, you can enjoy the big band music of Erskine Hawkins today at the Lincoln Hotel or the easier sound of William Adler's violin ensemble at the Rainbow Lounge atop the RCA building.

McCreery's in New York is selling men's slacks at $4.95 and slippers at $3.98. In the same store, a woman's circular haircut is $1.50 and a permanent wave is $10.00.

Selective Service head General Hershey's plan to release conscientious objectors while the country is still at war has been blasted by Selective Service groups.

That's the news this June 12, 1945.

And now today's news, June 13, 1945.

A report from Washington today says since 1939, the Allies have lost 4,770 merchant ships totalling 21 million tons including 1,500 U.S. ships. Six thousand American merchant seamen are dead, missing, or prisoners. Over half were sunk by enemy submarines. While 4.4 million U.S. soldiers were safely sent abroad on ships, 3,600 were lost on these ships.

As more Australian troops landed on Borneo, 3,500 Japanese troops have been killed on Okinawa in the last 9 days.

President Truman's special envoy to Russia, Harry L. Hopkins, has returned from Moscow reporting an ease of tension and a more positive attitude towards the Polish question. Next week Gen. Charles de Gaulle arrives in Washington from France to meet with Truman.

A report today says that had the war lasted 6 months more, the Germans would likely have had V-bombs accurate enough to bomb New York City from 3,000 miles away.

GI's passing through the U.S. from Europe to the South Pacific got a tax break today: no income taxes.

About Generals today: General Patton is visiting President Truman at the White House, General Jimmy Doolittle gets his first ride in a B-29, and General Eisenhower is being honored in Paris.

A C-54 has set the longest flight in history today—4,330 miles in 16 hours and 55 minutes from Natal to Casablanca. The previous record was a B-17 of 3,444 miles from Newfoundland to Oran.

At the movies are Bing Crosby, Betty Hutton and Sonny Tufts in "Here Come the Waves," Frederic March and Claudette Colbert are in "The Sign of the Cross," and Tallulah Bankhead, Anne Baxter, Charles Coburn, and William Eythe are in "A Royal Scandal." Fans of Al Jolson are likely to see him on Broadway again in a Mike Todd production being discussed.

Pan Am reports sales of $93 million with a net of 1.6 million while Northwest Airlines is running ads showing their 26 stops across the top of the U.S. from New York to Seattle.

That's the news this June 13, 1945.

169

Thursday, June 14, 1945

And now today's news, June 14, 1945.

Five hundred B-29's today hit Osaka with 3,000 tons of bombs as Japanese war leaders called upon all 100 million citizens to be prepared to sacrifice their lives in defense even as Premier Suzuki admits that Okinawa is lost. Meanwhile, General Jimmy Doolittle's European 8th Air Force will join the battle for Japan.

If you're in New York four days hence you can be one of millions to greet General Eisenhower in a welcome home parade.

Nine rings of racketeers have been flooding the East Coast with 30 million red point stamps—enough to supply 600,000 people for a month with rationed meat, butter, fats and oils.

In Washington, the U.S. Chamber of Commerce today endorsed a peacetime draft to ensure a lasting peace.

In England, Britain has recommended that India's reconstituted government should be all Indian excepting for a British Viceroy. On the continent Field Marshal Montgomery has relaxed fraternization rules for British troops so that they may speak to and play with German children. And, notwithstanding the war, Holland today says they will export 10,000 tons of tulips to the U.S. and Canada this fall.

World War I infantryman Harry S. Truman today saluted the U.S. infantrymen and their role in the war. And in Germany, Britain will be starting the first war trials in three weeks in the British zone.

In sports, veteran Joe Medwick, former Cardinal outfielder and currently on Mel Ott's New York Giants, is being traded to the Boston Braves. And, good news for the Detroit Tigers—Captain Hank Greenberg was released today to return at the same 1941 salary of $55,000, highest in baseball. The Red Cross tennis benefit at Forest Hills starting June 22nd will now include Mrs. Sarah Palfrey Cook.

Paul Muni and Claude Rains have been signed for "Angel on My Shoulder." Greer Garson and Gregory Peck are in "Valley of Decision" at Radio City Music Hall with the on-stage spectacular including the Corps de Ballet and the Rockettes.

Finally, "Ask the man who owns one" says Packard car ads. Fewer repairs, less service and something to keep in mind when new cars do become available.

That's the news this June 14, 1945.

170

And now today's news, June 15, 1945.

The Big Three will meet in Berlin next month and especially invited by Winston Churchill will be Labor Leader and political opponent Clement Attlee.

Joachim von Ribbentrop has been captured asleep in bed in a Hamburg lodging house with a small vial of poison strapped to his body.

The 10th Army's 7th and 96th Divisions and the 1st Marine Division are pushing the Japanese further back on Okinawa. Marine General Pedro del Valle says the enemy's morale is low and he expects to secure the entire island within two weeks.

It's now reported that the carrier U.S.S. Saratoga was badly hit off Iwo Jima two days after the invasion February 19th by suicide planes with 7 direct hits blowing open the hull. 123 men were killed or missing and 192 wounded.

General Eisenhower urges a peace time draft citing need for training and is backed up by Secretary of War Stimson. The General is to be made a citizen of Paris shortly.

There's been another 22 mile advance on Luzon as Santiago and Echague are liberated.

Up to V-E Day, the RAF reports the loss of 9163 bombers, 3558 fighters and 3600 other planes. 5735 were lost in the Mediterranean and the Mid-East.

It's now revealed that German U-boats laid mines in 1943 at the entrance of New York Harbor bottling up the port for three days. Mines were also laid at the entrance of the Panama Canal and 4 other east coast ports. Small countries at the Peace Conference in San Francisco have lost by 28 to 17 the right to revise the world charter within 10 years.

An extraordinary parade and drama occurred today on 5th Avenue in New York as 600 Purple Heart veterans rode in jeeps. The crowds were too deeply moved to cheer.

U.S. experts are extremely impressed with German synthetic rubber with superior quality and production process that will help the U.S.

Welterweight Ray Robinson has knocked out Jimmy McDaniels early in the second round at Madison Square Garden. Sam Snead, thinking he had a sprained wrist, had it taped, shot a 70, found out it was broken and withdrew from the Philadelphia Inquirer Invitational.

Brigadier General David Sarnoff believes within five years after the war that television will be a billion dollar industry.

That's the news this June 15, 1945.

Saturday, June 16, 1945

And now today's news, June 16,1945.

The 86th Black Hawk Division of 14,000 men is due in New York tomorrow from Europe as the first complete unit to then go to the Pacific.

The British fleet has attacked with ships and planes the Japanese held island of Truk, a major naval stronghold.

50% of the shipments of food, vital supplies and war materials in the Chicago area has been brought to a standstill by a strike of 6000 truckers.

General George C. Marshall and Admiral Ernest J. King concur with General Eisenhower that there should be a peace time draft.

Vice President Juan Peron of Argentina, also Secretary of Labor and Social Welfare, has been sharply criticized in papers across the country by principal organizations representing industry and commerce.

Hermann Goering says Hitler gave German plans for jets to the Japanese and delivered them by submarine.

1447 of 18,000 American prisoners from Bataan and Corregidor have been freed. Most others had been sent to Japan, China and Formosa.

Australian ground forces have advanced 4 miles more on Borneo and are now close to Brunei.

Japanese women have been told to fight in the front lines if there is an invasion.

An RAF C-54 has flown 9120 miles in 56 hours round trip from London to Karachi, India averaging 215 mph.

Generalissimo Franco says Spanish municipal elections will be held soon.

UNRRA plans to send 14,500 tractors to 11 European countries with less than half to be paid for.

The War Production Board has approved manufacturing of 50 types of electrical equipment from toasters to refrigerators.

United Press says U.S. Archbishop Francis Spellman will be made a Cardinal this fall.

A first performance of Gershwin's "Porgy and Bess" in Moscow has brought plaudits from composer Dimitri Shostakovich.

A New York film wholesaler says many retail film outlets will specialize in color film after the war.

Good news for European based soldiers. Families will be able to join you soon.

That's the news this June 16, 1945.

And now today's news, June 17, 1945.

Over the weekend, Joachim von Ribbentrop, Hitler's foreign minister, was captured in Hamburg, Germany, where he had been living for 6 weeks. American troops have seized the last 3 remaining Japanese-held hills on Okinawa, and American troops gained another 5 miles further south in the Philippines on northern Luzon.

The aircraft carrier, Saratoga, badly damaged in the battle for Iwo Jima, is repaired and back in action.

B-29's have started mass attacks again and hit 4 Japanese cities. Other bombers have hit Formosa and Shikoku.

The Russians say regulations in the World General Assembly will have to be changed before they sign the security charter.

Here at home, the OPA has cut sugar quotas to industry by 37% for the 3rd quarter of the year. Black market prices for oranges have soared to $4.00 a case.

Socialist premier Achille van Acker and his cabinet have resigned in Belgium in protest over the return of King Leopold's return to resume the throne.

General Dwight Eisenhower's triumphal return to New York day after tomorrow is expected to receive unprecedented coverage by the radio networks and independent stations.

India plans to send 500 native students to the U.S. in the fall to attend graduate schools.

Lawrence Tibbett, of the Metropolitan Opera, will replace Dick Todd as featured singer on "Your Hit Parade" starting next month. And, Brian Aherne will star in the radio series, "The Saint," on CBS, beginning this week.

In sports, Satchel Paige and his Kansas City Monarchs made their appearance at Yankee Stadium and beat the Philadelphia Stars, 3-1.

Finally, John Hartford, President of A&P has acknowledged that he had loaned Elliott Roosevelt $200,000 in 1939 and wrote it off in 1942 after a payment by the late President's son of only $4000.

That's the news this June 17, 1945.

Monday, June 18, 1945

And now today's news, June 18, 1945.

Lt. General Simon Bolivar Bruckner, Jr., was killed by a Japanese shell on Okinawa today. He died within ten minutes after being hit in the chest.

In London Lord Haw Haw has been formally charged with treason at his arraignment.

More than 1 million people cheered Gen. Eisenhower in Washington today. He was decorated by President Truman and then addressed a joint session of Congress. Tomorrow, he will be in New York and will attend the Braves-Giants baseball game.

A Japanese spokesman says his country will never accede to Allied demands for unconditional surrender. He also predicted an assault on Japan's mainland could come within a few months.

More than 400 uniformed soldiers are driving trucks in Chicago today. The government seized the trucks after a strike by drivers tied up shipping in the city.

President Truman will leave tomorrow for San Francisco to address the closing conference of the World Conference of Nations now known as the U.N.

Fifteen of sixteen arrested Polish underground leaders are said to have pleaded guilty as their trial began in Moscow.

In sports, Phil Marchildon is reported ready to rejoin the Philadelphia Athletics in about 2 weeks and be ready to pitch 3 weeks after that. The right-hander had been in a German war camp.

Actor Hugh Herbert, the one who says "woo woo," resumes his career tonight in "Oh, Brother." His co-star will be Arlene Whelan.

Finally, a bizarre destruction of a B-29 took place recently when the ship's instruments and controls were shot out, the crew had bailed out but the plane flew on. A U.S. Black Widow fighter pumped 775 shots into the superfort before it was destroyed as thousands on Iwo Jima below watched.

That's the news this June 18, 1945.

And now today's news, June 19, 1945.

Gen. Dwight Eisenhower was hailed by over 4 million people in New York's greatest welcome ever as he rode through 37 miles of the city's streets. He was made an honorary citizen of New York. The General then said after Japan is defeated, there will be other problems to face...jobs and peace.

Moscow has offered a compromise in its dispute over discussion in the proposed World General Assembly. Lots of problems pending there.

Trapped Japanese troops are said to be jumping off cliffs into the sea in southern Okinawa. This has been a pattern of suicide which had also occurred at Saipan and Tinian.

Chinese troops have rolled to within 19 miles of Liuchow in southern China and Japanese troops are preparing to abandon Amoy and Swatow.

President Truman has asked Congress to pass a bill changing the presidential Succession Act of 1886 so as to make the House Speaker first in line for the post after the Vice President.

Lt. Gen. Simon Bruckner, Jr., was buried today in Okinawa. He was killed yesterday by a Japanese shell. Just 10 days ago he was demanding surrender by the Japanese.

King Leopold of Belgium says he will not give up his throne. He will return to Belgium and will reassume his full constitutional powers.

Signing ceremonies for the new world charter of the United Nations will be held in San Francisco on Friday or Saturday and are expected to last about 8 hours. About 200 delegates will sign the document.

Leonardo da Vinci's "Last Supper" is again on display in Milan after being hidden during the war by walls of sandbags supported by steel scaffolding.

Babe Didrickson Zaharias has moved through first round play in the 16th annual women's Western open golf tournament in Indianapolis.

That's the news this June 19, 1945.

Wednesday, June 20, 1945

And now today's news, June 20, 1945.

The shooting on Okinawa is almost over as remaining Japanese forces are trapped in 3 pockets at the southern tip of the island.

Another General has been lost. Brigadier Gen. Claudius Easly, assistant commander of the 96th Infantry Division, has been killed in action on Okinawa.

The Queen Mary landed in New York with the largest single contingent of American fighting men and women to come home from the wars...some 14,500. That's a lot of people on one ship built to carry 3,000.

Two German prisoners have told their captors that Adolf Hitler and Eva Braun killed themselves in the Berlin Chancellery. The bodies were then saturated with gasoline and burned.

J. Andre Fouilhoux, designer of the Trylon and Perisphere of the New York World's Fair, was killed in a fall from the roof of a building he was inspecting in Brooklyn today.

The War Production Board has authorized manufacturing of 691,000 passenger cars between July 1 and March 31, 1946, by 10 auto makers. GM has the largest quota; Crosley, Graham-Paige and Willys Overland the smallest.

Former President Herbert Hoover says the meat shortage is due to bad organization. He has offered a 12-point program for increasing the meat supply.

Russia has accepted a temporary compromise at San Francisco to permit Assembly discussion. The final document will be signed next week and President Truman will address the conference.

Captain Hank Greenberg, back from the war, plans to be back in the Detroit Tiger lineup on June 30th.

The Broadway hit, "Follow the Girls," with Gertrude Niesen, will stage its 500th performance tonight.

That's the news this June 20, 1945.

176

And now today's news, June 21, 1945.

Okinawa has finally been captured after 82 days of bitter fighting. One thousand seven hundred Japanese troops have surrendered to American troops but others jumped into the sea rather than give up. American casualties are expected to total 50,000 in the battle for the island.

Gen. Vinegar Joe Stilwell has been named to lead the U.S. 10th Army to new battles against the Japanese.

Honshu has been hit by 450 American Superfortresses from bases in the Marianas. The Kure Arsenal was the main target.

Lt. Gen. Jimmy Doolittle has been barred from further combat flying because officers in full possession of strategic plans must not fall into enemy hands. And that, just after announcing his 8th Air Force is being redeployed from Europe to the South Pacific.

Yugoslavia is protesting against the slowness of the handling of Italian war criminals.

Supreme Allied Headquarters now believe that Hitler did indeed die in Berlin on May 1st, although no trace of his remains has been found.

The 7th War Loan Drive has reached almost 16 billion dollars nationally, topping its goal by almost 2 billion.

Admiral William Standley, former U.S. Ambassador to Russia, says he believes Stalin wants to cooperate with the U.S. and Britain in the post war world to assure a durable peace.

The Packard Motor Car plant in Detroit has been hit by a strike, and the government is taking action to draft those striking truck drivers in Chicago.

Veteran Connie Mack of the Philadelphia Athletics says he let catcher Frankie Hayes go because he didn't talk it up enough behind the plate.

The late movie star Lupe Velez's 12-room house was sold at auction for $41,750. Her collection of jewels and furs will be sold tomorrow.

That's the news this June 21, 1945.

Friday, June 22, 1945

And now today's news, June 22, 1945.

Texas Senator Tom Connally says there is no chance that the Senate can ratify the new World Charter from the San Francisco peace conference until this fall. Lord Halifax of England concurs for the English.

Justice Robert H. Jackson, U.S. Chief Counsel, says the trial of top Nazis will start later this summer in Germany.

While the U.S. has slaughtered 90,000 Japanese on Okinawa, today the Japanese have sunk two light U.S. vessels and damaged 3 others. 160 Japanese have committed suicide by hand grenades on the southern tip of the island.

In an unescorted daylight raid 450 Superfortresses have hit the naval arsenal at Kure and five aircraft factories on Honshu with the loss of four planes.

The Czechoslovakian government has seized 260,000 corporations and farms in the possession of Germans, Hungarians, traitors and Nazi collaborators.

Bernard Baruch told the Senate Military Affairs Committee today that Germany's heavy industry should be moved to other countries to end the Third Reich.

Thirteen state governors report that black markets in food is so rampant that immediate action is required.

A $38 billion war appropriations bill has been sent to the House with a declaration by General Marshall predicting 1000 plane raids on Japan.

15,000 more American troops went aboard the Queen Elizabeth en route home today. Most were 8th Air Force men. The Queen Mary landed in New York two days ago with 15,000 men.

Hermann Goering says Hitler always thought he could make peace with England until Winston Churchill became Prime Minister.

Professor Albert Einstein will lead a drive for funds to settle 30,000 Jewish war refugees in the Soviet Union.

The home of Washington Irving in Tarrytown, New York will become a national shrine thanks to financial aid by John D. Rockefeller, Jr.

The Labor Department says strikes have doubled since V-E Day.

Finally, in a Red Cross benefit in Forest Hills tennis, 52-year-old Bill Tilden beat Lloyd Budge, Elwood Cooke beat Frank Shields, and Sarah Palfrey Cook beat Dorothy May Bundy.

That's the news this June 22, 1945.

And now today's news, June 23, 1945.

American bombers have attacked Japanese positions in China on a 1300 mile front as Chinese prepare to battle for Liuchow.

Documents have been discovered telling how Japanese killed some 80,000 of their own wounded men in the Philippines by injection, by their own hands or by friends after allowing 24 hours for meditation.

Emperor Hirohito has told the Japanese people the present crisis is unprecedented in Japanese history and that he is satisfied with the valor of his people.

Rumors are that former South Carolina Senator James F. Byrnes will become Secretary of State replacing Edward Stettinius who would become envoy to London.

President Truman has commuted death sentences to life of two convicted spies—one an American and one German—who came ashore in a submarine in November 1944.

An alert has been issued in Seattle and Alaska to look out for floating Japanese mines.

A poll of the Senate would show 52 of 96 Senators approving the U.N. Charter.

General Charles de Gaulle wants to visit President Truman before the next Big 3 meeting. He says U.S.-French relations have to be improved.

The Big Four have agreed to admit Poland to the U.N.

The War Food Administration says civilians will get more meat due to less military demand, while the Petroleum Administration has asked the oil industry for a record output in July.

At today's Princeton University Commencement, London bacteriologist Sir Alexander Fleming, discoverer of penicillin, has been honored with a Doctor of Science.

Among new movies opening this week are "Rhapsody in Blue" starring Robert Alda as George Gershwin, James Cagney in "Blood On The Sun," and Fred MacMurray, Marjorie Main and Helen Walker in "Murder He Says," while "Crime Incorporated" features Leo Carillo, Tom Neal and Martha Tilton. George Murphy and Ann Sothern have been signed to star in "Up Goes Maisie."

Processors of food that is frozen say that the frozen food industry will mushroom from $90 million a year to over $500 million a year after the war.

Finally, another reminder. Have you donated blood to the Red Cross lately?

That's the news this June 23, 1945.

179

Sunday, June 24, 1945

And now today's news, June 24, 1945.

Japan will be subjected to daily 1000 plane attacks, says Army Chief-of-Staff Gen. George C. Marshall. He said almost 3 million tons of bombs would be dropped on Japanese targets in the fiscal year starting July 1. In keeping with his announcement, the entire Japanese-held area from Burma to the Kuriles was hit today by American and British planes.

Russia will demilitarize millions of men in the oldest age groups.

Twelve American generals, back from the War in Europe, say Germany is "through for 100 years."

Over the weekend, the House of Representatives voted to transfer to the Secretary of Agriculture almost all of the controls over food now held by the OPA.

General Dwight Eisenhower has denied that he has any idea of going into politics. He said when he takes his uniform off, he wants to be a civilian.

Lady Spears, wife of Major General Sir Edward Spears, former British minister to Syria and Lebanon, has been asked to leave France.

General Charles de Gaulle has proposed several dates during July when he would like to visit President Truman.

Moscow reports a new Polish government has been formed including five from London as well as men of the Warsaw Administration. There will be a three man council holding the Presidency.

In sports, Pancho Segura defeated William Talbert in the Red Cross victory tennis exhibitions at Forest Hills Stadium. Big Bill Tilden lost to Welby Van Horn in 3 exciting sets.

At the movies, Tom Drake will get the lead in the MGM screen version of "The Green Years."

In business, B.G. Erskine, Chairman of the Board and former President of Sylvania Electric Products, died at the age of 62 at his home in Emporium, Pennsylvania.

That's the news this June 24, 1945.

And now today's news, June 25, 1945.

Delegates to the San Francisco U.N. conference have unanimously adopted a new world charter for peace and security. The document will be signed today. President Truman will address the closing session.

B-29's hit targets in Nagoya, Osaka, Akashi and Gifu in great numbers and Tokyo has admitted that most of Formosa's cities have been reduced to cinders by air blows.

Tokyo has apparently written off Okinawa and the prisoner count continues to rise. The latest figure is almost 8,700.

A trap is closing on some 20,000 Japanese troops on Luzon.

In London, Lord Haw Haw who broadcast for the Nazis to Allied troops, says he is not a British citizen, but is American, having been born in Brooklyn.

The 7th War Loan drive has rolled past the $20 billion mark and is expected to break all previous war loan records.

Sean T.O'Kelly has been sworn in as the second president of Eire. The ceremony took place in the cream and gold St. Patricks Hall in Dublin Palace.

Construction of the proposed tunnel under the Narrows connecting Brooklyn and Staten Island is expected to take 5 years and cost $73.5 million.

A bill to extend Social Security to all gainfully employed persons has been introduced by Senator Theodore Green of Rhode Island.

The nation's restaurateurs are fighting further cuts in their food rations and predict further cuts will lead to increased black marketing.

Musicians of "Oklahoma" have changed their minds and have decided to donate their services to the war bond campaign in a special matinee to be given on July 10th.

In sports, Tami Mauriello knocked out Lou Nova in the first round of their scheduled ten-rounder in Boston today.

That's the news this June 25, 1945.

And now today's news, June 26, 1945.

President Truman challenged the new United Nations Conference to translate its words into deeds, telling the delegates "you have just created a structure upon which we can build a better world." The President will present the new U.N. charter to the Senate on Monday and urged its prompt ratification.

Belgium's King Leopold will announce within 48 hours his decision to abdicate or return to the throne.

In the war, nearly 50 B-29's hit plants on Honshu, striking at a huge refinery, Japan's last remaining aviation gasoline producer.

The bodies of the Japanese commander-in-chief and his chief-of-staff on Okinawa were found in shallow graves after they committed suicide.

All factions in India have reportedly accepted in principle new British proposals for a revised central government, including parity of caste Hindus and Moslems.

Former University of Michigan All-American Tommy Harmon and his wife, actress Elyse Knox, are the proud new parents of a baby girl, named Sharon Kristan Harmon.

The Boston Red Sox have given a contract and bonus deal to 17-year-old Ted Del Guericio of Newark. The contract will reportedly net him between $15,000 and $20,000.

Helen Hayes, tired from her coast-to-coast travels in "Harriet," plans to take a long rest and not appear on stage till a year from September.

"Children get ideas from radio, and entertainment helps to make ideas stick," according to the Child Study Association of America. The group says there is already conflict "between what children enjoy and what we want them to enjoy."

Erno Rapee, maestro of the Radio City Music Hall orchestra since the opening of the theater in December 1932, has died of a heart attack. He was 55.

That's the news this June 26, 1945.

And now today's news, June 27, 1945.

General Douglas MacArthur has announced the liberation of all of Luzon, 5 months and 19 days after the first landings in Lingayan Gulf.

It's revealed that two Japanese suicide planes crashed on the deck of the carrier Bunker Hill off Okinawa last month, killing 373 and wounding 264. American naval casualties for the entire Ryukyus campaign, through June 20, were 4,907 killed or missing and 4,824 wounded.

Japan has put all communications under government control and all postal, telegraph, telephone and radio communications will be strictly supervised.

For GI's anxious to get out of the service, the Army's requirements for discharge points should lower from 85 to 80 or 78 within a few weeks.

At least 50,000 GI's will leave Europe monthly for America or the Pacific until only about 500,000 are left to police the American zone in Germany.

Edward R. Stettinius has resigned as Secretary of State to become the U.S. Representative to the U.N. President Truman will nominate a new Secretary next week, likely to be James F. Byrnes.

Inefficiency by the War Food Administration has probably led to government losses in the millions in the storing and handling of food for war.

The Senate and House have agreed to extend the Price Control Act for another year through a compromise to make the Secretary of Agriculture a food "czar."

Auto pioneer Benjamin Briscoe has died at the age of 78. He helped finance the first Buick car.

Helen Keller celebrated her 65th birthday today and announced the establishment of the Council for Deaf/Blind.

And, the FCC has assigned 90 channels between 88 and 106 megacycles for frequency modulation, likely to be a new radio medium.

The ceiling price of red raspberries is up 4 cents to 38 cents a pint.

That's the news this June 27, 1945.

And now today's news, June 28, 1945.

Japan's naval base at Sasebo and 3 cities not hit before have been bombed by almost 500 B-29's dropping 3,500 tons of bombs.

Generalissimo Chiang Kai-shek is urging speedy American landings in China to open a supply route.

Special suicide corps and bases have been set up in Japan and secret weapons are being made to meet the expected American invasion.

German scientists said to have been working on weapons that could harness solar power have offered to continue their experiments for the U.S. and England.

General Mark Clark has been named Commander-in-Chief of U.S. occupation forces in Austria.

Poland's Warsaw Provisional government has quit and the new Government of National Unity has taken over.

Negotiations between the All-Indian Congress Party and Moslem League have broken down over the question of Hindu and Moslem representation.

Here at home, AT&T has announced a plan for mobile radio-telephone systems that would give motorists a 2-way communication capability.

The 7th War Loan has set a new record of $21,639,000,000 in sales.

The shortage of meat is expected to remain acute in July despite a 5% increase in total supply.

Major Edwin Armstrong, inventor of FM radio, says 400 new stations can start as soon as the FCC issues licenses.

That's the news this June 28, 1945.

Friday, June 29, 1945

And now today's news, June 29, 1945.

American patrols have invaded the little island of Kume 345 miles from the Chinese coast and President Truman has sent congratulations to General MacArthur for taking Luzon.

Planes of the American 5th and 13th Air Force have dropped 1000 tons of bombs in the past two weeks on oil fields in Netherlands Borneo and 280 tons on gun positions, barracks areas and supply dumps near the oil fields.

The world's largest ship, the Queen Elizabeth, arrived today in New York harbor with 13,113 GI's along with Princess Juliana of the Netherlands and 446 nurses.

The House has passed a bill by voice vote and cheering for the Present Speaker Sam Rayburn which would provide that the Speaker of the House become President in the event of death or disability of both the President and Vice President.

Acting Secretary of State Joseph E. Grew flatly denies any official or unofficial peace offerings by Japan. Japan is reported to have transferred much of its industry from Japan to Manchuria.

Paris says it is impossible to identify 330,000 prisoners and deportees killed or who died in Germany.

During a riot of 154 prisoners at Ft. Dix, New Jersey, 3 Russians captured while fighting for the Germans have committed suicide.

Mississippi Senator Eastland arguing against the Fair Employment Practice Committee says Negro troops were an utter and abysmal failure in Europe.

George Bernard Shaw, in a letter of support to a Communist candidate in England, says he is a communist.

President Truman met in Kansas City with 1936 Republican presidential candidate Alfred E. Landon who praised many of the President's foreign policies.

Ford Motor Company has shown 1946 Mercury and Lincoln models. Lincoln will have an electrically operated hydraulic mechanism for operating windows to become standard equipment. The car will have 12 cylinders.

There may be a Salzburg Music Festival this summer and Bruno Walter may be the conductor.

Welterweight Rocky Graziano knocked out Freddie "Red" Cochrane in the 10th round at Madison Square Garden. Cochrane is recently out of the Navy.

Finally, a father of 9 in Buffalo who makes $62 a week, is about to be inducted into the Army. His family allotment will be $240 a month.

That's the news this June 29,1945.

And now today's news, June 30, 1945.

President Truman has appointed James F. Byrnes as Secretary of State as Edward R. Stettinius has resigned to represent the U.S. at the U.N. Speedy Senate approval is expected.

The U.S. has lost its 44th submarine, the Keete. It is also the 320th naval vessel lost in the war.

Large paper balloons carrying bombs have been released by Japanese and carried on easterly winds over various places in northwestern Canada.

Chinese Premier T.V.Soong is meeting today with Marshal Stalin in Moscow.

American and British troops will begin withdrawing from the Soviet's official zone and will enter Berlin to share occupation with the Soviets.

Chinese troops have rewon Liuchow and are within 125 miles of Shanghai.

Director of War Mobilization and Reconversion Fred M. Vinson said today peace plans must consider both an early and later end of the war and called for modernization of tax laws, high wages, full employment, and public works.

Conservative candidate Prime Minister Winston Churchill says if he is defeated he will not serve under a Labor government.

The President of the South Carolina NAACP has challenged Senator Eastland's contention that Negroes were a failure, asks for documentation and that Eastland's remarks be stricken from the Senate record.

Lewis B. Swellenbach was sworn in today as Secretary of Labor replacing Frances Perkins.

In sports at Randalls Island, New York in the National AAU track championships, Henry Ewell ran the 100 meters in 10.3, Herb McKenley the 400 meters in 48.4, a three way tie in the high jump including Herb Albritton at 6-5 3/4 and a tie in the pole vault at 13 feet 6 by Lt. Albert Morcom and Robert Phelps.

A Book of the Month Club selection is "Up Front" by cartoonist Bill Mauldin at $3.00 while heading the General Best seller list is Ernie Pyle's "Brave Men."

That's the news this June 30, 1945.

And now today's news, July 1, 1945.

Allied armies in Germany are shifting their lines in accordance with an agreement on their respective occupation zones.

A BBC broadcast says Truman, Churchill and Stalin will meet on July 10th in Berlin.

General MacArthur says powerful fleets of aircraft and naval forces are hitting southeast Borneo and that Australian forces have landed at Balik Papan. Meanwhile, Chinese troops have recaptured Liuchow, the former American base in Southern China from the Japanese.

Here at home, as expected, President Truman has nominated James Byrnes as our new Secretary of State. Speedy Senate confirmation is expected. The President has also signed a bill giving federal employees a 15% pay hike. Mr. Truman has ordered seizure by the government of oil plants of the Texas Company in Port Arthur where a strike began Friday.

Price controls have been extended for another year, and the new Secretary of Agriculture, Clinton P. Anderson, promises improvement in the meat supply and food production generally.

New York's Mayor, Fiorello LaGuardia, has made his radio debut as a reader of the comics on Station WNYC for children deprived of the "funnies" by a strike of newspaper deliverers which began on Friday. New York stations and the networks have increased their news program because of the strike.

Ohio Governor Frank Lausche has ordered the Ohio Selective Service to induct into the armed forces striking Goodyear workers at Akron.

Alben Barkley has told the U.S. Senate it will not recess until the new world security charter is ratified.

In sports, Detroit beat the Philadelphia A's twice in a twin bill as Hank Greenberg hit a home run in his baseball comeback.

Ray Bolger will start a new variety program on CBS beginning this Friday and the American Forces Network, with stations in England and on the continent, will celebrate its 2nd anniversary this week.

That's the news this July 1, 1945.

Monday, July 2, 1945

And now today's news, July 2, 1945.

Advance American occupation forces have entered Berlin. The main forces are either on their way to the German capital or waiting for orders to move.

Allied Supreme Headquarters says the Big 3 conference in the Berlin area may be held without news coverage. A conference to determine the status of Tangier has been postponed and Russia says it wants to be included in the talks.

In the Pacific, Japanese resistance has stiffened in Borneo, and almost 600 B-29's have hit 4 Japanese cities in a record attack.

Chinese Premier Soong is going to Moscow, and his visit may produce a new Russian-Chinese pact.

In this country, President Truman will address the Senate today to urge speedy acceptance of the new San Francisco Security charter. New York Governor Thomas E. Dewey has also urged quick ratification.

James Byrnes has been unanimously confirmed by the Senate as Secretary of State. The War Labor Board has ordered New York's striking newspaper deliverers to show cause why the stoppage should continue.

On the way to the U.S. is Britain's first post-war automobile. Austin Motor Car Company says the 10 horsepower, 4-door sedan was shipped to an American distributor in New York.

A 2 day seminar conducted by the National American Christian Palestine Committee opened today in Princeton, New Jersey to discuss problems in the Middle East.

From now on, the Queen Elizabeth and Queen Mary will be used only to carry U.S. troops across the Atlantic releasing smaller ships for the Pacific.

The War Production Board has lifted controls on the manufacture of electric irons.

In sports, Phillies pitcher Hugh Mulcahy, the first major leaguer to enter the armed forces, is on is way back to Shibe Park and the major leagues. It's hinted that he may become manager of the Phillies.

Dinah Shore will be the featured singer tonight at the Philharmonic Symphony Orchestra concert at Lewisohn Stadium.

That's the news this July 2, 1945.

And now today's news, July 3, 1945.

The occupation of Berlin by American and British troops got underway today. Citizen reaction is reported mixed.

Poland's new government says "free and unfettered" elections will be held as soon as possible.

General Joseph Stilwell says the Pacific issue is no longer in doubt and hopes his troops will all be back home on next July 4th.

Meanwhile Shikoku, on the Japanese home island, has been hit by over 500 B-29's which dropped 3,000 tons of bombs on 3 cities.

Australian troops have seized a big airfield in Borneo.

Here at home Harry Hopkins has resigned as advisor and assistant to the President, saying the time has come to take a rest.

New Secretary of State James Byrnes says there will be no change in basic foreign and peace policies and no change in personnel until after the Big 3 Conference in Berlin.

President Truman has ordered all but 6 federal agencies to cut their work week from 48 to 44 hours. Some 2.5 million workers will be affected.

Dr. Theodore Leslie Shear, internationally known archaeologist for his work excavating the Agora in Athens, Greece and member of the Princeton University faculty, died today at Lake Sunapee, New Hampshire of a heart attack while boating on the lake,

A gray 2-door sedan is the first civilian car to come off the Ford assembly lines since February 1942. Henry Ford drove it off the line at the River Rouge plant.

Ethel Barrymore has signed with David Selznick to appear in 4 pictures over a 4 year period. Her first film will be "Some Must Watch."

Striking newspaper deliverers of New York were scheduled to meet with the War Labor Board today to show cause why their strike should continue.

That's the news this July 3, 1945.

189

Wednesday, July 4, 1945

And now today's news, July 4, 1945.

The 169th anniversary of the Declaration of Independence will be marked by a full day's work by millions of workers in war plants around the nation. Sixty-four thousand people in Yankee Stadium last night saw one of the biggest shows in war bond history. The Army Ground Forces presented its spectacular "Here's Your Infantry."

General Douglas MacArthur declares "the Philippines are now liberated" as American planes of all types have played havoc with Japanese shipping, industries and airfields, and Sakhalin Island has been shelled for 2 days.

Australian forces have captured most of Balik Papan on Borneo.

The American flag has been raised over the southwest part of Berlin and the British have occupied the western section.

France says it has informed the U.S. it has no objection to Russian participation in the Tangier conference.

A Sino-Russian aid pact is reportedly near as the Mongolian Prime Minister arrives in Moscow where China's Premier Soong has been conferring with Russian officials.

Australian Prime Minister John Curtin has died in his sleep. He was 60.

Gemma LaGuardia Gluck, the long-missing sister of New York's Mayor, has been discovered safe in Berlin with her daughter and grandson. She had been arrested in Budapest and put into a concentration camp.

British Chancellor of the Exchequer Sir John Anderson said today that Britain will never ask the United States for credits nor accept any obligation she cannot see her way to fulfill.

That's the news this July 4, 1945.

Thursday, July 5, 1945

And now today's news, July 5, 1945.

Henry Morgenthau, Jr. has resigned as Secretary of the Treasury, effective after the President returns from the Big 3 conference. And, Justice Owen Roberts has retired from the U.S. Supreme Court effective July 31st.

Not a single death from fireworks was reported yesterday and holiday fatalities from all causes was far below the pre-war level.

President Truman has congratulated Henry J. Kaiser as Chairman of the U.N. Charity Collection on the success of the drive for collecting clothing for war victims in Europe and the Far East.

The U.S. Navy has been ordered to take over and operate temporarily the Akron, Ohio plants of Goodyear Tire and Rubber Company whose workers have been on strike since June 16.

The War Labor Board has ordered New York's striking newspaper deliverers to take immediate steps to end their strike or face disciplinary action.

The U.S. has officially recognized the new Polish government of national unity in Warsaw.

The U.S military government in Germany has seized the 24 plants of I.G. Farben Industries.

Here at home, table grapes from California and Arizona are under a flat ceiling price of 30 cents a pound, half of what they sold for last July.

In sports, welterweight Tommy Bell will face Jake LaMotta in a 10 rounder tonight at Madison Square Garden.

Spencer Tracy, who hasn't been on a Broadway stage since 1930, will return in November in Robert Sherwood's "Out of Hell" and "A Bell for Adano" has its world premiere today at Radio City Music Hall. It stars John Hodiak, Gene Tierney and William Bendix.

That's the news this July 5, 1945.

Friday, July 6, 1945

And now today's news, July 6, 1945.

600 B-29's have hit Kofu, Chiba, Shimizu, Akashi and Shimotsu with 4000 tons of bombs. A total of 121 square miles of Japanese cites have been destroyed since the Tokyo fire raid on March 10th.

After an inspection aboard, the U.S. Navy has let a Japanese ship leave Wake Island with 874 wounded and starving men.

Marine General Roy S. Geiger says Japan is ripe for a necessary mainland invasion and that the U.S. could invade at any time. He believes Japanese industrialists would stop the war if they could.

In the 9th year of war on the Chinese mainland, Generalissimo Chiang Kai-shek says that notwithstanding any mainland Japan invasion, there are great hardships ahead for the Chinese to win at home.

General Charles de Gaulle will definitely visit President Truman in the latter part of August with an expected visit also to New York City.

Fred M. Vinson, Director of War Mobilization and Reconversion will become Secretary of Treasury after the Big 3 meeting to succeed Henry Morgenthau who has resigned.

The redeployment of the 9th Air Force from Reims France to the Pacific has started for 5612 men.

All naval bases in Brazil are being returned to Brazil and no U.S. combat units will remain.

Consolidated Vultee Aircraft has developed for the Army Air Forces a giant 6 engine cargo plane. The XC-99 has a wingspan of 230 feet, length of 183 feet. This compares with the B-29 141 foot wingspan 99 foot length.

An English newspaper reports that the Duke and Duchess of Windsor will return to England in late August with his brother King George's approval.

Tech Sergeant Joe Louis is back at Camp Shanks after a 21,000 mile tour to military installations throughout the U.S. and Canada.

In sports, Boston Braves' Tommy Holmes hits in a double header today breaking the National League consecutive games of hits record set by Rogers Hornsby in 1922. Bill Talbert and Pancho Segura have reached the finals in the National Clay Court Championships.

That's the news this July 6, 1945.

And now today's news, July 7, 1945.

The Chinese Central News Agency says Japanese have made a landing near Amoy 140 miles west of Formosa to prepare their defenses against an expected Allied landing. Winston Churchill predicts the day is not long off when Japan will be driven out of China. Japanese news sources also say they fear an Allied offensive to recapture Singapore.

American military authorities say Japanese ack ack has improved 100% in the past three months due to better radar tracking training. The Australian 7th Division has moved ahead another 6 miles in the Netherlands Borneo from the captured city of Penajam in oil refinery areas.

Dr. Andreas Hermes of Berlin is the last surviving member of the group that unsuccessfully plotted the death of Adolf Hitler in July 1944. He has revealed the names of most of the others involved including generals and past ambassadors. Only he and one other escaped execution.

In Honolulu the 10 pm to 5 am curfew that was imposed after Pearl Harbor has been lifted. It had prohibited anyone from being on the street until 5 am.

SHAEF—the Supreme Headquarters Allied Expeditionary Forces will be dissolved July 13th with American, British and French Forces reverting back to their own commands.

100 colleges and universities are developing an unprecedented re-education program for 370,000 German prisoners in this country hoping to instill basic American ideals and traditions in them before returning to Germany.

10,000 Berlin civilians who had demanded cessation of hostilities were drowned by Elite Guards who flooded the subways they were occupying.

480 U.S. soldiers of the 5th Army are living it up in a Lake Como villa being used as a peacetime rest camp.

The Munich Symphony Orchestra will present works by Felix Mendelssohn tomorrow for the first time since Nazis banned the music of the famous Jewish composer.

Postmaster General Frank Walker says the post office had a $150 million surplus last year.

Phil Silvers and Cornel Wilde open in "A Thousand and One Nights" this week, and nightclub comedian Jimmy Savo is now a feature on the NBC weekly Supper Show Monday evenings.

That's the news this July 7, 1945.

193

Sunday, July 8, 1945

And now today's news, July 8, 1945.

600 American B-29's again blasted the Japanese homeland today. Americans let a Japanese hospital ship remove 974 Japanese prisoners off Wake Island.

The 50th Fighter Group—the first to fly cover for the Normandy invasion a year ago...is on its way home.

If you're taking an overnight trip of more than 450 miles, you won't find any Pullman cars..they're needed for the armed forces. But the OPA says you'll have 10% more butter next month.

Signs of peace include the opening of London's famous Covent Garden to which food came from all over the world.

Casualties reported today include another 2,000 Army and 2,500 Navy men plus the names of another 181 freed American prisoners.

The Navy announced an experimental technique of transmitting photos via radio for fast on-the-spot pictorial reports.

For entertainment during this weekend, Alec Templeton performes the Grieg Concerto one night and Leonard Bernstein conducts the Philharmonic Symphony Orchestra another with music by Brahms at Lewisohn Stadium. At the movies, "Dillinger" has opened starring Dennis O'Keefe and Constance Moore while "Those Endearing Young Charms" stars Robert Young, Larraine Day and Ann Harding.

Finally, a front page New York Times story today tells of the first B-29 to bomb Tokyo that was on the way home with a crew that had finished 30 missions. It crashed on Kwajalein killing 10 of the 13 men aboard.

That's the news this July 8, 1945.

And now today's news, July 9, 1945.

The greatest assemblage of American aerial forces, 1,500 fighters and bombers, have hit Japan with some B-29's flying almost 4,000 miles round trip to hit Sendai 190 miles North of Tokyo. And, while the invasion of Iwo Jima cost 20,000 American casualties, already it has saved 1,500 B-29's and 16,000 men who use it as a halfway stopping point from targets.

The U.N. Charter approved in San Francisco is now in the U.S. Senate for confirmation. One Senator noted that World War I cost 37 million lives and this war 14 million so far.

President Truman and Jimmy Byrnes are en route to a Big 3 Conference near Berlin as his administration is asking for $25 a week jobless pay. Some states pay only $15.

In Germany, the I.G. Farben munitions plants may be used for the fight against Japan.

In sports, winners and losers in the National Clay Court Championships in Chicago are Bill Talbert over Francisco Segura, and in an upset, Mrs. Sarah Palfrey Cook over Pauline Betz.

At the movies Jimmy Cagney and Sylvia Sidney star in "Blood on the Sun," while a Bing Crosby Production called "The Great John L" stars Linda Darnell and Barbara Britton. Gladys Swarthout is singing "Carmen" at Lewisohn Stadium in New York.

On radio, popular programs include the Fred Waring Show, Maggi McNellis, The Answer Man, Vincent Lopez Orchestra, and the especially popular daytime soap opera, Ma Perkins.

And Oscar Levant, close friend of George Gershwin since 1925 until the composer died in 1937, today revealed new stories about Gershwin in an interview.

The Federal Communications Commission expects that AM, FM, and TV sets will be available this October as the fledgling TV industry with virtually no sets in the marketplace poses itself a question: Does it build up programs in hopes people will buy sets or wait until people buy sets and then build up programs?

The New York Times has featured an incredible GI named PFC Chester Salvatori who has been kept in observation for a month by Army doctors because he is the eating wonder of the Army who consumes as much as 10 ordinary men. His last huge meal cost $9.95.

That's the news this July 9, 1945.

Tuesday, July 10, 1945

And now today's news, July 10, 1945.

Admiral Bull Halsey's navy planes have destroyed another 173 planes as 1,000 planes hit Japanese airfields today. The Air Force in the Pacific has now been put under General MacArthur. Notwithstanding constant severe blows, Acting Secretary of State Joseph Grew has issued a statement denying any peace feelers from Japan. ·

The Senate is having a vigorous debate today as to the difficult problems facing the U.S. as part of the U.N. on the potential use of U.S. troops in any peace keeping action. Should the U.S. Delegate have authority to commit troops or should a two-thirds vote of the Senate be required?

Mrs. Harry Truman has become Honorary Chairman of the English classics Collection of Books for Russian War Relief to replace books destroyed by the Germans. A House committee today told military and civilian planners that they must work together to prevent vast scale starvation this winter in Europe.

Two months after the war is over, a German U-boat has surrendered in Argentina and a Tokyo radio station has criticized the government for not telling the Japanese people the truth of the island by island losses.

In sports, Byron Nelson, with an eagle and Johnny Revolta are tied at 138 in the PGA Golf tournament in Dayton, Ohio.

At the movies, Monty Woolley, Gracie Fields and Beatrice Lillie are in "Molly and Me," while Robert Cummings, Lizabeth Scott and Don Defore are in "You Came Along" at the Paramount with Stan Kenton's band on stage. Francis Lederer has been signed opposite Paulette Goddard for a new film as Ona Munson joins John Wayne and Vera Ralston to shoot "Dakota."

Radio shows not to miss this week are Perry Mason, Ethel and Albert, Pepper Young's Family, Eileen Farrell Sings, A Date With Judy, the Longine Symphonette and the Victor Borge Show.

The Queen Mary arrived in New York Harbor today packed with 15,000 homebound troops including 7,000 Canadians. Another 7 ships also arrived making a total of 35,000 GI's returning to New York in one day.

Finally, Barbara Hutton is suing her third husband for divorce based on mental anguish. He is movie actor Cary Grant.

That's the news this July 10, 1945.

And now today's news, July 11, 1945.

President Truman is aboard the cruiser Augusta en route to Potsdam for a Big 3 meeting and had long meetings with Secretary of State Jimmy Byrnes and Admiral Leahy. Tomorrow morning at 9:00 the Russians will hand over civil and military control to the Americans and British in their zones in Berlin.

A report today states that 27,000 Japanese planes have been destroyed since the start of the war—the Navy bettering the Japanese by a 9 to 1 ratio and the Air Force by 2 to 1. General Claire Chennault from China says the Japanese fliers have been wiped from the skies and have retreated back to Manchuria.

Three Swiss bank accounts totaling $250,000 have been found believed to have belonged to Adolf Hitler.

The Treasury Department is looking into those 6 loans made to Brigadier General Elliott Roosevelt by John Hartford, President of the A&P.

Eamon DeValera of Ireland said today that Ireland is a Republic which has started all kinds of questions as to the present and future relationship of Ireland to the British Commonwealth.

In Italy, Benito Mussolini's widow in an interview told of her husband's plans when they were newlyweds of emigrating to the United States. She says she regrets they didn't.

In sports, Byron Nelson has eliminated Gene Sarazen 4 and 3 in the PGA in Dayton. In Washington, Connie Mack of the Philadelphia Athletics and Clark Griffith of the Washington Senators are in town with other owners to vote on a new baseball commissioner.

At the movies, "A Bell for Adano" stars John Hodiak, William Bendix and Eduardo Ciannelli, while "Nob Hill" stars George Raft, Joan Bennett, Vivian Blaine and Peggy Ann Garner. And, "1,001 Nights" has premiered featuring Evelyn Keyes, Cornel Wilde, Phil Silvers and Adele Jergens.

Radio programs you shouldn't be missing in the daytime include Life Can Be Beautiful, evening news shows by Lowell Thomas, Fulton Lewis, and Robert Trout, police stories via Mr. District Attorney, and music and comedy with the Phil Harris Show.

Oscar Hammerstein today celebrates his 50th birthday on the same day that his great show "Oklahoma" arrives at its 1,000 Broadway performance.

That's the news this July 11, 1945.

Thursday, July 12, 1945

And now today's news, July 12, 1945.

Three thousand more tons of jelly incendiaries and demolition bombs have hit four cities in Japan by 500 B-29's. The intensity of the American attack continues to grow daily.

General Eisenhower arrived back in Europe today from his triumphal U.S. visit to help close the headquarters of the Allied Expeditionary Force. His British staff is giving him a farewell banquet tonight.

It's estimated that there are still over 2.5 million displaced persons in Europe.

In Washington Col. Oveta Culp Hobby, who organized and heads the Woman's Army Corps better known as the WACS, retires on September 3rd.

In Washington Republican Senator Robert Taft of Ohio today attacked the legislation passed by the House that would set up a $10 billion dollar Bank for Reconstruction and Development. He says its a guise merely to let the U.S. loan money abroad. Democrat Senator Alben Barkley of Kentucky says he'll debate Taft on the issue.

In Argentina the campaign for the President by Col. Juan Peron started today with a major labor rally in Buenos Aires.

Two Polish economists in London report that Poland is economically exhausted. They need manpower, machinery and food as the cost of living has gone up 120 times since 1938.

Well, the baseball world has a new Commissioner—he's Senator Albert B. "Happy" Chandler of Kentucky. The owners have voted him a $50,000 salary and a 7 year contract.

With his new bride Gloria Vanderbilt in the front row, maestro Leopold Stokowski conducted the Hollywood Bowl Orchestra last evening.

Actress Luise Rainer is being married today. She was previously married to playwright Clifford Odets.

Though 75% of Frankfort was destroyed, U.S. troops have helped get electricity, water and the trolley lines going again. Mail service will start soon, Nazi administrators have been replaced, and 2,000 tons of food a week is being brought in.

A realty sale today in New York for a 6-story, 160-room hotel, a 2,000 seat theater, plus stores and offices at 138th and Broadway went for $750,000.

That's the news this July 12, 1945.

And now today's news, July 13, 1945.

American Warships today shelled the Japanese homeland 275 miles north of Tokyo for the first time in the war in combination with 1000 planes. Kamaishi was the principal target.

The Senate Foreign Relations Committee has approved the U.N. Charter by a 20 to 0 vote. Three Senators did not vote.

The U.S. has advised the Japanese government that it takes full blame for the inadvertent sinking of the Awa Maru which was sailing under Allied safe conduct while delivering food and supplies for prisoners and civilian internees. It has extended sympathies to families of those who may have died. The U.S. submarine captain has been court martialed.

A violent June 5th typhoon has ripped off the prow of the cruiser Pittsburgh which made it to port. The huge storm damaged 5 aircraft carriers, 3 battleships, 4 cruisers and 9 destroyers with the loss of only 1 life.

Japanese radio in explaining suicides of their soldiers say they were taught to fight without anxiety or worrying about the future and with peace of mind compared to Westerners who they say commit suicide out of despair.

U.S. Supreme Court Justice Robert Jackson says Nazi war criminals will be required to testify at their own trials.

The British double summer time—a war time expedient—one hour more than daylight savings time—ends tomorrow and will not recur.

Marlene Dietrich has returned from an 11 month USO tour of North Africa, Europe, Iceland and Greenland. She often played to front line combat troops.

Linda Darnell has signed with Cornel Wilde to star in "The Captain From Castille" while Walter Brennan, Ward Bond and Grant Withers are added to the cast of "Dakota."

Paris is alive with excitement for tomorrow's first free Bastille Day since 1940.

The CIO has asked President Truman to raise the minimum wage to 65 cents per hour.

The House Un-American Activities Committee has assigned an agent to look into possible subversive activities in Hollywood.

Red Hill, the home of Patrick Henry in Richmond, Virginia will be developed as a national shrine.

And, Pan Am led the stock market today with 40,000 shares traded.

That's the news this July 13, 1945.

Saturday, July 14, 1945

And now today's news, July 14,1945.

For the second day the Missouri, Iowa and Wisconsin battleships poured shells on Hokkaido along with air attacks by 1000 planes under Admiral Nimitz.

The fraternization ban has been lifted permitting American troops to talk to German adults in public places.

President Truman arrived aboard the cruiser Augusta in the English Channel en route to Berlin via Antwerp for Big Three talks. Crews of escorting British ships sounded traditional 3 cheers.

Lt. Roy Wanger of Chicago is now a civilian and in appreciation of receiving 27 life saving pints of blood overseas has just donated his first pint back to the Red Cross.

Italy has joined the Allies in declaring war on Japan.

Japanese troops have covered 35 to 50 miles through Chinese defenses below Amoy and west of Hong Kong.

The German diet is inadequate at under 1550 calories a day and the Allies will have to import food this winter to avoid famine and disorder.

The 5,000-6,000 Jews remaining of the 200,000 living in Berlin when Hitler came to power in 1933 want the same eligibility for food rations as heavy workers.

The two week old Firestone Rubber strike is over as 6000 Tampa, Florida cigar workers went out on strike.

Republican Senator Hiram Johnson of California is the sole member of the Senate Committee to oppose the new U.N. Charter. He also opposed the League of Nations under Woodrow Wilson.

"Along Came Jones" starring Gary Cooper and Dan Duryea opens this week.

After losing a double header today New York Giants manager Mel Ott is going to change the line-up to come out of 4th place.

Edward Everett Horton starts a 13 week summer show on NBC with Jo Stafford.

Finally, the Carrier Corporation President says air conditioning offers a big potential after the war in industry, commerce and in homes.

That's the news this July 14, 1945.

And now today's news, July 15, 1945.

President Truman arrives in Berlin today for a Big 3 Conference as the war in the Pacific heats up. U.S. Navy battleships Iowa, Missouri and Wisconsin have shelled the Japanese mainland for the first time pounding Muroran on South Hokkaido and other warships shelling Kamishi 275 miles north of Tokyo. And two U.S. destroyers have knocked down 38 suicide planes off Okinawa.

Former Intelligence Officer in the Far East Capt. Ellis M. Zacharias broadcasting to the Japanese war lords says the U.S. unconditional terms of surrender are similar to those imposed by the Japanese in taking Singapore on February 16, 1942.

Fifty-four year old Gen. Claire Chennault, whose flying tigers cleared the Chinese skies of Japanese aircraft, will shortly be retired as head of the 14th Air Force.

In Europe King Leopold says he will not abdicate nor will he return to Belgium from exile at this time.

With fraternization rules relaxed some U.S. troops can now be seen holding hands with German girls.

In Frankfort analysis of German loot gathered since 1934 continues. Included is 90% of German gold, 20 tons of Hungarian silver, gold coins, jewels, gold and silver cigarette cases, pearls, gold and silver church crosses and, incredibly, two valises full of gold and silver teeth from victims at concentration camps.

The U.S. Senate today asked to raise the minimum wage from 55 to 65 cents.

Joe Louis has 71 of his 85 points to become a civilian but says he wants to stay in until the end of the war.

On Broadway, Frank Fay in "Harvey" had its 300th performance yesterday, Gertrude Niesen and "Follow the Girls" is in a second year, and movies today include "Frenchman's Creek" starring Joan Fontaine and Arturo de Cordova. Frank Sinatra and Gene Kelly's new movie "Anchors Aweigh" opens this week.

Arthur Murray's dance studios have new summer rates, Hearns Store in New York has heavy steel gauge kitchen cabinets from $19 to $43 and Gimbels has screen doors at $3.25, hardwood chairs at $2.94 and ironing boards at $2.39.

That's the news this July 15, 1945.

201

Monday, July 16, 1945

And now today's news, July 16, 1945.

A Tokyo newspaper today suggests Japanese war leaders should look hard at the current situation and consider Japan's future. Meanwhile, in Potsdam, President Truman and Prime Minister Churchill await the arrival of Stalin by independently taking a tour of the Berlin ruins.

Gen. Doolittle's Pacific 8th Air Force will start bombing with B-29's from Okinawa within a few weeks. Washington has reported 261 B-29 raids in the past 13 months, dropping 90,000 tons of bombs and destroying 127 square miles of 27 Japanese cities. 51% of Tokyo has been bombed out.

Secretary of Agriculture Anderson says U.S. citizens must eat 5% less this year than last due to food shortages. In a surprise announcement, Minority leader Representative Joe Martin proposes that all nations drop compulsory conscription.

In Guam 25 Australian and U.S. newsman differ on the end of the war. Some say this year, but most say a year from now in June 1946.

A British ship today delivered 1,164 Jewish war victims to Palestine, many of them still wearing German striped concentration camp uniforms.

On the West Coast Howard Hughes has let the public see his Hercules airplane for the first time. Made completely of wood, it is 320 feet to the tips of its wings, has 8 engines, can carry a tank or 750 infantrymen. A maiden flight is scheduled for next year.

In baseball, the Detroit Tigers lead the American league by 3 over the Washington Senators and Yankees while in the National League the Chicago Cubs lead the St. Louis Cardinals and the Brooklyn Dodgers by 4.

Today on radio is My True Story, Valiant Lady, Romance of Evelyn Winters, Light of the World. Tonight hear Ginny Simms, Big Town, A Date with Judy and the Falcon.

Pepsi Cola hits the spot at 5 cents a bottle, and soon KLM Royal Dutch airlines will be flying DC-3's throughout the West Indies.

Finally in Berlin today Foreign Secretary Anthony Eden pointed to a bombed out room and said to Winston Churchill "I had dinner with Hitler right there in 1935." Churchill's response was "You certainly paid for that dinner, Anthony."

That's the news this July 16, 1945.

And now today's news, July 17, 1945.

President Truman has been chosen to preside at the Potsdam conference with Stalin and Churchill as Foreign Ministers, Jimmy Byrnes, Anthony Eden, and Vyacheslav Molotov prepare the agenda.

British and American generals say European style round-the-clock bombing will begin shortly over Japan. In the Philippines, news has been released of the slaughter by the Japanese two months ago in the village of Infanta on Luzon of 2,000 men, women and children in their homes.

From Washington an announcement today that to meet the military requirements for transportation the country's entire railroad passenger coaches have been put at the disposal of the Army.

In Belgium the Chamber of Deputies today voted 90 to 6 to continue the regency under Prince Charles and to bar the return of King Leopold. Six Catholic cabinet ministers have resigned in protest.

The start of the trial of Marshal Petain in Paris has once again been delayed as word is received that Gen. de Gaulle will visit Washington after the Potsdam conference.

United Nations officials today estimated that 4 million Germans died in battle with a total of 13 to 14 million casualties.

A newspaper ad today by RCA communications says radio-telegraph communications have been resumed to Italy, France, Belgium, Holland, Norway, the Philippines and Czechoslovakia.

In sports, the mile record of Arne Anderson of 4.02.2 was broken today in Malmo, Sweden as Swedish ace Gunder Haegg beat Anderson with a 4:01.4 world record.

On radio today is Road of Life, Joyce Jordan, Amanda, Second Husband. Tonight there's Treasury of Music, the Billie Burke Show, Phil Harris Show and a talk by President Truman.

A Buenos Aires newspaper says they believe that Adolph Hitler and Eva Braun have landed in the Antarctic in U-Boat 530. The U.S. State Department is investigating.

Finally, the phone company asks you not to tie up lines and keep your long distance to five minutes maximum.

That's the news this July 17, 1945.

And now today's news, July 18, 1945.

Notwithstanding bad weather and intense enemy ack-ack, the U.S. Navy bombed, shelled, and torpedoed what may be the last part of the Japanese Navy today at Yokosuka at the mouth of Tokyo Bay. Fifteen hundred planes were also involved.

Another bombing raid over Kyushu involved 350 European U.S. veterans flying the new A-26 Douglas invaders. In China, 6 Chinese columns mowed down hundreds of Japanese troops gaining up to 12 miles towards Kweilin and imminent recapture of the 14th Air Force base there.

The rumor that Marshal Stalin is bringing a Japanese peace feeler to the Potsdam conference has been denied.

The OPA in Washington has unfrozen 347 brand new 1942 cars causing a flood of calls to those few dealers who have kept them since the war started.

A three month inspection by Red Cross officials at Red Cross installations in Europe says maintenance of our soldiers' morale is the greatest problem as GI's see destruction, human desolation and the horror of refugees. One Red Cross official said "I don't care how much you hate the Germans, it does something to your heart."

Captain Mildred H. McAfee, director of the WAVES and President of Wellesley College, will be married soon to Rev. Dr. Douglas Horton, Chairman of the Committee for World Council of Churches.

The Navy reports that it had 383 combatant vessels and 49 warships on July 1, 1941. Including 140 major ships lost thus far in the war its fleet is now 100,000 vessels including 1,500 warships.

On radio today is David Harum, Ted Malone and Aunt Jenny's Stories. Tonight try Suspense, Now It Can Be Told, Adventures of Topper or Gabriel Heatter.

Bloomingdales bargain sales has men's slippers at $2.99, coffee tables at $12.98, men's socks at 35 cents, suspenders at 85 cents and women's dress handbags at $2.89.

Rumors of peace knocked down the stock market today almost 5 points with last hour volume of 750,000 shares and a total of 1.5 million for the day.

That's the news this July 18, 1945.

And now today's news, July 19, 1945.

With a news blackout of the whereabouts of Admiral Bull Halsey's 3rd fleet, a record force of 600 B-29's firebombed Hitachi and Choshi, a principal food production center of Japan.

President Truman gives the first state dinner tonight for Stalin and Churchill in Potsdam. Lord Louis Mountbatten returns to India today after a three day visit with General MacArthur in Manila. Back in action after kamikaze damage which killed 144 men in January is the aircraft carrier Ticonderoga.

The diaries of Count Ciano, son-in-law of the late Benito Mussolini, say that Mussolini wanted to double-cross Hitler and hoped for a German defeat but he couldn't get out of Hitler's clutches.

On the home front over 500,000 women have lost their wartime jobs due to production cutbacks implemented by Senate vote of 61 to 16. Prominent psychiatrists report demobilization of war workers may pose more nervous instability than for returning GI's.

The United States becomes the first nation to ratify the Bretton Woods resolution establishing an international institution to maintain stable currency exchanges and long-term credits for reconstruction.

In sports, former Davis Cup star Frank Shields has moved to the quarter finals of the Eastern Clay Courts Championships along with other seeded players Sidney Wood and Elwood Cooke. Secretary Forrestal has asked baseball commissioner Happy Chandler to arrange for the World Series winner to tour the South Pacific this fall.

On radio today hear Our Gal Sunday, Mary Margaret McBride and Backstage Wife. Listen to news tonight with H.V. Kaltenborn, Cecil Brown, Fulton Lewis, Jr. and Ted Husing Sports.

Oscar Hammerstein who wrote the book and lyrics to Jerome Kern's "Showboat," says today that Billy Rose has backed out of sponsoring a proposed revival at his Ziegfield Theater. In Hollywood, Bruce Cabot, Howard DaSilva and Hattie McDaniels all signed for new pictures today.

John D. Rockefeller, Jr. has given $300,000 to the National War Fund to help servicemen and a Miami official states that the $35 million estate of William K. Vanderbilt has been taxed $25 million by the government, and another 5 million by New York State, leaving only $5 million for his widow.

That's the news this July 19, 1945.

Friday, July 20, 1945

And now today's news, July 20, 1945.

The American flag that flew over the Capitol in Washington on December 7th 1941 was raised today in Berlin as President Harry S. Truman said the United States wants no territory, only peace and world prosperity.

In Berlin there is a major drive by Americans, British and Soviet troops to quell the raging black market.

Francisco Franco of Spain has shaken up his cabinet as 9 ministers have resigned while new members are said to be less monarchistic.

The House has approved a tax relief bill to provide $5 billion to industry for post war conversion and expansion.

31,000 more troops have arrived on six ships in New York harbor including once again the Queen Elizabeth.

A Navy flier and a commander of a gun battery on Wake Island have described in detail the heroic 14 day stand in December 1941 of the battle for the island. Both were taken prisoners by the Japanese and beaten during their three year imprisonment.

94 P-51 Mustangs took a 1600 mile round trip from Iwo Jima to machine gun and rocket enemy airfields, factories and oil plants in the Nagoya-Osaka area.

Former French Premier Paul Reynaud blames Marshal Petain who succeeded him in 1940 for giving in to the Nazis. Petain had Reynaud arrested and imprisoned.

Two pianists performed for Stalin and Churchill in Berlin at the Big Three concerts. The first was noted pianist Sgt. Eugene List who was toasted and praised by Stalin and Churchill. He was followed by another noted pianist, Harry S. Truman, who played Beethoven's Minuet in G.

At the movies Tom Conway and Edward Brophy are in "The Falcon in San Francisco" and about to go in production is "The Common Sin" with Van Johnson and "Finnegans Folly" with Barry Fitzgerald. George Barbier who played bombastic businessmen and flabbergasted husbands in 40 movies is dead at 80.

Stage and screen pianist Hazel Scott will marry Congressman Adam Clayton Powell on August 1st with a reception at Cafe Society Uptown where she first became well known.

Finally, New York City plans to invest $160 million to build a new airport at Idlewild in Queens.

That's the news this July 20, 1945.

And now today's news, July 21, 1945.

Ships and planes of Admiral Nimitz's Third Fleet again shelled and bombed Japan this time 50 miles north of Tokyo and received no opposition.

Marine General Allen Turnage says Marines are being massed in the Mariannas, on Okinawa and Iwo Jima ready to go ashore in amphibious operations as strategy directs.

Nuremberg has been tentatively selected as the site for Nazi war criminals trial. A British victory parade with tanks and troops in Berlin today was reviewed by Winston Churchill.

2605 German war prisoners in the United States will be sent back to Germany as prisoners to use their past experience to mine desperately needed coal.

A new Glenn Martin giant flying boat called the Hawaii Mars has been publicly shown. 72¼ tons, with a wing span of 200 feet, this first of 20 supercargo planes will fly at 225 mph.

As a final message in his role as Supreme Commander of SHEAF, General Eisenhower today has bid farewell to U.S. and British staff. Meanwhile, Kansans have started the Eisenhower Foundation which will include maintaining the home he and his five brothers grew up in.

Tens of thousands of prisoners were killed and experimented on in so-called Nazi medical experiments in prison camps. American medical officers have found no positive contributions as a result.

The reconditioned giant ocean liner Europa, which for four years was used as a billet for German soldiers, leaves September 1st to bring back 5000 men.

President Day of Cornell University will have compulsory physical training for freshmen and sophomores in various sports. This evolved from 3 years of campus conditioning of Army and Navy personnel.

Tonight composer Sigmund Romberg, famed for "Up In Central Park," "The Desert Song," and "The Student Prince" will conduct the Philharmonic Symphony Orchestra at Lewisohn Stadium in New York with soprano Victoria School and baritone Robert Merrill.

A new movie this week is "Wilson" starring Alexander Knox as Woodrow Wilson with Charles Coburn, Thomas Mitchell and William Eythe.

Finally, leave it to the Americans. To serve ships too small to have their own ice cream facilities, the Navy is planning a $1 million barge capable of making 10 gallons every 7 minutes. In the hot Pacific, business should be brisk.

That's the news this July 21, 1945.

And now today's news, July 22, 1945.

Over the weekend, Generalissimo Francisco Franco shook up the Spanish cabinet as 9 of 13 ministers resigned.

At Potsdam, President Truman says the U.S. has no territorial or monetary ambitions, aiming only to bring peace and prosperity to the world as the Allied powers have agreed to hold a mass trial of leading war criminals in Nuremberg, the Nazi "shrine city." Finally, the Big Three has warned Japan it must consider unconditional surrender soon or miss the opportunity forever.

In the war, 30 Japanese ships have been bombed by planes from the Philippines off the coast of China and Malaya and an American destroyer force has sailed 5 miles beyond Majima Cape into Tokyo waters and has sunk 4 ships. Four Chinese armies are closing in on Kweilin, site of the most important American 14th Air Force base lost to the enemy last fall.

In New York, for the first time Tammany Hall has endorsed a Communist for public office. He is Benjamin Davies, Jr., running for re-election to the City Council.

The Office of Defense Transportation has banned organized group train travel, such as "all-expense tours," effective immediately.

A break for soldiers with slightly less than 85 points makes them eligible for discharge within a few days.

Washington announces that home heating oil is expected to be in short supply soon because of the war against Japan, but gasoline supplies will be adequate. Also, there will be no increase in lard, grease and fat supplies till next spring.

Marshal Henri Petain will appear in full uniform when his long postponed treason trial finally opens in Paris today.

In the movie world, actress Sally Eilers has been signed to star in "Make Yourself at Home" due in late September in New York.

That's the news this July 22, 1945.

And now today's news, July 23, 1945.

B-29's today dropped almost 4,000 tons of bombs on 80-square miles in the Osaka-Nagoya area in Japan. More than 600 Superforts took part in the raid. Chinese troops have captured 3 towns in the Kweilin area on the mainland of China.

Rioting broke out at the trial of Marshal Petain in Paris as he challenged the jurisdiction of the court and said he would not answer their questions. U.S. Ambassador Spruille Braden received an enthusiastic welcome today in Buenos Aires by thousands of Argentinians.

More than 80 thousand Germans have been arrested by 500 thousand American troops during a massive surprise search in homes and on highways for fugitives and contraband .

Japanese leaders are preparing the people for bad news in the form of "fresh, vigorous" Russian policy in the East. Russia and China are said to be nearing an understanding never achieved before by the two nations.

Here at home, Fred Vinson is being sworn in today as the new Secretary of the Treasury replacing Henry Morgenthau, Jr.

President Truman has set August 1st as Air Force Day to be observed throughout the nation and overseas wherever possible.

Congressional House members will not have to pay income tax on their $2,500 expense allowance if their returns state the money was "fully expended in the performance of official duties."

Administration officials are studying a plan that would establish a new department of Welfare and Security and a new secretary who would become the 11th Cabinet member.

In baseball, Yankee manager Joe McCarthy has tried to resign again saying he is sick but President Larry MacPhail simply refuses to listen.

A reduction of 1 or 2 points in the ration value of almost all cuts of beef, veal and lamb will go into effect on Sunday.

That's the news this July 23, 1945.

Tuesday, July 24, 1945

And now today's news, July 24, 1945.

At least 7 of Japan's remaining warships have been damaged during a carrier strike against the naval base at Kure and other ports of Japan's inland seas. The enemy homeland was also bombed.

Major General Curtis LeMay, former European Air Force General and designer of the low-level devastating March fire raids over Japan, has been promoted to Chief of Staff for General Spaatz, Commanding General of the Strategic Air Forces in the Pacific.

The Potsdam conference is going into recess to allow British representatives to return to England where the results of the recent election will be announced tomorrow.

Benito Mussolini's son Vittorio and his nephew Vito appear likely to face war criminal charges in Italy. Meanwhile, it's been revealed that 90% of Italy's art treasures escaped all injury during the war.

Here at home, Henry Morgenthau, Jr. says President Truman asked him to resign as Secretary of the Treasury against his wishes.

The Navy has announced the establishment of an age-service point system which will release some 35,000 older enlisted men and officers by December.

Membership pressure has forced Tammany Hall to withdraw the endorsement of Communist Benjamin Davies for re-election to the New York City Council announced just 2 days ago.

The Brotherhood of Locomotive Engineers and the Brotherhood of Railroad Trainmen have filed demands for a hike of 25% in wages with a minimum raise of $2.50 a day.

A new ration book, number 5, will be issued in December. You'll be glad to know it will be smaller in size and easier to handle.

New York Yankee Manager Joe McCarthy's personal physician says McCarthy is indeed in a greatly weakened and debilitated state but doesn't appear to have a serious ailment.

The famed Salzburg Music Festival, discontinued since 1939 because of the war, will resume on a restricted basis on August 12th.

Opening today at the movies, Betty Hutton stars in "Incendiary Blonde," the biography of Texas Guinan.

That's the news this July 24, 1945.

And now today's news, July 25, 1945.

Admiral Lord Louis Mountbatten has talked with the Big 3 following his Manila talks with General MacArthur. Rumors have it Mountbatten may be given a Pacific command leaving MacArthur free to pursue the war against Japan.

B-29's again have hit Japan's oil supplies, bombing 3 big refineries at Kawasaki 10 miles south of Tokyo.

Chinese forces have taken Hanshon and have driven into the former American air base at Yangso.

Tokyo Radio is reported as saying that if American peace terms were lenient enough Japan might call off the war.

Allied officials in Berlin have reached agreement on a number of items regarding uniform civilian control and the economy in Germany.

Marshal Henri Petain refused to answer questions at his treason trial about whether he had congratulated Hitler on the English defeat at Dieppe and asked Hitler's permission for French troops to fight with the Germans.

The U.S. Army will open a big school in England next week at Shrivenham with a student body and faculty of 4,000. A similar school will open August 20 at Biarritz, France.

A temporary truce has been called in the labor problems at Packard Motor Car Company in Detroit while 5 New Jersey plants of Wright Aeronautical Corporation have been hit by wildcat walkouts.

A multi-million dollar medium-rent housing project will be built just south of the Polo Grounds in Harlem after the war.

In sports, Del Webb, co-owner of the New York Yankees, says if Joe McCarthy quits as manager it will be because of illness, nothing else.

John Carradine will recreate John Barrymore's role in "My Dear Children," opening at the Brighton Theater August 5th.

That's the news this July 25, 1945.

211

Thursday, July 26, 1945

And now today's news, July 26, 1945.

In a stunning upset, Winston Churchill's Conservatives have been defeated by the Laborites. Liberal candidates were also defeated. As a result, Churchill has resigned as Britain's Prime Minister and has been replaced by Clement Attlee who has pledged to finish the war with Japan and to cooperate with the U.S. and Russia. Meanwhile, the Allies have warned Japan to surrender unconditionally or face prompt and utter destruction.

In the war B-29 incendiary bombs have set on fire the 3 industrial cities of Honshu, Shukoku and Kyushu.

President Truman, reviewing troops in Germany, says he will follow Franklin D. Roosevelt's ideas and pledge a free world.

A coal shortage is expected to hit northwestern Europe this winter and experts are urging an increase in the production of the Ruhr coal mines.

Here at home, there'll be more sugar and about 11% more meat available for civilians in August, but there may be fewer canned goods on grocery shelves.

Chrysler Company officials have refused to hear union grievances at the Dodge Plant until the workers call off their strike. Meanwhile, some 2,500 wildcat strikers at Wright Aeronautical plants in New Jersey have returned to work, but workers at the Paterson plant have voted to stay out.

The 2,200 ton destroyer "Joseph P. Kennedy," honoring the late son of Ambassador Joseph P. Kennedy, was launched today at Quincy, Massachusetts.

The first sheet of 1 cent Roosevelt memorial postage stamps was presented today to Eleanor Roosevelt.

Walter Winchell has declined an invitation to appear in "The Magnificent Heel." He says no play about a columnist has ever been successful.

Bethlehem Steel reports second quarter earnings of slightly over $8 million, equal to $2.15 a common share.

That's the news this July 26, 1945.

212

And now today's news, July 27, 1945.

20th Air Force Gen. Curtis LeMay today had B-29's drop leaflets on 11 Japanese cities announcing they would be bombed, four of them in the next few days. Saipan radio has repeated the unusual challenge.

A Japanese news agency says the Allied ultimatum to surrender will be ignored. A former American born war correspondent for the Japanese Domei Agency, Ken Murayana, says he believes Japan will surrender during the next few weeks. Marine General Holland Smith says he believes it will happen in six months.

It's now reported that the battleship California was hit by a kamikaze last January 9th in the Lingayan Gulf with 203 casualties including 32 killed and 3 missing.

Meantime, new Prime Minister Clement Attlee, bringing new Foreign Minister Ernest Bevin with him, has arrived in Berlin to replace Winston Churchill.

In the fifth day of the trial, former Premier Leon Blum of France told the High Court of Justice today in Paris that Henri Petain morally betrayed France. In Norway the trial of Vidkun Quisling begins August 1st.

The U.S. Chief of Air Technical Services at Wright Field says while the U.S. was ahead of Germany in most technical and medical areas, he praised their invention of an ejection seat for pilots to catapult them out in an emergency.

The National Convention of the American Communist Party will disband the organization and reconstitute the Communist party with a stern warning to past Executive Director Earl Browder.

Novelist and playwright Booth Tarkington wants a ceiling on armaments for all countries.

In Hollywood, MGM has acquired rights to the "A Date With Judy" radio show to star Jane Powell in a film version while Gregory Peck, Maureen O'Hara and Jeanne Crain probably will be signed for "Berkeley Square."

New movies this week include "The Frozen Ghost" with Lon Chaney, Douglas Dumbrille and Elena Verdugo plus "Christmas in Connecticut" with Barbara Stanwyck, Dennis Morgan, Sidney Greenstreet, and S.Z. Sakall.

In sports at the All American Golf Tournament in Chicago, Byron Nelson leads by 4 strokes over Gene Sarazen followed by Lt. Ben Hogan, Sam Snead, and Ralph Gudahl.

Finally, singer Grace Moore, back from 2 months overseas with the USO, says faithless wives of GI's at home ought to have their hair shaved off like the women in Nazi dominated countries.

That's the news this July 27, 1945.

And now today's news, July 28, 1945.

A B-25 bomber lost in the fog over New York City crashed into the Empire State Building this morning at 9:49. Hitting the 79th floor, it created an 18 x 20 foot hole, killed 13 and injured 26. Ambulances from hospitals and the Red Cross promptly responded to the tragedy as airplane gasoline set fires on the 78th and 79th floors and bodies exploded out the side of the building. The war decorated pilot flying from Bedford, Massachusetts to La Guardia was advised to land there but he asked for weather information at Newark apparently in hopes it would be clear.

Between 550-600 B-29's fired six cities today as promised yesterday by General LeMay. New B-32 bombers are now in action over Formosa.

A new British 12th Army claims a record kill of 5500 Japanese in one week in Burma along the Sittany River.

The Red Cross says 2400 Red Cross aides are now in the Pacific at 700 installations with plans for a total of 6000 in months to come.

In a secret recently uncovered 23-page book, Adolph Hitler's plans for what he expected to be a conquered England by September 9, 1940 included a plan to ship all Englishmen between ages 17 and 45 to the continent as labor to prepare for Hitler's later invasion of Russia.

While Hermann Goering had a heart attack two days ago, he has been advised he will be in court at the war criminal trials even if he has to be brought on a stretcher.

General Omar Bradley has been named to head the Veterans Administration.

A new movie this week features Beulah Bondi, Betty Field, and Zachary Scott in "The Southerner."

Finally, a few furniture prices in New York has Sterns selling a bedroom set with bed and two dressers for $145 to $195 and Simmons mattresses at $24.95. Over at Hearns is a 9 piece dining room set at $259. And, though it is summer time, Finchleys is selling woolen sports jackets for men at $35 to $50.

That's the news this July 28, 1945.

And now today's news, July 29, 1945.

Over the weekend, after warning pamphlets were dropped, six Japanese cities were set on fire by B-29 bombers. Additionally more than 1,000 American and British carrier planes smashed transport, airfield and other military targets in the Tokyo area as battleships shelled Hamamatsu. Japan, meantime, has rejected the warning to surrender.

The U.N. Security Charter has been ratified by the U.S. Senate, 89-2, 107 days after the death of Franklin D. Roosevelt. William Langer, of North Dakota and Henrik Shipstead, of Minnesota, were the two who voted against it. Both are Republicans.

The American Communist Party has shelved Earl Browder and Robert Minor, veteran party leaders in this country.

The French Consultative Assembly has defeated Charles de Gaulle's proposal for a referendum on a constitutional convention despite his threat to resign if it lost.

British Prime Minister Clement Attlee who has replaced defeated Winston Churchill, has taken his oath of office in London along with six ministers.

A "No Sunday Work" strike in England again inconvenienced thousands of British holiday makers. It was the 4th in a series of Sunday work stoppages.

The British 8th Army, which fought in North Africa and Europe, has been disbanded. The 13th Corps remains as an occupation force in Europe.

In sports, New York Yankee president Larry MacPhail is defending the sale of Hank Borowy to the St. Louis Cardinals for $100,000 in cash and players, and has dismissed criticism by Branch Rickey and Clark Griffith. Griffith wants an immediate waiver rule change because of the Borowy deal.

On the radio, CBS will launch a new game show, "Give and Take" with John Reed King as host at 10 am Saturday, August 25th.

That's the news this July 29, 1945.

215

Monday, July 30, 1945

And now today's news, July 30, 1945.

American destroyers have sailed into Suruga Bay and shelled Shimizu, 80 miles southwest of Tokyo. Meanwhile, an influential Tokyo newspaper has demanded that national defense be put on a priority basis following Japan's rejection of a surrender ultimatum.

Russian Premier Stalin is expected to rejoin the Big 3 conference in Berlin. He has been incapacitated for the past 2 days.

Chinese Premier Soong has resigned as Foreign Minister in a reorganization of the Chinese cabinet.

The Mediterranean Allied Forces that bombed Germans over a wide area have been disbanded.

The Arab office in London says Arabs would never agree to a Jewish home state in Palestine.

Justice Robert Jackson says he will resign as the U.S. representative if things don't speed up at the trial for international war criminals.

In this country, Brigadier General Elliott Roosevelt will leave the military on August 15. He has asked to be released.

A new wind tunnel at United Aircraft Corporation is expected to be a big help in building new planes that will fly at the speed of sound.

Republican leaders are calling for the appointment of more Republicans as Federal judges, particularly one to succeed Justice Owen Roberts who has resigned from the Supreme Court.

The main plant at Detroit and a subsidiary plant of U.S. Rubber Company has been taken over by the U.S. Army in an effort to halt a 17-day work stoppage. Bob Coleman has resigned as manager of the Boston Braves, although he has more than a year to go on his contract.

Byron Nelson captured the All-American open gold tournament with a record 72 hole total of 269, 19 under par.

Finally, experts are predicting a shortage of sugar for at least 9 months and perhaps for a year.

That's the news this July 30, 1945.

And now today's news, July 31, 1945.

Okinawa-based planes have hit shipping and airfields in Japan's Kyushu area, and the U.S. has warned Japan against moving American war prisoners and interned civilians to areas that are targets for bombing raids.

Meanwhile, Allied forces have now wiped out some 7,000 Japanese troops trying to escape a jungle trap in lower Burma.

Pierre Laval of France has surrendered to the U.S. Army in Austria.

President Truman plans to meet with King George VI before returning home from the Big 3 meeting. Russia's Premier Stalin, who has been ill, is attending today's session.

Sir Harold Alexander has been named Governor General of Canada succeeding the Earl of Athlone.

Lawyers for Marshal Petain are expected to ask for a delay in his treason trial so they can call Pierre Laval as a defense witness.

Elliott Roosevelt has strongly denied that his father had ever helped him with his financial dealings, particularly a $200,000 loan from John Hartford.

The Southern California Restaurant Association says lack of red ration points will force 90% of their restaurants to close within 2 weeks.

Gas stoves have been taken off the ration list but not the liquefied petroleum gas which many of them burn.

The shortage of experienced coal miners may produce a coal shortage and reduced work week this winter unless 30,000 miners are furloughed from military service.

U.S. Steel had income of $32 million in the first half of 1945, equal to $2.24 a share.

Fred Astaire has been named to replace Paul Draper in the musical "Blue Skies."

That's the news this July 31, 1945.

217

Wednesday, August 1, 1945

And now today's news, August 1, 1945.

General Curtis LeMay, before retiring as head of the 20th Airforce, has warned 12 Japanese industrial and rail cities that they will be firebombed in a few days.

Army Air Forces Day is being celebrated throughout the nation and by all Army Air Forces stations in the world marking the 38th anniversary of the AAF. The world's fastest airplane with the most powerful jet engine can be made ready for the Japanese war if needed. It is the Lockheed Shooting Star P-80, produced by Lockheed and GE which today, traveling at almost the speed of sound, flew from Dayton, Ohio to New York City in 62 minutes. Meanwhile, an Army transport C-69 has flown from New York to Paris in 14 hours 12 minutes. British heavy bombers will join the U.S. Air Forces in the Pacific as soon as there are airfields ready to handle them.

Chinese troops have captured the Japanese-held base at Pinglo in southeastern China.

About 50% of the $340 million that Rumania will pay Russia in reparations during the next 6 years will be in petroleum and oil products. Pierre Laval has been taken to the Fresnes (Fren) prison in Paris to await trial for treason. He is expected to be tried in about 2 months.

Here at home, William O'Dwyer has resigned as District Attorney of Kings County to devote his full time to his campaign to become Mayor of New York.

The government is promising 10 million pounds more butter in August than originally allotted, but the ration value will not be cut.

The Navy Seabee Magazine has suggested that the 1945 World Series be played in the South Pacific.

A new company, Selznick International Pictures of England, has been formed with J. Arthur Rank as Chairman and David Selznick in charge of production.

Finally, "A Bell for Adano" goes into its 5th week at Radio City Music Hall today.

That's the news this August 1, 1945.

And now today's news, August 2, 1945.

The Big 3 Conference in Berlin ended early this morning. There was no immediate communique, but a later announcement reveals that Germany will be decentralized economically and politically as soon as possible. New borders have not been released, though East Prussia and large areas along the Oder River will be taken away. A Council of Foreign Ministers, including those of France and China, has been created to propose tentative peace agreements for all European Axis countries besides Germany.

President Truman will meet today with King George VI in Plymouth, England.

Japan was hit early today by the largest single air attack ever struck as 830 B-29's dropped over 6,600 tons of bombs on 4 cities and a petroleum plant on Honshu. Other planes hit Kyushu and Nagasaki which was left in flames.

The trial judge has ruled that Pierre Laval must testify tomorrow at Marshal Petain's treason trial.

The Allied Commission has announced the freeing of almost all of Italy's foreign trade so other countries can deal directly with the Italian government and commercial agencies.

The Swedish motorship Gripsholm landed at Jersey City today with 1,509 passengers on its 14th trip of the war, and the Queen Mary brought almost 15,000 GI passengers to New York City.

Army Secretary Stimson says the Army discharge point system will not be revised till next year.

Pietro Mascagni, composer of "Cavalleria Rusticana," has died at the age of 81 of bronchial pneumonia and former Fordham basetball coach Edward Kelleher suffered a fatal heart attack in Munich today. He was 50.

Dodgers president Branch Rickey has proposed that his club and the Giants and Yankees enter a 5-year agreement not to play more than 7 night games a season.

That's the news this August 2, 1945.

Friday, August 3, 1945

And now today's news, August 3, 1945.

Every major Japanese harbor has now been mined and plugged up by B-29's mining operations. Major Korean ports have also been mined. A Japanese newspaper has predicted an Allied invasion within one or two months.

Chinese troops have captured Sinning and are within 12 miles of the former Flying Tiger airfield of Lingling. Lt. General Albert Wedemeyer says Chinese troops are ready for big offensives that will use paratroopers.

Gen. George C. Kenney's Far East Air Forces in the last seven months have destroyed 1375 enemy planes and sunk 2.8 million tons of Japanese shipping.

The War trials are now scheduled to start on September 1st at the German Palace of Justice in Nuremberg. Major war criminals will be held in the local jail.

Pierre Laval testifying at Marshal Petain's treason trial, himself known as the #1 French collaborator, says Marshal Petain approved Laval's broadcast of June 22, 1942 hoping for a German victory.

Hitler's half brother Alois has been released from 6 weeks detainment it being clear he was scared stiff of being associated with the Fuhrer. He was a Berlin bartender during most of the war.

As of July 30th over 4 million displaced persons in Europe have been repatriated.

Democratic Senator Burton K. Wheeler of Montana says as soon as U.S. troops leave Europe he expects revolutions all over. The War Department says so far there are no disorders by Germans in U.S. zones in Germany noting even respect is shown by most of them for the U.S military government.

Five troops ships have brought 6124 troops into Boston Harbor.

The French conservative assembly wants to break diplomatic ties with Franco Spain.

Yale University has adapted sweeping changes in its curriculum starting September 1946 that will include required summer reading courses, a first at any college.

Dr. Harold Taylor at age 30 has become one of the youngest college presidents in the country in assuming that position at Sarah Lawrence in Bronxville, New York.

The City of Memphis has banned the 8 year old film "Dead End" as not proper to show to youth feeling it would encourage crime. The city had already banned "Dillinger" for the same reason recently.

Only 500,000 shares traded on the New York Stock Exchange today, the lightest in 11 months. Graham Paige led with 36,000 shares traded.

That's the news this August 3, 1945.

And now today's news, August 4, 1945.

12 more Japanese cities totalling almost 1.5 million people have been warned they will be destroyed by fire bombs following similar warnings to 10 other cities and subsequent B-29 bombings this past week. In the South Pacific, P-38's from the Philippines blasted Surabaya in Java involving a 2300 mile mission.

For the first time General Douglas MacArthur has assumed control of the Japan mainland operation. However, Lt. General James Doolittle's 8th Air Force will be based in Okinawa remaining separate from General MacArthur's command.

Japanese radio says they expect 800,000 Allied troops to invade but that it would repel such an invasion with suicide pilots and newly developed wooden planes.

The first trainload of 70,000 Germans has left Norway to go home via Sweden in cattle cars. Required to bring their own food for the 48-hour trip to Trelleborg, the Swedes are providing them only water.

The majority Italian party—the Christian Democrats—are now on record in favor of a republic and not a monarchy.

The U.S. State Department says under the new U.N. mandate U.S. troops can be used without congressional approval.

Instead of using slower trains, 25,000 troops a month will be flown from the East Coast to the West Coast en route to the Pacific using 68 C-47's under the supervision of TWA, American, Northwest and United Airlines but flown by 200 Army Air Force pilots.

Moscow has revealed a new helicopter with double wings and two propellers, a speed of 100 m.p.h., landings at zero speed and capable of going backward.

New movies this week include Fred MacMurray and Lynn Bari in "Captain Eddie," a biography of World War I air ace Eddie Rickenbacker, and "West of the Pecos" starring Robert Mitchum.

Finally, Don Ameche will be back with Edgar Bergen and Charlie McCarthy this fall and Hollywood columnist Hedda Hopper will switch from CBS to NBC.

That's the news this August 4, 1945.

Sunday, August 5, 1945

And now today's news, August 5, 1945.

As American military men tell the Japanese which specific 12 cities next will be bombed, P-38 Lightnings have hit Java from the Philippines. An invasion jittery Japanese radio station has suggested if the Americans can land 300,000 men on Japan they probably will win.

The Navy has announced that the 24-year-old battleship West Virginia which was sunk at Pearl Harbor has been in the middle of battle since it was raised in shellings at Iwo Jima, Okinawa and the Philippines. Retribution at last!

Near the Philippines U.S. Navy personnel have boarded a Japanese Hospital ship with clear Red Cross markings. Aboard they found 1,500 men with no wounds under their bandages and stores of guns and ammunition in the sick bay.

In Paris, Pierre Laval has defended Marshal Petain at his trial stating that Petain secretly defied the Nazis in Africa ordering French troops to aid the Allies.

In New Haven, Connecticut, a special study committee has recommended to Yale University that it establish a strong post-war religion department to develop greater spiritual and ethical values among the students.

In Germany the son of the late Field Marshal General Erwin Rommel says his father—known as the Desert Fox—committed suicide to avoid the penalty of death for his involvement in the 1944 bomb plot to kill Hitler.

The fourth son of President Theodore Roosevelt, Lt. Colonel Archibald Roosevelt, is retiring. Three other sons gave their lives in service—Quentin in World War I and Theodore, Jr. and Kermit in the present war.

In sports, Byron Nelson today captured his tenth straight tournament, the $10,000 Canadian Open.

The City of Trenton, New Jersey today declared a quarantine for all children under 15 due to an outbreak of 185 cases of infantile paralysis. Eight have died. No youngsters at movies, stores, churches, Sunday Schools, or other gatherings.

That's the news is August 5, 1945.

And now today's news, August 6,1945.

An incredible announcement has just been made by President Truman from the cruiser Augusta—the world's first atomic bomb was dropped today on the city of Hiroshima, Japan by a single B-29 aircraft. This splitting of the uranium atom produced a bomb equal to 20,000 tons of TNT as a new age of destruction and peaceful power has been ushered in.

An impenetrable cloud of dust over Hiroshima has thus far prevented aerial photos to determine the degree of damage caused by this bomb estimated to weigh 400 pounds and equal to 2,000 times the destruction of any other existing bomb. President Truman's solemn announcement said that since the Japanese refused the ultimatum to surrender on July 26th, the atomic bomb was used to spare the Japanese population a rain of ruin never before seen. Winston Churchill has stated "By God's mercy Britain and American science have outpaced German efforts" in developing a similar bomb.

Overseas radio is telling Japanese what has been dropped on Hiroshima in hopes they will surrender. Secretary of War Stimson says the bomb will be a tremendous aid in ending the war.

The atomic theory of Princeton resident Professor Albert Einstein has now been put into practical use.

It was also announced that the first test occurred on July 16th near Alamagordo, New Mexico with scientists reaching into the unknown at least 10,000 feet away. The bomb vaporized an immense steel tower and sent a cloud 40,000 feet high. The $2 billion atomic project has involved almost 100,000 people in Oak Ridge, Tennessee, in a new town of 17,000 in Richland, Washington, and 7,000 in the new town of Las Alamos in New Mexico. Few employees knew what they were working on. Among those involved have been Major General Leslie Groves in charge of what has been called the Manhattan Project, Dr. J. Robert Oppenheimer, Dr. James B. Conant, Professor Harold Urey, Dr. Neils Bohr, Dr. Vannevar Bush and Dr. Enrico Fermi.

We repeat, the world's first atomic bomb has been dropped on a city in Japan named Hiroshima doubtlessly destroying most of the city.

As reaction comes in from around the world, we will report further on this incredible news—the splitting of the atom and the atom bomb dropped on Hiroshima today.

That's the news this August 6, 1945.

Tuesday, August 7, 1945

And now today's news, August 7,1945.

Reconnaissance photos of yesterday's atom bomb raid on Hiroshima shows that 60% of the city was wiped out. It's believed that much of the terrible destruction on this city of 343,000 was due to concussion of the bomb in a split second. Pilot of the B-29 Enola Gay, named after his 57-year-old mother, was Col. Paul Tibbets who besides the crew was joined by Captain Williams Parsons ordnance designer of the 400 pound bomb. The bombardier was Major Thomas Ferebee. The flash of the bomb, brighter than sunlight—was seen for hundreds of miles. The Vatican in Rome has deplored the use of the bomb noting it remains "a temptation for posterity."

Gen. Carl Spaatz says a B-29 atomic fleet is ready to go if necessary. An eminent French physicist Duc de Broglie says the fabulous energy of the atomic bomb will soon replace power generated by coal, oil and water. U.S. scientists say atomic energy in the distant future may power airplanes, while U.S. technical consultant Dr. Delya Bramis says peaceful power is a long way off. William B. Stout of the Society of Automotive Engineers says an atomic automobile engine the size of a man's fist is in the cards for the future. Professor Albert Einstein, on vacation at Saranac Lake, says he had no role in the development of the bomb and won't speak about it.

In the Pacific a man known as the "flyingist gunner in the Army Air Force" has been lost on a B-29 raid. He flew 107 combat missions in three theaters of war.

Tokyo Rose—known to hundreds of thousands of GI's as a radio personality talking about home-sweet-home, and girlfriends while she played Big Band music to presumably cause poor morale, has been given a Navy Citation by top brass for actually improving morale.

A major new development in research is reported today as Alfred P. Sloan, President of General Motors and his Vice President of Research, Dr. Charles F. Ketttering, have funded $4 million to start the Sloan-Kettering Institute for Cancer Research in New York City.

Finally, near Burbank, California two days ago, America's #1 air ace, Major Richard Bong, has been killed while testing a new P-80 jet fighter.

That's the news this August 7, 1945.

And now today's news, August 8, 1945.

In the shortest press conference on record today, President Truman announced that Russia has declared war on Japan as announced in Russia by Foreign Commissar Molotov. The Red Army has already hit the Manchurian Border as bombers hit inside China as well. Thirty-five nations are now at war with Japan.

Japanese radio today reported nearly every citizen was killed at Hiroshima even as another 385 B-29's bombed Tokyo arsenals. The U.S. Third Fleet hit Northern Honshu today with British carriers. President Truman will speak to the nation later tonight.

Dr. J. Robert Oppenheimer, involved in the atomic bomb development, says that he and other scientists find no reason to feel radioactivity will linger at the bomb sites.

In Washington, Bryon Price, Director of Censorship, says the atomic bomb project was the best held secret of the war. He praised newspapers, radio stations, magazine and books for voluntarily withholding any information about new secret military weapons. Notwithstanding freedom of the press, over 20,000 media outlets were so advised not to report on any military experiments or new developments and nobody did.

Washington reported another 550 Navy and Army casualties today.

Herbert H. Lehman, Director General of the United Nations Relief and Rehabilitation Administration—better known as UNRRA—says $1.5 million will be needed in 1946 to care for the helpless in Europe.

The Army has discontinued the use of powered sulfanilamide for wounds in battle stating after 3 experimental years it has not eliminated all infection. They have also discontinued dispensing 8 sulfa tablets to GI's who have hoarded them for improper self-treatment of gonorrhea.

On radio, current listening on the NBC station WEAF is Fred Waring with other features including David Harum, Don Goddard News at Noon, Maggi McNellis, Jack Smith Sings and Mary Margaret McBride at 1 pm.

"Captain Eddie," the biography of Capt. Eddie Rickenbacker, features Fred MacMurray and Lynn Bari, and Danny Kaye is in the 9th week of "Wonder Man" at the Astor in New York.

Finally, 37-year-old Justin Dart, President of United Drug, has turned down the Presidency of Montgomery Ward.

That's the news this August 8, 1945.

Thursday, August 9, 1945

And now today's news, August 9, 1945.

On nationwide radio President Truman today threatened Japan with atomic obliteration if they don't surrender, as today the United States dropped its second atom bomb on the Japanese city of Nagasaki. A mushroom cloud of dust still covers the city of 253,000. It is hoped this one-two punch today of Russian involvement and the second bomb may bring Japan to the surrender table.

B-29's have dropped millions of leaflets over Japan telling about the atomic bomb with promises of more to come as well as reporting on Russia's war declaration.

Notwithstanding the new Russian involvement, Admiral Lord Louis Mountbatten says he'll continue his battle plans in S.E. Asia. A story that now can be told from Sweden tells of B-17's and Norwegian saboteurs wrecking heavy water plants as Germans tried to develop their own atomic bomb.

Two church and civic leaders, Bishop G. Bromley Oxnam, President of the Federal Council of Churches and John Foster Dulles, Chairman of the Commission on Just and Durable Peace have urged cessation of any future use of atomic bombs before such warfare becomes commonplace and acceptable.

Under Secretary of War Robert P. Patterson says there are 400,000 Italian and German war prisoners in the United States who will be going home soon. Five thousand sick and wounded have already been returned.

The Committee of Catholics for Human Rights has assailed Sen. Bilbo of Mississippi for feeding the flames of bigotry and discrimination.

In sports, Manager Joe McCarthy returned to the Yankees today after a three week illness.

Good radio listening today includes Queen For A Day, Betty Crocker, Martha Dean, Ma Perkins, Pepper Young's Family, Right to Happiness and news at 4 with Westbrook Van Voorhees.

A plan to revolutionize nationwide FM and TV viewing was unveiled today by Westinghouse and the Glenn Martin Aircraft Factory proposing to transmit radio and TV signals to 14 airplanes who in turn retransmit to reach 78% of the U.S. Network officials agree this could make existing present networks a thing of the past and usher in a new age of entertainment.

Mild Kirkman soap is 5 cents, men can avoid 5 o'clock shadow with Gem blades, Canada Dry's new Spur Cola is 5 cents a bottle, and Phoenix Mutual has a plan to show how you can retire on $150 a month.

Finally, Amanda Siegel, the sister of Bob Ford, the man who shot and killed the famed outlaw Jesse James in 1882, died today at the age of 90.

That's the news this August 9, 1945.

And now today's news, August 10, 1945.

Japan has offered to surrender according to the Potsdam surrender ultimatum with a request for clarification on the status of Emperor Hirohito. The Domei News Services says the Japanese cabinet was unanimous in its vote. There may be strong feeling in the U.S. Congress to have the Emperor share in the blame for the war. The U.S. will hold all islands in the Pacific considered strategic to its future.

General Carl A. Spaatz, Commanding General of the USAAF, has stopped B-29 raids while the Navy has also ceased attacks. General MacArthur says he will continue fighting in the Philippines until further notice. Russian troops have advanced another 105 miles in Manchuria.

Gen. Spaatz also announced that 30% of Nagasaki was wiped out by the second Atomic bomb. Japan has filed a protest with the U.S. government on the use of such an inhuman weapon.

The Inter-American Judicial Commission in Rio de Janeiro says the German V-bombs are illegal weapons since they cannot be directionally controlled while the A-Bomb is legal since it could be guided so as not to hit undefended areas.

GI's in the Pacific are wild with joy regarding the surrender yelling "let them keep their Emperor" while GI's in Paris and London freely paraded through streets with equal enthusiasm.

The U.S. war cost has been 251,000 dead and 1 million casualties dwarfing all other U.S. wars at the cost of $300 billion.

John W. Snyder, Director of the Office of War Mobilization and Reconversion says a master plan is ready to put in place for transformation from a wartime to a peace time economy.

Robert H. Goddard, pioneer in rocket propulsion and Chief of Navy Research of jet propelled planes, died today in Baltimore at 62.

In baseball with two months to go, the Chicago Cubs lead the St. Louis Cardinals by 4½ games in the 8 team National League race and the Detroit Tigers lead the Philadelphia Athletics by one in the 8 team American League.

In business, Curtis Wright says upon formal announcement of the end of the war, all of their plants will close for 48 hours pending further advice from the government.

A sample listing of high grade municipal bonds nationally shows the city of St. Paul, Minnesota with a 1.10% return to a high of New York City at 2.4%. In the stock market, war issues faded today after news of the surrender as peace shares advanced with the Dow Jones closing off less than a point at 165.14.

That's the news this August 10, 1945.

Saturday, August 11, 1945

And now today's news, August 11, 1945.

The Allies have decided to let the Emperor remain subject to the occupation chief's implementation but will insist on free elections. General MacArthur has been designated to accept the surrender.

In the last month of the war Kamikaze planes sunk 20 U.S. ships and damaged at least 30 others. In Manchuria, the Russians gained another 50 miles.

Asserting that communism is sweeping throughout Europe, 71-year-old former President Herbert Hoover asks Americans to have faith in our system of freedom even as it has been estimated with peacetime conversation that some 5 million will likely lose their jobs.

Communications with the Japanese is time consuming and takes nine steps plus coding and decoding through the Swiss Legation in Washington, on to Berne, Switzerland to the Japanese Legation there and then on to Tokyo.

General Eisenhower and Marshal Zhukov flew from Berlin today to Moscow to be greeted by many Russians and American notables including U.S. Ambassador Averill Harriman and U.S. Reparations Commission head Edwin W. Pauley.

The surrender celebration on Okinawa has resulted in 6 deaths and 30 injured.

The Nagasaki atomic bomb made the Hiroshima bomb obsolete says Princeton Professor Henry Smythe who said they anticipated its destructive power which is heightened by the mid-air explosion.

The new giant supercargo Martin Hawaii Mars flying boat that sunk last week after a hard landing opened up its hull cost $2 million.

American Social Security has dispensed $8.7 billion in its first ten years.

Secretary of the Interior Harold Ickes proposes Alaska become our 49th state.

The 17 story Hotel Ansonia on 74th Street, New York has been sold for $2.5 million.

On radio, Bing Crosby, due to a movie commitment, won't be back with his Music Hall until mid-season, Andy Russell will be part of the Joan Davis show and the Arthur Godfrey morning show will be extended to 45 minutes.

Byron Nelson leads Herman Barron and Sam Snead at the Spring Lake, New Jersey pro-member tournament. The winning pro gets $1500.

That's the news this August 11, 1945.

And now today's news, August 12, 1945.

Big news over the weekend. Japanese offered to surrender presumably with full agreement to the Potsdam surrender ultimatum. The Allies are studying the offer including how to handle Emperor Hirohito who is divine to the Japanese people. Manila went hysterical, London went wild while most U.S. citizens are waiting to see. The war continues, however, as Russians move on the China front and MacArthur presses to the south. Otherwise, raids were held back over Japan.

Truman has met with his cabinet and others including Secretaries Clinton P. Anderson, Agriculture, Fred Vinson, Treasury, Henry A. Wallace, Commerce, Robert E. Hannegan, Postmaster General, Henry L. Stimson, War, James Byrnes, State, Tom Clark Attorney General, and James V. Forrestal, Navy.

Yesterday the Allies decided to let Hirohito remain and named General MacArthur as Supreme Commander for surrender purposes. Yesterday's Japanese newspaper hinted at a grave situation without reference to peace. Even as a premature wild celebration took place in Honolulu, Chinese and Russian troops kept fighting.

Today the U.S. cancelled plans for renewed attacks on Tokyo but President Truman is irked at Japanese delays and has threatened them with overwhelming attacks and more atom bombs unless they promptly respond.

General Eisenhower today stood by Marshal Stalin in Red Square in Moscow reviewing 40,000 troops.

In baseball, the American League champions, the St. Louis Browns elected a new president. In New York Mayor LaGuardia has sent up a 10 man committee including Larry MacPhail President of the Yankees, and Branch Rickey, President of the Dodgers to study color lines and discrimination in baseball.

It's reported that up to 5 million workers may be out of a job when war production end. Further it is expected 5 million GI's will be out of service and also looking for work within the year. GI's released on points will not be eligible for the draft.

That's the news this August 12, 1945.

Monday, August 13, 1945

And now today's news, August 13, 1945.

The Federal Communications Commission has been monitoring lengthy messages from the Japanese to the Swiss and while no official word has yet been received by President Truman, Japan's surrender is expected momentarily.

Plans for the Japanese indicate the Allies will ask Emperor Hirohito to also sign the surrender documents.

Meanwhile, 400 B-29's have blasted the island of Honshu again as the Red Army races towards Harbin in China.

A Japanese radio report today minimized the damage done to Hiroshima. The U.S has reported that neither Canada nor the British yet have atomic bomb capabilities. In Washington, Dean Acheson has resigned as Assistant Secretary of State.

In Germany, 15 of the top Nazis have been flown from Nuremberg to Munich and, like common criminals, are now in jail. They include Field Marshal Hermann Goering, Franz Von Papen, Joachim von Ribbentrop, Field Marshal William Keitel and Arthur Seyss-Inquart.

General Charles de Gaulle of France will arrive in Washington on August 22nd to visit with President Truman.

The world's mightiest aircraft carrier, the Midway, is about to be launched. Its deck is the length of 3 football fields.

Maestro Arturo Toscanini and the NBC Symphony Orchestra are preparing a major special V-J broadcast. Irene Dunne, Charles Coburn and Alexander Knox are in "Over 21" at Radio City Music Hall as Clark Gable has been signed to a sequel to "Mutiny on the Bounty" called "Christian of the Bounty."

New books include "Alexander Woollcott: His Life and His World" by Samuel Adams for $3.50 and "Dragon Harvest" by Upton Sinclair at $3.00.

Associated Broadcasting Corporation of Grand Rapids is suing the American Broadcasting Company who want to prevent them from using ABC as an identity.

Volume on the New York Stock Exchange today was 970,000 shares with Graham Paige heading the list with 20,000 shares at 10 7/8.

Finally, pianist and Staff Sgt. Eugene List performed at Potsdam for the Big Three—with President Truman turning the pages for him.

That's the news this August 13, 1945.

And now today's news, August 14, 1945.

Japan has surrendered! The announcement was made today by President Truman at 6:10 pm after Japan had accepted the unconditional terms set down at the Potsdam conference in July by forwarding their acceptance through the Swiss in Berne, Switzerland. The terms will deprive Japan of 80% of the territories held at the time of Pearl Harbor and will require Japan to demobilize and demilitarize the nation. Times Square today is filled with hundreds of thousands celebrating the news, Washington has erupted in noise as has San Francisco, Boston and Havana. Banks and the stock market will be closed tomorrow and government workers will have the next two days off as churches are filled throughout the land.

Emperor Hirohito read news of the surrender over the Japanese radio even as War Minister Korechika Anami committed suicide.

Prime Minister Clement Attlee announced the news at midnight London time and Canada has set Sunday as a day of prayer.

As five Japanese aircraft approached the United States Pacific fleet, they were promptly shot down today as American forces remain on the alert until V-J day.

The last B-29 raid yesterday involved 800 airplanes dropping 6,000 tons of bombs on the island of Honshu.

Gen. Chennault in China says the end came not because of the bomb but because of Russia's recent entry into the war. Gen. Chiang Kai-shek has invited communist Gen. Mao-Tse-Tung to meet with him in Chungking in order to try and avoid a Chinese civil war.

Among the 15,000 American prisoners expected to be released soon will be Gen. Jonathan Wainwright who was captured at Bataan.

A major naval tragedy has just been announced. The 16,000 ton cruiser Indianapolis which delivered the atomic bomb to Tinian in July was sunk on July 30 by a Japanese submarine with a loss of 1,196 men.

In Paris, 89-year-old Marshal Henri Petain has been convicted of treason and sentenced to death.

The secrets of radar—radio detection and range—the most powerful weapon until the A-Bomb—were revealed publicly today in Washington. It sees through fog and storms. Sir Stafford Cripps says radar won the war for the British.

And finally, Social Security started 10 years ago today.

That's the news this August 14,1945.

Wednesday, August 15, 1945

And now today's news, August 15, 1945.

A tragedy in Alaska 10 years ago today as one of America's favorite humorists, Will Rogers, was killed in an air crash with his friend and pilot Wiley Post.

Kantaro Suzuki's Japanese cabinet has resigned stating the need for a new cabinet to work under surrender terms being worked out by Gen. Douglas MacArthur. Japanese radio stations are cooperating with American forces as MacArthur has cautioned troops to beware of treachery.

The last Navy dogfight two days ago bagged 38 Japanese airplanes as the Russians continue to fight in Manchuria claiming Japan has not yet ordered its troops to surrender. In Luzon, isolated bands of Japanese continue to fight and kill Americans there today.

The Army says 5 million men will be out by year end, the Navy says up to 2.5 million, and the Marines will be released on points.

John W.Snyder, Director of War Mobilization, outlined today the beginnings of conversion from wartime to a peace economy. The London Parliament met today with labor proposing historical changes including nationalizing banks and the coal industry as well as ratifying the U.N. charter.

Good news for us all today. Gas and fuel oil rationing has ended and shortly there'll be no more coupons and ration books.

J.A. Krug, head of the War Production Board, says all war time controls on industry will be off by the end of the week as $6 billion in war time Navy contracts have been cancelled. Sixty-five thousand men at the Brooklyn Navy yard have a holiday today.

The planning for the formal Japanese surrender will probably include the giving up of Samurai swords by Japanese delegates. Since semi-religious rites surround the forging of these swords this is expected to have great impact on the Japanese.

The French government has advised the Allies it wishes to take over Indo China now that the war is over.

Gen. Charles de Gaulle is considering a life sentence for treason-convicted Marshal Petain.

In Princeton, New Jersey a 30,000 word historical report by Professor H.D. Smyth has been released describing details of the development of the atomic bomb.

Gen. Omar Bradley has been sworn in as head of the Veterans Administration as the war time Office of Censorship has been closed down.

That's the news this August 15, 1945,

And now today's news, August 16, 1945.

Even as Russia counterattacks in Manchuria, Emperor Hirohito has issued another order to Japanese forces to cease all war operations. His cousin Prince Naruhiko Higashi-kuni has formed a new cabinet.

On Luzon, Americans are spreading leaflets and using loud speakers to urge Japanese fighters to surrender. In one of his greatest speeches, Member of Parliament Winston Churchill said today it was a mistake to have given Poland much of East Germany. He continues to show distrust of Russian Communism.

In Washington, President Truman has asked for free and open settlement by Jews in Palestine. Truman has also asked Congress to establish universal military training. Gen. Brehan Somerville revealed today that 4 million troops have already arrived home including 2.5 million from Europe and 1.5 million from the South Pacific.

Today many transportation restrictions were lifted permitting auto racing, increased taxi service and car rentals.

Under Secretary of State Joseph C. Grew resigned today and was replaced by Dean Acheson. In London, Foreign Secretary Ernest Bevin says the atomic bomb has changed the conception of the United Nations.

More than 800 well known college, amateur and professional athletes were killed in the war including Niles Kinnick, All-American at Iowa, Lou Zamperini, great miler, polo star Tommy Hitchcock, 100-yard dash star Charley Paddock, amateur golfer Jack Burke and football players Clint Caselberry of Georgia Tech and Howie Seymour of Yale.

Pitcher Hal Newhouser won his 19th game for the Detroit Tigers today beating the Washington Senators 9-2. And Leo the Lip Durocher, Manager of the Brooklyn Dodgers is getting a $5,000 bonus from President Branch Rickey for every 100,000 in attendance over 700,000 for the season. This is on top of his $25,000 salary.

Liberty for 100,000 Navy men in San Francisco was cancelled today after riots and celebrations had killed 10 people in that city.

The Air Force has cancelled $9 billion in contracts for 7,650 bombers and 13,500 fighters.

That's the news this August 16, 1945.

And now today's news, August 17, 1945.

New Japanese Premier Prince Naruhiko Higashi-Kuni has issued an order to all officers and men to strictly observe the cease fire. Tokyo is sending an emissary to Manila to meet with General MacArthur regarding surrender there. 20,000 Japanese troops in Manchuria have surrendered even as Soviet troops are closing in on Harbin.

Vice Admiral Takijiro Onishi who originated the idea of Kamikaze attacks took his own life today.

In New York City over 100,000 workers were surprised to be laid off as a result of cutbacks as the war winds down.

Secretary of Agriculture Clinton P. Anderson says meat rationing may stop in the fall.

The War Production Board has cancelled almost all allotments of copper, steel and aluminum as a result of huge military cutbacks. The Office of Transportation has rescinded travel curbs on sporting events, and President Truman held a decisive meeting today to end lend-lease.

Viscount Halifax will return to Washington soon as British Ambassador.

Pearl Harbor skies tonight looked like a wartime battle zone as colored flares and fireworks lit up the skies in celebration.

Total American combat casualties are now 1,070,138, an increase of almost 2000 since last week.

This past week workers of the Budd Manufacturing Company in Philadelphia were spot welding bomb fins. 48-hours later they were working on auto side panels.

Charles Vidor will direct the new Rita Hayworth movie "Gilda."

The Dow Jones average closed today at 164.38, off .41 with volume of 1,210,000 shares led by Radio Corporation at 14 up one quarter with 51,700 shares.

Finally, President Truman has designated this Sunday as Prayer Sunday and will participate in a Prayer of Thanksgiving as millions of Americans do the same in churches and synagogues across the land.

That's the news this August 17, 1945.

And now today's news, August 18, 1945.

Foreign Minister Shigemitsu has told the Japanese people they are a beaten nation and must obey the terms of the Potsdam declaration. Thousands more are surrendering to the Soviets in Manchuria.

Allied Headquarters hope to speed the liberation of 155,000 troops and civilians in 100 Japanese prison camps in Japan and Asia. Lt. General Jonathan Wainwright who was captured while at Bataan and Corregidor may have been released from a Manchurian camp. Col. James P. Devereux, veteran of Wake Island, is with approximately 7000 other men, women and children in a Mukden Manchuria prison camp.

American B-32 reconnaissance planes were again attacked by Japanese Zeros with 1 airman killed and 2 wounded. Two zeros were shot down.

A nationwide speed limit of 35 m.p.h. was started on September 26, 1942 and now the Office of Transportation has ended it effective tomorrow and urges the public to be careful with higher speeds.

President Truman has asked that when VJ Day is proclaimed it be a working day, not a holiday. In keeping with the President's Day of Thanksgiving tomorrow, most broadcasters will present special programs of music and devotion.

Some 3000 Japanese-American Nisei troops will lead the VJ Day parade in Leghorn, Italy.

100 Miles of the Rhine River have been opened following blasting to clear debris and remains of 19 destroyed bridges.

Almost 76, Bernard Baruch says our U.S. scheme of free enterprise is the best in the world and that prosperity is ours for the making.

In an 8 week season at the Hollywood Bowl in Los Angeles, the Hollywood Symphony Orchestra will be conducted by Leopold Stokowski. Guests artists will include Isaac Stern and Sol Hurok's Ballet Theater.

A new movie is "Bewitched" with Phyllis Thaxter and Edmund Gwenn. In two recent pictures after her hit debut in "Gaslight," Angela Lansbury has enjoyed the company of fellow actress, her mother Moyna MacGill.

Finally, if you'd like a U.S. Army canteen many can be bought at specialty stores for $1.69 each.

That's the news this August 18, 1945.

And now today's news, August 19, 1945.

Japanese emissaries have arrived on the island of Ie off Okinawa to receive the conditions for Japan's surrender. It's announced that Japanese forces in China will surrender tomorrow.

A House Naval office subcommittee has recommended that the U.S. claim full title to the Pacific islands where U.S. bases are located.

With the end of the war, censorship has been lifted in 14 countries and is expected to end soon in about 10 others.

France has agreed to return to China some leased territory west of Hong Kong held under a 99-year lease.

Air Force General Hap Arnold may retire soon and says the next war will mean destruction of civilization due to new scientific weapons including a monster bomber being developed dwarfing the B-29 that seeks out targets by radar and television.

A war summary today says B-29's flew 32,600 sorties, destroyed major portions of 59 Japanese cities, laid 12,000 mines in waters, destroyed or damaged 2,285 planes and incurred a loss of 3,000 men and 437 bombers.

Marshal Petain's death sentence in Paris has been commuted to life imprisonment on an island off the Riviera.

Austria's first war criminal trial has sentenced 4 Nazis to hang as yet another German submarine U-boat has surrendered in Argentina 102 days after the end of the European war.

Secretary of State James Byrnes says Bulgaria has been warned that the U.S. cannot recognize the new government unless the August 26th elections are free and open to all democratic elements.

Here at home, rubber companies will not operate at full capacity for at least 6 months and tire rationing will not be lifted until after the first of the year.

In sports, the government has lifted curbs on traveling to sporting events and Cleveland Indians pitcher Bob Feller is eligible for release from the Navy and is expected to be pitching soon.

That's the news this August 19, 1945.

And now today's news, August 20, 1945.

A 16 man Japanese delegation has landed in Manila and was greeted with rigid formality by American officers.

All organized Japanese resistance in Manchuria has ended and Admiral Mountbatten has ordered Japanese envoys to appear in Rangoon this week to arrange for the surrender of Japanese forces in southeast Asia.

A Tokyo radio broadcast says Japanese acceptance of the Allied surrender terms is resented by a large portion of the military men and Allied occupation of Japanese territory may be too much for some of the officers to bear.

Emperor Hirohito has ended censorship and blackout restrictions in Japan. General Jonathan Wainwright is alive and well. He is in a prisoner-of-war camp in Manchuria.

At the treason trial of Vidkun Quisling in Oslo, he claims he was the "savior of Norway."

British Foreign Secretary Ernest Bevin says there will not be any radical changes in Britain's foreign policy.

On the home front, the War Production Board has removed 210 controls from such things as trucks, radios, refrigerators, stoves and electric fans. But, according to Donald Gordon, Chairman of the Prices and Trade Board, there is no immediate prospect of meat rationing being discontinued, thus discounting reports that it might end by Fall.

The Andrews Sisters have returned from entertaining troops in Africa and Italy and are wondering how they are going to work for ordinary civilians again. The Army-Navy football game will be played in Philadelphia's Municipal Stadium on December 1st, and London is now the likely site for the 1948 Olympic Games.

Massachusetts Senator Walsh asked Secretary Forrestal today for all Pearl Harbor files for a full investigation which involved Rear Admiral Husband E. Kimmel and Major Gen. Walter C. Short who have continued to await court martial since January 1942.

That's the news this August 20, 1945.

Tuesday, August 21, 1945

And now today's news, August 21, 1945.

Signing of the Japanese surrender treaty is expected to occur within 10 days. The 16 man Japanese delegation is returning to Japan. American occupation of Japan will be made with large armadas of planes and ships and men. Occupation will start Sunday when airborne troops land at Atsugi airport southwest of Tokyo. Additional landings will occur next week in the Yokosuka area, according to the Japanese government.

Tokyo radio has appealed to Japanese suicide flier groups to accept Japan's surrender.

Meanwhile, Japanese officials have met with Chinese officials in west Hunan to negotiate their surrender.

Admiral Mountbatten has demanded that the Japanese southern army in Burma end all hostilities.

Labor members of the British Parliament are calling for international control of the atomic bomb.

In Oslo, Vidkun Quisling has been charged with being an army deserter and giving defense secrets to the Nazis.

The properties of 20 American corporations in the American sector of Berlin have been taken over by the U.S. Army and will eventually return to them. They include GE, IBM, Ford Motors and others.

President Truman has ended the lend-lease program, and has revoked an executive order that provided premium pay for war workers remaining on the job on national holidays.

Despite continuing layoffs, the War Manpower Commission says job orders on file outnumber job seekers 3 to 1.

General Charles de Gaulle arrives in Washington today to discuss many problems affecting relations between the U.S. and western Europe.

Jerome Kern and Oscar Hammerstein have announced plans to present "Show Boat" at Billy Rose's Ziegfeld Theater in New York early in December.

Popular movies showing are Gary Cooper and Loretta Young in "Along Came Jones," Frank Sinatra, Gene Kelly and Kathryn Grayson in "Anchors Aweigh," Jean Gabin in "Pepe Le Moko," Robert Donat and Madeline Carroll in "The 39 Steps" and Walt Disney's "Pinocchio."

That's the news this August 21, 1945.

And now today's news, August 22, 1945.

The U.S., Britain and Russia are preparing for joint political action to avert civil war in China. Meanwhile, Chiang Kai-shek's troops are preparing to occupy Hong Kong, Formosa, northern Indochina and a part of Thailand.

Russian airborne forces have occupied the ports of Port Arthur and Darien in Manchuria and Shimushu in Kurile Islands. Gen. MacArthur will enter Japan next week, heading a mighty force of Allied planes and ships. He will land at Atsugi Airport, outside of Tokyo. The formal surrender will be signed 3 days later on the battleship Missouri in Tokyo Bay.

The two atom bombs dropped on Japan are said to have killed 70,000, wounded 120,000 and rendered 290,000 homeless.

The King of Rumania has asked the Big 3 to help that country form a new government they could recognize and sign a peace treaty with.

President Truman has proposed that Puerto Ricans be given an early opportunity to settle future relations with the U.S. though free choice.

Gen. Charles de Gaulle came to Washington today and paid his first visit to President Truman.

The 8th and final War Loan drive gets underway October 29 with a goal of eleven billion dollars.

Government regulations on wholesale and retail motor truck deliveries will end November 1, and controls on lumber will be lifted September 30.

The U.S. Navy does not plan to have any permanent bases in Europe and is abandoning present ones as rapidly as possible. Meanwhile, the Army Air Force expects to discharge almost 1½ million men in the next year.

Broadway's Winter Garden Theater will be converted into a first run movie house and will open October 1 with Noel Coward's "Blithe Spirit."

Bob Feller is being released by the Navy today. He says he is ready to pitch Friday night against leading Detroit.

Five thousand telegrams were sent today from Washington cancelling orders to 186 textile firms. And, finally, Treasury Secretary Fred Vinson says there may be an income tax cut in 1946. We will hold our breath.

That's the news this August 22, 1945.

And now today's news, August 23, 1945.

President Truman says the proclamation of V-J Day, probably August 31st, will mark victory over Japan but not the formal end of the war. That's up to Congress.

Japan is preparing to disarm her ships and ground her planes while more than 7,500 American troops are preparing to land in Japan next week with General MacArthur.

Russian Premier Stalin has announced that Red troops have completed the conquest of Manchuria and the southern half of Sakhalin Island.

According to Tokyo Radio, Allied air attacks wrecked 44 cities, killed 260,000, injured 412,000 and left homeless over 9 million people.

American, British and French troops have entered Vienna to occupy their respective zones in the Austrian capital.

The British government says it has no interest in giving up Hong Kong or even in considering the question at this time.

Chinese Communist troops are rumored to be gathering for an all-out offensive against government forces, while Chiang Kai-shek's troops received the surrender of over 1 million Japanese.

President Truman has ordered government seizure of the Illinois Central Railroad to stop a threatened strike by engineers and firemen. Meanwhile, the president, in blunt terms, says we don't like Spain's Generalissimo Franco or his government. He also scolded the French press for being unfair to the U.S.

New York is making plans for its formal welcome to Gen. de Gaulle next week.

Price controls have been suspended on washing machines, ironers and aluminum kitchen ware, but sugar rationing will continue for the rest of the year.

In sports, Tommy (Rocky) Graziano is favored to beat Freddie (Red) Cochrane in their 10-round bout tomorrow night at Madison Square Garden.

The Cleveland Indians have signed pitcher Bob Feller to a new contract said to be worth $40,000. Feller was released from the Navy yesterday.

That's the news this August 23, 1945.

And now today's news, August 24, 1945.

Surrender plans have been postponed in Japan for two days due to typhoons around Japan. Now the first U.S. troops landing are due this Tuesday with the formal surrender scheduled for September 2nd.

Tokyo radio says that due to radio activity and ultra violet rays 30,000 lives have been lost at Hiroshima due to aftereffects. American scientists had previously discounted such possibilities.

Chinese communist forces under General Chou En-lai along with Generalissimo Chiang Kai-shek's men continue to move forward in China against the Japanese. Chiang Kai-shek says the Chinese will not occupy Hong Kong to avoid disputes with the British and hopes settlement can be reached through legal procedures.

General Charles de Gaulle and French Foreign Minister Georges Bidault spent an hour today conferring with President Truman and Secretary of State James Byrnes seeking cooperation to solve European and Asian problems.

Prime Minister Clement Attlee says the abrupt termination of lend-lease by the United States puts Britain in a very serious financial position.

The first of many gaps in Dutch dikes caused by bombings have been sealed up.

78-year-old Arturo Toscanini is returning to Milan for the La Scala opening in February.

President of the Federal Council of Churches Bishop G. Bromley Oxman and Chairman of a Just and Durable Peace Commission John Foster Dulles have issued a joint letter grateful for Japan accepting the peace without more Atomic bombs noting "We have given a practical demonstration of the possibility of atomic energy bringing war to an end. If that precedent is constructively followed up, it may be of incalculable value to posterity."

Gertrude Stein is writing a new book about GI's called "Brewsie and Willie."

Bob Feller struck out 12 as the Cleveland Indians defeated the Detroit Tigers 4 to 2 in Feller's first outing in nearly four years of being in the Navy.

Brooklyn Dodger manager Leo Durocher will join Danny Kaye on a USO tour of the South Pacific and will miss the World Series. The Dodgers won't be there since they are 10½ games out of first place.

Henry Cotton, twice British Open Golf Champion, shot a final 74 today to win the $6000 British PGA tournament.

The Dow Jones at 169.68 closed today at the highest since April 1940 on 1,320,000 shares.

That's the news this August 24, 1945.

Saturday, August 25, 1945

And now today's news, August 25, 1945.

Ships of the U.S. Navy have entered Sagami Bay below Tokyo as reports of many suicides have taken place in front of the Emperor's Palace. The Japanese people simply can't comprehend they have lost the war. A fleet of 401 Allied ships, of which 383 are U.S., began a triumphal entry into the lower harbor.

Bundles of food and medicine are being dropped by Navy planes to prisoners of war in Japan as local citizens come out to wave at the planes flying over.

The city of Tokyo's population has been reduced by 63% since the bombing raids started due to evacuation and deaths. 70% of the city is destroyed.

Generalissimo Chiang Kai-shek's armies have moved into Shanghai and Nanking as rival communist army forces are moving in on Canton and Hong Kong.

Two 5th Air Force P-38 pilots were the first to land on Japanese soil as one was running out of gas. They made a landing on south central Kyushu Island, spent 2½ hours chatting with Japanese officers and enlisted men waiting for a B-17 to arrive with gasoline before taking off for home base on Okinawa. They said the Japanese were fascinated by the B-17 and did seem to realize they had been defeated.

Three weak and haggard fliers on the April 18, 1942 Doolittle raid off a carrier over Tokyo have been liberated by paratroopers in Chungking.

The U.S. had 200 submarines operating during the war and lost 52 of them. They sank 1187 ships including 146 combat vessels.

7000 Negro troops will be leaving Marseille, France shortly for home.

President Truman has ordered the return of 24 private mostly small businesses which were seized in March 1942 to halt or avert interruptions of work.

Nelson A. Rockefeller has resigned as Assistant Secretary of State to be replaced by Spruille Braden.

7 Nazi prisoners in Ft. Leavenworth, Kansas have been hung after being convicted of killing a fellow Nazi prisoner they considered a traitor to Germany. All embraced the Catholic faith before dying in the largest mass execution of prisoners in U.S. history.

At the movies Edward Arnold is in "The Hidden Eye," George Sanders and Geraldine Fitzgerald are in "Uncle Harry" and a lively musical film, "State Fair" has come to the screen with music and words of Oscar Hammerstein and Richard Rodgers and starring Charlie Winninger, Jeanne Crain, Dana Andrews, Dick Haymes, and Vivian Blaine.

That's the news this August 25, 1945.

And now today's news, August 26, 1945.

Over 400 U.S. warships are assembling in Sugami Bay to assist occupation forces. American planes are dropping gifts, food and medicine to Americans in prison camps and large numbers of Japanese are committing suicide in front of the Emperor's palace.

Twelve hundred planes of Admiral Bull Halsey's fleet are guarding the American fleet as 21 grim-faced Japanese have boarded the USS Missouri to receive occupation instructions.

Three American prisoners captured on the famous Doolittle B-25 raid over Tokyo in 1942 have been freed and are in Chungking, China. They noted some of their fellow prisoners had been executed. Heroes of Bataan and Wake Island have been brought from Mukden, China to Kunming, many with tuberculosis and malnutrition. Most had never heard of President Truman or Dwight D. Eisenhower.

American journalists including W.H. Lawrence of the New York Times flew in a B-17 today over Nagasaki to view the destruction and desolation of the atomic bomb.

General de Gaulle is in Hyde Park today and was greeted in New York City by Grover Whelan and made an honorary citizen of the city by Mayor LaGuardia.

German war secrets today indicated considerable progress had been made by the Germans in developing an atomic bomb as well as intercontinental missiles.

Washington says they will continue a monthly draft of 50,000 men.

In medicine a doctor in Curacao says he had cured leprosy with penicillin.

Chester Bowles of the OPA says prices of 1946 cars will be similar to the last models produced in 1942.

Amateur tennis star Billy Talbert won his 9th consecutive tournament today at Southampton.

John Garfield, Eleanor Parker and Dane Clark are starring in "Pride of the Marines" and CBS has announced a new technique for color TV by Peter Goldmark.

That's the news this August 26, 1945.

Monday, August 27, 1945

And now today's news, August 27, 1945.

America's first 150 troops have landed in a giant C-54 in Japan to prepare landing fields for U.S. arrivals as 10 ships have entered Tokyo Bay. The Allies have been cautioned to take over gradually and with cooperation with Japanese government officials.

Tragically, 20 U.S. communication experts were killed taking off from Okinawa today en route to Tokyo.

Japanese officials today said the dropping of the atomic bomb convinced them to surrender.

Japanese forces on the once formidable islands of Truk, Yap and Rota that were bypassed have given up.

The hero of Bataan, Gen. Jonathan Wainwright is now free and in Chungking, China.

Two million today hailed Gen. Charles de Gaulle in a New York City parade as Governor Dewey says he's getting ready to run again in 1946.

Thirty-one Icelandic war brides and their 21 children arrived today in New York.

The carrier Enterprise, known as the Big E, has been called the fightingest ship of the war. Reportedly sunk 6 times by the Japanese, it was seriously hit 15 times, shot down 911 Japanese planes, sunk 71 ships, damaged 191 more and now is in Puget Sound Harbor.

National Housing Administration head John Bladford says there is a need for 400,000 houses for men who can only afford from $20 to $40 per month for housing.

Thirty-seven Giant football players reported today for duty minus Mel Hein and Ward Cuff who have been delayed. Maj. Andy Gufstason and Herman Hickman of the Army coaching staff were on hand watching.

On radio tonight is Ginny Simms, The Falcon, Alan Young, Inner Sanctum, the Man Called X with Herbert Marshall, Connie Boswell is on stage at the Roxy, Rita Hayworth has signed for a new movie called "Gilda."

AT&T has filed for $160 million in debentures to pay 2 3/4%

That's the news this August 27, 1945.

And now today's news, August 28, 1945.

Gen. MacArthur landed in Okinawa today en route to Tokyo as preparations for the surrender on September 2nd proceed. The Flagship Missouri is now in Tokyo Harbor with Admiral Bull Halsey proudly leading the way.

The first naval fliers have landed at Atsugi Airport and been greeted by Japanese generals in full dress. Lt. Commander Harold Stassen, former Governor of Minnesota, is in the advance guard beginning discussions with the Japanese.

Good news from a prison camp in Thailand. Word has been received that there are as many as 300 survivors of the cruiser Houston that disappeared presumably with loss of all hands in the battle of the Java Sea on February 28, 1942. Communist General Mao Tse Tung has met with Gen. Chiang Kai-shek in hopes of reconciliation between the rival Chinese forces.

Freed war prisoner Gen. Jonathan Wainwright has expressed grateful thanks for the Philippines. He likely will join Gen. MacArthur on the Missouri for surrender ceremonies.

A late report on the battle of Saipan says 4 top Japanese generals died, three by suicide.

A New York Times reporter flying over Tokyo says the previous reports on damage done by the B-29 raids was underestimated. He called the devastation "a shocking understatement of aerial warfare."

One of America's top war aces, Marine Major Gregory Boyington who shot down 26 Japanese planes and was lost on January 3, 1944, has turned up alive in Tokyo.

In Germany, the British have refused to let former world heavyweight boxing champion Max Schmeling publish a book designed to re-educate German youth.

In sports, Byron Nelson is tied with Sammy Snead at the halfway mark of the $10,000 Oakmont, PA. Open. Former ace Gene Sarazen is 14 strokes back.

26-year-old Leonard Bernstein has been named music director of the New York Center of Music for the 1945-46 season.

Top trades on the New York stock exchange today were Baldwin Locomotive, Radio Corporation, Graham Paige, Socony Vacuum and Radio Keith Orpheum.

That's the news this August 28, 1945.

Wednesday, August 29, 1945

And now today's news, August 29, 1945.

Gen. MacArthur has arrived in Tokyo in his gleaming C-54 plane named the Bataan along with Lt. Gen. Eichelberger and Lt. Gen. Sutherland. Upon arrival he said "Well, we got here, didn't we."

U.S. and British soldiers have come ashore at Yokosuka Naval base and raised the American flag. Eighty-six Red Cross workers have also arrived as first U.S. prisoners are being evacuated.

A full report on the disaster at Pearl Harbor was released today including a 15-page detailed report in the New York Times. The report criticizes Lt. Gen. Walter Short, Admiral Husband Kimmel, Adm. Harold Stark, Cordell Hull, Gen. Marshall and General Gerow. Secretary of War Stimson, backed by President Truman, says criticism of Gen. Marshall is unjustified. The report speaks of America's unpreparedness, lack of cooperation between the services and a divided foreign policy towards Japan.

Shanghai is wildly celebrating its freedom from the Japanese today after 8 years of occupation. In Germany 24 top Nazis have been indicted for crimes against peace, against humanity and war crimes. Justice Robert H. Jackson on a four power international committee says they will be tried in a Nuremberg court.

Secretary of State Jimmy Byrnes today says the Japanese were beaten even before the bomb was dropped.

The Japanese government has moved to provide freedom of the press and, as an added touch, the American flag which Commodore Perry raised in Tokyo 93 years ago is being delivered to Admiral Halsey for use on the Missouri during the surrender. Another American flag today was raised on Mili Atoll in the Marshall Islands.

U.S. prisoners reaching Rangoon today tell of Japanese atrocities and death by disease. An American bomber pilot was hung by his thumbs for 30 minutes recently.

Madame Chiang Kai-shek visited today with President Truman in Washington and is leaving shortly for China. An interesting war statistic released today says that an average of two tons a minute was flown over the hump from India to China during the war.

Twenty-four cases of polio have been reported in New Jersey bringing this year's total to 503.

And Maxwell House coffee is advertising an amazing new product called instant coffee—a spoonful in hot water and there you have it—a cup of coffee.

That's the news this August 29, 1945.

And now today's news, August 30, 1945.

Gen. MacArthur has opened up U.S. headquarters in Yokohama, Marines have come ashore, the Yokosuka naval base is under U.S. control and the Japanese seem to be acting in good faith with the Americans.

President Truman has now read the entire Pearl Harbor report released yesterday and says all Americans must share in the blame for not wanting nor supporting preparedness before the sneak attack. Congress is demanding hearings.

British naval vessels are back in control again in Hong Kong and the two largest submarines in the world each weighing about 5,000 tons have been surrendered by the Japanese.

The Army has taken over Japanese radio stations and a U.S. reporter notes that many Japanese are taking the defeat very hard, but remain polite.

The government has cut the federal budget by $33 billion due to the end of the war and the 1945 debt will be $15 billion less than forecast.

The government has also cut back red points needed for meat, butter, cheese and margarine.

A Brooklyn federal court judge has upheld the right of a returning GI to get his old job back even if it is at the expense of someone with seniority.

Radio shows tonight include Blind Date, the Aldrich Family, Adventures of the Thin Man, It Pays to be Ignorant, and over the weekend you can hear the National Barn Dance, the Hit Parade, Can You Top This, Judy Canova, Grand Ole Oprey, Manhattan Serenade, Double or Nothing, James Melton, Phil Spitalny All Girl Orchestra, Take It or Leave It, We the People and Meet Me at Parky's.

Gary Cooper and Madeline Carroll star in "Northwest Mounted Police" and a new movie called "State Fair" features Jeanne Crain, Dick Haymes, Dana Andrews, Vivian Blaine, Charles Winninger, Fay Bainter, Frank McHugh, Frank Morgan and Percy Kilbride. While the Rodgers and Hammerstin music is wonderful once again and the movie looked good to this reporter, the New York Times review says the movie didn't quite make it.

Seventeen thousand more men arrived home today.

Barbara Hutton divorced Cary Grant today saying, among other things, that the actor snubbed her dinner guests by eating his dinner in his bed.

That's the news this August 30, 1945.

247

Friday, August 31, 1945

And now today's news, August 31, 1945.

General Prince Naruhiko Higashi-Kuni, Premier of Japan and cousin of Emperor Hirohito, will sign final surrender documents for Japan aboard the battleship Missouri tomorrow, September 2nd, Japanese time—exactly six years after Germany started the war by attacking Poland. General Jonathan Wainwright has arrived at General MacArthur's headquarters to witness the surrender noting "Now, the shoe is on the other foot." American troops are quickly expanding their occupation of the Tokyo Bay area.

A large number of Japanese suicide boats tried to escape from Hong Kong after a British naval force arrived. Carrier planes attacked them promptly.

President Truman has abolished the Office of War Information and instructed Secretary of State James Byrnes to create a program to keep foreign countries informed of U.S. developments.

Commander Harold Stassen reports incredibly cruel conditions in Tokyo prisoner camps including bestial treatment. 1494 prisoners have been liberated so far.

Harvard educated Toshikazu Kase of the Japanese Foreign Office says Japan is ready to pay the price of defeat but will react if treated too severely. He said that Japan had been defeated even before Russia declared war and before the atomic bomb was dropped and that Japan had sought peace through Russia. He described Japan as a shocked nation, one day ready to die in battle and now suddenly it's over.

The prosecutor in the trial of Norwegian traitor Vidkun Quisling has called for the death penalty on three counts.

Gene Tierney and Cornel Wilde have been chosen for leads in "Claudia and David" at 20th Century Fox, and Bing Crosby has resumed work on the Irving Berlin movie "Blue Skies" at Paramount. Gravel-voiced Andy Devine starts his 20th year as a Universal Pictures contract player. And, if you haven't see their latest, the Marx brother's new "Horse Feathers" is great fun.

Opera singer Rise Stevens has had her voice insured for $1 million—$3000 a week if her voice gives out at a premium cost of $10,000 per year.

Finally, tournament after tournament Byron Nelson has led the pack. Today Ben Hogan shot a 64 in the Nashville Open to lead Nelson by 4 strokes.

That's the news this August 31, 1945.

And now today's news, September 1, 1945

Japan unconditionally surrendered today—September 2nd—Japan time—on the Battleship Missouri. With scores of the top Admirals and Generals aboard the ship and overseen by General Douglas MacArthur, it took 20 minutes to conclude. Foreign Minister Shigemitsu signed for the Japanese government and General Yoshijiro Umezu for the Emperor. General MacArthur accepted on behalf of the United Nations. Some Toyko aides wept at the sight.

We know now that the Japanese army had opposed the surrender but even as War Minister Korechika Anami committed suicide, Emperor Hirohito overruled the military.

In Washington President Truman sees an era of international peace and Secretary of State James Byrnes foresees a peaceful Japan. Secretary of War Henry L. Stimson called General MacArthur the architect of victory.

Seriously ailing Allied prisoners of war in Tokyo were used as guinea pigs and tortured in so-called medical experiments which are being compared to the sorcery and cruelty of the Middle Ages.

Military chiefs of the United States are divided on the future of Italian colonies including Eritrea, Libya and the Italian Somaliland as to whether they should go back to Italy, become Allied mandates or be put under U.N. administration.

About 85,000 V-12 Navy students taking medical, dental and theological training will be released on November 1st with another 25,000 remaining as apprentice seamen continuing their studies until graduation.

A new record for a non-stop flight from Honolulu to Washington today as the B-29 plane "The Lady Marge" took 17 hours and 31 minutes.

New movies are "Duffy's Tavern" with Bing Crosby, Sonny Tufts, Betty Hutton and in "Our Vines Have Tender Grapes" are Edward G. Robinson, James Craig, Margaret O'Brien and Butch Jenkins.

On radio this week the Great Gildersleeve and Edgar Bergen return on Sunday nights on NBC, Lum and Abner return on the American network, Sherlock Holmes on Mutual, and the Life of Riley moves next Saturday to NBC followed by Truth or Consequences.

In sports at the U.S Tennis Championships at Forest Hills, Pauline Betz and Sarah Palfrey Cooke are finalists after beating Doris Hart and Louis Brough. In the men's finals will be Sgt. Frank Parker and the winner of the Pancho Segura and favored Bill Talbert match.

That's the news this September 1,1945.

And now today's news, September 2, 1945.

President Truman has designated surrender day as V-J Day. Gen. MacArthur aboard the USS Missouri in Tokyo Bay accepted the Japanese surrender terms. First, the Japanese signed—for Emperor Hirohito Foreign Minister Shigemitsu and for the Imperial General Staff General Umezu—the first Japanese defeat in its 2,600 year history was witnessed by aides in tears. Then 12 Allies signed headed by Gen. MacArthur who said at 9:07 am "It is my earnest hope and indeed the hope of all mankind that from this solemn occasion a better world shall emerge out of the blood and carnage of the past." Others on hand included Admirals Halsey and Nimitz, and Generals Eichelberger, Curtis LeMay, Jimmy Doolittle, Carl Spaatz and freed prisoner General Jonathan Wainwright.

Disliked and guilty of committing many blunders, most Japanese expect former Premier Tojo to be tried as a war criminal. And Japanese General Yamashita, known as the Tiger of Malaya, surrendered today.

When the Queen Elizabeth arrived two days ago in New York harbor with 14,800 passengers it included former New York Governor Herbert Lehman, now head of the United Nations Relief and Rehabilitation Association, and film star Col. Jimmy Stewart.

In sports, while 6th ranked Doris Hart of Miami did beat Margaret Osburne at Forest Hills in the finals Mrs. Sarah Palfrey Cooke beat 3-year winner Pauline Betz.

President Truman has abolished the Office of War Information, and the Army and Navy have ended censorship of mail. The supply of gas this Labor Day weekend is plentiful for the first time since 1941 as Americans by the millions have hit the roads.

Sixty-five year old actor and playwright Frank Craven died yesterday. He was best known as the Manager in "Our Town."

Yesterday was the 6th anniversary of the invasion by the Nazis of Poland starting World War II.

Today the churches are full throughout the world celebrating the formal surrender of the Japanese on the USS Missouri.

That's the news this September 2, 1945.

And now today's news, September 3, 1945.

U.S. occupation troops are in command of 720 square miles around Tokyo as the Japanese announced a free and democratic election in January.

As the Union Jack is raised again today in Singapore, 2,000 Allied prisoners in Japan have been released. An estimated 9,000 remain on the mainland.

Air Force Generals LeMay, Doolittle and Twining today flew low level over Tokyo to look at the damage done by B-29's. This was Gen. Doolittle's first flight over Tokyo since his famous April 1942 B-25 raid with planes launched from a U.S. carrier.

The Hawaiian V-J Day celebration has ended with a re-enacted mock attack on Pearl Harbor by planes of the the Air Force, Navy and Marines. With firecrackers adding atmosphere, the loudest cheers were for the 100th Infantry Battalion of Japanese-Americans who fought so bravely in Italy.

The Labor Day weekend death toll was 341, 30% more than last year.

The Soviet magazine New Times urges the U.S. to share atomic information to insure peace for all. This seems to be a hint of an atomic race between the two nations.

Premier Chiang Kai-shek, says he wants a Chinese constitutional democracy and says he'll consult all parties including the communists before establishing a National Assembly.

While Hitler claimed to be a servant of his people, records disclosed today he had an income from various sources from $2 to $6 million a year.

In sports, the New York Giants beat the Phillies 3-2 and 9-0. Giant Mel Ott hit his 21st homer and pitcher Sal Maglie claimed a shut-out. The Yanks beat the Philadelphia Athletics 4-1 and 7-6 led by George Sternweiss and Charley Keller. Texas bantam golfer Ben Hogan today won the Nashville Open in his first effort out of the Air Force. Byron Nelson faded towards the end while seeking his 17th win of the year.

Sammy Kaye's Orchestra is at the Astor Roof in New York and Vincent Lopez is at the Taft Grill. And that $6 million Big Eye 100 inch telescope for Mt. Palomar in California to search the universe is back underway after the war and is scheduled for use in 1947.

And here's good news for everyone: heavy cream comes back tomorrow with prices similar to 1942 when it was banned.

That's the news this September 3, 1945.

Tuesday, September 4, 1945

And now today's news, September 4, 1945.

Twelve hundred Japanese surrendered today as the American flag was raised once again on Wake Island with a small U.S. force present. A New York Times reporter today visited the 60% destroyed city of Hiroshima and reports that 100 people are dying each day with the present total from the first atomic bomb now 53,000. It may rise to as high as 80,000.

Secretary of State Jimmy Byrnes says the U.S. has tacitly agreed to Soviet possession of Sakhalin Island and the Kuriles in the Pacific. Gen. MacArthur today moved into the New Grand Hotel in Yokohama which will be his headquarters. The New York Times has a photo today worth a thousand words—GI soldiers leaving a prison camp as Japanese guards are bowing to them. The prisoners tell of beatings while standing at attention.

There are 115,000 prisoners in Southeast Asia including 800 U.S., 30,000 British, 31,000 Dutch, 24,000 Indians. On mainland China, 50,000 Japanese are still holding Nanking awaiting formal surrender.

Good news for stateside GI's: 665,000 of you won't be sent abroad including those over 37-years-old, those with 45 or more points, and those with one year or more of service and at least 34 points.

In sports, 44 men have turned out at West Point for football practice under Army Head coach Red Blaik and line coach Herman Hickman. Familiar faces returning including the touchdown twins Glenn Davis and Doc Blanchard.

Joseph Schildkraut has been signed as the villain in a new Bob Hope movie "Monsieur Beaucaire," Joseph Cotton and Jennifer Jones are starring in "Love Letters" while at the Paramount in New York "Duffy's Tavern" stars Ed Gardner on screen with the Andrews Sisters on stage.

Other New York entertainment includes "I Remember Mama" at the Music Box, "Oklahoma" still at the St. James, and "Life With Father" in its sixth year at the Empire. Billy Rose has a new show at his Diamond Horseshoe and Tommy Dorsey with his orchestra and Buddy Rich are at the 400 Restaurant.

National Airlines will fly you to Jacksonville in five hours and Pan Am will fly you in their four engine Constellation Clippers to Lisbon. And, the man in the house can get a fine Mallory hat for $6.00-$7.50.

Washington reports that there will be more meat, butter and bacon on railroad dining cars shortly as well as more Pullman space as military demands on the railroads continue to decrease.

That's the news this September 4, 1945.

And now today's news, September 5, 1945.

Through the Swiss government, the United States has lodged protests with the Japanese regarding atrocities, barbaric executions, filth and starvation of Allied prisoners. Among specifics was the massacre of 150 Americans by fire, behead-ing, and denial of food. Released Doolittle fliers from China today have told of 40 months of hell in solitary confinement while survivors of the USS Houston say 3,500 died on a 140 mile death march in Thailand as part of a total of 20,000 dead captives out of 56,000.

Reconnaissance troops are in Tokyo today planning occupation and the First Cal-vary will occupy the Emperor's palace. Even as Japanese Prime Minister Prince Higashi-Kuni today told the Diet that the Japanese were fast losing the war even before the atomic bomb, the U.S. revealed it broke the Japanese code in 1942 just before the battle of the Coral Sea May 4th.

Tokyo Rose, who broadcast music, advice and comments to GI's in the Pacific, has been taken at the Tokohama Bund Hotel. She is 29-year-old U.S. citizen Iva Togari, a California born Nisei who had a degree from UCLA. Claiming to be one of four women known as Tokyo Rose, she says her honey-voiced chitchat and sour propaganda was not disloyal to the U.S. and her citizenship.

The Navy says it will keep Naval bases in 15 areas including Guam, the Aleutians and Bermuda.

Gen. Chiang Kai-shek today greeted his wife on her arrival from the U.S. Her sister, Mrs. Sun Yat Sen also was on hand. Gen. Carl Spaatz, Commander of Strategic Air Forces in Japan, arrived back home in San Francisco today. Lt. Gen. Wainwright is due this weekend. And, President Truman has appointed the Joint Chiefs of Staff on a committee to study the merger of the Air Force, Army and Navy into a single Department of Defense.

There's fear in Europe of famine and chaos this winter if rail and waterways are not repaired very soon. The Commerce Department says it is putting up $300 million of war surplus materials at fixed prices for the public to buy—everything from film to bulldozers.

Navy Secretary Forrestal today said, sorry, fellows, the Navy won't let its person-nel wear civvies off duty quite yet.

While the war is over for most, today's casualty list of 297 brings sadness to families with notices of recent as well as earlier deaths and injuries.

That's the news this September 5, 1945.

Thursday, September 6, 1945

And now today's news, September 6, 1945.

President Truman today addressed Congress proposing 21 points for legislation and predicting the greatest prosperity ever.

His requests include: Increasing unemployment compensation up to $25 per week, increasing upwards the 40 cent per hour minimum wage, fair employment practices, Selective Service for 18-25 year-olds for 2 years of service, programs to benefit veterans, and an increase in congressional pay up to $20,000 a year.

Meanwhile, the Senate has voted to have a Pearl Harbor inquiry.

Disarmament of 7 million Japanese is under way and, according to Gen. MacArthur, they will be returned to their homes by October.

OPA Administrator Chester Bowles says price and rent control must stay to prevent inflation but most rationing will be over by the end of the year.

In Germany, the Allies have arrested 40 German industrialists as accomplices of the Nazi war effort.

Just four days after being present at the Japanese surrender on the USS Missouri in Tokyo, Admiral John McCain, who had been head of Task Force 38, died at his home in San Diego of a heart attack.

In New York, Police Commissioner Lewis J. Valentine has resigned after 42 years to become Chief Investigator and narrator of radio's "Gang Busters."

President Truman today appointed War Manpower Commissioner Paul V. McNutt to be High Commissioner of the Philippines.

Czechoslovakia's first war criminal was hung today as in Norway Vidkun Quisling gave his summation at his trial for treason.

The IRS will be giving preference to veterans in hiring 5,000 people to go after wartime income tax evaders.

Lois Collier and Charles Drake have been signed for the next Marx Brothers film "A Night in Casablanca," Ida Lupino will star with Errol Flynn in "Station Road," Air Force veteran Van Heflin's first role will be "Bridget," and Columbia has a new 7 year contract with Rita Hayworth. Todd Duncan, Negro baritone noted for playing Porgy in Gershwin's "Porgy and Bess" has signed for his operatic debut in "I Pagliacci" with the New York City Opera.

That's the news this September 6, 1945.

And now today's news, September 7, 1945.

General Robert Eichelberger, commander of the 8th Army, directed the ceremonies today in Tokyo as the stars and stripes were raised to formalize General MacArthur's authority in the name of the U.N.

For the first time in six years no war communiques were issued anywhere in the world.

The formal surrender in Nanking of one million Japanese on mainland China on Sunday will be a 100% Chinese show with the Americans in the background.

Secretary of War Henry L. Stimson today presented the signed Japanese surrender documents personally to President Truman in Washington.

Senate Finance Committee Chairman Walter George indicates a 15% to 18% tax cut on individuals is planned in the new tax bill.

22 people including 9 soldiers were killed in an Eastern Airlines crash in a dense swamp near Florence, South Carolina today about 2 am.

House Republican leaders led by party leader Martin of Massachusetts and Halleck of Indiana have already analyzed President Truman's legislative message of yesterday for 1946 political ammunition.

In major cutbacks, the Army has cancelled all orders for 163 million packs of cigarettes valued at $8.15 million, 20 million half package of peanuts valued at $3.5 million, and 20 million packages of gum valued at $600,000.

Black markets and inflation is running rampant in Japan since the end of the war.

12 of German's leading war criminals are in solitary confinement in a special wing of the Nuremberg jail and are being treated as common criminals.

The Orly Airfield the French plan to build will be one of the largest in the world.

In Berlin the military might of four Allies joined in a VJ day parade through the battered streets of the city.

So far, 5 million Russians have been repatriated from enemy countries.

New movies include "Isle of the Dead" starring Boris Karloff and Ellen Drew plus "Love, Honor and Goodbye" starring Virginia Bruce, Victor McLaglen and Helen Broderick.

Buster Crabbe has been signed for "Swamp Fire" in which he will have an underwater fight with lead actor Johnny Weissmuller.

Finally, 40,000 Brooklyn Navy yard workers celebrated VJ day today with an emphasis on sports including boxing matches refereed by Sgt. Joe Louis.

That's the news this September 7, 1945.

Saturday, September 8, 1945

And now today's news, September 8, 1945.

As American troops spread throughout a subdued Tokyo with bayonets ready, other soldiers have gone ashore in Korea which has been under Japanese control since 1910.

There's a hero's welcome today in San Francisco for General Jonathan Wainwright back after five years including 40 months in a Japanese prison camp. He was wearing his new 4 star general stars and told how he kept his mind active in prison by playing 8,642 games of solitaire.

Lt. Lou Zamperini, great U.S. miler in the 1936 Olympics who was given up for lost after a major sea search 28 months ago, is on his way home after having been found following 47 days in a raft and subsequent cruelties in a Japanese prison camp.

The head of the Japanese Naval Ministry says Japan did not invade Honolulu after their Pearl Harbor bombing because they had not expected such success.

A description of the Nagasaki atom bomb drop by New York Times Science Editor William L. Laurence notes he was on one of two non-bomb carrying B-29's that accompanied Bocks Car that dropped the bomb. After flying through a severe electrical storm and enemy flak, the bomb caused a seething pillar of fire 60,000 feet high that rocked the planes.

3 members of the staff of Yank Weekly, including cartoonist Sgt. George Baker creator of Sad Sack, moved into Tokyo a week before anyone else to print a souvenir edition complete with photos of the Battleship Missouri surrender..

Eyewitness reports in Singapore say the Japanese killed between 100,000 and 150,000 Chinese by lopping off their heads with swords or machine gunning groups. The Chinese natives taught their children to chant "English come, Nippons go" as they tagged along with the Japanese troops who, hearing the children, imitated the children's chanting without knowing what the words meant.

The London War Office reports the daring glider and paratroop attack on Vermork, Norway on February 2, 1943 so damaged the heavy water supplies of the Germans who were feverishly trying to develop their own atomic bomb that they discontinued work on it.

A new East-West continental record was set today by a Lockheed Constellation in 8 hours and 39 minutes averaging 272 m.p.h. Major Alexander de Seversky held the previous 10 hour and 2 minute record flying a fighter plane in 1938.

At the movies, John Wayne is in "Back to Bataan" and among fall radio shows with stars returning are Bob Hope, Hildegarde, Frank Sinatra, Kate Smith, and Gary Moore with Jimmy Durante.

That's the news this September 8, 1945.

And now today's news, September 9, 1945.

Over the weekend, American troops entered Tokyo and raised the American flag over Gen. MacArthur's headquarters in the American embassy. MacArthur says the Japanese will be allowed to govern themselves as long as they and the Emperor follow orders. The General, who has not been home since 1937, may visit the U.S. soon.

The Japanese have formally surrendered their million man force in China. A Pleasantville, New York B-29 pilot lays claim to his airplane dropping the last bomb of the war north of Tokyo as a result of his plane being the last to arrive on target at 3:15 am, August 15th.

Inflation and the black market are running wild in Japan since the end of the war.

The U.S. Army has cancelled all contracts for cigarettes, peanut butter and chili con carne, and has cut back orders for chewing gum, cereals and corn starch. President Truman has ordered an end to the program for training nurses by the U.S. Public Health Service.

The Bell Telephone Company has announced that long-distance dialing to almost any place in the country may be ready within 4 years.

Congressional leaders have promised to abolish Daylight Savings Time or War Time by September 30th.

Canada is restoring meat rationing to make sure there will be enough for export to the United Kingdom and liberated countries.

Ambassador Spruille Braden says the U.S. attitude toward Argentina will remain critical till full democracy is restored.

The U.S. and Great Britain will open a series of financial and trade talks tomorrow to help Britain out of its worst financial crisis in a century.

General Jonathan Wainwright has revealed that the Japanese had threatened to kill him while in prison.

Bess Myerson is the new Miss America. She claims she has no interest in offers from stage, screen or modeling agencies. On radio tonight is Pic & Pat, Dinah Shore, Gladys Swarthout, Rise Stevens and the Lone Ranger.

Dick Fowler, recently discharged from the Canadian Army, has pitched a no-hitter for the Philadelphia Athletics to beat the St. Louis Browns, 1-0 in the 2nd game of a doubleheader.

On a sad and historical note, 102-year-old Annie Underhill of Palisades, New York has died. She attended President Lincoln's first inaugural ball.

That's the news this September 9, 1945.

And now today's news, September 10, 1945.

Vidkun Quisling has been sentenced to death for high treason in Norway. He was also found guilty of larceny and receiving stolen property.

Gen. MacArthur has ordered the abolishment of the Japanese Imperial General Headquarters, and said he would close all news and radio agencies that continue to report false or deceptive propaganda criticism of the Allies.

Gen. Wainwright has received a hero's welcome today in Washington and was given the Congressional Medal of Honor by President Truman.

All German officials and agents in neutral countries have been recalled by the Allied Control Council.

The foreign ministers of the Big 5 will meet in London tomorrow to begin talks on peace problems. The series of conferences could last for 2 years.

Demonstrations have broken out in Korea protesting U.S. Army orders which leave Japanese overlords in office.

The Soviet Union says its casualties in killed and wounded totalled some 30,000 in the short war with Japan.

The Argentine Supreme Court says it does not have the authority to withdraw recognition from the military regime of President Farell.

Former heavyweight champion Max Schmeling has been acquitted in Germany of charges of making improper statements about his plans for publishing books to re-educate German youth.

Rumors indicate that the rationing of meat and shoes may end about October 1st. The United Rubber Workers Union says industry should support a 30 hour work week with no reduction in pay.

Soaps on radio today include Bachelor's Children, Amanda, Second Husband, and A Woman's Life. Young opera singer Mimi Benzel who made her Met debut January 5th is engaged.

The liner Ile de France has sailed from New York for Europe on her first peacetime voyage in 6 years. She should reach Southhampton this weekend.

A decision is expected soon on whether new cars will be released from rationing or limited to essential users.

That's the news this September 10, 1945.

And now today's news, September 11, 1945.

Former Japanese Premier Hideki Tojo has tried to kill himself. The suicide attempt came after Gen. MacArthur had ordered his arrest as a war criminal. American blood plasma is expected to save Tojo's life. In addition to Tojo, MacArthur has ordered the arrest of 40 persons classified as war criminals. Meanwhile, Vice Premier Prince Konoye has declared that war could have been avoided if the military clique had not interfered.

Disarming of the Japanese is continuing at a rapid rate, but the surrender of Hong Kong has again been delayed by the Japanese commander.

The Allied Control Council for Austria has adopted the minimum daily ration scale of 1,500 calories for Vienna citizens.

The Foreign Ministers Council has opened in London and work has started on a peace treaty with Italy.

The Chinese government is less optimistic about reaching an agreement with the Communists. Only limited progress is reported so far.

American and British trade and financial representatives will consider trade policies and termination of Lend-lease when they start talks in Washington.

The House Ways and Means Committee has voted to start working on an interim bill to provide relief from war taxes in the next calendar year.

A black market has broken out in fuel oil as Eastern states homeowners rush to convert from coal to oil heat.

Many New York retailers are charging 10 to 25 cents a pound over ceiling prices for meat and poultry.

Rubber manufacturers are predicting some kind of unrationed tires for motorists by the end of the year.

The United Steelworkers have announced they will ask for a pay hike of $2 per day.

On radio tonight you can hear Mr. and Mrs. North, The Saint, Bert Wheeler, Billie Burke, Dr. Christian, Crime Photographer, Mr. District Attorney and the Phil Harris Show.

That's the news this September 11, 1945.

Wednesday, September 12, 1945

And now today's news, September 12, 1945.

Japanese Field Marshal Gen. Sugiyama and his wife have committed suicide and Admiral Shimada has been arrested.

Japanese Gen. Hideki Tojo, who tried to kill himself this week, is in "very satisfactory" condition but still not out of danger.

Gen. MacArthur has ordered the Black Dragon Society disbanded and 7 of its leaders arrested.

Admiral Lord Louis Mountbatten has told his troops to be tough with surrendering Japanese armies.

The original Japanese surrender documents, signed on the battleship Missouri went on display today in the National Archives Building in Washington.

Marine ace Gregory "Pappy" Boyington came home today after 20 months in a Japanese prison camp.

Francis Biddle, former Attorney General, will be the American judge on the international tribunal trying war criminals.

American airlines are ready to start flying from New York to Europe, India and foreign countries in the near future.

Secretary-treasurer George Meany of the AF of L attacked the CIO before the British Trades Council and was booed when he criticized unions in Russia.

500 food dealers and 5 gangs in Manhattan and Brooklyn are said to be involved in large-scale racketeering in forged ration currency checks.

The United States Lines new ship Courser was launched today in New York and will take food, clothing and medical supplies to the Philippines.

President Truman is expected to be on hand for the opening game of the World Series on October 3rd in the city of the winner of the American League.

Gimbels is selling a Hearns five tube super heterodyne AC-DC radio for $27.30, stainless steel sauce pans at $1.93 and a 10 x 12 foot wooden storage or playhouse for $208. Up the street Sterns has real English leather wallets at $1.98—one to a customer, please.

Shirley Temple has revealed that she'll become a bride next week at the age of 17 when she marries war hero Sergeant John Agar.

That's the news this September 12, 1945.

And now today's news, September 13, 1945.

General Jonathan Wainwright visits New York today. He'll get a hero's welcome and be honored at a dinner tonight.

Japan's propaganda Minister Ogata has been removed from his office by the Japanese cabinet, and a purge of Japanese officials in Korea is underway. General Hideki Tojo is in "quite satisfactory" condition today, but had nothing to say about his upcoming trial as a war criminal.

And the Japanese have finally surrendered in Burma.

U.S. troops are expected to occupy major cities in China until the internal situation become stabilized.

Russia has presented a bill for 679 billion rubles as the cost of German's invasion and a basis for reparations.

Russia, meanwhile, is expected to demand a Red Sea port for herself, Trieste for Yugoslavia, and southern Tyrol for Austria at the foreign ministers meeting in London.

Here at home, President Truman has withdrawn from sale or other disposal all public lands containing radioactive materials used in atom bombs.

Gen. John J. Pershing of World War I fame is 85 today.

The Army expects to release about 1.5 million more men by Christmas. The aircraft carrier Saratoga docked at Alameda Navy Base today with 3,710 returning serviceman.

The Senate Finance Committee has further watered down the Kilgore unemployment compensation bill.

Nearly 30,000 workers are now idle in the 4-day old strike at Westinghouse plants in 6 states.

An additional 270,000 workers were laid off last week, bringing to 2,370,000 the number idled nationally since the end of the war.

The United Rubber Workers will ask for a hike of $.30 an hour, a 6-hour day and a 30-hour week in their new contract talks.

A great tropical storm, with winds over 100 miles an hour, is headed for the Bahamas, and south Florida has been put on the alert.

And if you didn't have your radio on last night, you missed Hobby Lobby, Suspense, Phil Vance, the FBI in Peace and War, Rudy Vallee, and the All Stars versus the Green Bay Packers.

That's the news this September 13, 1945.

261

And now today's news, September 14, 1945.

A stern General MacArthur says Japan will be made to carry out her terms of surrender in an uncompromising manner and he pledges a firm rule.

Ford Motor Company has stopped production in all plants and laid off 50,000 workers. The company blames strikers at suppliers. Labor officials in Washington regard a national labor crisis as a possibility.

For generation New Yorkers have had trolleys. They all will disappear by the end of next year to be replaced by 700 busses.

A survey by the New York Times suggested that colleges and universities across the land will spend $2 billion on post war building programs.

Communist armies in China have made sweeping gains from the Yangtze valley to areas west and north of Peiping.

U.S. Steel President Benjamin Fairless says the CIO Steel Workers demand of $2 a day wage increase would only require material price increases.

New York Senator Mead says he will join Senator Kilgore of West Virginia to increase unemployment benefits to $25 a week for 26 weeks.

The Army plans to release 13,000 doctors, 3500 dentists and 25,000 nurses by January 1st as General Eisenhower says most European GI's should be home by New Years.

Premier Higashi-Kuni says if the U.S. will forget Pearl Harbor, the Japanese will forget the atomic bomb and both can start anew.

General Eisenhower in Frankfort on the Main has warned GI's of severe punishment for black market activities.

The Duke and Duchess of Windsor left New York today for France and he will then go alone to England to visit his mother the Queen Dowager for the first time in 9 years.

Staff Sergeant Joe DiMaggio was released by the Army today at St. Petersburg, Florida. Whether he will play for the Yankees next year is only conjecture.

In the American League Detroit leads the Washington Senators by half a game and in the National League the Chicago Cubs lead the St. Louis Cardinals by 3½.

A new movie is "Lady on a Train" starring Deanna Durbin, Ralph Bellamy, and Edward Everett Horton and Allen Jenkins.

That's the news this September 14, 1945.

And now today's news, September 15, 1945.

Vice President Walter Reuther of the United Auto Workers CIO says a strike fund of $4 million has been set aside to make General Motors a test case in demands for a 30% wage increase. 213,000 are now idle across the country mostly in the related automotive field.

From Independence, Missouri, President Truman says a first step on returning to Washington is to see what can be done about the strikes across the land.

A violent hurricane has lashed south Florida and the Keys at 143 m.p.h. The Navy says scores of planes, blimps and hangars have been destroyed at Richmond 30 miles from Miami.

General MacArthur has put tight censorship on Japanese news sources and says that Japan cannot think of itself as an equal but as a defeated enemy. Virtually every member of the Japanese Diet is ill, has been arrested, or has committed suicide. Lt. General Masahara Homma, Commander at Bataan and Corregidor and now in custody says they felt the battle was being lost until they saw the white flag of surrender raised by the Americans over the "Rock."

The Big Five Ministers are about to agree in a surprise decision to strip Italy of all of its colonies.

Civilians are rushing to make airline reservations as 4 priority classes have been reduced to 1. United Airlines says 90% of their seats are now open.

Studebaker has shown 4 new body types with 6 cylinder engines adopted from the famous war Weasel.

The 50-year-old, 320 foot one-time President yacht earlier known as the Mayflower was used as a training vessel during the war in Boston and Norfolk.

715 Germans have been deported including Fritz Kuhn who was the leader of the German-American Bund and a former convict.

A 8400 foot airstrip was built in Hokkaido for the purpose of launching 4 engine suicide bombers to fly non-stop into U.S. cities like Chicago, Detroit and New York. The Japanese Domei News Agency has quoted a Dr. Hishina as saying that radioactivity is not a problem to human beings except at the time of and by direct damage caused by the explosion. A Tokyo newspaper has an ad for 3000 Geisha girls to entertain occupation troops.

In sports, Yankee Manager Joe McCarthy argued too strongly with Ump Cal Hubbard and was banished from the field during the first of two games at Yankee Stadium against the St. Louis Browns.

That's the news this September 15, 1945.

Sunday, September 16, 1945

And now today's news, September 16, 1945.

Japanese Prince Higahi-Kuni has asked Americans to "forget Pearl Harbor," at the same time the Japanese commander during the Bataan death march arrived in Tokyo to surrender as a war criminal.

Chinese Communists claim to have made large territorial gains in China. Poland has denounced its concord at the Vatican.

A committee of 10 Congressional members, all lawyers, will investigate the Pearl Harbor disaster.

The U.S. Navy has announced it will use the Japanese battleship Nagato in an atom bomb test.

Gen. MacArthur has ordered the Japanese premier to impound and report on all Axis and satellite properties in Asia. Meanwhile, the Japanese have finally surrendered the crown colony of Hong Kong.

Four Russian fighter planes attacked and shot down an American B-29 over Korea last month. Russian army officials say it was a "mistake" and issued regrets.

Josef Kramer, director of Belsen concentration camp, goes on trial tomorrow.

Ford Motor Company has halted production at all its plants, blaming "irresponsible labor groups" for strikes against its suppliers. 50,000 workers have been laid off. Meanwhile, CIO-United Rubber Workers have voted 4-1 to end their 10-day strike at B.F. Goodrich in Akron, Ohio, but workers at Montgomery Ward are threatening a nationwide strike.

The United Auto Workers are demanding a 30% wage hike, but the Big 3 auto makers are expected to reject the demand.

A weekend hurricane caused $50,000,000 damage in south Florida.

New York trolley cars will disappear from Manhattan and most of the Bronx by the end of the year.

Sammy Snead won the Southwest Invitational Golf Tournament and collected $2,000 in war bonds.

Dr. Frank Lovejoy, chairman of the board of Eastman Kodak, has died at 74.

Finally, the great Irish tenor, John McCormack, died in Ireland at the age of 61.

That's the news this September 16, 1945.

And now today's news, September 17, 1945.

Yugoslavia will submit today to the Foreign Ministers Conference in London her demands for Trieste, Fiume and other Italian territory.

In Japan, Tokyo reports that Premier Shigemitsu has resigned and has been replaced by Shagima Yoshida. Meanwhile, Gen. Wainwright says Japan must be occupied for 20 years.

The Army expects to release 765,000 men and 75,000 officers by Christmas, and the 6th Armored Division has been "inactivated." All draftees in the Japanese theater will be released with 6 months.

The trial of Josef Kramer, the Beast of Belsen, got underway in Germany today, and the trial of Lord Haw Haw for high treason started in London.

Former president Herbert Hoover has prepared a 5 year plan for the settlement of all war debts to the Allies.

China has announced she will eject all Japanese civilians from that country.

The CIO United Steelworkers claim the industry profits were over $2 billion in the five years of war and want a 25 cents hourly wage hike.

President Truman says he is ready to accept the best compromise he can get in the unemployment compensation bill now under study in Washington. Meanwhile, the President has decided to reorganize the Labor department and will give details tomorrow.

In sports, Jake LaMotta stopped George Kochan in the 9th round of their scheduled 10 round bout last night, and Tami Mauriello was awarded a TKO over Gunnar Barlund in New Orleans.

The New York football Giants will take on the Boston Yanks in a charity game tomorrow night in Lynn, Massachusetts.

In Hollywood, there are rumors that Will Hays will retire and be succeeded by Eric Johnston as head of the Motion Picture Producers and Distributors of America.

Finally, good news for New Yorkers. Mayor Fiorello LaGuardia has ended meatless Tuesdays and Fridays.

That's the news this September 17, 1945.

And now today's news, September 18, 1945.

Secretary of War Henry Stimson has resigned. His replacement will be Robert Patterson. Ohio Senator Harold Burton has been nominated to the Supreme Court by President Truman.

The War Labor Board, Office of War Mobilization and Reconversion, and Office of Economic Stabilization have been merged into one office and the National War Labor Board, U.S. Employment Service, and War Manpower Commission have been incorporated into the Labor Department.

The UAW has authorized local unions to accept less than the 30% wage demand if companies promise to add increases depending on the settlement with General Motors.

CIO oil workers have gone on strike, idling some 200,000 workers.

Senator Richard Russell, of Georgia is demanding that Japanese emperor Hirohito be tried as a war criminal and Japanese Prince Higahi-Kuni has promised to abolish the War and Navy ministries.

Gen. MacArthur has suspended the Tokyo newspaper Asahi for 2 days for "slanting the news."

Chinese government and Communist negotiators are said to be nearing agreement on avoiding a civil war.

Russia wants to be the sole trustee over Tripolitania in North Africa and probably Eritrea.

Housewives here will be getting a lot more shortening, cooking and salad oil, but sugar will continue to be rationed. And, despite the biggest crop in history, turkeys are still scarce and costly, but there should be enough by Thanksgiving. Meanwhile, government restrictions on the building of homes, public works and commercial buildings will end on October 1.

In baseball, Frankie Frisch is reported to be on his way out as manager of the Pittsburgh Pirates and will be replaced by Al Lopez.

Finally, 3 B-29's have taken off from Japan trying to fly non-stop to Washington.

That's the news this September 18, 1945.

And now today's news, September 19, 1945.

Acting Secretary of State Dean Acheson says the U.S. government, not the army of occupation, will determine policy towards Japan.

In London, Lord Haw Haw has been found guilty of high treason and sentenced to be hanged.

Those three B-29's flying from Japan had to stop in Chicago for fuel and it thwarted their efforts to fly nonstop to Washington.

Gen. MacArthur has slapped a 24 hour suspension on the Nippon Times for failing to submit copy for censorship before publication.

The Navy announced it has been ordered to hold up using the Japanese battleship Nagato in an atom bomb test.

Britain's Prime Minister Clement Attlee has told the Indian people that steps will be taken to give them self-government after the upcoming Indian elections.

In South America 250,000 Argentines shouted "Death to Peron" in a mass rally for liberty.

The French have received assurances that China will respect French sovereignty in Indochina.

Spain's Generalissimo Francisco Franco says he will retire when he chooses to.

U.S. occupation forces in Korea have lifted Japanese-imposed restrictions on religion, the press and politics.

And President Truman says the size of the occupation army cannot be estimated accurately until next spring.

The U.S. Senate has voted against retaining the $25.00 weekly benefit in the Kilgore Unemployment Compensation bill.

U.S. Airlines says they will soon be offering 10-hour coast-to-coast flights, and 11-hour flights to Europe.

The Nash-Kelvinator plant in Kenosha, Wisconsin, has been closed by a wildcat strike nationwide. Over 200,000 workers in various industries are now idled by strikes.

Finally Dr. Elwood Channing Huntington, father of College athletics, has died.

That's the news this September 19, 1945.

Thursday, September 20, 1945

And now today's news, September 20, 1945.

The critical point score for Army discharge will be lowered from 80 to 70 on October 1st, then to 60 points on November 1st.

The Senate has passed the Kilgore Unemployment Compensation bill and sent it to the House. It provides $15-$28 per week for as long as 26 weeks.

Spreading strikes are threatening to shut down 2 of the country's largest oil refineries.

The OPA has raised the price of imported silver to 45 cents an ounce.

The French luxury liner, Normandie, has been declared surplus property and turned over to the Maritime Commission for disposal.

OPA Chief Chester Bowles says price controls should be maintained long enough to prevent inflation.

Nearly 3/4 of Japan's army has been demobilized in one-half the allotted time.

All restrictions on fraternizing between Germans and Allied soldiers will be lifted on October 1, but there will be reservations on intermarriage and billeting.

General Brehon Somerville has requested retirement effective the same day Gen. George Marshall steps down as Chief of Staff.

President Truman has terminated the Office of Strategic Services, effective October 1, and ordered creation of a permanent foreign intelligence service under the State Department.

Two Senators have delayed Dean Acheson's nomination to be Under-Secretary of State saying he insulted Gen. MacArthur.

Representative Joseph Martin has recommended a cut in 1946 federal taxes of at least 20%.

Finally, Studebaker Corporation says it is aiming for a production rate of 300,000 cars a year.

And finally, rationing of lower grades of beef will end October 1st.

That's the news this September 20, 1945.

And now today's news, September 21, 1945.

General MacArthur says the war criminal trials will start soon and the Japanese army will be abolished October 15th. He also ordered the arrest of Kenji Diohara, commander of the First Army, known as a master of murderers and recent successor to Field Marshal Gari Sugiyama who committed suicide September 12th.

Japanese sources say Emperor Hirohito is stronger than ever in Japanese public opinion as a result of his leadership in his nation's surrender.

The Senate Military Committee has postponed changing the draft law to see how voluntary enlistments develop.

The World Council of Churches in Geneva, Switzerland will establish an extensive food and clothing organization for Europe.

The All-India Congress has met in Bombay for the first time since 1942 and is demanding freedom from imperialistic domination.

Professor Tran Duc Thao, Vice President of Indochina government, says only France menaces the independence of Indochina and it will be resisted.

Major General Leslie Groves who was in charge of the atomic bomb development, says the U.S. should keep its secrets at least for a few years as a guarantee of peace.

Chancellor Robert Hutchins of the University of Chicago says an institute has been established there to apply the discoveries of atomic research regarding cancer, heredity, and growing old.

General Eisenhower was acclaimed today by tens of thousands in the streets of Warsaw, Poland. He was there to receive the Supreme Polish Award called the Virtuti Militari.

Among books published today are "The Ghost and Mrs. Muir" by R.A. Dick at $2.00 and "Atomic Energy for Military Purposes" by Professor Henry Smythe at $1.25 paperback and $2.00 in cloth.

Frank Sinatra has signed a five year contract with MGM. His first feature will be "Till the Clouds Roll By." Dean Jagger has been signed for "Sister Kenny" with Rosalind Russell and Alexander Knox.

In sports the St. Louis Cardinals beat the Chicago Cubs in a double header today now only 2 games out of first place with 8 games to go and the two teams meeting again next week. Detroit is 1½ games ahead of the Yankees. Byron Nelson shot his second 66 in a row to stay ahead of Ben Hogan by four strokes in the Esmeralda Open in Spokane, Washington.

That's the news this September 21, 1945.

Saturday, September 22, 1945

And now today's news, September 22, 1945.

The U.S. government has sent a directive to General MacArthur that Japan is a menace to the world and must be restricted politically, militarily and economically. Prince Konoye says the Japanese people may not be ready for elections in January and predicted the Emperor will not abdicate.

President Truman has sent a letter to the British Cabinet asking to allow 100,000 Jews to enter Palestine immediately.

Under an American plan, Trieste would remain Italian and Italy should not be asked to pay reparations. The views were presented to the Council of Foreign Ministers in London today.

The War Production Board headed by J.A.Krug will go out of existence October 31st.

Contrary to popular belief, Kamikaze pilots could turn back if it wasn't possible to cause damage to the target. They would then be sent on another suicide mission. All Kamikaze pilots who did not come back got promoted two grades.

Assistant Secretary of the Navy John L. Sullivan says carriers were the deciding factor in the Pacific victory and will continue to be one of our most potent weapons.

In Luxembourg, Germany Polish-Jewish physician Ada Bimko testified today in the trial of Josef Kramer known as the Beast of Belsen, that he kicked and beat sick and dying prisoners as they were led to the gas chamber.

5441 United Mine Workers are on strike in Pennsylvania as well as 25,000 more at Westinghouse—a total of 34,000 strikers in Pennsylvania.

Senate Finance Committee Chairman Walter George is advocating a 50% cut in income taxes. He says the government shouldn't take more than 50 cents out of a dollar.

Winston Churchill today spent a day sketching on the Riviera near Monte Carlo.

Dr. Nicholas Murray Butler is retiring as President of Columbia University at age 83.

Now, would you believe that Macys New York is selling airplanes? It's called the Ercoupe, flies at 110 m.p.h. with a range of 500 miles, takes two passengers, is spin proof, and sells for $2994.

Two new movies this week. Joan Crawford is in "Mildred Pierce" and Hedy Lamarr and Robert Walker are in "Her Highness and the Bellboy."

That's the news this September 22, 1945.

270

And now today's news, September 23, 1945.

Life Magazine reports this week that Governor Thomas Dewey knew about but did not reveal Pearl Harbor information that could have so damaged President Roosevelt that Dewey could have been elected President.

President Truman has accepted Secretary of War Stimson's recommendation that the recent war be known officially as World War II.

Viet Nam, the Indochinese resistance movement, has set up government in Hanoi and want the French out.

Gen. MacArthur says Japan is doomed, never again to be a world power, militarily or commercially. Gen. Wainwright today called them savages.

Wake Island defender Lt. Col. James Devereux is back from 4 years of prison.

The Japanese deny the aviatrix Amelia Earhart is alive.

General Eisenhower was cheered by thousands today during a Warsaw, Poland Parade.

In Los Angeles there was a demonstration today of using radar to guide airplanes in blind landings.

The banished Duke of Windsor looked at England through binoculars in the English Channel en route to Paris.

On Friday twenty-eight year old Henry Ford II replaced his 82-year-old grandfather Henry Ford as President of Ford Motor Company.

A new automotive firm is being formed by Henry J. Kaiser and Joseph Frazer to market the Frazer auto.

Sgt. Joe Louis will receive the Legion of Merit as a model soldier and Frank Sinatra has a new five year exclusive MGM contract and is about to start filming "Till the Clouds Roll By."

That's the news this September 23, 1945.

Monday, September 24, 1945

And now today's news, September 24, 1945.

Emperor Hirohito says he is now for peace and blames War Minister Tojo for the war.

In Oslo, Norway, Vidkun Quisling is appealing his death sentence for treason.

The 50,000 ton German liner Europa arrived in New York today manned by a Navy prize crew and jammed full of returning GI's. 140,000 troops were demobilized last week.

Dean Acheson has been confirmed Under Secretary of State by 69-1.

Archbishop Spellman is in Chungking, China.

China and the British still want United Nations headquarters in Geneva, though the Russians have agreed to a U.S.location.

There's concern for the Nazi underground movement in Argentina with the government there doing little about it.

Col. Jacob Ruppert, late founder of Ruppert's beer, left an estate of almost $5 million.

Singer Vaughn Monroe is at the Commodore Hotel in New York and Mexican screen actor Ricardo Montalban has been signed to be in "Fiesta" with Esther Williams.

GE lamp bulbs today start at 10 cents and up, $1 buys 10 Persona blades, and the new plastics industry which grew 325% from 1939 to 1945 is expected to grow 25% per year.

AT&T sold out its $160 million of 2¼ per cent debentures as the stock market today traded 890,000 shares.

Finally, Navy day on October 26th will feature some 40 to 50 ships in New York Harbor including the surrender ship, the Missouri.

That's the news this September 24, 1945.

And now today's news, September 25, 1945.

Russian Foreign Minister Molotov dropped a bomb today demanding joint Allied control of Japan. Secretary of State Byrnes bristled. Gen. MacArthur predicts a long U.S. occupation.

President Truman has asked for a 28 billion dollar slash in War Department appropriations.

Strikes are spreading. Sixty-seven soft coal mines are closed affecting 10,000, 1,400 Phelps Dodge workers are out in Elizabeth, New Jersey, the elevator strike in New York City has paralyzed the garment industry, 500 Pan Am maintenance workers are threatening, the UAW is demanding a 30% increase from Chrysler, and the United Electrical Workers are demanding a $2 a day raise from Westinghouse.

In San Francisco Gen. MacArthur with handpicked 80 survivors of the Bataan Death march received a roaring reception.

Due to a lack of materials, there will be no boat show in New York. The last one was in January 1941.

A new movie has opened called "The House on 92nd Street" featuring William Eythe, Lloyd Nolan, Gene Lockhart, Leo G. Carroll and Signe Hasso.

Washington reports that wages for women during the war went up 60% while men went up 39%. And those women can buy the popular brown and white saddle shoes at I.Miller for $5.95.

That's the news this September 25, 1945.

273

Wednesday, September 26, 1945

And now today's news, September 26, 1945.

An unprecedented meeting took place today in Tokyo as Emperor Hirohito with top hat on his head called on Gen. MacArthur for a 40 minute social visit.

Gen. George Patton's recent comments belittling the importance of ousting Nazis from high positions in industry and commerce has aroused Gen. Eisenhower who has summoned Patton to explain his public stand.

Under Secretary of State Dean Acheson today revealed a letter from the late President Roosevelt to Spanish government officials that the United States would not provide economic aid nor friendship so long as Franco is in power.

In Paris, actor Maurice Chevalier has been cleared of collaboration charges. Lack of fuel in that city may keep the Louvre closed this winter.

In Copenhagen, Denmark King Christian was cheered on his 75th birthday.

Almost all of the 32,000 Allied prisoners in Japan have left for home even as details are learned of the execution of 3 Doolittle raiders after a 30 minute mock trial in October 1942 following their carrier-based raid over Tokyo.

In Germany, witnesses testified against Belsen concentration camp guard Irma Grese.

In China, a victory bonus has been declared for all soldiers equal to $1.50 in American money.

In New York, famous Hungarian composer Bela Bartok had died at age 64.

Finally, 55-year-old U.S. Army Major Paul Hitler has had enough. He and his wife have legally changed their name to Harrison.

That's the news this September 26, 1945.

And now today's news, September 27, 1945.

Argentina's military dictatorship continues to arrest freedom fighters who are speaking out.

General George C. Patton has met with General Eisenhower who says Patton must yield his viewpoints on the Nazis or step down.

Robert P. Patterson was sworn in today as Secretary of War succeeding Henry Stimson.

Marshal Zhukov of Russia will be visiting President Truman in Washington, October 4th.

Former President Herbert Hoover says the U.S. should keep its atom secrets to itself.

King Christian of Denmark has honored metropolitan opera star Lauritz Melchior.

Promoter Sol Hurok announces that 55-year-old famed ballet dancer Vaslav Nijinsky will appear at the Met next month.

Skater Sonja Henie's 5 year marriage to Marine Capt. Dan Topping II seems to be breaking up and 21-year-old Angela Lansbury will be married tomorrow to 35-year-old actor Richard Cromwell.

Hedy Lamarr, Robert Walker, June Allyson and Agnes Moorhead are in a new movie called "Her Highness and the Bellboy."

A 3 run homer by Yankees pitcher Red Ruffing helped beat the Philadelphia Athletics and the New York Giants have signed manager-player Mel Ott to a five year contract.

Finally another 594 war missing Americans have turned up alive.

That's the news this September 27, 1945.

And now today's news, September 28, 1945.

In Tokyo General MacArthur has ordered the Japanese government to stop taking action against a free press and suppressing public opinion in writing or spoken word and that includes not printing an American interview with Emperor Hirohito. Headquarters says 4 combat divisions will start home within 7 weeks with 1.5 million home by spring.

The British are rushing troops to Java where some Indonesians have revolted while other troops will be sent to Indochina where the Annamese have been rioting.

Under agreements between Russia and Chiang Kai-shek and Communist leader Mao Tse-Tung "a complete central unified government will be created for the whole of China with early elections."

With the non-fraternization with German citizens lifted, American soldiers and German girls have produced a pro-German attitude among many occupation troops along with a rise in social diseases.

President Truman has proclaimed exclusive mineral rights to the Continental shelf to an offshore depth of 600 feet. Fishing grounds will also be regulated.

William H. Davis, former director of Economic Stabilization says the legal minimum wage of 40 cents an hour is inadequate saying it should be a minimum of 65 cents and 75 cents in two years.

Philippine President Sergio Osmena is in California today en route to Washington to meet with President Truman.

From Mongolia to Indochina during the war 85 Army, Navy and Marine officers and men with a hundred other agents of the AGAS (the Air Ground Air Section) along with tens of thousands of friendly Chinese saved 898 fliers who bailed out or crashed.

A German doctor-internee testified today how he found evidence of cannibalism in the Belsen concentration camp by inmates starving to death. He said conditions there were far worse than at Buchenwald.

A C-54 Globemaster started a regularly scheduled around-the-world passenger service with 8 passengers aboard. It will take 151 hours, leave on Friday and return next Thursday with a dozen crews and 3 airplane changes.

Auto deaths are up 26% over August of last year which this month took 2430 lives. In cities over 10,000 deaths were up 57% in largest part to old cars, poor roads and driving too fast.

That's the news this September 28, 1945.

And now today's news, September 29, 1945.

President Truman has ordered General Eisenhower to stop the abuses of Jews that includes poor food and insufficient, unsanitary conditions for those still behind barbed wire in Austria and Germany outside the Russian zone.

The Russian government through the Peoples Commissar for Foreign Affairs Vyacheslav M. Molotov has remained rigid in a contrary position to the others in Big Five meetings regarding the Potsdam peace agreement. Some say this impasse may require scrapping the treaty making plans devised at Potsdam.

The Arab League has protested the proposed trusteeship of Russia over Tripolitania and it would ask for immediate independence for Palestine if Britain tried to transfer her mandate there to an international trusteeship.

The National Industrial Council says that in the midst of many strikes there are 150,000 jobs going begging throughout the country with 25,000 available in Kansas City alone. At one time in the war there were 1.7 million shipyard workers. With 221,000 laid off in August alone, their numbers are down to 871,000.

6 German civilians and 10 POW's have arrived in Boston under tight security brought here for their transportation talents in research and development.

The State Department says the U.S. is ready to recognize Hungary now that they've agreed to free elections.

The U.N. Executive Committee in London has still not made a decision on a permanent site for U.N. headquarters and Russia is pushing for a discussion of specific sites.

33-year-old American born Rita Louisa Zucca, known to European GI radio listeners as "Axis Sally," has been sentenced to 4 years and 5 months by an Italian military tribunal.

Now that the DC-4 and Lockheed constellation have proved their capacities and range, they'll provide a whole new era of flying comfort for commercial airlines.

In sports, Army beat the Army Air Force Personal Distribution Command in football today 32 to 0. Coach Earl Blaik's Black Knights ran over the opposition at West Point led by Felix "Doc" Blanchard and Glenn Davis. And Charlie Grimm's Chicago Cubs have clinched the National League for the World Series.

That's the news this September 29,1945.

And now today's news, September 30, 1945.

Gen. George Patton has met with Gen. Eisenhower regarding possible discipline following Patton's recent outspoken comments about Germany.

Sixty-two year old Admiral Bull Halsey will retire soon.

The Air Ground Air Section saved 90% of the Navy and Army fliers who crashed or bailed out in Asia during the war—almost 1,000 men.

Eleanor Roosevelt has endorsed William O'Dwyer for Mayor of New York where 6th Avenue will soon be known as Avenue of the Americas.

Irving Berlin has been honored for "God Bless America" as the best wartime song.

The new Joan Crawford movie "Mildred Pierce" features Jack Carson, Zachary Scott and Eve Arden.

Columbia's Lou Little has a new wing-T offense which didn't help in a weekend loss to Lafayette 40 to 14 as Penn beat Brown 50 to 0.

One day out of the Navy, pitcher Virgil Trucks started for the Detroit Tigers, was relieved by Hal Newhouser as Hank Greenberg hit a grand slam homer giving the Tigers a win over the St. Louis Browns and the American League title. They'll meet the National League champs Chicago Cubs coached by Charlie Grimm in the World Series.

That's the news this September 30, 1945.

And now today's news, October 1, 1945.

Treasury Secretary Fred Vinson has proposed a 5 billion dollar tax cut even as unemployment may hit 8 million in 1946.

The administration has goals of a 40-50% increase in output of civilian goods.

A Jewish doctor has testified at the war crimes trials in Germany that 80,000 Jews were put to death in one night at a Polish concentration camp.

The Navy says the U.S. lost a total of 701 ships during the war.

Chief Justice Harlan Stone has welcomed newest justice Harold M. Burton to the bench.

Irving Berlin was given the Legion of Merit today by Gen. George C.Marshall for "This is the Army" show for which he wrote the book, lyrics and music.

For the first time in history, a woman has addressed the Italian Parliament.

Canadian Prime Minister Mackenzie King has recommended Vancouver Island as U.N. headquarters.

Two new movies are "Blithe Spirit" starring Rex Harrison and Constance Cummings, and "The Story of GI Joe" featuring Robert Mitchum and Burgess Meredith about the life of Ernie Pyle.

Radio shows tonight include Amos and Andy, Jo Stafford and the Bob Hope Shows.

That's the news this October 1, 1945.

And now today's news, October 2, 1945.

Gen. Eisenhower has removed Gen. George C. Patton as head of the Third Army and command of Bavaria for speaking out on Germany.

Characterized as a dismal failure, the Big Five peace conference has ended after 22 days in London with no conclusions.

Illness has cancelled Soviet Marshal Zhukov's trip to Washington.

Pope Pius said today the difference in civil and ecclesiastical law is that one springs from man, the other from God.

Henry A. Wallace's new book speaks to its title "60 Million Jobs."

Nicholas Murray Butler has retired as President of Columbia University. No successor has been announced.

A.N. Spanel, President of International Latex, is suing King Features for $6 million for libel.

Army Sergeant Joe Louis has been discharged and expects to be at the World Series.

A new book for $2.75 by Sinclair Lewis is called "Cass Timberlane."

"Weekend at the Waldorf" is at Radio City Music Hall starring Ginger Rogers, Lana Turner, Van Johnson and Walter Pidgeon.

Radio shows tonight include Eddie Cantor, Kay Kyser, Can You Top This, Inner Sanctum and Fibber McGee and Molly.

That's the news this October 2, 1945.

And now today's news, October 3, 1945.

The soft coal strike is spreading, an outlaw Longshoreman strike has paralyzed New York Harbor, and a possible temporary telephone strike tomorrow could affect long distance and network programming.

President Truman says the Navy will seize operation of 11 oil refineries on strike. He has also proposed an Atomic Energy Commission be established to regulate atomic development.

Britain and France want Geneva as UN headquarters as the executive Committee has voted 9 to 3 to have it in San Francisco.

Roy Rogers headed the 20th Annual Madison Square Garden Wild West Show last night. The 104th New York Philharmonic season has opened with conductor Artur Rodzinski. Today is the 75th anniversary of the YWCA.

In sports the Detroit Tigers beat the Chicago Cubs 9 to 0 in the first World Series game.

Pedigree pups are $40 each at Gimbels and Wanamakers plans to sell Piper Cub airplanes.

Radio shows tonight include Abbott and Costello, Rudy Vallee, Burns and Allen and Jack Haley and Andre Kostalanetz with Lily Pons.

Finally, word is out about an exact look-alike for Britain's Field Marshal Montgomery, who, to fool the Germans, masqueraded as Montgomery in Algiers on June 4, 1944 just two days before D-Day.

That's the news this October 3, 1945.

And now today's news, October 4, 1945.

A New York State tax commission recommends repeal of the state income tax.

Gen. MacArthur has abolished the Japanese secret police and all restrictions on freedom of speech and religion. Also today the entire Japanese cabinet has resigned.

Air Force General Curtis LeMay has declined appointment as Senator from Ohio replacing new Supreme Court Justice Harold Burton.

Pierre Laval was ordered out of the Paris courtroom today for vehement protests.

A C-54 Globemaster has completed a round-the-world flight of almost 24,000 miles in just under 150 hours.

Emerson Radio has a portable radio with no outside wires or antenna and new tube developments for $25, while Maytag has a new product line including an automatic washer, automatic dryer, and an electric food freezer.

Frederic March closes in Broadway's "A Bell for Adano" after 296 shows and Humphrey Bogart and Lauren Bacall are signed for "The Devil Was A Lady."

Radio shows tonight include Kate Smith, Frank Munn, The Lone Ranger, and Duffy's Tavern. Tomorrow night Jessica Dragonette sings with Gus Haenshen's orchestra.

The Detroit Tigers tied the world series today beating the Cubs 4 to 1.

That's the news this October 4, 1945.

And now today's news, October 5, 1945.

Admiral Chester Nimitz received a thunderous welcome today in Washington. Hundreds of thousands lined the streets before he spoke at the Washington Monument and was then greeted by a joint session of Congress.

The Navy has released the names and dates of the loss of all naval vessels during the war. They include battleships Arizona and Oklahoma sunk at Pearl Harbor, carriers Hornet, Princeton, Wasp, Lexington and Yorktown to 7 heavy cruisers, 6 escort carriers, 3 light cruisers, 52 submarines, 69 PT boats and 71 destroyers.

Phone service in all 48 states and Washington, DC was interrupted today for as much as four hours in the first nationwide strike of phone workers. Just returned veterans at Camp Shanks, New York trying to reach their loved ones resented the 100,000 workers involved.

73-year-old Baron Kijuro Shidehara, a former Ambassador to the United States and a known liberal, has been invested as Premier by Emperor Hirohito.

In a nationwide address, Secretary of State James Byrnes says the United States is firmly against a peace conference only by the Big Powers and hopes Russia would agree since at the moment Russia seems suspicious of the Western Allies.

2700 west coast drivers of Pacific Greyhound Bus walked off their jobs. Not a bus is moving. There are now 200 strikes involving 491,000 workers nationwide.

The censorship started in Germany in 1933 is about to end as restoration of a free press in Bavaria starts momentarily and will include the melting down of the original metal plates of Hitler's "Mein Kampf."

Students in Cairo are rioting to make British troops withdraw from Egypt. They also back Arab rights in Arab countries including Palestine.

After having spent $10,000,000 during the war, the Army is returning Newark Airport to the city and commercial flights of four airlines starts October 15th.

Mass picketing at Warner Brothers film studios in Hollywood between differing unions in a 7 month old strike erupted today into riots that included knifings, clubbing and gas as police restored order.

Discontinued by the war, the Tanglewood Music Festival starts again this summer in the Berkshires with 22 year veteran conductor Serge Koussevitsky at the podium.

Finally—and possibly very finally—13 civil war veterans of the Grand Army of the Republic have met in Columbus, Ohio. Their ages ranged from 96 to 102.

That's the news this October 5, 1945.

283

Saturday, October 6, 1945

And now today's news, October 6, 1945.

As part of controlling post war Japan the U.S. policy will be to see that National Shintoism is rooted out as a state religion. The constitution of the Emperor also is to be radically modified. Japan's new Premier Baron Shidehara says he wants all cooperation possible from Japanese citizens and wants to fully cooperate with General MacArthur.

The Communist newspaper Pravda in Moscow says if France is permitted to participate in the peace treaties of the Balkans, then Poland, Yugoslavia and Czechoslovakia should be included.

While the coal mine operators blame John L. Lewis for calling a strike, Lewis says he didn't call workers out and has rejected the operators request to put them back to work.

For the second time in 3 days former French Premier Pierre Laval has been ejected from his treason trial courtroom for staging turbulent scenes.

Combat veterans across the country are mad at the number of strikes and workers off the job. Mrs. Roosevelt told 100 women union members they should be community citizens first rather than workers with special interests.

Providence Attorney John A. Pastore became Governor of Rhode Island today when J. Howard McGrath resigned to become U.S. Solicitor General.

Students at four universities in Argentina are flying rebel flags and holding out against the state military dictatorship. Over 1000 have been arrested along with some professors. Many protests are directed at Vice President Juan Peron.

The Navy has revealed it had a secret torpedo driven by an electric motor that left no identifiable wake and which successfully attacked hundreds of enemy vessels.

Col. Stafford L. Warren, Rockefeller University lecturer on medicine, says upon returning from Japan that radioactivity in Nagasaki is only 1000th that of a luminous watch dial.

On Broadway, lead performers Howard Keel and Betty Jane Watson are celebrating the 1100th performance of "Oklahoma" while nearby John Raitt and Jan Clayton celebrated the 200th performance of "Carousel."

That's the news this October 6, 1945.

And now today's news, October 7, 1945.

Admiral Chester Nimitz who led the Pacific fleet to victory was honored two days ago in Washington with a huge parade, 1,000 planes flying overhead and honors by President Truman.

Two hundred strikes nationwide have idled almost 500,000 workers. Combat veterans are bitter about the strikes.

In Paris, Pierre Laval has blamed Marshal Petain for the wartime Vichy dictatorship.

In London the Duke of Windsor has received a tumultuous welcome after a six year absence.

Survivors of 6 U.S. submarines lost in the war with all hands presumed lost have been found in prison camps.

At a lunch with Netherlands Queen Wilhemina, Gen. Eisenhower presumably has said he believes Hitler is alive.

General Motors president Harlow Curtice has shown the 1946 Buicks and Cadillacs with sweeping fenders and massive front ends.

Fred Allen is back on radio after a year and Maureen O'Hara has been signed for a 1946 production of "Sinbad the Sailor" with Douglas Fairbanks, Jr. to cost $2 million.

New movies are "Weekend at the Waldorf" starring Ginger Rogers and Van Johnson and "George White's Scandals" starring Jack Haley and Joan Davis

Yesterday Army overwhelmed Wake Forest 54-0 with All-Americans Glenn Davis and Doc Blanchard each scoring a touchdown and Columbia's Lou Kusserow scored three touchdowns in beating Syracuse 32 to 0.

In the world series, the Detroit Tigers yesterday beat the Chicago Cubs 4-1 to even the series and today went ahead by winning 8 to 4.

That's the news this October 7, 1945.

And now today's news, October 8, 1945.

President Truman says the United Nations will not share its atomic energy engineering secrets with other nations.

The government plans to sell 650,000 housing units to the public that it built for wartime purposes.

Rudolf Hess who parachuted into Scotland in May 1941, has been returned to Germany for war crimes trial.

The Beast of Belsen Josef Kramer testified today he was only being an obedient Nazi.

In Wiesbaden, Germany, two German women described the deaths of 400 Poles and Russian slave laborers by hypodermic needle and poison pills.

GE scientist Dr. Irving Langmuir told a Senate Committee today by 1965 the Russians will have push-button capability of bombing the United States.

Former Japanese Premier Prince Higashi-Kuni said today Emperor Hirohito did not know about Pearl Harbor in advance of the attack.

The New York City Symphony opened its concert season today under new, young conductor Leonard Bernstein. Artur Rubenstein appears in Town Hall, October 28 and Marian Anderson on November 11th.

The Cubs tied the world series by beating the Tigers 8 to 7 today.

On radio tonight listen to Vox Pop, Gabriel Heatter, Cavalcade of America, Hedda Hopper and Lum and Abner.

That's the news this October 8, 1945.

And now today's news, October 9, 1945.

Gen. George C. Marshall in a major report on the war warns that the U.S. could face future disaster by disarming. He also revealed plans how the U.S. would have invaded Japan on November 1st.

The House Military Affairs Committee says the U.S. has a five to twenty year head start on atomic developments.

In Paris, Pierre Laval was sentenced to death today, without appeal, for plotting with the enemy.

Col. Juan Peron, Argentina's Vice President, has resigned after a military coup.

Readership of Hitler's Mein Kampf has been banned by a German committee.

Admiral Chester Nimitz paraded down Park Avenue and Broadway today to City Hall to roaring crowds and was made an Honorary Citizen of New York by Mayor LaGuardia.

Army faces Michigan this Saturday at Yankee Stadium featuring its famous backfield of Arnold Tucker, Glenn Davis and Doc Blanchard.

On Broadway Josephine Hull completes her 400th performance in "Harvey" tonight. Victor Moore will be in a new Broadway show "Nelly Bly" on October 15th.

Charles Coburn and Ginny Simms star in a new movie "Shady Lady" and on Radio tonight you can listen to Lowell Thomas, Raymond Graham Swing, Kenny Baker Sings and the Jo Stafford Show.

That's the news this October 9, 1945.

And now today's news, October 10, 1945.

Despite the devastating wartime raids, 75% of German industry has survived but cannot operate fully due to lack of coal and transportation.

U.S. Senator William Fulbright is being considered as President of Columbia University to succeed Nicholas Murray Butler.

U.S. Senator Happy Chandler of Kentucky has resigned following his confirmation as baseball commissioner.

The USO hasn't ended with the end of the war. It is sending 86 shows overseas for occupation troops.

While one million GI's are being released each month consumers are benefitting with the release of 80 million pounds of butter by the Army.

Pitcher Hal Newhouser led the Detroit Tigers to win the World Series today beating the Chicago Cubs 9-3.

Admiral Nimitz was on TV station WNBT New York today and was televised to war wounded in area hospitals using 59 TV receivers.

An incredible 110-year-old edition of the New York Daily Mirror newspaper of 1835 has been found with an anonymous editorial predicting that gunpowder eventually will become obsolete as a powerful new destructive force will be developed capable of killing a million men in an hour forcing international settlements. Other predictions included stratosphere flying in pressurized cabins, a huge bridge that will be built across the Hudson River, and that New York City's population will be over 10 million—all by the year 3000.

Finally, on radio tonight enjoy Jack Smith, Ellery Queen, Ezio Pinza records, the Billie Burke Show, the Bert Wheeler Show or the Frank Sinatra Show.

That's the news this October 10, 1945.

And now today's news, October 11, 1945.

A tax cut bill was overwhelmingly passed today by the House to save $5.3 billion that also frees 12 million from the tax rolls.

The editor of the Communist newspaper, the Daily Worker, has resigned and renounced all connections with Marxist ideology and has joined the Catholic church.

Gen. Eisenhower was honored with a cheering parade today in Prague.

14 men were honored today as President Truman presented each with the Congressional Medal of Honor.

The FCC today announced the achievement of a television miracle as CBS told the FCC they have sent a color TV signal from the Chrysler Building across town to the CBS building. It is said the color was bright and the picture clear. CBS expects to publicly demonstrate color TV in January.

In sports, New York Giants football Coach Steve Owen today especially saluted his two veterans Ken Strong who has played for 12 years, and Mel Hein 15 years. Notwithstanding injuries, the Dartmouth football team left today to meet undefeated Notre Dame in South Bend.

Frank Parker and Robert Falkenburg are in the tennis semifinals in Mexico City.

Universal and Warner Brothers studios have been closed by strikes.

On radio tonight hear Dinah Shore's Open House, the Jack Kirkwood Show and the Andre Kostalanetz Show featuring Oscar Levant and Dorothy Kirsten.

Men's wool or camel-hair top coats are $48.25 at Macy's and men's Oxford shirts at Franklin Simon are $2.50 each.

That's the news this October 11, 1945.

Friday, October 12, 1945

And now today's news, October 12, 1945.

German General Anto Dostler has been sentenced to death by a firing squad at an American Military Court in Rome. He was convicted of shooting 15 American soldiers without a trial.

The Argentine government is in a state of crisis. President Edelmiro J. Farrell has accepted resignations of all cabinet members with the exception of the newly appointed Minister of War who has permitted the Army to place recently ejected Vice President Juan Peron under arrest. It's believed he's on a gunboat under strict surveillance prior to a trial.

With the return of the Queen Elizabeth and the Aquitania to British service, the U.S. has lost 125,000 spaces for troops to return home. It will cause several months delay of the planned schedule.

General Eisenhower emphatically says no Nazi will be allowed to vote and that the Army "will uproot Nazism in every shape and form."

The Japanese cabinet is starting a major overhaul of their constitution geared to General MacArthur's demands.

The Cuban Senate has ratified the U.N. Organization Charter by 34 to 2.

General Eisenhower has clarified his statement reporting Hitler might be alive. He said he had said "There's every presumption that Hitler is dead but not a bit of positive proof he is dead."

Among the men President Truman honored with the Congressional Medal one was to a conscientious objector, Corporal Desmond T. Dodd of Lynchburg, Virginia. A medical corpsman, he showed supreme heroism in aiding wounded comrades on Guam, Leyte, and Okinawa including saving the lives of 75 casualties bringing them one by one down a cliff by a rope ladder.

While 261,608 were killed in the war, at home during the same period 355,000 were killed in accidents and 36 million injured. Traffic alone caused 94,000 deaths.

Following this week's destructive typhoon that isolated 150,000 U.S. troops in Okinawa, 50 B-29 Superfortresses are flying in emergency food and supplies.

In a Wiesbaden, Germany trial, an attendant at the Hadamar Insane Asylum has told how he and an assistant killed 400 Russian and Polish men, women and children by poison or by injection.

President Truman has condemned the DAR for denying their Memorial Constitution Hall to Negro performer and pianist Hazel Scott.

Dan Duryea has signed for "Come On Along" with Eddie Cantor and Joan Davis.

That's the news this October 12, 1945.

290

And now today's news, October 13, 1945.

400 scientists who helped develop the atomic bomb foresee bombs thousands of times more powerful than those just dropped. They say to try and keep it from the rest of the world "will lead to unending war more savage than the last."

The Norwegian Supreme Court has upheld a lower court death sentence by firing squad for traitor Vidkun Quisling. Execution is likely for next Saturday.

From Batavia, Java, the Commander of Indonesian People's Army has called for an all out guerrilla warfare against the Dutch, Eurasian and Ambonese. They want freedom from the Dutch. Japanese military police there posted barricades and set up machine guns.

China and France are negotiating in Chungking for an agreement reaffirming French political rights in Indochina.

Hearings on Pearl Harbor are expected to start in a month.

In an order dated December 10, 1944, Japanese headquarters approved their soldiers in the field eating dead enemies but not dead comrades.

The Japanese Cabinet has agreed to amend the election law to permit women to vote.

Allied Headquarters this week revealed a highly secret U.S. army intelligence unit consisting mostly of Japanese-Americans who risked their lives and likely that of relatives in Japan with their undercover work. Many have received top decorations.

U.S. Judge Advocate General E.C. Betts in Europe says veterans are law-abiding men and will not contribute to crime just because they know how to use guns.

Chain-smoking Pierre Laval has written letters of farewell to his wife and daughter while awaiting death by a firing squad. His wife continues appeals.

The founder of the worlds best known chocolate, Milton S. Hershey, has died in the town he founded, Hershey, Pennsylvania at age 88. After two failures and one major success making caramels, he retired only to roll up his sleeves and start the chocolate company in 1903. His largest philanthropy was a $60 million gift to found the Hershey Industrial School in 1918.

Another Army victory, this time over Michigan with its All American Twins Doc Blanchard scoring on a 68 yard run and Glenn Davis on one for 70 yards.

That's the news this October 13, 1945.

Sunday, October 14, 1945

And now today's news, October 14, 1945.

Violence has flared up in Buenos Aires and Juan Peron was arrested.

In Germany, General Dostler has been sentenced to be shot while Gen. Charles de Gaulle says he will not order a new trial for Pierre Leval.

The Japanese General Staff headquarters has been dissolved.

British troops, led by tanks, have raided the black market in Tiergarten, Germany.

Syria and Lebanon are considering further restrictions against Jews.

Herbert Hoover says harsh treatment of Japan and Germany is not the way to secure lasting peace.

Here at home, the AF of L and CIO continue to struggle for control of the New York waterfront.

Transit workers have gone on strike in Massachusetts, stranding 600,000. Gov. Tobin has seized the lines.

Sample of CBS color TV sets should be ready by the end of January.

The 27,000 aircraft carrier, USS Oriskany, was launched yesterday in the Brooklyn Navy Yard.

Strikers in Hollywood have hit 2 more studios.

Barry Fitzgerald starts a new radio show "His Honor the Barber" Tuesday written by Carleton E. Morse.

Star football player Charlie Trippi is being discharged from the Air Force because he is "surplus."

Incredible Byron Nelson continues his domination of golf by winning the $10,000 Seattle Tournament with rounds that included a 62 and 63.

Turkish and huck towels will return to stores by mid-November.

That's the news this October 14, 1945.

And now today's news, October 15, 1945.

With Admiral William F. "Bull" Halsey standing on the deck of the battleship U.S.S. South Dakota, his Third Fleet steamed into San Francisco Harbor today as tens of thousands looked on.

Pierre Laval was executed today before a firing squad, not before, however, he attempted suicide when he heard his time had come. His stomach was pumped out and then he was shot and, as observers noted, he died bravely.

General MacArthur says Japan has been totally disarmed and is no longer a world power. His headquarters also announced that live Allied prisoners had been used for bayonet practice.

A Reuters dispatch says a Japanese Navy staff officer says Hitler had made plans to escape to Japan with Eva Braun.

Generalissimo Chiang Kai-shek says the U.S. Marines will be withdrawn from China soon.

The British are experimenting with rocket missiles found in Cuxhaven, Germany that can be aimed at targets 150 miles away.

Thirteen Congressmen returning from Russia urge closer ties with the Soviet Union.

Representatives of 40 countries began arriving today in Quebec for the first session of the U.N. Food and Agriculture Organization created to eliminate worldwide hunger through better distributing of world resources.

Washington announces that 4.75 million men will be out of the service by year's end equal to half of peak Army war time strength. Recently discharged Joe Louis has signed a contract with promoter Mike Jacobs to fight Billy Conn next June.

Head Michigan football coach Herbert O. "Fritz" Crisler says the rules should be changed to permit freshmen to play varsity football.

With the lifting of all priorities on the airlines, all flights are booked solid. Delivery of surplus C-54's by the Army will increase capacity from the DC-3's 21 passengers to 44 passengers and when the new Douglas DC-6 is delivered soon capacity will be 52 passengers.

Television must be on the horizon as radio repair man William Bundy Still is building his own TV station with FCC approval for an experimental license W2XJT in Queens, New York. He even adapted a film projector to TV standards so as to show films.

And that's the news this October 15, 1945.

293

Tuesday, October 16, 1945

And now today's news, October 16, 1945.

A flight of 101 Navy planes flew over New York today, heralding the arrival of 10 fighting ships to Presidential review on Navy Day.

President Truman has asked Congress to allow Puerto Ricans to vote on their independence.

The War Labor Board will end its work by January 1st.

Edward Stettinius has flown home from London for treatment of gallstones.

An Argentine report says Juan Peron was never arrested, but he would be released from protective custody to go to a hospital.

A state of siege has been reported in Hungary.

The Netherlands is reported ready to grant dominion status to Indonesia.

Japanese in Tokyo have staged a hunger strike calling for food and demanding death for war leaders.

General Eisenhower says Germany is on the brink of economic disaster because of inflation.

Pan-Am's new fare from New York to London will be $275 one way and $495 round trip starting Saturday.

The Philadelphia A's have traded Dick Seibert to the St. Louis Browns for George Quinn.

The "Red Mill" will open tonight for 8 weeks at the Ziegfeld Theater in New York.

A new film firm, Sam Goldwyn Productions, has been formed in Hollywood.

The Queen Mary will continue as a troop transport at least until the first of the year.

That's the news this October 16, 1945.

And now today's news, October 17, 1945.

Negotiations resume today in New York's dock strike as thousands of workers are back on the job.

John L. Lewis has suddenly called off the soft coal strike.

Over 1,00,000 American soldiers will be discharged this month.

President Truman has asked Congress to revive the Public Works Program.

In his annual harvest festival amnesty Japanese emperor Hirohito has released about 1,000,000 Japanese.

In Argentina, Juan Peron has gotten his henchmen back into the Cabinet.

Russia has started withdrawing its troops from Manchuria, and say they want an Allied Control Council in Tokyo.

Archbishop Damaskinos has temporarily assumed the premiership in Greece.

Billy Conn has not signed a contract to fight Joe Louis in June because of a dispute over a clause barring tune-up fights.

Jimmy Foxx and Gus Mancuso have been dropped by the Phillies, and the A's have sold Don Black to Cleveland.

American Airlines will start New York to London service on Tuesday.

The popular radio show, Mr. District Attorney, will soon be on the movie screens with Franchot Tone in the starring role. Adolphe Menjou and Michael O'Shea will also be featured.

That's the news this October 17, 1945.

295

Thursday, October 18, 1945

And now today's news, October 18, 1945.

A military tribunal in Berlin has indicted 2 German war leaders and 7 Nazi organizations on war crimes charges.

Pro-Peron mobs are in power in Buenos Aires after a night of shooting, as Peron forces now control Argentina.

Britain and the U.S. are reported ready to recognize the Hungarian government.

In Japan, Gen. MacArthur has outlawed all activity in narcotics and ordered drug crops destroyed.

Tokyo Rose has been transferred to a jail in Yokohama. She will be tried for treason.

Flying the Hump in the Himalayas will stop November 15th.

Marshal Tito is said to be massing military forces in the southern part of Yugoslavia.

Task Force 62 is in New York waiting for the battleship New York which arrives tomorrow.

The New York dock strike is over.

Butter prices will go up 5-6 cents a pound on November 8th.

Billy Conn has now agreed to fight Joe Louis in June. Welterweight Tony Janiro takes on Al Guido tomorrow night at St. Nick's Arena.

The Davis Cup competition will resume next year, 7 years after its suspension because of the war.

Finally, the Senate Finance Committee has voted to repeal the excess profits tax.

That's the news this October 18, 1945.

And now today's news, October 19, 1945.

The battleship New York arrived in New York Harbor today 31 months and 4 major battles later to be dismantled by cutter's torch or possibly to be used in research for a test of the atomic bomb on naval vessels.

The Senate Finance Committee plans to give all individuals a 5% tax cut more than the house version and take 12 million off the tax rolls.

Indictments have been handed down for 23 German war criminals for their trials due to start in November. They include Reich Marshal Hermann Goering, Rudolf Hess once the #3 man in the country, Field Marshal Wilhem Keitel, Grand Admiral Erich Raeder, Alfred Rosenberg, Arthur Seyss-Inquart, Foreign Minister Franz von Papen, Foreign Minister Joachim von Ribbentrop, Col. Alfred Gustav Jodl, Julius Streicher known as the Jew baiter, and Minister of Economics Walter Funk who broke down in tears on hearing the indictment. Still missing is Hitler's deputy Martin Bormann.

The Dutch are trying to put together an Army for subduing the unruly Nationalists in the East Indies.

90% of the 589,852 Marines in service served overseas.

Management walked out of the UAW bargaining meeting for 90 minutes today protesting the presence of the press. Union leader Walter Reuther says something less than a 30% increase may be possible.

General H.H. "Hap" Arnold says there should be a single Defense Department with equal status for the Army, Navy and the Army Air Force.

An RAF Glouster Meteor jet has set an unofficial world's speed record of 600 m.p.h beating the 1939 record of a German at 469 m.p.h.

A secret railroad car #140 was used by President Roosevelt and then by President Truman. It contained equipment for phone calls anywhere in the U.S., radio teletype with unbreakable code transmission at 100 words per minute for transmission around the world, and capability to send and receive messages from ships at sea.

Adlai Stevensen, American Delegate to the U.N. Executive Committee, says 39 countries have now signed the UNO Charter.

New movies feature Claude Rains in "Strange Holiday" written by Arch Oboler, and Constance Bennett and Gracie Fields in "Paris Underground." "Duffy's Tavern" radio star Ed Gardner says he will produce a film "Murder in Duffy's Tavern."

The stock market today traded a heavy 1,730,000 shares with the DJA off 1.44 at 185.34. Commonwealth Southern led activity with 99,000 shares.

That's the news this October 19, 1945.

Saturday, October 20, 1945

And now today's news, October 20, 1945.

General Eisenhower has recommended destroying the I.G. Farben munitions plant in Germany as well as breaking up German cartels.

Rebel airplanes bombed Caracas, Venezuela today as heavy street fighting continued between rebels and national guard units loyal to the deposed President Anganta. 300 are dead and 1000 injured in the last 36 hours.

During the next 3 to 5 year period General Motors has proposed a 5-8% pay increase to the United Auto Workers Union. GM President Charles E. Wilson discussed the proposal with President Truman in Washington.

Indonesian leader Achmed Sukarno has asked President Truman to stop the Netherlands from using American equipment in the independence fighting.

6th Avenue in New York City is no more. Today its name was changed to Avenue of the Americas with dedications by Mayor Fiorello LaGuardia and Chilean President Juan Antonio-Rios. Together they reviewed a large Navy parade down the Avenue.

Great Britain today ratified the U.N. charter leaving only Russia among the Big Five to do so.

Some 40 to 50 Germans connected with the Dachau concentration camp will go on trial next month in Wiesbaden, Germany.

The Japanese internment camps in California have released more Japanese-Americans leaving 12,000 plus 16,000 in a special camp for those considered as possibly disloyal. They expect to close all camps by December 15th.

Three B-29's landed in Washington today 59 hours and 30 minutes after flying 13,167 miles from Guam west around the world. They had stops in Karachi, India and Frankfort, Germany.

Dr. Syngman Rhee, former President of the Korean Provisional Government, returned to Seoul today after 33 years in the United States determined to resist the country's separation at the 38th parallel.

Former Postmaster General and head of the Democratic National Committee James A. Farley is in New York today campaigning for William O'Dwyer for Mayor. Mrs. Wendell Willkie is in town doing the same for opponent Newbold Morris.

New movies include Claudette Colbert in "Guest Wife," Constance Bennett in "Paris Underground" and Walter Abel and Shirley Temple in "Kiss and Tell."

In sports, Army beat the PT Raiders from the motor training center in Rhode Island 55-13 with Blanchard and Davis each scoring 3 touchdowns.

And that's the news this October 20, 1945.

And now today's news, October 21, 1945.

Returns from France's first election since 1936 today indicate General Charles de Gaulle has a threefold victory.

British Gurkha troops have occupied Semarang in Java after a three hour battle with native forces.

Juan Peron's opponents in Argentina have gone into hiding and police are patrolling streets in Buenos Aires.

General MacArthur's chief legal officer says Emperor Hirohito and his household will be tried as war criminals if evidence develops against them.

The U.S., Britain, France and Russia have officially recognized the provisional government of Austria.

Venezuelan rebels have gained full control of the country headed by its provisional President Romulo Betancourt.

A survey in Germany indicates many young girls under 19 want Nazism back and claim Hitler merely had bad advisors.

Pope Pius XII says women should go into public life or at least vote and to oppose doctrines that threaten the home.

A new word has been coined by a Duke University Professor Raphael Lemkin during an indictment against German war criminals. It is "genocide" from Latin and Greek words meaning killing of races.

Price controls have been lifted on many consumer items but red point rationing will probably continue for the rest of the year.

While during normal times hundreds would graduate, Princeton University is still on an accelerated program. Just 17 men from the classes of 1943 to 1947 will constitute the smallest graduation group since Colonial times as they get their degrees right in the President's office. It is expected Princeton and other accelerated schools will be back to normal graduation next June.

Yankee Stadium will have night baseball starting in 1946.

Newell Convers Wyeth, well-known illustrator and painter was killed in a train accident today near Chadds Ford, Pennsylvania. He was 62.

In pro football, Slingin' Sammy Baugh of the Washington Redskins tossed for three touchdowns while beating the Philadelphia Eagles 24-14. The Cleveland Rams, behind first year quarterback Bob Waterfield, whipped the Chicago Bears 41-21.

That's the news this October 21, 1945.

And now today's news, October 22, 1945.

French voters overwhelmingly okayed a constituent assembly in yesterday's national elections.

General MacArthur has abolished military and "ultranationalistic" instruction in schools in Japan.

Romulo Betancourt has had himself declared President and Minister of the Interior in Venezuela.

New elections have been promised in Argentina that will be "absolutely free and honest."

A force of 1,200 Navy planes will fly over New York as President Truman reviews the fleet in the Hudson River on Navy Day.

Western Union Telegraph Company plans to establish thousands of super high frequency radio beam stations on towers across the country to replace its wire system.

Production has stopped at 12 Libbey Owens Ford plants.

Teamster President Daniel Tobin is threatening a strike of milk truck drivers.

The GI show, "This is the Army," held its last show last night in Honolulu.

The U.S. Senate has confirmed the appointment of Spruille Braden as Assistant Secretary of State for Latin American affairs.

General Motors has conceded that a labor walkout is inevitable while the UAW has asked for a Senate investigation of what it calls the company's strike-provoking activities.

That's the news this October 22,1945.

And now today's news, October 23, 1945.

President Truman has asked that Congress consider 1 year of military service for all males some time between ages of 17 and 20.

The U.S. Navy is trying to arrange a sea test of an atom bomb attack on a group of warships to test its effect.

The U.S. Steel Corporation says ceiling prices and wage stabilization make wage hikes impossible.

James Petrillo, President of the American Federation of Musicians union, is demanding more jobs for musicians on radio stations that duplicate their live programs on the new FM stations.

Pan Am will not put its $275 trans-Atlantic fare into effect on Saturday. A new application will be filed in a few days.

A new outbreak of violence in the motion picture strike has resulted in 13 arrests and injuries to 50 people.

The battleship Missouri has joined the growing fleet for Navy Day in New York.

Vidkun Quisling has been executed by a firing squad in Norway.

The U.S. is considering whether to recognize the new regime in Venezuela. Official circles indicate that conditions appear to be favorable.

The British labor government has promised tax relief to individuals and corporations next year.

The U.S. Senate Finance Committee has okayed a plan to cut taxes for Americans by over $5 billion.

Russia will participate in the 1948 Olympics if Russia accepts its invitation to membership.

Jackie Roosevelt Robinson has signed a contract with the Montreal Royals making him the first Negro in organized baseball.

That's the news this October 23, 1945.

Wednesday, October 24, 1945

And now today's news, October 24, 1945.

The U.S. Senate has passed a tax reduction bill of about $6 billion and sent it to the House for conference.

With Russia's ratification of the document, the U.N. Charter has become the "law of nations."

Secretary of Labor Schwellenbach is urging a 65 cents minimum wage, and reports progress in getting labor to think about productivity as well as wages and hours.

American Airlines has suspended service in and out of Chicago as the UAW is attempting to represent their maintenance workers. Meanwhile, American has launched European service with the completion of the first commercial flight of land planes from North America to Europe.

U.S. Navy ships are moving into position in New York for the big Navy Day celebration at which President Truman will christen the carrier Franklin D. Roosevelt.

Arab states have threatened retaliatory moves against American oil interests in the near East due to the Palestine issue.

Starting next week, all FM stations will drop all network programs containing music as a result of a demand by James Petrillo that more musicians be hired.

Clark Gable will star in the film "Lucky Baldwin," and John Garfield has signed a contract with RKO for one picture a year for 5 years.

Branch Rickey denies that the Brooklyn Dodgers organization was forced to hire Jackie Robinson, the first Negro in organized baseball.

That's the news this October 24, 1945.

And now today's news, October 25, 1945.

Nazi Labor Front leader Dr. Robert Ney has committed suicide in his cell to avoid trial as a war criminal.

Russia is expected to join a modified Allied Advisory Council for Japan which would leave Gen. MacArthur in power.

Paraguay, Ecuador and Cuba have recognized the new regime in Venezuela.

Loose German mines are threatening the liner Queen Mary in a heavy storm off the French coast. Fierce winds have already wrecked an American Liberty ship.

The Nobel Prize for medicine has gone to Sir Alexander Fleming, discoverer of penicillin, and to two co-workers.

President Truman will disclose his wage and price policy in a nationwide radio address next week.

General Motors workers have voted almost 6-1 to strike, if necessary, to win a 30% wage hike.

Mass picketing, which interrupted service at LaGuardia Airport in New York, has been banned by police as mediation talks get underway.

All picketing has ended in the Hollywood movie strike.

Starting Sunday, only 8 red points will be needed to buy a pound of butter.

AT&T has opened a new phone service between the U.S. and New Zealand.

That's the news this October 25, 1945.

Friday, October 26, 1945

And now today's news, October 26 1945.

In a tax reduction bill review, House conferees in Washington have agreed not to tax enlisted men's pay and to defer officer's taxes for three years. The United Steel Workers CIO union representing 766 companies have filed with the NRLB to strike.

The U.N. Executive Committee in London still has no decision for a permanent site for the U.N. after 4 hours of wrangling. An October 3rd draft recommending the United States was bitterly opposed by Britain, France and the Netherlands who want it in Europe.

Foreign Minister Ernest Bevin and the House of Commons have made it clear that the British people are horrified by the expected misery and starvation of the German people this winter, a remarkable attitude turnaround considering England was being hit by V-bombs just a few short months ago.

Tomorrow is Navy Day in New York when 47 warships will pass in review for President Truman. More than 2 million men have been released since V-E day.

The Curtis Wright Research Lab has announced it has flying devices that can go 1400 m.p.h. with likely speeds for regular aircraft at 500 to 600 m.p.h.

The town where executed Norwegian traitor Vidkun Quisling was born will not permit his ashes to be buried there.

The French report that 300,000 died during the war including 150,000 French soldiers, 100,000 civilians and 40,000 shot or massacred by the Germans. French men and women who died in German concentration camps are not included.

A new Sherlock Holmes movie is "Pursuit to Algiers" with Basil Rathbone and Nigel Bruce while just discharged from the Navy Victor Mature will star in "Three Little Girls in Blue" with June Haver, Celeste Holm and Vera Ellen. In sports, Billy Conn is in training with warm-up bouts before he meets Joe Louis next June.

Finally, Albert Einstein in an "Atlantic Monthly" article says the secrets of the atomic bomb should not be given to the UN or to the Soviet Union but only to a world government created by the U.S., Britain and the Soviets.

And that's the news this October 26, 1945.

And now today's news, October 27, 1945.

As one million people crowded into New York's Central Park, President Truman gave a major policy address on Navy Day. He said the U.S. will not recognize any government imposed on a nation by a foreign power, that present difficulties among the Allies will work out, and that the U.S. holds the atomic bomb as a sacred trust. His talk, the first time a President has been televised, was transmitted to Schenectady, New York and Philadelphia for those few people with TV sets. 12.5 million across the country listened on radio as newsreel companies filmed the occasion for use in movie theaters.

The President then took a 7 mile ride up and down the Hudson reviewing 47 warships as 1200 planes flew overhead. He also christened the new 45,000 ton Franklin D. Roosevelt carrier as 5 million people up and down the river watched.

A B-29 is expected to take off momentarily to attempt the first non-stop flight from Tokyo to Washington, DC. An earlier attempt ran out of gas.

Admiral Ernest King says as many as 100 U.S. Naval vessels may be used in an isolated Pacific spot as atomic bomb targets in a research project.

Of some 1000 marriages between Americans and New Zealanders, less than 5% have resulted in divorce probably due to an Army and Navy checkup system of planned nuptials.

In Tokyo General Yamashita will become the first Japanese to be tried on war crimes starting on Monday.

Tuberculosis is now claiming 10,000 lives a month in Poland.

On Broadway "Life with Father" has reached its 2500th performance as "Harvey" completes its first year. New movies include "Spellbound" with Gregory Peck and Ingrid Bergman, "This Love of Ours" with Charles Korvin and Merle Oberon, and "And Then There Were None" with June Duprez, Louis Hayward, Roland Young and Barry Fitzgerald.

Classical performances upcoming at Carnegie Hall and Town Hall in New York include Issac Stern, Artur Rubenstein, Rudolf Serkin, Dorothy Maynor, and Marian Anderson.

Gene Autry is out of the Navy and back on radio and this Thursday Fred Allen's "Allen's Alley" will especially feature Minerva Pious as Mrs. Nussbaum.

And that's the news this October 27, 1945.

Sunday, October 28, 1945

And now today's news, October 28, 1945.

A Chinese Communist spokesman says the war between the Central Government and Communist troops has spread to 11 of China's 28 provinces.

General MacArthur has ordered restoration of Christian teachings in St. Paul's University in Tokyo and will have all other Christian institutions in Japan surveyed to report on war-time changes and restrictions.

In an unprecedented action, the Japanese newspaper Yomiuri Hochi has released the annual income of Emperor Hirohito at 6,275,000 yen or about $1.6 million.

The ABC, NBC and CBS networks have decided to close down their New York City FM stations due to the requirements of the American Federation of Musician's President James C. Petrillo requiring standby musicians. Additionally, the FCC is requiring all FM stations to change frequencies imposing large new transmission costs.

While an RAF fighter has now flown 540 m.p.h., Curtiss-Wright has revealed a 1400 m.p.h. flying machine has been tested. They expect 500-600 m.p.h. commercial planes to be flying in years to come.

Oxford University has honored General Eisenhower and U.S. Ambassador John G. Winant. Eisenhower says atomic secrets should not be shared with Russia or the U.N. but with a world government.

Secretary of the Navy James V. Forrestal has revealed Japanese task force commanders were given specific orders a month before Pearl Harbor.

Vice President Walter Reuther of the United Auto Workers Union has rejected General Motors' President C.E. Wilson's proposal that Congress establish a 45-hour work week during the post-war reconstruction period.

In Hollywood, John Payne has been signed as detective Phillip Marlowe in "High Windows" and Jack Benny will be in a gag sequence in Claudette Colbert's upcoming movie "Thanks, God, I'll Take It From Here." And, Basil Rathbone and Nigel Bruce are in a new Sherlock Holmes movie, "Pursuit to Algiers."

In pro football the Redskins Slingin' Sammy Baugh did it again, this week completing 19 of 23 passes to beat the New York Giants at the Polo Grounds 24-14. One of the all-time great receivers, Don Hutson once again led the Green Bay Packers to a 33-14 win over the Chicago Cardinals scoring 3 touchdowns on receptions.

Finally, there should be no housing shortage now that Anchorage Homes in Westfield, Massachusetts is setting up a plant to prefabricate homes using new methods perfected during the war. One to four bedroom houses will cost from $3625 to $7525.

That's the news this October 28, 1945.

306

Monday, October 29, 1945

And now today's news, October 29, 1945.

The Chinese civil war between the Central Government and Communist troops has spread to 11 of the 28 provinces. The Russians may help the Chinese Communists massing on the Manchurian border.

The President of Brazil, Gutulio Vargas, today resigned.

American Military prosecutors of Gen. Yamashita, the Tiger of Mayala, plan to bring mutilated, bayoneted witnesses to the trial on stretchers.

An analysis of the wealth of Emperor Hirohito reveals a past income of $1.6 million, now $425,000 per year. He owns over 3 million acres of Japanese pasture and forestry.

A Victory War bond campaign was kicked off today by Mrs. Eleanor Roosevelt, Actress Merle Oberon, Secretary of the Treasury Morgenthau, and Wake Island Marine hero Lt. Col. James Devereaux.

While GI's may have been writing home about being entertained by Geisha girls, Japanese police revealed most were fakes since of the real 1500 Geisha girls, most are married or have moved away.

On the radio today you can hear Constance Bennett, Galen Drake, Jack Smith Sings, Ted Malone, and Mary Margaret McBride.

Women's cotton brunch coats are $2.50 at Gimbels, Women's alligator bags at $34.50 at Macy's and pictures of the 1946 Packard Clipper have been released that will be available in November.

That's the news this October 29, 1945.

Tuesday, October 30, 1945

And now today's news, October 30, 1945.

President Truman today has advocated higher salaries without any price increases. Neither labor nor industry is happy with the prospect.

The War Department today announced a proposal of consolidating the Army, Navy, and air groups into a single Armed Forces Department.

Prime Minister Clement Attlee of Great Britain is scheduled to meet in Washington with President Truman on November 11th to discuss atomic energy and the atomic bomb.

In the Nuremberg trials of German war criminals, Franz von Papen is the first indicted war criminal to retain a personal attorney for his defense.

A famous submarine has been decommissioned. Originally called the Squalus which sank in the Atlantic in 1939 with the loss of 26 lives, it was raised, refitted, and did battle during the war as the Sailfish.

MIT today revealed a giant robot mathematician which will do rapid calculations beyond ordinary human means. In secret operation since 1942, its capabilities baffle scientists and experts. It weighs 100 tons, has 2,000 electronic tubes, and 150 motors. Many peacetime uses and calculations of all kinds are expected.

Soprano Dorothy Maynor performs tonight at Carnegie Hall, Spencer Tracy opens on Broadway on November 2nd in Robert E. Sherwood's new play "The Rugged Path," and Ralph Bellamy and Ruth Hussey open November 11th in "State of the Union."

And, the Reynolds Miracle Pen which guarantees no refilling for two years is selling for $12.50.

That's new news this October 30,1945.

308

And now today's news, October 31, 1945.

Secretary of State James Byrnes today absolved his predecessor Cordell Hull of any responsibility of the Pearl Harbor attack because of a November 26, 1941 note he initiated.

Edwin Pauley, head of the American Reparations Commission says that a large amount of Emperor Hirohito's $100 million fortune will be used for reparations. Also in Tokyo, a large black market ring has been smashed involving 4 GI's that involved women, liquor and smuggling.

In China, American troops helping to maintain order in Japanese surrendered sectors may be in danger because of the civil war.

Famed Flying Tiger General Claire Chennault who operated out of China was honored yesterday in New York by Mayor LaGuardia.

The Independent Rochester Telephone Company has contracted to buy new automatic rotary telephones to put in use soon.

Capital Airlines is advertising non-stop flights to Pittsburgh, and the Liberty Music shops in New York has in stock the new Victor unbreakable records.

Beardsley Ruml has been elected Chairman of R.H. Macy's.

Jeanette McDonald will be featured in the life of Jerome Kern called "Till the Clouds Roll By" also starring Edward Arnold and Van Johnson.

On radio today is Stella Dallas and tonight is the Bob Burns Comedy Show, Patti Clayton Sings, Fulton Lewis, Jr. News, and Boston Blackie Mystery.

That's the news this October 31, 1945.

And now today's news, November 1,1945.

Four B-29's arrived in Washington today in the first non-stop flight from Tokyo. The flight of 6,500 miles took 27½ hours.

Terrorists today sabotaged railways and communications killing 6 in Palestine.

The Provisional President of Venezuela, Romulo Betancourt, says a new constitution will soon be written.

Some German leaders are critical of the retroactive laws which have been created by Justice's Jackson's tribunal to try German leaders as war criminals.

Three famous U.S. air aces met in Dayton, Ohio yesterday—Capt. Don Gentile, with 30 planes to his credit, Capt. John Godfrey with 37, and Lt. Col. Francis Gabreski with 31.

An investigation continues in Illinois into a straw field which still had radioactivity 23 days after the first atomic bomb explosion in New Mexico.

West Point's Athletic Director says its unbeaten football team may not entertain any post season games including the Rose Bowl.

A 75th anniversary party of the first Y.M.C.A. was held today in New York with 300 guests. 28,000 others celebrated throughout the city.

Gregory Peck and Ingrid Bergman open today in Alfred Hitchcock's new thriller "Spellbound." The Trapp Family singers will perform at Hunter College on December 15th.

On radio tomorrow night is Leave It to the Girls, Gangbusters, and The Hit Parade, and on Sunday Gene Autry, Manhattan Merry-Go-Round, and Walter Winchell.

A 6 piece sterling silver flatware Gorham set is $22.50.

A new buying wave raised stock volume today to 2,210,000 shares with the Dow Jones up $2.24 to 188.84.

That's the news this November 1, 1945.

And now today's news, November 2, 1945.

President Truman is backing a 20% pay raise for all Federal officials except the President involving about 860,000 people. Top officials would get raises of as much as $10,000.

Already Republicans are challenging Democrats on the Pearl Harbor hearings scheduled to start November 15th charging the Democrats are withholding confidential records of the late President Roosevelt.

In Cairo Jewish families have been stoned and a synagogue sacked during general strikes called by anti-Zionist organizations. Ten have been killed, 350 hurt. The outbreak is timed a year after the Balfour Declaration pledging the British to help establish a national home in Palestine for Jews.

General Lucius D. Clay, deputy to General Eisenhower, is in Washington to talk about a four power rule in Germany and reports the French are causing problems preventing a unified administration.

11,500 more GI's arrived in Boston today along with 4 dog platoons and 79 dog handlers. The dogs will be sent to Camp Kilmer, New Jersey for retraining before being returned to their owners. These and other GI's may find a problem converting to civvies in light of the current clothing shortage.

General George C. Kenney testified before the Senate Military Affairs Committee in favor of a unified command in the future for the Army, Navy and Air Forces.

In Tokyo Major Alexander de Seversky compared Hiroshima's atomic bomb to 200 B-29 bombers saying it would take many atomic bombs to devastate a city such as Chicago. He says we will still need the Army, Navy and Air Force.

In Korea 43 political parties are asking the U.N. to end the division of Korea in two parts. They want a unified whole nation.

In sports, Navy Lt. Bill Dickey, great Yankee catcher, may be the next Boston Braves manager. Major football games tomorrow include Army versus Villanova, Navy-Notre Dame, Penn-Princeton, Michigan-Minnesota, Yale-Dartmouth, and Syracuse-Penn State. In golf Bobby Cruikshank leads Ben Hogan and Ed Porky Oliver by one and three ahead of Sam Snead.

Charles Boyer and Lauren Bacall are opening in "Confidential Agent," while in Hollywood Cary Grant and Ingrid Bergman have signed for Alfred Hitchcock's "Notorious."

The Dow Jones closed at 188.62, down 22 cents on 1,840,000 shares.

And that's the news this November 2, 1945.

311

Saturday, November 3, 1945

And now today's news, November 3, 1945.

Since the arrival of the U.S.S. Missouri in New York on October 23rd over 635,000 have visited the Mighty Mo. For souvenirs visitors have stripped the Japanese surrender ship of name plates and anything that could be pried off with pliers or screwdrivers. Most of them were taken by some of the 60,000 school children aboard on one day. Even the commemorative surrender plate was assailed.

General Motors with its cash reserves and the United Auto Workers with over $100 million have set aside war funds for an extended strike which is expected to start shortly. Strikes by the AFL and CIO Machinists union in San Francisco Bay are holding up repairs on ships capable of bringing home 22,000 GI's.

Elections take place this Tuesday across the land with special attention to New York City where William O'Dwyer is expected to win and to Boston where 71-year-old former governor and congressman James Curley is hoping to win. In San Francisco the first Negro to run for office is getting support in a rally from Joe Louis and comedian Rochester.

The wonder drug penicillin is being given out now by the War Production Board on a priority basis due to a shortage.

Secretary of Labor Lewis Schwellenbach has asked the U.S. Steel Corporation and U.S. Steel Workers Union CIO to settle their dispute over a $2 a day wage increase proposal. A strike vote is scheduled for November 28th. A Presidential emergency board has recommended a 10 cent per hour increase for 7500 teamster employees of Railway Express who are now making $49.96 a week in New York.

In Nuremberg, Germany 42 members of the Dachau concentration camp have been indicted for using prisoners for inhuman medical treatment. In Manila a U.S. Military Commission has accused Lt. Gen. Tomoyuki Yamashita of deliberate destruction of Manila, slaughter of 6000 Filipinos and infamous orgies of torture, rape and murder.

In football today Notre Dame and Navy tied at 6 apiece, Michigan 26-0 over Minnesota, Penn State 28-Syracuse 0, St. Marys 26-S.California 0.

A new movie this week is "The Spanish Main" starring Paul Henreid, Maureen O'Hara and Binnie Barnes.

And radio is celebrating its 25th year this week recalling the Harding-Cox presidential election returns over KDKA Pittsburgh on November 2, 1920.

And that's the news this November 3, 1945.

And now today's news, November 4, 1945.

The British today reported they believe Hitler and his bride Eva Braun died by their own hands in a Berlin bunker April 30th.

The French provisional cabinet of Gen. Charles de Gaulle is stepping down, the U.S. has recognized the Hungarian government, France has asked for control of 3,200 German warplanes, the fight to get the Netherlands to give independence to President Sukarno's Indonesia has 30,000 bandit troops fighting British troops, and Dr. Sygman Rhee of Korea has pleaded with the United Nations to let North and South Korea unite.

OPA administrator Chester Bowles says raising the minimum wage to 65cents would have little effect on prices.

The Conservatives in Belgium believe that King Leopold will return once again as king next spring.

A milestone in aviation history today as a DC-3 has flown from the West Coast to the East with totally refrigerated vegetables, flowers and lobsters.

U.S. Senator Bilbo of Mississippi has attacked Hunter College students as "Communistic, mongrel congregations."

Archeologists digging in Iraq have found evidence that civilization may have started 2000 years earlier than the presumed period of 6000 B.C.

Lt. Gen. Jimmy Doolittle has flown a B-29 from Oakland, California to Washington in 6 hours and 59 minutes, just one minute short of Howard Hughes 1944 record.

The $10,000 Richmond Golf Tournament has been won by Ben Hogan, followed by Dick Metz, Vic Ghezzi, and Johnny Bulla.

That's the news this November 4, 1945.

Monday, November 5, 1945

And now today's news, November 5, 1945.

Secret papers have been found documenting how German's Hermann Goering and Joachim von Ribbentrop duped Neville Chamberlain in 1938 with assurance that Czechoslovakia would not be taken over as was Austria.

42 members of the German Dachau concentration camp have been indicted. If convicted, they will face decapitation.

A forced landing of a Pan Am clipper flying boat in calm waters near Honolulu has resulted in safely picking up all 26 passengers.

Because of a shortage of penicillin, it is being allocated to hospitals on a priority basis.

Railway Express workers are likely to settle for their demand of 10 cents an hour raise.

Gabby Hartnett, former Chicago Cubs catcher and manager, will become manager of the International League team Buffalo Bisons next year.

A new Bob Hope and Bing Crosby song and gags record is out for $1.05. One side has "Road to Morocco" and the other has "Put It There."

Barry Fitzgerald, Louis Hayward and Walter Huston star in "Then There Were None" and Charles Boyer and Lauren Bacall are in a new movie "Confidential Agent." Irene Dunne has been signed to star in "Anna and the King of Siam" with Rex Harrison.

Finally, word has been received that 61-year-old composer Jerome Kern has been rushed to a hospital. He presently is out of a coma and in critical condition.

That's the news this November 5, 1945.

And now today's news, November 6, 1945.

William O'Dwyer who became well known as New York District Attorney who indicted and convicted Murder, Incorporated, has been swept into office as Mayor of New York in today's elections. In Boston 71-year-old Representative James Curley was elected Mayor for the 4th time.

Russia's Foreign Minister has rebuked the United States' atomic policy and has told the Russian people they'll have their own atomic devices.

Even though Italy surrendered two years ago on September 3rd, the long awaited suppressed armistice with the U.N. has finally been signed.

London is going through the worst crime wave since post World War I. Six murders have been reported in the past two weeks.

Mayor Kelly of Chicago has recommended a new airport site northwest of the city which he hopes will rival New York's huge Idlewild Airport.

While General de Gaulle and his cabinet have resigned in Paris today, their re-election is held to be certain.

Bell Labs and New York Telephone have demonstrated a new wireless multi-channel communications system called microwave which was secretly used during the war. They expect it may be widely used in the future.

3 years ago yesterday composer George M. Cohan died. Among those attending a memorial service were "Harvey" actor Frank Fay, sportscaster Clem McCarthy, columnist Ed Sullivan, and former New York Mayor Jimmy Walker.

Sylvia Sidney has signed to star in Lillian Hellman's "The Searching Wind" with Robert Young, Paul Henried, and Walter Slezak.

That's the news this November 6, 1945.

315

Wednesday, November 7, 1945

And now today's news, November 7, 1945.

The Senate Foreign Relations Committee today has voted to permit U.S. participation in the United Nations giving its representative the right to vote.

A House Committee on Un-American Activities has started to review scripts of 7 radio commentators with a view to holding hearings on their political views. They include Raymond Graham Swing and Cecil Brown.

Republicans scored heavily in New Jersey in yesterday's elections as they took the State Senate 17 to 4 and the Assembly 42 to 19.

British Air Chief Sir Arthur Tedder and Lady Tedder were greeted today in Washington by Gen. Carl Spaatz.

British radio traitor Lord Haw Haw has lost his death sentence appeal.

November 7th was the 25th anniversary of the start of radio by KDKA in Pittsburgh which reported the Presidential returns of Harding and Cox. Other early historical radio events included Billy Jones and Ernie Hare known as the Happiness Boys, Douglas Fairbanks Sr. and Mary Pickford dramas, and Graham MacNamee who broadcast the first world series in 1924 and the first Rose Bowl game coast to coast.

Dunhill's Denicotea claims to filter out almost 80% of the tars and nicotines from cigarettes.

Former St. Louis Cardinal Manager Billy Southworth becomes manager of the Boston Braves next season.

Finally, Hotpoint expects to sell dishwashers at 30% less than their 1942 models due to new mass production techniques.

That's the news this November 7, 1945.

316

And now today's news, November 8, 1945.

President Truman has directed all government and armed forces personnel to cooperate fully and provide any and all information to the Pearl Harbor investigating committee.

The Nazi saboteurs who landed via submarine on the Atlantic Coast in June 1942 had as targets to destroy the Hell Gate Bridge in New York, the Ohio River locks, and the Pennsylvania Railroad station in Newark.

Admiral Bull Halsey visited the Pingry School in New Jersey today where he was a student in 1900.

An RAF Gloster Meteor plane has set a world speed record of 606 m.p.h. The War Department reports that while over 1.5 million men were in Britain at one point, only 77,000 remain.

Fewer than 20,000 autos have been produced in Detroit in the last 4 months due to parts shortage and strikes.

While Cary Grant originally brought the script to the studio and was to have starred, the lead in a new movie to be called "It's a Wonderful Life" will be Col. Jimmy Stewart's first postwar role.

On radio tonight hear People are Funny, Eddie Cantor Show, Jimmy Durante and Garry Moore, It Pays to be Ignorant and tomorrow night you can hear Lionel Barrymore as Mayor of the Town, Truth or Consequences and Break the Bank.

Finally, Eastman Kodak has announced a new color process which will require only one hour to develop the first print with copies taking only ten minutes each, only one-eighth of the present time. It should be available sometime next year.

That's the news this November 8, 1945.

Friday, November 9,1945

And now today's news, November 9, 1945.

General Jimmy Doolittle before the Senate Military Affairs Committee today says the Air Force must be on an equal basis with the Army and Navy in the future under a unified command. He said "It was not carrier strength that won the air war. Our B-29 boys are resting uneasily as a result (of such comments)." Secretary of the Navy James Forrestal promptly objected to Doolittle's statements.

Walter Reuther, Vice President of the CIO United Auto Workers has point by point rejected General Motors' offer of a cost of living wage increase.

Fourteen American B-29 flyers were executed just two days before the Japanese surrender. Other prisoners said they had been tortured for two months before their deaths.

Chinese Communist troops have warned the National troops of Generalissimo Chiang Kai-shek to stay out of Manchuria.

The FBI reports it handled 525,000 draft violation cases during the war involving enough men to make up 30 divisions. 12,789 men were convicted and given sentences averaging 3 years.

FCC Chairman Paul Porter says he can do nothing about the demand of James C. Petrillo, President of the American Federation of Musicians, to require a double musicians crew if a musical program is simultaneous over AM and FM.

In New York at Billy Rose's Diamond Horseshoe is a new show called "The Toast of the Town." At the Paramount in New York the movie is "Hold That Blonde" starring Eddie Bracken and Veronica Lake with Frank Sinatra on stage with Jan Savitt's band.

Tomorrow Army's Head Coach Col. Earl Blaik brings his undefeated team with Doc Balanchard and Glenn Davis into Yankee Stadium to face undefeated Notre Dame with its acting coach Hugh Devore and the country's best quarterback and team captain Frank Dancewicz. The front lines of both teams average just over 200 pounds per man.

The Dow Jones average ended down 26 cents at 191.46 on 1,830,000 shares with the Curb Exchange having 1,360,000 shares traded.

The Rockefeller Center skating season has opened in New York. If you don't skate you can dine at either the Cafe Francais or the English Grill and watch skaters while dining for dinner starting at $1.50.

For a lighter subject, GE lamp bulbs start at 10 cents for 25 to 40 watts, 100 watt bulbs are 15 cents, 150 watt bulbs are 20 cents and 3-way bulbs are 55 cents.

And that's the news this November 9, 1945.

And now today's news, November 10, 1945.

After arriving in Washington on a C-54 Skymaster from London, Prime Minister Clement Attlee immediately started discussions with President Truman and Secretary of State James Byrnes.

Fighting has become more intense between Chinese Nationals and the Communists at Shanhaikuan, the gateway to Manchuria.

Senator Alben Barkley, Chairman of the Joint Congressional Committee Investigating Pearl Harbor, says nothing will be withheld. An imposing list of witnesses will appear including former Secretary of State Cordell Hull and New York Governor Thomas E. Dewey.

The Metropolitan Museum of Art in New York will spend over $10 million renovating and adding on to their building in New York on the occasion of its 75th anniversary. It will include a new wing, a 1200 seat auditorium, a radio and TV broadcasting studio, and new facilities for displaying art objects valued at between $500 million and $1 billion.

Premier Kijuro Shidehara has complimented General MacArthur in "moving in a fair and effective manner." Many Japanese hope the Americans will bring freedom and lasting peace to Japan.

British planes and artillery along with Indian troops have blasted Surabaya in a battle against Indonesians who had rejected a British ultimatum to surrender.

On the 170th Anniversary of the U.S. Marines, a statue symbolizing the fight for Iwo Jima was unveiled today in Washington by Marine General A.A. Vandegrift.

Five German civilians were hanged today in Bruchsal, Germany for the murder of 6 American flyers parachuted from damaged planes on August 26, 1944.

Detroit is celebrating 50 years since the automobile started production—that's 88 million cars ago at a value of some $63 billion.

In New York, Sterns has women's nylon blouses at $3.50 and women's black suede shoes are $4.35 at A.S. Beck.

Adolphe Menjou and Pat O'Brien are in a new comedy "Man Alive," Franchot Tone stars in "That Night With You" and Sol Hurok will present Marian Anderson at Carnegie Hall on December 30th in her 10th anniversary concert. Negro pianist Hazel Scott today cancelled her appearance at the National Press Club in Washington because Negro journalists are barred from the organization.

Army today crushed Notre Dame 48-0 with 3 touchdowns by Glenn Davis and Navy beat Michigan 33-7.

Finally, Lewis J. Valentine continues as host on radio of "Gangbusters" on ABC.

And that's the news this November 10, 1945.

319

Sunday, November 11, 1945

Prime Minister Clement Attlee, in Washington, has proposed internationalization of all scientific developments, including the atomic bomb.

Russia has lifted censorship on all outgoing news dispatches.

Yugoslavs have elected a Constituent Assembly and Marshal Tito is expected to be heavily favored in the voting.

British troops in Java have occupied most of Surabaya in light fighting.

Allied Headquarters in Japan is expected to order dissolution of Japan's feudal landholding system.

The U.S. has an agreement with France whereby this government can be reimbursed by France for any losses incurred by over-evaluation of the franc.

The Chinese government is negotiating with the Soviet Union for permission to fly Nationalist troops into Manchuria.

Armistice Day was observed by a world largely at peace for the first time in 7 years.

U.S. Steel President Benjamin Fairless says his company has not declined to bargain collectively, but rather that the union has demanded a "yes" or "no" answer.

Because of illness, Marian Anderson has postponed her concert tonight at Carnegie Hall.

Army, Navy and Penn are the top rated football teams in the country.

Finally a great American composer, Jerome Kern, has died of a cerebral hemorrhage at the age of 60.

That the news this November 11, 1945.

And now today's news, November 12, 1945.

British Prime Minister Attlee says the U.N. Security Council has to be trusted with the atomic bomb.

Former Secretary of Commerce Henry Wallace and former Postmaster General Farley are urging international agreements to avoid economic warfare.

General Eisenhower says maintenance of adequate occupation forces in Germany is needed to help secure the peace.

Europeans are facing one of their worst winters because of the lack of coal, food, houses and clothing.

Gustav Krupp is so old and ill he may not be able to stand trial as a war criminal. Britain wants to try him in absentia.

King Farouk says Egypt is determined to bring about withdrawal of British troops and win sole rule of Sudan.

In Java, British warships and planes are attacking Indonesian positions in Surabaya.

Communist sources in China say Nationalist troops are increasing their attacks against Shanhaikwan.

A Japanese Communist leader has called Emperor Hirohito a war criminal who should be deported to China.

Figures released today show the American Baseball League played before some 5.5 million fans, the largest paid attendance in its 45 year history.

For the first time since the 1942 models, models of the new 1946 Pontiac will go on display in New York on November 18.

That's the news this November 12, 1945.

Tuesday, November 13, 1945

And now today's news, November 13, 1945.

Prime Minister Attlee addresses a joint session of Congress today and is expected to outline Britain's nationalization program.

Chungking forces are said to have captured Shahaikwan, the gateway to Manchuria.

Destruction of German war industries is underway with the blowing up of 2 Farben plants in Bavaria.

General de Gaulle has been unanimously elected president of the French government.

Yugoslavia's Marshal Tito, following his overwhelming win at the polls, says his country will not become a Russian satellite.

In Argentina, that country's elections have been moved up from April 7 to February 24.

Russia is evacuating Manchuria and has given China permission to fly 1,500 troops daily into Changchun.

U.S. Steel has refused to attend a meeting called by Labor Secretary Schwellenbach with a federal mediator and the Steelworkers Union.

Price Administrator Chester Bowles says auto dealers will not be permitted to raise prices.

The Army-Navy football game in Philadelphia on December 1 will be televised for New York television set owners.

Finally, Boeing Aircraft has introduced a new fighter plane that can go up to 450 miles an hour.

That's the news this November 13, 1945.

And now today's news, November 14, 1945.

The U.S., Britain and Canada have agreed to turn over the secret of atomic energy to the United Nations.

Russian scientists have reportedly discovered that cosmic rays can knock off protons in lead, which could lead to atomic power or bombs.

France and Russia now support America's stand of substituting Alfred Krupp for his father, Gustav, as a defendant in the war crimes trials.

Two have died and 57 people were injured in Tel Aviv in protests against Britain's new Palestine Policy.

Foreign Commissar Molotov has renewed Russian demands for a control council in Japan.

Chinese Communist forces control Manchuria as Nationalist forces have been unable to get there.

The U.S. Maritime Commission is planning to add 11 superliners to this country's merchant fleet.

Governor Thomas Dewey took a ride in a new Bell Aircraft helicopter and predicted it would become a widely used form of transportation.

Princeton University will observe its 200th birthday with an elaborate program starting next September and continuing through the academic year to June,1947.

Phil Cavaretta, the Chicago Cubs first baseman, has been named the National League's most valuable player for 1945.

Eldridge Reeves Johnson, founder of the Victor Talking Machine Company of Camden, has died of a stroke suffered a few days ago. He was 78.

That's the news this November 14, 1945.

Thursday, November 15, 1945

And now today's news, November 15, 1945.

The U.S., Britain and Canada are ready to share their atomic secrets with the U.N. on a reciprocal basis and with inspections provided.

Chinese Communists are said to be closing in on Changchun to keep Nationalist troops from landing in Manchuria.

The U.S. reportedly knew 6 months before Pearl Harbor of Japanese plans to sweep from Indochina through the Netherlands, Indies and Singapore.

British troops are in Tel Aviv to halt burning and looting of building and stores by rioters.

Gen. Eisenhower told the House Military Committee "nothing affects Russian policy so much as a desire for friendship with the U.S."

The old World's Fair site in New York has been offered as a permanent headquarters for the United Nations.

The auto industry is facing a strike as Ford turns down a union request for a 30% wage hike.

The UAW has rejected GM's offer of a 10% pay hike to salaried employees making less than $500 a month.

The U.S Bureau of Censorship goes out of existence tonight.

Basil O'Connor, president of the American Red Cross, has been named president of the board of governors of the League of Red Cross Societies.

The war crimes tribunal has postponed the trial of Gustav Krupp, but 40 members of the Elite Guard have gone on trial at Dachau concentration camp.

In Finland, the ex-president, 2 former premiers, and 5 other men have gone on trial in Helsinki.

Night baseball is coming. The owners of the New York Yankees have signed a contract for the installation of lights at Yankee Stadium.

That's the news this November 15,1945.

And now today's news, November 16, 1945.

At the Pearl Harbor hearings in Washington charges were made that the crew of the U.S ship Boise saw the Japanese fleet before December 7th and failed to report it because of orders for radio silence.

Marine Lt. General Albert Wedemeyer, Commander of U.S. forces in China, has told the Communist forces that air strafing missions will start if they don't stop firing on U.S. troops.

Secretary of State James Byrnes says a U.N. atomic energy commission could be set up in 60 days a program to rescue the world from a desperate armament race.

More than 1500 B-29 flyers are missing in combat over Japan in addition to the 837 who have been freed from prison camps.

Australia's Foreign Minister Dr. Herbert Evatt says it's time for smaller nations to share in voting and policy decisions currently being made only the Big Three.

In Walnut Ridge, Arkansas over 5000 combat planes--excepting B-29's--are being scrapped representing billions of dollars in original cost.

A British military court has found guilty the Beast of Belsen, Josef Kramer, and 29 of his staff who conducted inhuman atrocities. Sixteen were women including blonde 22-year-old Irma Grese who picked victims for the gas chamber. Fourteen were acquitted.

Jewish riots in Tel Aviv have caused 6 deaths. Soldiers and police now patrol the city and provide protection for British buildings.

General Charles de Gaulle in France has submitted his resignation as President after failing to form a cohesive and independent government. The assembly will meet Monday to decide if a new President should be elected.

A children's Christmas party in Hartford, Connecticut has been cancelled after James C. Petrillo and the American Federation of Musicians insisted they have a 12 piece orchestra if any vaudeville acts performed.

Movie and aquatic star Esther Williams will marry Sgt. Ben Gage on November 20th. He has been Bob Hope's announcer. A new movie is "Mexicana" with Leo Carillo, Constance Moore and Tito Guizar. Marlene Dietrich is physically and mentally tired after two years on the road entertaining troops and will not return to Hollywood for some time.

Stocks hit a new high for the year with the Dow Jones ending at 192.13, up one dollar on 2.3 million shares with 1,440,000 shares traded on the Curb.

And that's the news this November 16, 1945.

Saturday, November 17, 1945

And now today's news, November 17, 1945.

At the Pearl Harbor hearings in Washington it was reported that Japanese carrier pilots were secretly briefed by Admiral Yamamoto on October 5, 1941, two months before Pearl Harbor though when the fleet left November 26th they had orders to return if the American and Japanese negotiations had ended amicably.

Gen. Charles de Gaulle says he'll continue to serve as President if the French constituent Assembly wants him to try and set up a new government.

Over 500,000 American troops are expected back from Europe this month.

Admiral of the Fleet Chester Nimitz says he is opposed to a single department of Armed Forces saying it would hinder the Navy and its sea power role.

Marshal Tito in Yugoslavia says the national election last week was tantamount to rejection of a continued monarchy and urges King Peter to renounce his throne.

In Japan with runaway inflation and shortage of food and consumer goods combined with the devastation of its cities and manufacturing capabilities, many feel it will be years before Japan can become competitive to American and British world markets.

The U.S.S. Bridge hit a mine off Japan and as it foundered, its crew and its 102,000 pounds of Christmas and Thanksgiving turkey were transferred to another ship for delivery to American troops in Japan and Korea.

Eyewitnesses say Charles Lindbergh personally modified and upgraded the capabilities of the Corsair plane in the Pacific but contrary to rumors as a civilian did not fly combat missions.

Ingrid Bergman and Gary Cooper are in a new movie "Saratoga Trunk," another new one is "Abbott and Costello in Hollywood."

In sports, Army won its 17th in a row 61-0 over Penn with All-America's Glenn Davis and Doc Blanchard each scoring three touchdowns. West Point superintendent Gen. Maxwell Taylor is undecided about post season offers.

Finally, the pending sale of the Pullman Company sleeping car business to 27 railroads is on hold pending a review by a Federal court.

And that's the news this November 17, 1945.

And now today's news, November 18, 1945.

Over the weekend, Charles de Gaulle submitted his resignation in a tiff with the Communist Party.

Mamie Eisenhower has been hospitalized with pneumonia.

Yesterday Josef Kramer and Irma Grese were sentenced to hang for murder and atrocities at Belsen and Oswiecim concentration camps.

Bus drivers tied up key routes on Staten Island affecting 125,000 riders.

Predictions have been made that the U.S. sugar supply will hit bottom in the three months starting December 1.

A rebellion has broken out in northern Iran. Russian trucks are said to be distributing weapons to the rebels.

Chinese troops are making a strong effort to drive into Manchuria after capturing Shanhaikwan from the Communists.

Japan has ordered the arrest of 11 war leaders and the halting of all civil aviation and air training.

Crowds have demonstrated in Greece against American recognition of Albania.

Rabbi Hillel Silver has been elected president of the Zionist Organization of America.

Opening night performance of the Metropolitan Opera will be broadcast in its entirety from eight to midnight November 26 on the American network.

Comedian Al Pearce will start a new show from 3:00 to 3:30 daily on the American Network, starting December 3.

Retail prices for new Chrysler cars will go up 1%, Fords 2%, Studebakers 9%, while GM prices will be cut 2½.

That's the news this November 18,1945.

And now today's news, November 19, 1945.

The UAW has suggested arbitration in its dispute with General Motors.

Phone service in Indiana and Illinois has been crippled by a strike of 16,000 workers.

The OPA says black markets are still flourishing strongly in this country.

In Java, fighting has broken out in Batavia, while Chinese troops are pouring into Manchuria and have penetrated 40 miles beyond the Great Wall.

The war crimes trials are scheduled to get underway in Nuremberg tomorrow.

In France, the 3 major parties will meet with President de Gaulle to form a new government.

Iran's new ambassador has charged Russia with engineering the revolt in northern Iran.

Britain's Labor Government plans to nationalize all public utilities except shipping.

President Roosevelt reportedly said in October, 1940, that Japan would make a mistake and force the U.S. to enter the war.

Admission to the all-star Victory Loan Bond Show December 3rd at Madison Square Garden will be through the purchase of Victory Bonds.

Repairs to bomb-damaged Wimbleton Tennis Courts will cost about $24,000.

Philco Corporation will produce 4,000,000 radio receivers next year.

President Truman has asked Congress to act immediately on a 5-point health and social welfare program.

And, conductor Leonard Bernstein has charged the New York Symphony with being a "complete fraud."

That's the news this November 19, 1945.

And now today's news, November 20, 1945.

The war crimes trials got underway today in Nuremberg with 20 top Germans facing charges.

Russian troops have stopped Iranian forces trying to relieve garrisons in Azerbaijan Province.

Greek premier Canellopoulos and his Cabinet have resigned.

Chinese troops continue to pour into Manchuria, but the Communists have cut their lines of communication.

British planes have bombed Indonesian Nationalists in the heart of Semarang.

In Brazil, mayors of all municipalities have been removed from office until after the December 2nd elections.

General Eisenhower has been named Chief of Staff and Admiral Nimitz Chief of Naval Operations succeeding Gen. Marshall and Admiral King who resigned.

It is now reported that President Roosevelt considered a naval blockade against Japan in 1940.

The U.S. Senate has turned down President Truman's request that the U.S. Employment service be kept for another year before giving it back to the States.

Joe DiMaggio has signed his contract with the New York Yankees for next year. He'll get $42,500.

The Ivy League will institute a rigid, new football sports code next year to avoid overemphasis and to preserve the values of the game.

James Water, who played Jack Goldberg on the famous radio program, "The Goldbergs," has died in Woodmere, Long Island.

A B-29 has flown in record time from Guam to Washington, DC. in 35 hours 5 minutes.

That's the news this November 20, 1945.

329

Wednesday, November 21, 1945

And now today's news November 21, 1945.

UAW members are on strike against General Motors. The unions says the strike is 96% effective.

Washington transit workers have gone on the second wildcat strike in a month, and President Truman has ordered the government to take over the system.

Montgomery-Ward Company workers have called a one-week strike for next week.

French President de Gaulle has formed a new Cabinet with an equal number of members from the three main parties.

Regent Damaskinos has resigned in Greece and the Sophoulis Cabinet has taken over his duties.

U.S. Marines are in China to disarm the Japanese, while Chinese troops are threatening to overrun Hulutau, in Manchuria, now held by the Communists.

Russia has condemned the single-handed supervision of Japan by the U.S.

Lt. General Alexander Patch Jr., has died of pneumonia at the age of 55and Robert Benchley, well-known humorist, has died of a cerebral hemorrhage. He was 56.

Welterweight fighter Al "Bummy" Davis was shot to death by 4 holdup men in a New York tavern.

Detroit pitcher Hal Newhouser has been named the American League's Most Valuable Player.

Under a new FCC plan New York will have 7 television stations instead of 4.

President Truman has been asked by the OPA to decide whether to end meat rationing.

"Saratoga Trunk," starring Ingrid Bergman and Gary Cooper, has opened its run at the Hollywood Theater in New York.

That's the news this November 21, 1945.

And now today's news, November 22, 1945.

Today is Thanksgiving Day and the nation is at peace for the first time in four years.

Anthony Eden is urging repeal of the Big Five's veto power in the U.N. and has criticized Britain's new policy on Greece.

President de Gaulle says nationalization of credit and electric systems and administrative reform are high on his priority list.

In Japan, former War Minister Araki and Yoshishisa Kuzu, head of the Black Dragon Society, have been arrested.

Japanese forces have been fighting in Java under British orders. Peace negotiations have been called off.

Twelve American soldiers have been injured in riots in Calcutta, India.

A Labor Department official predicts the GM strike will be over by January 14.

The OPA is investigating a new black market in the purchase of new cars.

Northrop Aircraft has announced development of a new jet-propelled buzzbomb and a twin-fuselage military fighter with a range of 2,500 miles.

Gimbels is advertising Taylorcraft airplanes for $2,295 including 8 hours of flying instruction.

The possibility of a state-wide blackout faces New Jersey tonight because of a possible strike by PSE&G workers.

Turkey has warned that a leftist government will be formed in Iran if America and Britain do not stop Russian intervention.

Fred Astaire and Lucille Bremer premiere in a new movie today at the Capitol Theater on Broadway called "Yolanda and the Thief." Jimmy Dorsey's band is on stage.

That's the news this November 22, 1945.

Friday, November 23, 1945

And now today's news, November 23, 1945.

At the Pearl Harbor hearings former Secretary of State Cordell Hull says he put the U.S. Cabinet on alert November 7th, 1941 warning that "The United States should be ready for a Japanese attack anywhere at any time" though no one had suggested to him Hawaii might be a target.

Good news for everyone. Red point rationing is over meaning meat, butter, fats and oils are now unburdened though sugar remains rationed at least until 1946.

General Charles de Gaulle obtained unanimous backing with a vote of confidence by the French Constituent Assembly today.

Captured German documents outlined an agreement in February 1941 between Hitler and the then Japanese Foreign Minister Yosuke Matsuoka by which Japan would attack the U.S. as soon as possible.

Bishop William T. Manning says Elliott Roosevelt cannot be a Vestryman in the Hyde Park Episcopal Church apparently based upon his two divorces. His father President Roosevelt was a Vestryman there for 35 years.

General Motors has refused to accept arbitration saying it would abdicate control. They also withdrew the offer of a 10% wage increase. As 80 of 93 GM plants are already idle, its impact on suppliers may cause Ford and Chrysler to close down.

Across the land the sale of Victory E. Bonds is being heavily promoted. So far $2.754 billion has been sold toward the $4 billion goal. With a good college education including living expenses at $1250 per year, an investment of $3750 now will provide a full $5000 for four years of college expense in 10 years.

In Hollywood, Sir C. Aubrey Smith will star with Jennifer Jones and Charles Boyer in "Cluny Brown."

Gimbels New York is having a book sale of best sellers for $1.00 each including Anya Seton's "Dragonwyck," Max Shulman's "Barefoot Boy With Cheek," Pearl Buck's "Dragon Seed," Daphne Du Maurier's "Frenchman's Creek" as well as her "Rebecca," Ernest Hemingway's "For Whom The Bell Tolls," Betty Smith's "A Tree Grows in Brooklyn," Marion Hargrove's "See Here Private Hargrove," and "God Is My Co-Pilot" by Col. Robert Scott.

And that's the news this November 23, 1945.

And now today's news, November 24, 1945.

At the Pearl Harbor hearings it was noted today that Winston Churchill on November 30, 1941 urged President Roosevelt to serve notice on Japan that further aggressiveness would lead to the gravest of consequences. There was no indication that Roosevelt did so.

640,000 United Steel Workers will take a strike vote on Wednesday. Informants say a strike is likely. Union leaders have told their members no wildcat strikes.

Walter Reuther of the United Auto Workers says General Motors is trying to become an industrial economic dictatorship by means that could lead to a third world war.

With the lifting of red ration points, restaurants across the land are preparing to put steaks, chops and butter back on their menus.

President Truman is considering replacing his personal chief of staff 70-year-old Admiral William Leahy with 65-year-old retiring General George C. Marshall.

General MacArthur says Japan will not be permitted to reconstitute her former world trade organization which will now be under Allied control.

Russia intends to at least triple its auto output by the end of its next 5 year plan.

With the war over, there's expected to be a surplus of both natural and synthetic rubber for a few years.

In Nuremberg Rudolf Hess does indeed have amnesia according to Russian, French and American psychiatrists though it apparently was self inflicted. He likely will still stand trial on war crimes.

Finally, the on-going investigation of the tragic Coconut Grove fire in 1942 that killed 498 people indicates that many died of toxic fumes from burning synthetic leather.

And that's the news this November 24, 1945.

Sunday, November 25, 1945

And now today's news, November 25, 1945.

Former Secretary of State Cordell Hull says he warned President Roosevelt the Japanese might attack the United States almost anywhere. And on November 30, 1941, Prime Minister Churchill asked Roosevelt to warn the Japanese.

In Japan U.S. Marines today seized and started to destroy 5 cyclotrons with which Japanese scientists had experimented with atomic energy and were on the trail of an atomic bomb.

Rockets from RAF planes have blasted an Indonesian extremist radio station.

In Tel Aviv armed terrorists believed to be Zionists blew up coast guard stations today.

The Dean of Canterbury, the Very Reverend Hewlett Johnson, is visiting President Truman today in Washington even as the President's mother turned 93 today vowing to live to 100.

Former Vice President John Nance Garner and his wife celebrated their golden wedding anniversary today in Uvalde, Texas.

U.S. epidemiologists say they have a complete cure for cholera involving blood plasma and sulfadiazine which was used in a recent Calcutta epidemic.

Pan Am's 4 engine land clipper costs $265 to London compared to their pre-war flying boat rate of $375. Trans-Canada Airlines now has DC-3's 3 times daily between Toronto and New York.

Alabama will play in the Rose Bowl and key weekend games saw Yale beat Princeton 20 to 14 before 35,000 people at Palmer Stadium, Columbia beat Dartmouth 21-0 and Harvard blasted Boston University 60-0.

For radio entertainment tonight try Edgar Bergen and Charlie McCarthy at 8 pm.

That's the news this November 25, 1945.

Monday, November 26, 1945

And now today's news, November 26, 1945.

Former Ambassador to Japan Joseph Grew vigorously denied the statement by former Secretary of State Cordell Hull that Grew had helped touch the button causing the Japanese to attack Pearl Harbor.

Documents have been found showing that Germany was ready to invade Czechoslovakia in September 1938 even as Prime Minister Neville Chamberlain was returning to England with his famous "Peace in our time" statement.

Idaho poet Ezra Pound is one of 8 American citizens branded as traitors for broadcasting from Axis nations during the war.

New England educators say colleges and universities will be swamped by retuning GI's.

General George C. Patton has been made an Honorary Citizen of France.

The Senate Judiciary Committee has approved an official pledge of allegiance to the flag.

In New York, Mrs. Harry Truman and daughter Margaret attended last night's opening of the Metropolitan Opera.

Shipstead and Johnson Ice Follies are at Madison Square Garden. Vaughn Monroe's Orchestra is at Warner's Strand, Brian Aherne and Arlene Francis will open in "The French Touch" on Broadway December 5th, and Rise Stevens and Eleanor Steber open Friday at the Met in "Der Rosenkavalier" with Helen Traubel featured tonight in "Lohengrin."

Finally, steaks and butter are returning to restaurants with the end of red-point rationing.

That's the news this November 26, 1945.

Tuesday, November 27,1945

And now today's news, November 27, 1945.

Ambassador to China, Patrick Hurley, has resigned denouncing bitterly the administration's China policy. President Truman has appointed retiring General George C. Marshall to replace Hurley.

General Eisenhower has been given a gift by grateful Scottish people of the top floor in historic Culzean (Culleen) Castle in Ayrshire.

30,000 going-home GI's have been frustrated waiting 6 days on the west coast for trains to take them east due to railroad car shortages.

The U.S. is now capable of producing more synthetic rubber per year at lower prices than the entire pre-war world production.

Col. Paul Tibbets, commander of the Enola Gay B-29 that dropped the first atomic bomb over Hiroshima, will speak on the subject tonight at the Waldorf Astoria.

The government announced today that most all of the U.S. warplanes built at a cost of 17 billion dollars are obsolete and will be junked.

Because of a jurisdictional dispute, the new Idlewild Airport in New York will not open as scheduled in 5 days.

Pianist Hazel Scott's Carnegie Hall appearance last night featured both classical and popular music. At Radio City Music Hall, Van Johnson, Lana Turner, Ginger Rogers, and Walter Pidgeon star in "Weekend at the Waldorf" and new books include "The Robe" by Lloyd C. Douglas at $2.50 per book.

Gimbels has a double mattress pull-out bed for $49.95, a box of 25 Havana cigars for $6.43 and nylon blouses at $2.90.

Oppenheim Collins has silver fox coats at $369, black Persian lamb coats at $489 and Wild mink at $2135.

That's the news this November 27, 1945.

And now today's news, November 28, 1945.

As a result of Ambassador Patrick Hurley's resignation, Congress is demanding a hearing of U.S. policies on China.

New York Times correspondent William H. Lawrence said today that the war in Japan was won principally by U.S. bombers.

Navy Captain Charles McVay, skipper of the cruiser Indianapolis which delivered the A bomb to Tinian and was later sunk with a loss of over 1100 lives, will be court-martialed as a result of the sinking disaster.

In Congress, Representative John Sparkman of Alabama in his 5th term of office will become House Democratic Whip.

Steel workers today voted 5 to 1 for a nationwide strike.

A TWA plane has flown in record commercial time across the Atlantic from Gander, Newfoundland to Iceland in 6 hours and 45 minutes.

World War I flying Ace and Eastern Airlines President Capt. Eddie Rickenbacker has been elected to the Board of Foremost Dairies.

Macys is selling International Silver 6 piece place settings from $17 to $21, in the record department it has 3 ten inch Walt Disney records for $1.77, and 3 Alice in Wonderland records featuring Ginger Rogers at $3.44.

Hathaway Furniture has a 3 drawer drop lid desk at $89.50, a glazed leather chair at $295, and a leather top coffee table at $59.50.

At the Roxy in New York, Betty Grable, John Wayne, and June Haver are starring in "The Dolly Sisters."

Finally, make an investment in peace, join the nationwide effort and buy victory bonds.

That's the news this November 28,1945.

Thursday, November 29, 1945

And now today's news, November 29, 1945.

Yugoslavian citizens revoked their monarchy, ousted King Peter and proclaimed themselves a republic.

President Truman today says that if the U.N. works right there will be no need for further Big 3 talks.

Maj. General Miles today said that before December 7, 1941 the U.S. intercepted critical Japanese intelligent messages but that they were not decoded until after the Pearl Harbor attack.

A report today tells how U.S. airplanes losses were cut 75% over Germany by scattering tinfoil to disrupt German radar.

The War Labor Board today says it approves of the principle of equal pay for men and women in the same job. The decision affects 100,000 women at GE and Westinghouse.

A radio repairman in Queens has put up a 200 foot tower and granted an experimental TV station license by the FCC.

The first series of 10 year bonds issued by the government in 1935 come due tomorrow yielding 2.9%.

Henry Fonda will play the lead as Wyatt Earp in "My Man in Gray." New movies include Dorothy Lamour in "Masquerade in Mexico," Charles Laughton starring in "Captain Kidd," and "The Man in Grey" starring new British idol Farley Granger.

Finally U.S. Senator Wherry of Nebraska has publicly reprimanded Texas Senator Tom Connally for using the word damn on the floor of the Senate. Senator Connally has apologized.

That's the news this November 29, 1945.

And now today's news, November 30, 1945.

The then Army commander in Hawaii Major General C. Short was not told that 3 days before Pearl Harbor the Japanese were burning their codes and while the Navy had sent this information to Admiral Husband E. Kimmel in Hawaii it was not forwarded to Gen. Short.

In the Nuremberg trials, Rudolf Hess made a dramatic statement today by standing up and saying he faked his amnesia, is sane, and accepts full responsibility for all he has done.

The British government suddenly has advised Pan American World Airways that it cannot have 5 flights a week into England and will be restricted to two. The action apparently is in retaliation for low Pan Am fares. Pan Am will direct other flights into Shannon, Ireland.

An A-26 bomber has just circled the earth in 96 hours and 50 minutes flying westward and landing back at Washington.

In Manila, General Yamashita disclaimed any responsibility for atrocities by his troops in the Philippines saying he was too busy fighting to oversee everything.

200,000 Chinese communists have moved deeply into Shantung Province along a 200 mile front in the south as a major battle is expected in the north above Peiping.

Here at home, the Army has reduced discharge points from 80 to 70 for medical units making 15,000 doctors and 5,000 dentists eligible for discharge.

Dr. Irving Langmuir, Nobel Prize physical chemist, testified today in Washington warning of an atomic bomb race and noting that the Soviets could gain supremacy in 3 years.

Of 2700 Germans about to be extradited from Stockholm, Sweden back to Germany, 600 were hospitalized today after violence in which 100 tried to commit suicide.

Western Union Telegraph employees have voted 5277 to 478 to strike. The company has turned down the union demand of a 10 cent per hour increase.

A movement in Congress to end the draft is based upon increased volunteer enlistments.

100,000 in Philadelphia Municipal Stadium tomorrow will watch highly favored Army play Navy. It will be broadcast to armed forces throughout the world.

Finally, 85-year-old Erie Railroad Conductor Samuel Snyder made his last run today 2,500,000 miles and 69 years after he started. His train was the only one to reach Jersey City in the blizzard of 1888.

And that's the news this November 30, 1945.

Saturday, December 1, 1945

And now today's news, December 1, 1945.

In Nuremberg, Hermann Goering says flatly he still is a Nazi and would support the Fuerher as he knew him in 1933. The top ten German industrialists have been taken from their opulent homes and apartments to be interrogated for their role in the war with possible prosecution as war criminals.

A Labor-Management conference in Washington has found no panacea for the many strikes across the country. Congress is considering repressive action.

The Army has cut discharge points from 60 to 55 for enlisted men permitting another 800,000 to get out.

Representative of railroad brotherhoods will present demands this week for a 30 cent per hour increase equal to $2.40 a day with a 6 day week for one million non-operating employees.

2934 companies nationwide have signed a pledge created by the Industry for Veterans to rehire former employees who went into the service. San Francisco citizens have finally concluded that others who refer to their city as Frisco are really being affectionate and won't fight it any more.

Katharine Lenroot, chief of the Children's Bureau of the Department of Labor, has just returned from the Continent and says the U.S. must save the children in Europe. Thousands may die from lack of food and clothing this winter.

Just before German General Anton Dostler was executed by a firing squad today in Aversa, Italy, the names of the 15 American soldiers he had shot on March 26, 1944 were read aloud to him. As he was roped to the stake he said "Long live Germany!"

The U.S. still has 1.5 million Germans as prisoners of war though 2.3 million have already been released and another 1.7 million transferred to other nations. Another 9 ships arrived in New York Harbor today with 21,673 GI's aboard.

In a matinee today Ezio Pinza and Nadine Connor sang in the "Magic Flute" at the Met in New York, and this evening Dorothy Kirsten and Jan Peerce will be in "La Boheme."

In college football Army beat Navy 32 to 13 with all five touchdowns scored by Doc Blanchard and Glenn Davis. Yale beat Harvard 28 to 0.

And that's the news this December 1, 1945.

And now today's news, December 2, 1945.

17-year-old Shirley Temple had tea today at the White House, Alcide de Gasperi has formed a new Italian government, and street cars are running again in Hiroshima.

550,000 are now on strike nationwide.

In Japan 59 men designated as war criminals will be put on trial soon.

As atom conferences continue, it is predicted that atomic energy will be harnessed for power to replace present sources.

A survey of German people indicates considerable dislike and even hatred of American occupation troops due to fraternization, inequities, and clashes with local civilians.

Chinese forces are approaching Mukden in Manchuria even as the Communist troops moved forward.

The French National Constituent Assembly has nationalized the Bank of France.

In yesterday's Army-Navy football classic which was attended by President Truman and top military leaders, the 32-13 win by Army was televised by NBC back to New York City using a new image orthicon tube.

In pro football, Slingin' Sammy Baugh passed for three touchdowns in the Redskins win over the Steelers, Bob Waterfield fired two touchdown passes as the Cleveland Rams beat the Boston Yanks, Sid Luckman led the Chicago Bears over the Chicago Cardinals, and Ben Hogan has won the $10,000 Orlando Open.

Mayor Fiorello LaGuardia of New York may be paid as much as $100,000 a year by NBC for a nationwide radio series.

Finally, 1000 cases of Australian beer went down with the ship in August of 1944 off North Borneo. It's now been raised, bottles unbroken, and good to the last drop.

That's the news this December 2, 1945.

Monday, December 3, 1945

And now today's news, December 3, 1945.

A report today states that Hermann Goering was personally responsible for the famous Reichstag fire in Germany in 1933.

A government report today says the Army and Navy Intelligence Committee scheduled to start October 1, 1941, did not start until after December 7th due to controversy between the services.

Alabama today says its Jim Crow Law that provides equal but separate facilities for Negroes and whites will be rigidly enforced.

Berkeley says the cyclotron will point the way to curing certain types of cancer even as other reports say the atom will provide heat and power in the near future.

Jack Bailey's "Queen for a Day" on Mutual radio originated from New York this past week.

Conductor Erich Leinsdorf will conduct the New York City Symphony tonight in his first New York appearance.

On Broadway Maurice Evans opens in "Hamlet" on the 12th, Betty Field in "Dream Girl" on the 14th, and Ken Murray's "Blackouts" has finished three years at El Capitan theater in Hollywood.

In college football, plunging back Doc Blanchard of Army was awarded the Heisman trophy today beating out his teammate Glenn Davis who came in second.

Finally, tis the season for Bing Crosby's newest music. For $3.41 you can buy 5 ten-inch records with Crosby's great Christmas songs. Add 22 cents for mailing.

That's the news this December 3, 1945.

And now today's news, December 4, 1945.

The Senate today voted 65 to 7 to give the U.S. full and active participation in the United Nations.

Dr. Vannevar Bush, Director of the Office of Scientific Research and Development says the atomic bomb will stop future wars. Quoting General Eisenhower he said "it might blackmail the world into peace."

Word today that President Roosevelt told Francis Sayre, then U.S. High Commissioner to the Philippines on November 16, 1941 to expect Japanese aggressiveness soon, possibly in Thailand.

The cost of the war for all nations has been estimated at one trillion dollars.

The Army has revealed a decoy technique used during the war of pneumatic tubes shaped in the form of men, trucks, and field artillery contributing to winning many battles.

The U.S. Senate Judiciary Committee today passed a resolution designating January 5th to honor Negro scientist George Washington Carver.

Communist pickets in Washington are demanding the resignation of Secretary of State Jimmy Byrnes, withdrawal of troops from China, and no U.S. support of Generalissimo Chiang Kai-shek.

Bing Crosby opens tomorrow in "Bells of St.Mary" and Ray Milland is starring as an alcoholic in the "Lost Weekend."

If you're looking for Christmas presents, try Virgin Wool blankets for $9.98 at Gimbels or imported Moroccan leather wallets from $1 to $10 each and Bloomingdales will sell you 55 pounds of Florida fruit for $8.18.

That's the news this December 4, 1945.

And now today's news, December 5, 1945.

The government today says manufacturers can adjust salaries and prices based upon 33% inflation since 1941.

500 business leaders and the Army have set up conference centers to counsel returning GI's about job opportunities.

General MacArthur has ordered the arrest of three-time premiere Prince Konoye and 7 others for war crimes even as Konoye reveals the Pearl Harbor attack was planned in October 1941 as USA negotiations continued.

Lt. General Jimmy Doolittle, citing the rise of air power, is pushing for one defense department. 3 naval aviation leaders are among 7 new admirals.

Young U.S. fighter pilots used to making $400 per month are finding a difficult adjustment to civilian jobs at $25 to $27 per week.

Fraulein Hanna Reitsch, Hitler's personal pilot, says the Fuehrer with little comprehension of his failures, raged insanely at the end in the Berlin bunker saying Himmler and Goering were treasonous.

New York's Mayor O'Dwyer says he will use the two-way radio communications technology of the Army during the war to fight crime on the streets.

Sen. McCarran of Nevada has introduced a bill to create one international airline. Sen. Bilbo of Mississippi says it is monopolistic and favors Pan Am.

Film stars Eddie Albert and Margo were married today.

On radio tonight try Hildegarde Sings, Frank Sinatra Show, Eddie Cantor, Kay Kyser and his Kollege of Musical Knowledge, or Dr. Christian.

Dan Topping has been awarded a franchise in the new All American Football league for the New York Football Yankees.

Macys has converted Naval officers coats at $46.58. GI army cots are $4.95 at Modells, and GE has a new light exposure meter for your camera at $23.75.

That's the news this December 5, 1945.

Thursday, December 6, 1945

And now today's news, December 6, 1945.

In Japan, Gen. Yamashita has been convicted of atrocities during the war in Philippines and will be hanged.

The U.S. will write off $25 billion of lend-lease to Britain and loan them another $4.4 billion at 2%.

MIT President Karl Compton has criticized the Army for destroying the Japanese cyclotrons saying Gen. MacArthur had a plan for the Japanese to continue their nuclear research under supervision. A Michigan professor says the Germans lagged way behind the U.S. in atomic development.

Scientific and business leaders today said atomic energy will be competitive with coal within 3 to 25 years.

Radar is being urged to replace instrument landings at airports.

The head of the OPA says GI's are getting sullen as they can't find housing.

Rookie Bob Waterfield of the Cleveland Rams has been named to the UP all-Pro team.

A New York Times photo today shows the giant Valparaiso, Indiana basketball team averaging 6 foot 5 inches.

Herbert Marshall has been signed with Claire Trevor and Pat O'Brien for "Crack Up." On radio tonight Jack Kirkwood, Jack Haley, Hobby Lobby, Abbott and Costello, Dinah Shore or the Green Hornet. Over the weekend hear the Lone Ranger, Blind Date, Kate Smith, Jimmy Durante and Gary Moore, First Nighter, Grand Old Opry, Break the Bank and The Hit Parade.

Secretary of the Interior Ickes has presented a back pay check of $7,400 to a teacher who spent 3 years in a Japanese prison.

Finally, the wife of retired Chief Justice Charles Evans Hughes died today at 81.

That's the news this December 6, 1945.

Friday, December 7, 1945

And now today's news, December 7, 1945.

On this 4th anniversary day of Pearl Harbor, Joseph L. Lockard, the soldier in Hawaii who gave an unheeded warning of the Japanese attack, is at home in Williamsport, Pennsylvania with his wife and two young children.

The Big Three Foreign Ministers will meet in Moscow on December 15th with atomic controls on the agenda. France once again is dismayed that it is not included in these meetings.

Poland and Canada want the United Nations headquarters in Europe casting doubt as to whether there are enough votes to put it in the United States.

Republican Minnesota Governor Harold Stassen has asked President Truman to immediately convene an economic conference to plan a 10 year cooperative venture between labor, business and farmers.

General Eisenhower has been made Chief of Staff even as 1000 generals will be cut from the army total of 1540.

Marine Lt. General Roy Geiger and Assistant Secretary of the Navy H. Struve Hensel separately gave speeches today against unification of the armed forces.

Convicted General Tomoyuki Yamashita says he will make an appeal to the U.S. Supreme Court. In Tokyo General Hideki Tojo, Japanese Premier at Pearl Harbor time, will be among the first war criminals to be put on trial next month.

In Nuremberg, the hypocrisy of the Germans was revealed through their stalling for time by signing mutual agreements with Scandinavia, the Low countries, Russia, Yugoslavia and Greece. It was also revealed that Foreign Minister Joachim von Ribbentrop proposed to the Japanese on March 2, 1941 that the Japanese attack the United States.

The $4 million Memorial Cancer Center Fund campaign in New York will not only enlarge Memorial Hospital but permit more cancer research, treatment, prevention and education.

The $10,000 Miami Open golf leader is Henry Picard followed by Dutch Harrison, amateur Frank Stranahan, Ben Hogan, and Jim Ferrier. Sam Snead is 6 strokes back.

New movies are "The Daltons Ride Again" with Alan Curtis, Lon Chaney and Noah Beery, and "Too Young to Know" with Joan Leslie, Robert Hutton, Harry Davenport, and Craig Stevens.

Stocks were up 24 cents today to 194.08 on 2,050,000 shares with Packard heading the list on 79,000 shares up over 1 to 11 and a quarter.

And that's the news this December 7, 1945.

And now today's news, December 8, 1945.

At the Pearl Harbor hearings General George C. Marshall said today one reason he did not use the telephone to talk to Hawaii on December 7, 1941 with any warnings was that the Germans had been tapping phone conversations between Roosevelt and Churchill and he was concerned with security.

President Truman's request today to end the General Motors strike has been rejected by the United Auto Workers Union.

British forces will use a stronger hand to restore and maintain peace in Java. In Buenos Aires 4 were killed and 40 wounded by supporters of Col. Juan Peron trying to disturb a meeting of the Democratic Union.

An experimental plane, the XB-42, has crossed the U.S. west to east in 5 hours and 17 minutes. Helped by tail winds the 2 engine, dual rotation, pusher propeller plane cut 46 minutes off the previous record.

1944 wages were the highest in history with half of all Americans making more than $2700, up from $1900 in 1941. A break even income for city dwellers rose to $1950. Families averaging three persons spent an average of 22 cents per meal, $30 a month for housing, fuel, and refrigeration, and paid $119 in taxes.

The National Safety Council says war time speed limits should be retained until new safer cars get on the highway.

In Herford, Germany today, Josef Kramer and 10 Nazis from the Belsen concentration camp lost an appeal of their death sentence.

386 women marines have left Hawaii where they say they had wonderful wartime duty. Fleet Admiral Ernest J. King reports in Washington in an accounting of the war that of 12 Japanese battleships, 11 were sunk; of 26 carriers, 20 were sunk, of 43 cruisers, 38 were destroyed. He said the Okinawa campaign was the most difficult of the Pacific war.

German Grand Admiral Erich Raeder in the Nuremberg trials says he personally ordered the scuttling of the Graf Spee off Montevideo, Uruguay on December 17, 1939 rather than do battle with awaiting British cruisers.

New movies feature Lawrence Olivier in "Adventure For Two" and Yvonne de Carlo and Rod Cameron in "Frontier Gal." A tribute to the late Jerome Kern will be on CBS tonight with Bing Crosby, Judy Garland, Hildegarde, Patrice Munsel, Dinah Shore, Nelson Eddy and Frank Sinatra.

In sports, the Big Ten will restore peacetime rules permitting freshmen on varsity teams. Finally, President Truman is off for the weekend on the Presidential yacht Williamsburg,

And that's the news this December 8, 1945.

347

Sunday, December 9, 1945

And now today's news, December 9, 1945.

General George Patton has been seriously injured in an accident in Germany. His car ran into a truck outside Mannheim.

Rudolf Hess says he flew to Britain to try to stop the war, and not to ask for Britain's help against Russia.

Russia says it will not withdraw its troops from Iran by January 1 as requested by the U.S.

The UAW has rejected a GM offer of a 10% wage hike as well as President Truman's fact-finding plan.

CIO steelworkers will decide this week whether to strike for a $2 a day wage increase.

Electrical workers will take a strike vote this week, but promise no strike before Christmas.

Pan Am has increased fares from New York to London by $100 to $375.

Sak's Fifth Avenue is advertising king-size men's ties for $1.50, and Gimbels has silk ties for $2.99.

Singer Johnny Desmond will have his own radio show Saturday mornings at 11 on NBC, and Elmer Davis will return to the air Sundays at 3:15 and Tuesdays and Wednesdays at 8:15 pm after an absence of 3 years.

Steve VanBuren scored 20 points and gained 100 yards as the Philadelphia Eagles walloped the Boston Yanks, 35-7, at Shibe Park.

Dr. Alfred Lucas, archaeologist who survived the famous King Tut curse, has died of a heart attack at the age of 79.

That's the news this December 9,1945.

And now today's news, December 10, 1945.

General Motors has cancelled its contract with the automobile workers union.

John L. Lewis says labor legislation of any kind is unnecessary. He also says General Motors is "dishonest" and that auto unions are "stupid."

The U.S. Supreme Court has ruled it an unfair labor practice for an employer to ask for authority to raise wages without dealing with the union it did not recognize.

Congressional leaders have introduced a bill to create an independent Air Force under a civilian Cabinet Secretary.

The Army and Navy have announced joint tests with the atomic bomb against naval vessels at an unspecified date.

In Iran, rebels have captured 3 more towns, extending their control in Azerbaijan.

General Patton is in critical condition following his accident yesterday and is paralyzed from the neck down.

Russek's in New York has ladie's mink hats for $38.50, and Hearns is advertising Hiram Walker bourbon for $3.67 a fifth.

Sugar stamp #38 is now good for 5 pounds through December 31.

Butter production has reached a 23-year low and the shortage is expected to get worse.

Avery Brundage has been re-elected president of the US Olympic body.

"The Dolly Sisters" is now showing at the Roxy in New York, and Gregory Peck and Ingrid Bergman are in "Spellbound" at the Astor.

Former U.S. Secretary of State Cordell Hull has been presented the Nobel Peace Prize for 1945 in Stockholm.

That's the news this December 10, 1945.

Tuesday, December 11, 1945

And now today's news, December 11, 1945.

Leaders of the steelworkers union have decided to call a nationwide strike on January 14.

Ford Motor Company is considering a proposal to substitute an annual wage for hourly wages.

General George Patton's condition is slightly improved and there has been a lessening of paralysis.

President Truman has warned police chiefs of the U.S. at their convention in Miami that juvenile deliquency is the most alarming problem facing the nation.

A B-29 has crossed the U.S. in the record time of 5 hours 27 minutes.

American Red Cross chairman Basil O'Connor has denied rumors of kickbacks to the AF of L and CIO.

Under a new "set-aside" order, the U.S. Army will take 30% of the production of better grades of beef. Sheets, pillowcases and blankets should soon be more plentiful on store shelves.

Gimbels is advertising Van Heusen men's white shirts for $3.45.

Signe Hasso will replace Lynn Bari in the lead in "Strange Triangle," and actor Alan Baxter returns to the New York stage later this month in "Home of the Brave."

Major league baseball owners have decided not to make the Pacific Coast League a third major circuit.

Fordham University will return to collegiate football ranks, fielding a team next year.

Finally, Father Divine has taken full responsibility for atomic energy but says he has it under control.

That's the news this December 11, 1945.

And now today's news, December 12, 1945.

Secretary of State Byrnes leaves for Moscow today. He will discuss an early peace conference, trouble in Iran, and Russian participation on the atomic bomb commission.

Iran's Premier plans to fly to Russia to discuss the trouble in Azerbaijan.

President Truman has appointed a fact-finding commission to look into the General Motors strike, and Ford says it can't afford to give a pay raise now.

Legislation fixing the prices of new homes is being demanded.

General Patton is listed in satisfactory condition, but he is still paralyzed from the neck down.

Asbestos millionaire Tommy Manville has taken bride #8. She is 27-year-old Georgina Campbell.

The U.S. Conference of Mayors wants federal rent controls continued beyond next July 1st.

Baseball Commissioner Happy Chandler has voted against limiting the number of night baseball games.

The Phillies have purchased infielder Lamar (Skeeter) Newsome from the Red Sox for $15,000.

Hollywood's Louis B. Mayer is the nation's leading wage earner with a salary of $908,000.

The Office of Price Administration says the black market in meat is now worse than ever, but the ban on heavy cream may soon be lifted.

"Adventure for Two," starring Laurence Olivier, opens today at the Winter Garden Theater in New York.

That's the news this December 12, 1945.

Thursday, December 13, 1945

And now today's news, December 13, 1945.

France and Britain have agreed to withdraw their troops from Lebanon and Syria and to turn over Mideast problems to the United Nations.

Iran has asked the U.S., Britain, and Russia to take up the Iranian situation.

Thirty-six of the Dachau concentration camp defendants have been sentenced to death by hanging, one to life in prison, and three to 10 years in prison.

Admiral of the Fleet William Halsey will be honored with a parade in New York tomorrow.

General Patton's condition continues to improve. A report blames careless driving for his accident.

The last issue of "Yank," the weekly Army publication, rolled off the presses in New York today.

RCA held the first public demonstration of color television today but said it would be 5 years before it is ready for practical use.

The Poughkeepsie Regatta will not be renewed in 1946, and there is no decision for 1947.

Beau Jack is favored to beat Willie Joyce in their fight tomorrow at Madison Square Garden.

Rumors in Washington say Edwin Pauley will succeed James Forrestal as Navy Secretary.

Retail prices of men's and boys' shorts, shirts and pajamas will be about 5% lower after January 1st.

That's the news this December 13, 1945.

And now today's news, December 14, 1945.

In freezing temperatures and 3 inches of snow, Admiral William "Bull" Halsey got a 15 mile hero's parade in New York today from Flushing to Park Avenue. Another whirling snow storm outside of Moscow today caused Secretary of State James Byrnes' airplane to be lost for an hour before finding a landing spot.

Charges and countercharges continue among Army, Navy, and Air Force interested parties over the proposal to have a common defense department.

Disillusioned by the prevention of much pertinent evidence, Chief Counsel for the Pearl Harbor hearings William D. Mitchell and his staff have resigned.

At the Nuremberg trials prosecutors showed that 6 million Jews were exterminated by the Germans. The Beast of Belsen concentration camp, Josef Kramer, his 22-year-old aide Irma Grese and 9 others were hanged today in Germany.

The Senate has voted down a 33% pay increase for all members of Congress by a 2-1 vote. It would have set the annual rate at $13,500 for members and $19,950 for the Speaker of the House and President ProTem of the Senate.

President Truman is considering appointing Eleanor Roosevelt to a position with the U.N.

Vice Admiral L.E. Denfield told Congress today that he expects defenses to atomic bomb missiles in flight to be perfected within 5 years.

Sgt. Melford Fabrikant is the one millionth soldier to pass through Camp Kilmer, New Jersey from overseas. Another 11,287 troops arrived today on the Queen Mary with 14 British war brides.

General George C. Patton will be flown in 4 to 6 weeks to the U.S. from Heidelberg, Germany for special care at Walter Reed Hospital in Washington or Cushing General in Boston. Still, he will be partly paralyzed for the rest of his life from a broken neck in an auto accident two weeks ago.

Robert Merrill, young American baritone, makes his Metropolitan opera debut tomorrow in Verdi's "La Traviata."

For the first time in 73 years Yale University has signed a football coach for more than one year. Howie Odell got a five year contract. The Brooklyn Tigers pro football franchise has been forfeited with 120 of its players transferred to the Boston Yankees.

In movies, Ray Milland will be the lead in "The Last Man in the World."

Finally, 1946 Mercury cars will average 4% over 1942 models with the new 2 door sedan going for $1,114 and the club convertible at $1,320.

And that's the news this December 14, 1945.

Saturday, December 15, 1945

And now today's news, December 15, 1945.

In Japan Prince Fuminaro Konoye, three times Japan's premier, has taken his life with poison rather than surrender as a suspected war criminal.

In London the Preparation Commission of the U.N. Organization has voted to put the U.N. headquarters in the United States by a 30 to 14 vote with 6 abstentions. U.S. Head Delegate Adlai Stevenson promptly proclaimed that the "U.S. will not fail to meet the challenge implicit in the decision." The specific site has not been selected. James J. Lyons, Borough President of the Bronx, New York already jumped the gun and has proposed to the U.N. Preparatory Commission that virgin territory in Riverdale on the Hudson be the site for U.N. Headquarters.

With James Byrnes out of the country, acting Secretary of State Dean Acheson has, for the first time since 1939, received a Spanish ambassador, Dr. Juan Negrin, a Franco opponent.

The President of the International United Auto Workers has appealed to the British government to support the union against General Motors.

Contrary to previous inferences, the cruiser Boise was never within 1400 miles of the Japanese Navy just before Pearl Harbor and the crew could not, therefore, have seen or reported it. Another Pearl Harbor hearing document today was a copy of a message sent by President Roosevelt to the Japanese Ambassador August 17, 1941 warning against further aggression.

Special envoy to China, General George C. Marshall, is on his way to Peiping to meet with Generalissimo and Mrs. Chiang Kai-shek.

Admiral Ernest E. King has retired as Chief of Naval Operations and has been succeeded by Admiral Chester Nimitz.

Security has been tightened around the 21 major German war criminals in prison in Nuremberg now that they know the consequences they face.

A new movie is "The House of Dracula" with Lon Chaney and John Carradine. A popular daytime Hollywood radio show is "Breakfast With Breneman." Host Tom Breneman chats with the ladies and always gives an orchid to the oldest lady in the audience.

Radio shows tonight include the New Dick Tracy Show, First Nighter, the Dick Haymes Show, A Christmas Carol with Lionel Barrymore, the National Barn Dance, and Break the Bank.

Finally, golfer Mrs. Mildred "Babe" Didrickson Zaharias has been voted woman athlete of the year by the Associated Press. She also won it in 1932 for track.

And that's the news this December 15, 1945.

And now today's news, December 16, 1945.

The Florida-bound Silver Meteor train ran into the northbound Sun Queen in South Carolina today. At least 7 have been killed.

The Army's superplane, "Mixmaster," has crashed in a field in Maryland.

UAW President R.J. Thomas has asked the British government to intervene in the General Motors strike as a stockholder.

Sinclair Oil has given its workers an 18% wage increase.

Sugar is expected to be in short supply until the second quarter of next year.

The U.S. is facing a fuel oil shortage because of heavy demands for gasoline by motorists.

The Office of Defense Transportation expects railroads and airlines to be jammed the rest of the year because of troops pouring in from overseas.

Admiral Chester Nimitz has taken over as Chief of Naval Operations, succeeding Admiral Ernest King, who has retired.

General George Patton's condition continues to improve in Germany.

Gimbels and Macys are advertising precision-built homes for as low as $2400. Macys will take applications shortly after January 1st.

Tickets go on sale today for the Sonja Henie ice show next month at Madison Square Garden. Prices range from $1.25 to $6.00

That's the news this December 16, 1945.

Monday, December 17, 1945

And now today's news, December 17, 1945.

General Motors has demanded 11 major contract changes in it negotiations with the auto workers.

Venezuela expects a big reduction in its oil production because of cheaper oil from Iran.

In Iran, a new government is moving swiftly to consolidate its position by creating a "people's militia."

Japanese General Yamashita has received a stay of execution from the U.S. Supreme Court.

The Big 3 foreign ministers held another meeting today, but there is still a news blackout on what they're discussing.

Charles Lindbergh has called for a world organization backed by military power.

Brothels in Paris have been given 3 months to close their doors.

General George C. Marshall will go to Chungking this week as Ambassador.

The U.S. Senate has adopted a resolution urging the U.S. to back establishment of a Jewish Commonwealth in Palestine.

Marine Tyrone Power is expected to rejoin 20th Century Fox soon. He has already signed for two new films.

National Football League officials have ratified the forfeiture of the Brooklyn Tigers franchise and have awarded the players to the Boston Yanks.

The famous workhorse airplane of the war, the DC-3 airplane known affectionately by some as the C-47, Old Methuselah, Dowager Duchess, the Dakota, and the Gooney Bird is ten years old today. Originally a 21 passenger commercial day plane and 14 passenger Skysleeper, it looks like it will fly on forever all over the world.

That's the news this December 17, 1945.

And now today's news, December 18, 1945.

Ford Motors has offered a 12% wage increase, but the union has rejected it. General Motors workers still want 30%.

President Truman will ask his fact-finding board to consider prices and profits in wage recommendations.

Iran has formally charged Russia with interferences in Azerbaijan.

The British House of Lords has rejected Lord Haw Haw's appeal of his death sentence.

Randolph Churchill's wife has been granted a divorce on grounds of desertion.

Sir. E. Farquhar Bussard, medical attendant to three British kings, has died at 74.

A freight embargo has been imposed on Buffalo, New York, after a 4-day blizzard.

Army's Doc Blanchard and Navy's Dick Dudden are among players to receive awards at the Touchdown Club's annual dinner.

Frankie Sinkwich, University of Georgia and National Football League great, says his football career is over because of a knee injury.

The ice cream industry expects to sell a billion gallons of ice cream in 1950.

Paramount films will produce 20 feature films in 1946 at a cost of $32 million.

Barry Fitzgerald and Betty Hutton are currently starring in "Stork Club" at the Paramount Theater in New York, with Woody Herman and his orchestra on the stage.

That's the news this December 18, 1945.

Wednesday, December 19, 1945

And now today's news, December 19, 1945.

Eleanor Roosevelt will be one of the American delegates to the United Nations General Assembly in London next month.

Premier Stalin has conferred separately with James Byrnes and British Foreign Secretary Bevin in Moscow.

Russia will withdraw from Iran if the US and Britain get out of Greece, Palestine, Egypt, China and Indonesia...that's all they want.

Congress has been asked by President Truman to merge the armed forces into a single unit under civilian control.

The U.S. Senate, by one vote, has extended the President's wartime power for another 6 months.

General Motors will not meet with the President's fact-finding board if prices and profits are considered in its wage dispute.

Members of the Senate Foreign Relations Committee say Russia must agree to international inspection before we give her more information about the A-bomb.

Representative Robert Doughton says an unbalanced budget is not a good thing for the country.

The New York Yankees of the All-American Conference have offered the Chicago Bears $25,000 to play them.

See the four Marx Brothers in "Monkey Business" at the Laffmovie in New York. Robert Montgomery and John Wayne are in "They Were Expendable," showing at the Capitol Theater with Tommy Dorsey's orchestra on the stage.

That's the news this December 19, 1945.

And now today's news, December 20, 1945.

Russia is demanding a large chunk of Turkey at the Big 3 Foreign Ministers meeting in Moscow.

General George C. Marshall has arrived in Shanghai, and the Chinese Communists have proposed a truce while differences are discussed.

General George Patton has suffered a respiratory infection, taking a turn for the worse.

President Truman says ability to pay is always relevant to an increase in wages.

At least 25,000 war veterans on the West Coast are waiting for east-bound transportation to get home for Christmas.

The famous 82nd Airborne Division will stage a parade up 5th Avenue in New York on January 12th.

For the holidays, a 3-pound Jane Parker fruit cake is $1.65, Florida grapefruit 7 cents each, stuffing bread 12 cents a loaf, and turkeys 45 to 52 cents a pound.

Agriculture Secretary Anderson says the only way to get more butter on the market is to increase the price to 65 cents a pound.

Menasha Skulnik is starring in "Wish Me Lunch" at the 2nd Avenue Theater in New York City.

Golfer Byron Nelson has been named the #1 male athlete in the world in 1945. Heisman trophy winner Doc Blanchard of Army placed second.

That's the news this December 20, 1945.

Friday, December 21, 1945

And now today's news, December 21, 1945.

60-year-old General George Patton died in his sleep today in Heidelberg, Germany from a blood clot. The former Third Army Commander was in an emergency hospital that once was a German calvary barracks. Narrowly escaping death 3 times during the war, his auto accident two weeks ago paralyzed him. The funeral will likely be Monday and burial somewhere in Germany near the site of his victories.

The Federal Housing Administration will give 400,000 GI veterans priority for moderate priced homes in 1946 costing less than $10,000 including land.

A political crisis continues in Iran due to the splitting off of the Soviet occupied Azerbaijan as an autonomous state.

The program for disarmament and reform of Japan under the Potsdam agreement is virtually complete according to General MacArthur's headquarters.

The International Association of Machinists has asked Connecticut Governor Raymond E. Baldwin to seize Yale and Towne in Stamford if the company refuses to bargain in good faith.

Some 7000 troops coming home and still at sea may not make it for Christmas.

A social and political reform development in Poland has been compared to the same ideals which guided the American revolution.

A union demand for a $2 daily wage increase was countered by General Electric with a 10% increase which was turned down by the union.

The top tennis rankings for the year 1945 for men are, in order, Sgt. Frank Parker, William Talbert, Pancho Segura, Elwood T. Cooke, Sidney B. Wood, Gardner Mulloy and Francis X. Shields. For women it was Mrs. Sarah Palfrey Cooke, Pauline Betz, Margaret Osborne, Louise Brough, Mrs. Pat Todd and Doris Hart.

And here's a perfect Christmas gift. In honor of a major political figure who once was Governor of New York State, a Memorial Album record album honoring Alfred E. Smith has been made with music selected by close friends Eddie Cantor, Eddie Dowling, Abel Green and Gene Buck. For $3.90 you can hear Al's favorites including "My Gal Sal," "Easter Parade," "The Bowery" and "The Sidewalks of New York" and many more.

And that's the news this December 21, 1945.

Saturday, December 22, 1945

And now today's news, December 22, 1945.

The U.N. Preparatory Commission has voted 25 to 5 with 10 abstaining to make U.N. headquarters in the United States east of the Mississippi. The site seems likely to be in the Boston area or within 50 miles of New York City with Britain favoring the Boston area and the Soviets New York.

With Christmas upon us, some 43,000 GI's aboard ships due to arrive in New York within 3 days won't make it home in time to celebrate. One of the great holiday jams in history is occurring in all forms of transportation across the country with 168,000 particularly frustrated GI's on the west coast trying to get home.

President Truman has issued a directive to expedite admission of displaced persons and refugees providing 3900 visas a month for this purpose.

While the U.S. has joined Britain to recognize Marshal Tito's government in Yugoslavia, it is critical of Tito's curbs on freedom.

The War Department has revealed a weather detector that can spot a thunderstorm within 2000 miles and 2 degrees using spheric stations and a static direction finder. The technology was used during the war at sites in Red Bank, New Jersey, Bermuda and St. Johns, Newfoundland.

At Kwajalein today, eyewitnesses told how 98 civilian employees of Pan American Airways were blindfolded and executed by the Japanese on Wake Island October 7, 1943 in advance of the U.S. invasion.

A U.S. Air Force sergeant, Frank Hirt, has been arrested as a Nazi spy. Once a Nazi storm trooper, he came to the U.S. in 1939 and joined the Army Air Corps.

The idea of atomic power for automobiles seems possible according to the Society of Automotive Engineers but is far in the future.

New Broadway shows include "Pygmalion" with Gertrude Lawrence and Raymond Massey, and "Home of the Brave" with Alan Baxter.

Baron von Trapp and the Trapp Family Singers are appearing with a Christmas show at Town Hall in New York.

And that's the news this December 22, 1945.

Sunday, December 23, 1945

And now today's news, December 23, 1945.

General George Patton, the audacious, unorthodox, vivid leader of the Third Army, who died over the weekend as a result of his car accident two weeks ago, was feared by the Germans, and respected for his leadership by his troops. The church in Europe was filled today by GI's at his funeral.

Gen. MacArthur has denied rumors he'll resign over Russian occupation proposals regarding Japan.

President Truman has sent his best wishes to Premier Stalin in Russia on his 66th birthday two days ago.

Ezra Pound has been declared insane and will not be tried for treason for his pro-Nazi wartime broadcasts.

Founder Henry Ford today joined his grandson and new President of Ford Motors, Henry Ford II, at an employee party.

The FCC has assigned three TV channels to New York City including CBS for WBCW Channel 2, NBC for WNBT Channel 4, and Dumont for WABD Channel 5.

A UN Study commission agrees that the permanent site of the U.N. should be east of the Mississippi. San Francisco has been eliminated, the Russians favor somewhere near New York City and the British favor the Boston area.

Francis J. Spellman has been named a Cardinal for the New York area. Four other American Cardinals were also named.

In basketball over the weekend, Penn beat Princeton 66-30 in the converted Hobey Baker hockey rink being used until the 1944 fire-damaged old gym is rebuilt.

Finally, Christmas sales are up 30% over 1944.

That's the news this December 23, 1945.

And now today's news, December 24, 1945.

Former Under Secretary of State Sumner Welles has stated he is in favor of a Jewish state in Palestine. He says the U.N., rather the U.S. and Britain, should work out details.

Gen. George Patton has been buried today in a U.S. cemetery next to a Private among his troops in Luxembourg.

President Truman tonight lit the first White House outdoor Christmas tree since 1941.

The Big 3—Russia, Britain and the U.S, have finally agreed to include France in drafting the peace treaty with Germany.

Well-known movie star and comedian Joe E. Brown who entertained troops all over the world during the war was involved in a skirmish on Luzon last summer when Japanese troops attacked. Handed a carbine, he killed two of the attackers.

Harvard has beaten Yale in chess 3½ to 4½.

Harmonica player Larry Adler is at the City Center in New York with dancer Paul Draper.

At stores in the New York area, women's nylon girdles are $10 at Arnold Constable's, you can learn the popular Rumba at Arthur Murray's dance studios, and while blended whiskies are plentiful at liquor stores, there's a shortage of scotch, bourbon and straight whiskies this season.

75-year-old Dr. Arthur Korn has died. A Nazi refugee who came to the U.S. in 1939, he transmitted the first photo by wire in 1906 from Paris to Lyon and back to Paris. He is also credited with founding facsimile.

Finally, the weather outlook for Christmas in New York and throughout the East is what the youngsters have ordered. Expect a White Christmas.

That's the news this December 24, 1945.

Tuesday, December 25, 1945

And now today's news, December 25, 1945.

On this, our nation's first Christmas free of war since 1940, there are a lot of GI's overseas in Germany and Japan who remain behind even though most overseas GI's have come home.

Worldwide broadcasts today include a message from King George VI of England, and from Pope Pius in Rome. President Harry S. Truman is at his home in Independence, Missouri with his family.

Happily, 40,000 GI's were released yesterday so they could be home for Christmas. Meanwhile thousands of Americans have sent gift packages to friends in England—a country still with many acute shortages.

For those in New York City, you can have a full turkey dinner at Horn and Hardart's Automats for 75 cents and a fancier full course meal at Reuben's for $3.

Current Broadway hit shows include "Oklahoma," "Carousel," "Showboat," "Song of Norway," "Bloomer Girl," "Up In Central Park," "Life With Father," "Harvey," "Voice of The Turtle" and "Glass Menagerie." And, the Trapp Family is singing this week at Town Hall.

At the movies is Robert Montgomery and John Wayne in "They Were Expendable" with Tommy Dorsey's Orchestra on stage, Hal McIntyre's Orchestra is at the Strand, Rise Stevens performs tonight at the Met in "Lucia Di Lammermoor," and Lily Pons will be in "Carmen" Friday night.

Finally, a popular Christmas gift is the amazing new Teletone 5 tube superheterodyne radio with an enclosed antenna for $27.55.

That's the news this December 25, 1945.

And now today's news, December 26, 1945.

Word today that many of the 170,000 GI's stranded on the West Coast due to a train car shortage, were entertained in thousands of private homes yesterday.

New U.S. Envoy to China Gen. George C. Marshall was toasted today in Shanghai.

In Buenos Aires, Col. Juan Peron has opened his campaign for the Presidency by declaring he is a leftist.

In a freak accident, an Army C-47 iced up, the entire crew bailed out, and the plane continued to fly 900 miles from Ohio to Nebraska before it crashed into an open field.

Music union head James C. Petrillo has banned use of any music from foreign countries except Canada on U.S. radio stations. Further, he hopes to get 441 stations to hire full time musicians for live music.

The William K. Vanderbilt estate on Fisher's Island at Miami Beach has been sold. It includes a large home, seaplane hangar, 9 hole golf course, tennis court, pool and private power plant. Built in the twenties for an estimated $1.5 million, it went to sportsman Edward S. Moore for $500,000.

New movies include "Leave Her to Heaven" starring Gene Tierney, Cornel Wilde and Jeanne Crain, "Junior Miss" with Peggy Ann Garner and two Disney productions— "The Enchanted Forest," and "Pinocchio."

"Pygmalion" opens this week on Broadway with Raymond Massey and Gertrude Lawrence.

Finally, Empire Airlines starts flights today from LaGuardia to Utica, New York.

That's the news this December 26, 1945.

And now today's news, December 27, 1945.

The Big Three have re-established unity and agreement on treaties, the atom, Japan and China, the end of the Korean partitioned nations and then set up the Bretton Woods Bank.

Principal candidates to become the U.N.'s first Secretary General include Lester Pearson of Canada, Paul-Henri Spaak of Belgium and Van Kleffens of the Netherlands. Britain is recommending General Eisenhower.

The Graham Paige Motor Car Company will introduce a totally new car next month called the Frazer in honor of the President of the company, Joseph Frazer.

120-year-old Rev. James Wilson, a former slave, has died. He remained a farm hand until he was 116.

Alcoa Steamship Line starts Caribbean cruises shortly with ships released from active way duty.

New movies include "Cornered" starring Dick Powell and Walter Slezak, "What Next Corporal Hargrove" with Robert Walker, "Snafu" with the four Marx Brothers.

On radio tonight and this weekend, try the Fred Allen Show, Jack Benny, Take It or Leave It with Phil Baker, Edgar Bergen and Charlie McCarthy and the phenomenal Quiz Kids Show.

On Sunday you can hear the CBS program, the "Family Hour" featuring singers Patrice Munsel, Jack Smith tenor, Earl Wrightson, baritone, and Al Goodman's Orchestra.

That's the news this December 27, 1945.

And now today's news, December 28, 1945.

President Truman today assured Congress that atomic bomb secrets will be kept at least until there are proper safeguards. He flew back to Washington from Kansas City, signed 63 bills, and took off for a five day cruise on the Presidential yacht Williamsburg. He will address the nation on radio January 3rd.

In the on-going labor dispute, General Motors today walked out of a Fact Finding Board meeting in Washington set up by President Truman and in the process struck a blow at the President's efforts.

In light of on-going strong-arming, Congress is considering setting up curbs on James C. Petrillo and the American Federation of Musicians Union.

Labor unions in Connecticut may unite for a city-wide stoppage in Stamford over the Yale and Towne and union dispute. 200,000 building trade workers in New York City may go on strike.

The Office of Price Administration has approved a 10 cent per ton hike in coal and coke prices. Also, OPA head Chester Bowles has protested to the White House that too many Federal agencies are showing marked resistance to the employment of Negroes.

1500 have been taken into custody in Jerusalem after last Thursday's terrorist outbreak which took 10 lives. The Jewish Agency has disclaimed any knowledge of the terrorist activity.

The de-Nazification of Germans in the Russian zone is going more smoothly than in the American Zone apparently due to more flexibility, less dogmatism and less confusion.

Dr. Alcide de Gasperi has held his first foreign press conference since becoming Italian Premier December 4th.

The National Safety Council's slogan for New Year's Eve is "If your liquor you feel, stay away from the wheel." Traffic deaths for 1945 are estimated at 29,000.

84-year-old H.H. Baxter died today in New Rochelle, New York. Donor of the famous Baxter Mile track trophy in 1910, he held the pole vault record from 1888 to 1892 at 11 feet 5 inches.

The 8th Annual Blue-Gray football game is tomorrow in Montgomery, Alabama.

A new movie is "San Antonio" with Errol Flynn, Alexis Smith and E.Z. Sakall.

Among classified ads for houses in Brooklyn, New York, a one family, 7 room, detached stucco house is $10,000, in Flatbush a 6 room house is $9,500 and in Seagate a 2 family modern brick house is $14,000.

And that's the news this December 28, 1945.

367

And now today's news, December 29, 1945.

Lt. General Matthew Ridgeway will represent General Eisenhower on the Big Five Military Board next month in London to plan an international peace force.

Hitler's private will dated April 29th has been found including his marriage contract with Eva Braun. It anticipates his suicide by stating he "chose death to escape the disgrace of being forced to resign or surrender." It also accused international Jewry for the world conflagration and called on German hatred of Jews for centuries to come.

U.S. delegates are pushing the U.N. to adopt freedom of the press worldwide.

Brazilian President-elect Enrico Gaspa Dutra says he will re-establish full democracy and military cooperation with the United States.

A current seaman shortage in New York has 500 merchant vessels choking the harbor with 121 ships on delayed arrivals.

Virtually all auto production in Detroit is closed down at least until Wednesday due to parts shortages.

The 29th Marine Regiment of the 5th division which stormed Mt. Suribachi on Iwo Jima sailed into San Diego harbor today.

Most Filipinos don't want unqualified independence on July 4, 1946 feeling they are unprepared and that there will be disorder.

A revival of Jerome Kern's "Showboat" at the Ziegfield Theater this Saturday stars Jan Clayton, Carol Bruce, Ralph Dumke, and Buddy Ebsen. Eddie Foy, Jr. is in "The Red Mill" at the 46th Street Theater.

New Year's Day football games include Alabama and Southern California on NBC radio from the Rose Bowl, Miami-Holy Cross Orange Bowl on CBS, Oklahoma Aggies against St. Mary's over ABC in the Sugar Bowl and Texas-Missouri over Mutual from the Cotton Bowl. Other bowl games are the East-West, Oil Bowl, Gater Bowl, Raisin Bowl, Vulcan Bowl, Flower Bowl and the Coconut Bowl.

A National Conference of Business Page Editors forecasts a big economic boom in 1946 when the strikes are settled and an unprecedented period of prosperity thereafter.

As we come to the end of this momentous year and peace after 4 years, think of those in need and reach out to your local fund to help the less fortunate.

And that's the news this December 29, 1945.

And now today's news, December 30, 1945.

President Truman has returned from his home in Independence in his C-54, the Sacred Cow, amid criticisms he was flying in poor weather and the plane had to fly on instruments. He has assured Congress this weekend the U.S. will keep its atomic secrets under proper safeguards.

The OPA has approved a 10-cent per ton increase on coal and solid fuels. Fleet Admiral Chester Nimitz says the post war Navy must be prepared at all times to be able to strike.

Papers have been filed this past week to set aside 1,280 acres owned by the Rockefeller family to become a wildlife preserve in Jackson Hole, Wyoming.

Hitler's will noted that he had expelled Goering and Himmler from the party for planning to seize control.

Noted American author Theodore Dreiser, author of "American Tragedy," died Friday at age 74.

All American back Y.A. Tittle played on the losing end of the North-South game today won by the North.

American Airlines has ordered 100 new DC-3's from Consolidated Vultee. They will hold 40 passengers.

George Raft, Signe Hasso and Claire Trevor are in a new movie "Johnny Angel," and George Whelan, the last of 3 brothers who started the United Cigar store chain in 1901, died Friday at age 80.

Earl Wrightson and Patrice Munsel are on CBS today with Al Goodwin's Orchestra in the weekly "Family Hour."

A million shares traded on the New York Stock Exchange today as Firestone reported over $16 million in earnings for the year.

That's the news this December 30, 1945.

And now today's news, December 31, 1945.

In an historic document, Emperor Hirohito of Japan has disclaimed his divinity and says it was a matter of legends and myths. He calls upon Japanese citizens to put the evils of the past behind and look to the future.

Former Secretary of War Henry Stimson says the uninvolvement of the United States in the post World War I League of Nations is a major cause for the coming of World War II.

In Pearl Harbor hearings, Admiral Stark says Admiral Kimmel in Hawaii had 11 messages in 3 months before the Japanese attack indicating peace was running out.

1946 is expected to be the year for TV as over $100 million is to be spent in manufacturing TV sets and putting on new TV stations in New York, Philadelphia, Schenectady, Los Angeles and Washington.

A U.N. Committee has selected either metropolitan Boston or New York as the permanent site for the U.N.

Mayor Fiorello La Guardia ends his 12 years as Mayor of New York tonight when William O'Dwyer takes office.

Sports stars of 1945 include the World champion Detroit Tigers and pitcher Hal Newhouser, Bob Waterfield who led the Rams to the pro football title, in tennis Mrs. Sarah Palfrey Cooke and Sgt. Frank Parker, collegiate football's Doc Blanchard and Glenn Davis from Army, athlete of the year Golfer Byron Nelson, and woman of the year, Babe Didrickson Zaharias.

For a New Year forecast, 83-year-old Philadelphia Athletics' Connie Mack, born Cornelius McGillicudy, says Babe Ruth's home run record will be broken by the year 2000.

Finally, as we wind down 1945, there will be over one million in Times Square tonight celebrating the conclusion of a momentous year in U.S. history and welcoming in a new year of peace.

That's the news this December 31, 1945.